LIVE & WORK IN

CHINA

LIVE & WORK IN

CHINA

Jocelyn Kan &
Hakwan Lau

Distributed in the USA by
The Globe Pequot Press, Guilford, Connecticut

Published by Vacation Work, 9 Park End Street, Oxford
www.vacationwork.co.uk

LIVE & WORK IN CHINA
By Jocelyn Kan & Hakwan Lau

First edition 2004

Copyright © Vacation Work 2004

ISBN 1-85458-308-5

Cover design by mccdesign ltd

Typeset by Brendan Cole

Publicity by Charles Cutting

Printed and bound in Italy by Legoprint SpA, Trento

CONTENTS

MAINLAND CHINA

SECTION I
LIVING IN MAINLAND CHINA

DAILY LIFE

RETIREMENT

SECTION II
WORKING IN MAINLAND CHINA

HONG KONG

SECTION I
LIVING IN HONG KONG

RETIREMENT

SECTION II
WORKING IN HONG KONG

EMPLOYMENT

FOREWORD

People around the world are fascinated by China for a variety of reasons. They go to China for the exciting business opportunities, for its rich and varied culture, for its long and colourful history, or even just for an experience of 'something different', all of which China never fails to deliver.

In recent years, the Chinese economy has become one of the most dynamic in the world and the Chinese government has opened its doors to foreign investors who can bring skills and expertise and enter partnerships with local businesses and institutions and so develop the huge potential wealth of a country with a population of over a billion people. Vodafone has linked up with China Mobile, Shell is working with CNOOC, a leading Chinese oil company, while 65% of the Chinese automobile production now comes from international joint ventures. These developments are being repeated across the country daily, not only to serve the huge local market, but also to generate exports on a massive scale. The increase in local wealth is typified by the fact that car ownership is currently doubling every four years.

The growth of the Chinese economy is such that by 2050, it is expected to overtake that of the United States and, to achieve this, the Chinese government is easing the immigration process for high-skilled personnel and, most recently, making long term or permanent residence a genuine aspiration. In short, the opportunities for living and working in China have never been better and are likely to continue to improve. The primary aim of *Live & Work in China* is to show where the greatest opportunities lie and to explain how best to pursue them.

China isn't just a country, it's a different world with regions and people that differ hugely in natural and demographic factors and with an area that makes it the third largest country in the world after Russia and Canada. To know its people and to explore the dynamics of China's ever changing economy, you need to be there and, if possible, to learn the language. You need to understand too that some of the western myths about China, such as *guanxi* (social connections) and *mianzi* (face), are to a large extent just that – myths. In *Live & Work in China*, we explore these issues and try to give readers a flavour of what they should expect in China from finding accommodation, to education and the health service, and from business etiquette to looking for work.

Live & Work in China also includes a special section on Hong Kong and we are proud to present the information about our vibrant home city to you. Compared to mainland China, Hong Kong is probably less daunting to most Westerners, mainly due to its colonial past. However, Hong Kong is by no means a watered down version of mainland China, nor is its culture much Westernised at a conscious level. It is a city with its own distinct character, brimful of people, skyscrapers and opportunities, and yet it remains extremely safe and hassle-free.

The geographical size of the city is small, but everything is three-dimensional and you should really expect nothing less than what you will find in New York or London.

Jocelyn Kan & Hakwan Lau
Oxford
June 2004

ACKNOWLEDGEMENTS

Thanks are due to Clare Passingham, Anna Tai and Sian Alexander for helping with the research and writing of this book. Clare has read the drafts of almost all the chapters and has helped with our use of the English language. Thanks also to the Institute for Chinese Studies at the University of Oxford for providing an extremely friendly and supportive working environment while we have been writing this book. Many colleagues have also provided very valuable information that could not be found anywhere else. In addition we thank our friends for sharing their experiences in China with us. Records of their interviews can be found in the final section of this book.

MAINLAND CHINA

Section I

LIVING IN MAINLAND CHINA

GENERAL INTRODUCTION

RESIDENCE AND ENTRY REGULATIONS

SETTING UP HOME

DAILY LIFE

RETIREMENT

GENERAL
INTRODUCTION

CHAPTER SUMMARY

- **Politics.** The People's Republic of China (PRC) was established on 1st October, 1949.
  - The National People's Congress (NPC) is the highest authority of the country.
- **Economics.** The growth rate in 2003 was 9%, which was about four times the world's average growth rate.
  - Foreign direct investment (FDI) has increased by more than 20% since China joined the World Trade Organisation (WTO) in 2001.
  - Special Economical Zones and technological development zones were set up to encourage foreign investments.
  - Beijing will host the 2008 Olympic Games.
- **Geography.** China is the third largest country in the world after Russia and Canada.
  - There are 22 provinces, 4 municipalities, 5 autonomous regions and 2 Special Administrative Regions on mainland China.
  - The Yangtze River is the world's third longest river.
- **Population.** The current population is 1.3 billion, which the highest in the world.
  - 92% of the population is Han Chinese.
  - China adopted the 'One-Child Policy' in 1979.
  - In a few years time there will be 20% more men than women.
  - China is an ageing society. Currently, about 7% of the population is aged 65 or above, and it is expected that this figure will reach 20% by 2050.
- **Climate.** Apart from the south and the east, the climate can be very extreme.
  - About 40% of cities face serious air and water pollution.

PROS AND CONS OF MOVING TO CHINA

China is probably the fastest growing economy in the world and is also one the few countries that has continued to grow during the world economic recession of the last few years. Although it is geographically far away from Europe and the USA, many investors find this fast-growing market irresistible and have started their businesses in China. From the late 70s, the Chinese government has set up favourable policies to attract foreign investment. A number of investment incentives are now available for foreigners, and more and more cities have been opened to foreign investment. Since entering the World Trade Organisation (WTO) in 2001, many tariffs and quotas have also been removed in China. In addition, the low land and labour costs are a great advantage for doing business in China. There are also plenty of opportunities for foreigners to be employed, as the country is currently actively seeking experts and highly-skilled personnel. Although you may find the salaries in China relatively low, this is matched with the low living costs. If you earn 5,000 *yuan* (US$600/£360) a month, you can probably enjoy a very good living standard in China. The general standard of living in China may not be as high as that of western Europe or North America, but in big cities it is becoming quite attractive. Many cities have been developing at such fast a rate that problems have been created. The percentage of car ownership has increased drastically in the last decade, and congestion has become a real problem in many big cities. Industrial developments have also caused serious pollution; it is estimated that over 40% of the cities are suffering from serious air and water pollution. Due to the unfavourable geographic conditions in the west and the extreme weather in the north and the northeast, most people prefer to live in the south and the southeast and as a result, you may find the cities along the coastline very crowded. If you plan to stay in China for a longer period, you will probably need to learn the Chinese language, as English is not commonly used in daily life.

Pros:	Cons:
o Low cost of living.	o Low salaries.
o Cheap housing.	o The language difference.
o The fast growing economy provides plenty of opportunities for investment and employment.	o Distance from home
	o Serious pollution
	o Serious congestion in big cities
o Many investment incentives available for foreign investors.	o Crowded, especially in coastal cities.
o Easy acceptance for staying as the country currently needs foreign experts.	o A complicated tax regime.

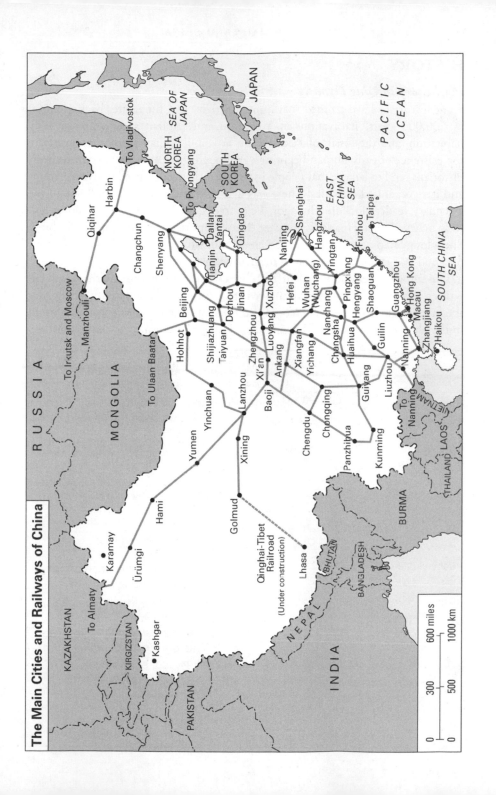

The Main Cities and Railways of China

HISTORY

Pre-history to Qing Dynasty

Some historians have claimed that human activity in China dates back 500,000 to 600,000 years. Excavations at Yuanmou and Lantian show signs of early habitation, and the fossils of Peking Man at Zhoukoudian further demonstrate the existence of early human beginings. Although there were no written records, historians tend to believe that people in pre-historic times started to live in groups and have organised activities. There was usually a leader of a group. Some of the legendary leaders include Huangdi, Fuxi, Yao Di, Shun Di and Shenlong Shi. It is believed that Huangdi invented the compass; Fuxi introduced clothing; Shenglong Shi pioneered herbal medicines; and Yao Di and Shun Di were famous for good leadership and were kind to their people.

The imperial period started in the Xia Dynasty. Even though there was no written record, excavations have showed the existence of the dynasty. Shang was the first dynasty with a textual record and the first form of writing was also found in the Shang Dynasty. The following table is a quick summary of past dynasties:

THE DYNASTIES OF CHINA		
Dynasty	**Period**	Remarks
Xia	2200 –1700BC	○ No written record has been found but there is archaeological evidence for the dynasty.
Shang	1700 –1027BC	○ The first dynasty with textual records ○ Ancient writing has been found on tortoise-shell (first written language).
Zhou	1027 – 2211BC	
Western Zhou	1027 – 771BC	
Eastern Zhou	770 – 221 BC	○ Confucius gained influence among the emperors.
Qin	221 –207BC	○ Writing, measuring units and currency were unified. ○ The Great Wall was built to prevent the invasion (or incursions) of 'barbarians'. ○ 'The burning of books and burying of scholars' (213BC); many valuable books of history, literature and medicine were destroyed.
Han	206BC – AD220	

Western Han	206BC – AD9	o Dong Zhongshu developed a system of cosmology called Wuxing (the Five Elements: metal, wood, water, fire and earth), which allegedly can predict the rise and fall of dynasties. o Sima Qian wrote the first Chinese history book: *Records of the Grand Historian* (*Shi Ji*).
Xin	AD9 –24	
Eastern Han	AD25 – 220	o Buddhism was first introduced into China. o Records of contacts with other countries including Japan, India, Persia and Rome have been found. o The Silk Road became an important route for trade between east and west.
Three Kingdoms	AD220 – 280	o The history of this period was the basis of the novel *The Romance of Three Kingdoms*, which is one of the 'Four Classics'.
Wei	AD220 –265	
Shu	AD221 – 263	o Liu Bei invited Zhuge Kongming as the Prime minister.
Wu	AD229 – 280	
Jin	AD265 – 420	
Western Jin	AD265 – 317	
Eastern Jin	AD317 – 420	
Southern & Northern Dynasties	AD420 – 589	
Southern Dynasties	AD420 – 589	
Song	AD420 – 479	
Qi	AD479 – 502	
Liang	AD502 – 557	
Chen	AD557 – 589	
Northern Dynasties	AD386 – 581	
Northern Wei	AD386 – 534	
Eastern Wei	AD534 – 550	
Northern Qi	AD550 – 577	

Western Wei	AD535 – 556	
Northern Zhou	AD557 – 581	
Sui	AD581 – 618	o The Grand Canal was built. o The Great Wall was reconstructed
Tang	AD618 – 907	o The best three hundred poems were collected into a book, 'The Three Hundred Tang Poems' (Tang Shi San Bo Shou), and were made popular among the public. o Revival of Confucianism. o Queen Wei became the first female emperor in China. Foreign trade was particularly active during her rule. o All Buddhist temples were destroyed and monks and nuns were forced to leave in AD 845.
Five Dynasties & Ten Kingdoms	AD907 – 960	
Later Liang	AD907 – 923	
Later Tang	AD923 – 936	
Later Jin	AD936 – 947	
Later Han	AD947 – 950	
Later Zhou	AD951 – 960	
Ten Kingdoms	AD907 – 979	
Liao	AD907 – 1125	
Song	AD960 – 1279	o The weakest dynasty in history with the smallest territory. o Economic and cultural developments such as Song Ci (lyrics), astronomy, geography, painting, calligraphy, philosophy, etc, flourished. o Zhu Xi established Neo-Confucianism.
Northern Song	AD960-1127	
Southern Song	AD1127-1279	
Jin	AD1115 – 1234	
Yuan	AD1206 – 1368	o The territory expanded as far as Europe. o Classification of the population into four groups, in which Mongolians were the most superior, while the Han-Chinese were given the lowest status.

Ming	AD1368 – 1644	o Zheng He explored 'The Western Ocean' with his fleet at least seven times. Visited Southeast Asia, Sumatra, Java, Ceylon, India, Persia, the Persian Gulf, Arabia, the Red Sea as far north as Egypt, and Africa as far south as the Mozambique Channel. o The length of the Great Wall was increased by 600 miles. o In 1557, Macau became a colony of the Portuguese and remained so until 1999.
Qing	AD1644 – 1911	o Further expanded territory. o Re-introduced the State Examination System. o Men were forced to dress their hair the Manchurian way (to shave the front hair and keep a pigtail at the back), which became a trademark for the Chinese in the West. o Hong Kong was ceded to the British in 1942 after China lost the First Opium War. o In June 1858, the Tianjin Treaty was signed and eleven more ports were opened to Western trade, in addition to the first five Treaty Ports. o Empress Dowager Cixi held the real power, on ruling the country for 40 years (1956 – 1908).
Republic of China	AD1911 – 1949	(see below)
People's Republic of China	AD1949 – present	(see below)

The Chinese people call themselves 'Han *ren*' or 'Tang *ren*' (*ren* means people) because the Han and the Tang Dynasties were the most powerful dynasties ruled by the Chinese. Although the Yuan and the early Qing Dynasties were perhaps more powerful, they were ruled by ethnic minorities who came from the northern part of China. Han-Chinese and other minorities have never mixed well, then or now. Intermarriages between different ethnic groups happen, but they are not very common.

The Fall of the Qing Empire

The late Qing Dynasty was weak and parts of the territory were leased or ceded to foreign countries. The dissatisfaction of the people grew strong, and political movements started to appear in different areas. Sun Yat-sen actively fomented revolution. He was born is Xiangshan County in Guangdong Province, and received his education in Hawaii and Hong Kong. He received his medical degree in Hong Kong and practised medicine for a few years there. He gave up being a medical practitioner and started *Xingzhonghui*, his first political group, in 1894 to start planning for the revolution. Unfortunately, his first attempt failed and he had to go into exile in Europe, the United States, Canada and Japan to raise funds for the future revolution. He joined *Tongmenghui* later in Japan and eventually became its leader. On 10th October, 1911, the uprising in Wuchang that was organised by the *Tongmenghui* succeeded in taking control from the Qing emperor and this put an end to the Dynasty period.

The Republic of China was founded on 10th October, 1911 and Sun Yat-sen was elected as the provisional President in December the same year. The Qing Dynasty was still in power in some of the provinces in the north. Since Sun had no military power, he finally sought the help of Yuan Shikai, who controlled the military in northern China. Sun offered the presidency in exchange for Yuan's help. Yuan was a dictator and pronounced himself as Emperor of the Chinese Empire, which led to strong opposition. Yuan died in 1916 due to kidney failure. In 1921, Sun Yat-sen was elected president of a self-proclaimed national government in Guangzhou city. He delivered a speech of the 'Three Principles of People' (*San Min Zhuyi*) in 1923 as the foundation of the country. The 'Three Principles' refer to Nationalism, Democracy and Socialism.

By the 1920s, the Kuomingtang was the dominant political party in eastern China. Through the influence of the Comintern (the Soviet Communist International), the Chinese Communist Party was formed in 1921. The Chinese Communist Party and the Kuomingtang formed a temporary alliance to prevent the invasion of Japan in 1924. However, after the death of Sun Yat-sen in 1925, the two groups headed in different directions and this finally led to the Civil War. The Civil War lasted for more than twenty years. The Japanese invaded and occupied China between 1937 and 1945. The two parties agreed to jointly fight against the Japanese during that time, but actually there was no real cooperation and the tension remained high between the two parties. World War II ended in 1945 and wars between Kuomingtang, led by Chiang Kaishek, and the Communist party, led by Mao Zedong, finally broke out a year later. Mao defeated the Chiang troops in 1949 and proclaimed the foundation of the People's Republic of China on 1st October and he became the leader of the country. Chiang fled to Taiwan with his remaining army and continued to call his government there the Republic of China.

People's Republic of China (PRC)

The PRC had a very difficult start: after years of war, the country was in chaos and was financially very weak. However, taking the Soviet Union as a model, economic and social reforms were introduced. The economy started to grow in 1953 after inflation was halted, and the country developed rapidly. The first five-year plan was successful, but Mao was not satisfied with the agricultural yields. He believed mass cooperation was the key to success, and he introduced the *Great Leap Forward* in 1958, which aimed at rapid growth in industrial and agricultural production. Mao insisted on putting most of the resources into the steel industry although many other government members, especially Premier Zhou Enlai, preferred agricultural incentives. Mao believed the Great Leap Forward would make China into a major steel producer and the total production would surpass that of Britain in 15 years. He got people to build backyard furnaces and the whole nation was enrolled in steel production. However, the Great Leap Forward proved to be a disaster. The supply of iron ore in China was limited, and people had to look for alternative 'resources', so farming tools and other iron household necessities were melted in those backyard furnaces. Due to the varied supply of resources, the steel produced was of very low quality and was of no market value. The three years under the Great Leap Forward programme put the country into a serious economic downturn and more than 40 million people starved to death.

The Soviet Union and the PRC signed a mutual defence agreement in 1950 and established a friendly relationship over the following eight years. However, the relationship between the two deteriorated after 1958. In 1959, the Soviet Union restricted the flow of scientific and technological information to China and removed all Soviet professionals from China in 1960. The two countries began to have open disputes in international forums.

Mao resigned as the head of state after the failure of the Great Leap Forward and Liu Shaoqi became president of the PRC. Although Mao was no longer the head of state, he was still the leader of the Chinese Communist Party and was *de facto* in power. Liu Shaoqi and Deng Xiaoping reformed government policies and focused on agricultural incentives and economic development. Liu and Deng received increasing support from party members and also from the general public. Mao became aware of the potential decline in his political status and he started to attack Liu and Deng. He openly criticised them for the restoration of capitalism and the introduction of social classifications. The Gang of Four, including Yao Wenyuan, Wang Hongwen, Zhang Chunqiao and Mao's wife Jiang Qing, supported Mao's criticisms of Liu and Deng, and these four were the initiators of the Cultural Revolution. The Cultural Revolution was actually begun after Jiang Qing criticised a play called '*Hai Rui Dismissed from Office*'. Jiang claimed that the play was in fact a satire of the 'poisonous' kind, which aimed at attacking Mao. Jiang and Yao started writing criticisms in newspapers, and their criticisms soon extended to officials in the PRC and other members in the Party. In May

1966, a formal notice was issued to launch the Cultural Revolution. Jiang and Yao went to universities and colleges to criticise the university administrations. They formed the Red Guards, who were students given red armbands and the 'little red book' (the *Quotations from Chairman Mao*). The number of Red Guards increased rapidly and they were given the authority to get rid of intellectuals and political opponents of Mao. During the period of the Cultural Revolution, schools were shut down, temples and churches were burnt. Thousands of teachers, artists, and writers were physically abused and were sent to re-education camps, often in remote parts of the country. Books, history records and works of art were burnt. The Cultural Revolution did not completely end until Mao died in 1976.

Deng Xiaoping regained his position with the help of Zhou Enlai in the early 70s. However, he was dismissed by Mao again after Zhou's death. Not until Mao's death did he return to the position of Vice-Premier and Vice-Chairman of the Party. Deng focused on economic development and introduced the 'Four Modernisations' (agriculture, industry, military and defence, and science) and the 'Open Door' policy. Since then, the PRC has been developing rapidly.

POLITICAL AND ECONOMIC STRUCTURE

Government

The Chinese government is basically divided into central administration and local administration. The central government sets laws, regulations, and policy directions, and manages the budget and personnel changes. Local governments carry out the policies and laws set by central government. The primary bodies of the government include the National People's Congress, the President and the State Council.

National People's Congress (NPC). This is the highest authority of the People's Republic of China (PRC); the NPC general meeting is held once every five years. The Central Committee of NPC consists of 300 delegates, who are all elected by the provincial people's congresses, for a term of five years. They meet for two weeks every year to produce work reports for the present year and to approve proposals for the coming year.

The President of the country is elected by the NPC, which also has the power to impeach or replace a President. The proposals of the State Council have to be approved by the NPC before they are carried out. The NPC selects the central committees for the Politburo (political bureau) Standing Committee and they, in turn, select about 500 members of the NPC to form the Standing Committee. The current Politburo Standing Committee includes nine members, with President *Hu Jintao* and Premier *Wen Jiabao* as part of the Committee. The Standing Committee has the constitutional authority to modify legislation within limits set by the NPC and it also has the power to interpret the laws of the PRC.

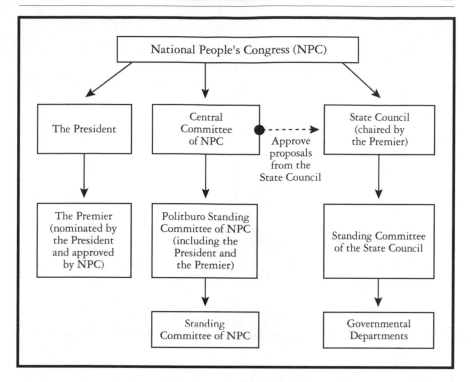

President. The President of the state is elected by the NPC. In practice, the top leaders of the Chinese Communist Party (CCP) discuss and make a nomination to the NPC for an appropriate candidate and the delegates vote to support or reject the nomination in the general NPC meeting. Up until now, all the nominations for previous and current Presidents were supported by the NPC. The President, also serves as the General Secretary of the CCP. The Premier and other members of the State Council are nominated by the President and approved by the NPC. The current President of the PRC is *Hu Jintao*, who commenced his work in March 2003.

State Council. The State Council is chaired by the Premier, currently *Wen Jiabao*, and is the central administrative body of the State. The State Council Standing Committee consists of the Premier, four vice-premiers, five state councillors, and the secretary-general. Other members of the State Council include the heads of each governmental department and agency, and the total number adds up to about 50. The State Council meets once a month while the Standing Committee meets twice a week. Members serve five years in one term, and they are not allowed to serve more than two consecutive terms. The main functions of the State Council are to formulate and implement laws, draft and submit proposals to the NPC, formulate tasks and responsibilities of ministries and commission of

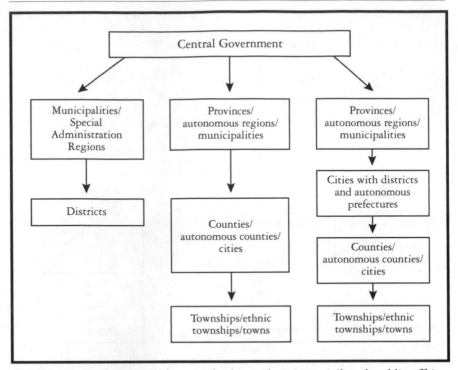

the State Council, prepare the state budget, administer civil and public affairs. The Premier is nominated by the President and approved by the NPC. Other members in the State Council are nominated by the Premier, but they have to be approved by the NPC as well. Although the President is not included in the State Council, he has the power to remove any member from it.

Local Administrations. There are several categories and levels of local administration. They can be separated into two-level, three-level and four-level administrations ('Central Government' is not counted as one of the levels):

The delegation of authority to local governments aims to implement the laws and regulations of the State more effectively. Since each province, city or town faces different economic and environmental advantages and disadvantages, contingency adjustments have to been made to ensure these laws and regulations run smoothly in different regions. Moreover, provinces, cities and towns may come across problems for which the central government does not normally provide guidance. The procedures for marriage between ethnic minorities can be one example. In such cases, local legislation is needed, but they must not violate the laws of the Central Government. There are two major principles in setting up local legislation: (a) it should be set up according to the local economy, politics, legal system, culture, customs, and conditions of the people. It should also be suitable to the actual local situation; (b) it must specifically solve the obvious issues that are not covered in the legislation and regulations of the Central Government, or issues that are not suitable for the central authorities to settle.

Political Parties

The biggest political party is the *Chinese Communist Party (CCP)*. The Party was founded in 1921 and it is estimated that about 5% of the population (more than 60 million people) are members of the *CCP*. The People's Republic of China was set up by Mao Zedong, who was a *CCP* leader, and since that time the *CCP* has held power. In general, the President of the government is also the General-Secretary of the *CCP*. There are eight legally registered non-Communist parties in mainland China. Rather than acting as opposing powers, these parties take a more positive approach to coexist with the *CCP* and engage in mutual supervision towards other parties as well as devoting themselves to the good of the country. Members of non-Communist parties, as well as some other non-party bodies, are called to the Chinese People's Political Consultative Conference (CPPCC) for consultations. The eight non-Communist parties include the *Revolutionary Committee of the Chinese Guomindang*, founded in 1948 and composed mainly of former Kuomingtang members or those who have historical connections with the Kumingtang and many of whom now live in Taiwan; the *China Democratic League*, established in 1941 by intellectuals at more senior levels; the *China Democratic National Construction Association*, formed in 1945, members are mainly businessmen and academic specialists; the *China Association for Promoting Democracy*, started in 1945 by intellectuals in cultural, education (primary and secondary schools), scientific and publishing fields; The *Chinese Peasants' and Workers' Democratic Party*, composed of people who work in public health, culture, education, and science and technology, was set up in 1930; the *China Zhi Gong Dang*, founded in 1925 and whose members are mainly overseas Chinese, relatives of overseas Chinese and specialists or scholars with overseas connections; the *Jiusan Society*, founded in 1945, whose members are dominated by college or university professors working in science and technology, culture and education, or public health; and finally the *Taiwan Democratic Self-Government League*, which was formed in 1947, which consists of people born or with family roots in Taiwan but who are currently living on the mainland.

Economy

At the time of the establishment of the PRC, the country was in a poor financial situation. This was mainly due to the Japanese invasion and the Civil War, but it was also a result of the poor financial management of the Kuomingtang before 1949. During the Maoist period, the economy of China was basically closed to foreign investment. Mao adopted the Soviet Union's model and preferred the self-reliant development approach. State-owned enterprises were set up and economic development was controlled by the central government. Foreign investments were not welcome and free trade, to Mao, implied handing the industries to foreigners. The first five-year plan was successful and the economy started to grow in the early 50s. The Great Leap Forward was introduced in 1958 but proved a failure and China experienced serious economic downturn. Mao resigned from the Presidency after the Great Leap Forward. The new President Liu Shaoqi and the party General Secretary Deng Xiaoping introduced agricultural incentives and the economy of China gradually recovered in early 60s. However, Mao, who was still in power in the CCP, did not agree with the approach of Liu and Deng and he started to criticise them seriously. Finally, the Cultural Revolution broke out in 1966 which brought the economic development of the country to a complete halt.

Not until the death of Mao in 1976 did the Chinese economy recover. Deng Xiaoping regained his position and control over the CCP, and he introduced a series of economic reforms. Instead of the self-reliant development approach, Deng encouraged foreign trade and foreign investment. He introduced the 'Four Modernizations' (agriculture, industry, science and technology, and the military) in 1978, and then exports started to flourish. Since the opening-up of the economy, the GDP of China has recorded 9% growth on average between 1978 and 1994, marking China as one of the fastest growing economies in the world. Industrial reform took place in the 80s and many TVEs (township and village enterprises) were set up in rural areas, becoming one of the driving forces for national economic development. TVEs are different from State-owned enterprises. TVEs are run by local authorities in the mode of a private business, which means the local authorities are responsible for losses and have to face competition. On the other hand, if the TVEs make money, profits go to the local government instead of the central government. Deng has also set up several Special Economic Zones, as part of the economic reform, to encourage foreign investment. Foreign investors are provided with extra investment incentives to start their businesses in these areas. These Special Economic Zones include the following cities: Shenzhen, Zhuhai, Shantou, Xiamen and Hainan. In addition, the government established 15 free trade zones, 32 state-level economic and technological development zones, and 53 new- and high-tech industrial development zones in the late 80s to early 90s. The establishment of the Shanghai Pudong New Zone has turned Shanghai into a major centre in banking and financial development and further stimulated the Chinese economy. China reached an average 9.7% growth through the 80s and the 90s. Even when suffering from the Asian financial crisis and SARS outbreak in 1997 and 2003, China recorded 7% and 9% growth respectively. The growth rate in 2003 was actually about four times the world average in the same year. The Foreign direct investment (FDI) has increased by more than 20%, since China joined the World Trade Organisation (WTO) in 2001 and Beijing being made the host of the 2008 Olympics Games will encourage even more foreign investment to mainland China.

THE MIDDLE CLASS

[btb]It is estimated that about one-fifth of the population in mainland China is considered middle class. The figure has only increased by 4% between 1999 and 2003 but is now rising rapidly. These people on average possess assets that are worth US$18,000 to US$36,000 (£10,000-20,000). The increase in the size of the middle class has changed the consumption pattern and many companies have now chosen this sector of society as their target market. The increase in sales of vehicles, properties, travel, etc, has stimulated economic growth and many middle class households have also started to run their own businesses. Recently, new laws have been implemented to provide legal protection for private property, due to the rapid increase in home ownership. The Chinese government also aims at increasing the number of middle class households by cutting the taxes of the poor and allowing more people from rural areas to work in cities. It is believed that the increase in the average income of households, and the low living costs, will result in a middle class society that is beneficial for the economy. It is expected that around 40% of the population will fall into the category of middle class by the year 2020.

GEOGRAPHICAL INFORMATION

Area

China is the third largest country in the world (after Russia and Canada) and is 9.6 million square kms, which is about the size of the USA. Russia is to the northeast of China and there are train connections between the two countries. To the north lies Mongolia while Xinjiang is next to Pakistan, Tajikistan, Kyrgyzstan, Kazakhstan and Mongolia. Vietnam, Laos and Myanmar (Burma) are located to the south of Yunnan. North Korea is connected to Jilin and Liaoning. Tibet is only separated from Nepal and India by the Himalayan mountains. The country is surrounded by the sea to the south and the east, and by desert in the north and mountains in the west and the southwest. The west is mainly composed of highlands. The average height of the Plateau of Tibet and Plateau of Qinghai is 4500m above sea level, and Tibet is known as 'the Roof of the World'. The Himalayas have peaks on average 6000m above sea level. The world's highest peak is Everest, lying on the border of Tibet and Nepal, and reaching 8848m above sea level. The middle and southeast mainly consist of lowland, which is good for agriculture. These areas have a high population density and they are also the source of the main supply of food for the whole country. Water flows from the mountains in the west to the eastern part of the country and then to the Pacific Ocean. The two major rivers, the Yangtze River (Chang Jiang) and the Yellow

River (Huang He), link the west and the east of the country and are the major water supply for the country. The Yangtze River (6300 km) is the world's third longest, and it flows from Qinghai to Jiangsu while the Yellow River (5460 km) starts in Qinghai and flows northwards to Shangdong. The Yangtze is also called 'the lifeline of China' as it is the major source of water supply to many provinces. The Yellow River is named because of the colour of the water. It is probably the world's most muddy river, which carries plenty of loose soil. It is the second longest river in China and is also the origin of the civilisation of the country. The Han Chinese started to settle along the Yellow River thousands of years ago since it was a major water supply and the loose soil was good for vegetation. Excavations around the Yellow River have shown that there were organised human activities in these areas. However, the Yellow River nowadays is more a burden than a source of life to the Chinese. The loose soil often blocks the mouths of tributaries and causes frequent flooding. One of the most serious floods happened in 1998 and caused more than 3,000 deaths and made 14 million people homeless.

Regional Divisions

The whole of mainland China is divided into 22 provinces, five autonomous regions, four municipalities and two special administrative regions. The government of China also considers Taiwan as a province and this brings the total number of provinces to 23. There is a capital in each province or region and it is usually the most famous city of that area. Each province, autonomous region, municipality or special administrative region has its own local government. These act independently when handling local affairs and are allowed to refine the laws of the State within certain limits.

Municipalities. The four municipalities are Beijing, Shanghai, Tianjin and Chongqing. Beijing is also the capital of China. It is in the northeast of the country and is in the middle of the Hebei Province. It has been the capital for more than 800 years. You will find the greatest number of imperial buildings in Beijing and they are very well preserved. The municipality is currently undertaking a number of renovations for the preparation for the 2008 Olympics Games. Shanghai, probably the fastest growing economic region, is located along the coast in the east. Shanghai aims at becoming the major finance centre for Asia, or even the world. Some people believe that Shanghai is going to replace Hong Kong and become the most important financial centre of China in twenty to fifty-years time, even the central government believes that both places are of equal importance to the country. Both Chongqing and Tianjin are major industrial centres of China. They may not be the most favourable tourist cities but the products from the two areas are famous for good quality. Chongqing, situated in the centre of the country, is the largest motorcycle producer in China, while the coastal municipality of Tianjin is famous for its bicycles and watches.

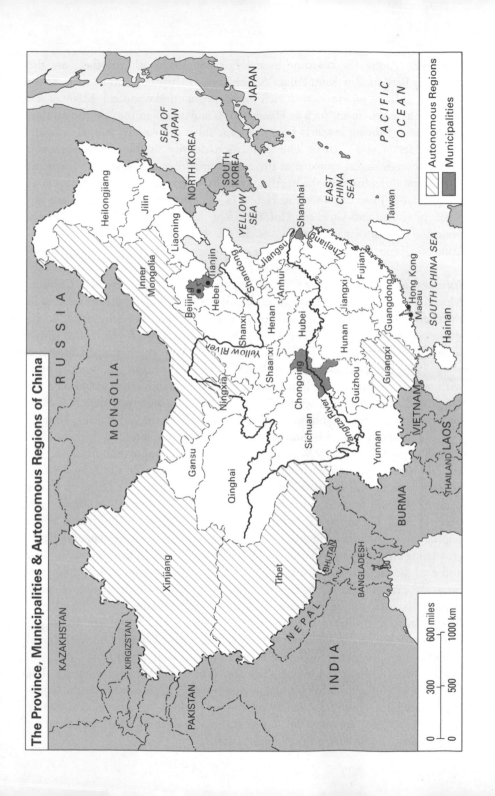

The Province, Municipalities & Autonomous Regions of China

Provinces. Along the coastline in the east and the southeast, there are the provinces Jiangsu, Zhejiang, Fujian, Shangdong, Guangdong and Hainan. These are more affluent provinces with rich supplies of natural resources. Many of the cities in these provinces, such as Hangzhou, Ji'nan and Nanjing, are also famous for tourism. Moving inwards from the east, there are Anhui, Jiangxi, Hunan, Hubei, Henan and Shanxi. The population density in these areas are quite high, although not as crowded as the coastal provinces. They are also the main regions for agriculture. In the northeast of China, you can find the provinces of Heilongjiang, Jilin, Liaoning and Hebei. In the centre of the country, there are Shannxi, Gansu and Guizhou. Unfortunately, the middle of China is relatively poor due to lack of natural resources. In the southwest, there are Sichuan and Yunnan. Qinghai is located in the west of China.

Autonomous Regions. Over 90% of the population in China are Han Chinese. Most live along the coastline or in the central regions, leaving the boundaries of the country for the ethnic minorities. Due to the differences in cultures and social values, the Chinese government set up autonomous regions for provinces with a high minority ratio to the Han Chinese. Guangxi is in the south of China and about 75% of the population are non-Han. *Zhuang* is the major group in Guangxi, with over 15 million people living in the province. Guangxi is actually called the Guangxi Zhuang Autonomous Region. There is also a sizable population of *Miao* and *Yao* living in the region but they remain mainly in the hill regions. Ningxia Hui Autonomous Region is located in the northwest of China and in the middle section of the Yellow River. More than one-third of the population in this region are *Hui*, who are descended from Arab and Iranian traders in the Tang dynasty. However, the population is still dominated by the Han. In the far north of the country, you will find the Inner Mongolia Autonomous Region. Mongolia (not part of China) lies to the north and Russia to the northwest. About 15% of the population in the Inner Mongolia Autonomous Region is Mongolian and others are mainly Han with a small number of *Hui* and *Manchu*. In this region, you will also find the biggest area of grassland in China. Tibet Autonomous Region has been a popular choice for foreign travellers in recent years. Its strong religious culture and the unique geographical location (at the base of the Himalayan Mountains) are probably the reasons for its popularity. There are about 2.5 million people living in Tibet and over 90% of them are Tibetans, but you should still expect to see quite a number of Han in Lhasa as well. Apart from Tibet, you can also find Tibetans in Qinghai, Sichuan, Gansu and Yunnan provinces. The full name of Xinjiang is Xinjiang Uygur Autonomous Region, which is the largest region of China. There are about 19 million people living in the region and more than 90% of them are non-Han. *Uygur* is the major ethnic group but there are over 40 other minorities in this region, as well.

Special Administrative Regions (SARs). The two SARs refer to Hong Kong and Macau, both located in the southeast of China and within Guangdong Province. The two regions have a high degree of autonomy and were granted the right to have their own legal systems under the 'one country, two systems' policy. Macau was once a Portuguese colony and was returned to China in November 1999. However, while Portuguese is still one of the official languages there, it is not a compulsory school subject and you should not expect locals to speak the language. There are many Portuguese buildings in Macau and, along with the casinos, they are the major landmarks of the city.

Population

Although China is slightly smaller than Canada, its population is 40 times greater. It is also five times that of the USA and 20 times that of the UK. The population in early 2004 was approximate 1.3 million. The population density on average is 135 people per square kilometer. However, quite a large area of China consists of mountains and deserts so the actual population density is much higher than this. In addition, most people prefer to live in the south and east of the country, which further boosts the local population density in these regions. For example, the population density in Beijing is 820 people per square kilometer, while that of Shanghai is up to 2,082 people per square kilometer. It is believed that the central part of Shanghai has 34,000 people in every square kilometer. According to the statistics of 2003, the natural growth rate is about 0.62% and the birth and death rates are 1.29% and 0.67% respectively. Life expectancy is 72, on average, but women in general live longer (to 74 years) while men usually live up to 70 years. The country's population is dominated by the Han Chinese, who account for about 92% of the total population, the remaining 8% being minority groups including mainly *Zhuang*, *Hui*, *Miao*, *Yao*, Tibetan, *Uygur* and Mongolian.

By the end of 2003, the male to female ratio was 1.16, which is above the warning point of gender balance at 1.07. In the 70s, the total population of China increased at a rapid rate. This led to a worry that the food supply would not be sufficient to feed the fast-growing population in the future. There would also be unemployment pressures and resource distribution problems, such as education, if the population continued to grow rapidly. In 1979, the government introduced the One-Child Policy to slow down population growth. Apart from the ethnic minority groups or couples who are both only children, who were allowed to have two children, other couples were limited to one only. The Government claims that the policy was a great success and that it prevented at least 250 million potential births between 1980 and 2000. However, the policy has created the problem of gender imbalance since it was introduced. The male to female ratio has kept rising in the last 20 years and the number of men will be 20% more than that of women in the future. Due to traditional preference and the need for manual labour, parents prefer to have a boy rather than a girl.

Under the limitation of the One-Child Policy, many mothers aborted their babies if they were known to be girls before birth. The abortion rate increased sharply from 1980. There were about 200,000 abortions a year before 1980. However, the number rose to 500,000 in 1987. In some cases, babies were even found killed after birth. As the problem is getting worse, the government is considering loosening the regulations, such as allowing second marriages where they have one child already to have a second one and allowing a couple to have a second child if their first child is handicapped.

About 70% of the population is aged between aged 15 and 64. However, the ratio of elderly over 65 is increasing. Currently, the number of those aged 65 or above represents 7.5% of the total population. According to the world standard, by which 7% is the borderline, China is an aging country. It is believed that, by the year 2050, the elderly group will be about one-fifth of the total population. The aging problem is also a result of the One-Child Policy mentioned above. Further discussion about the aging problem is covered in the chapter on *Retirement*.

Climate

The weather in the north and the west is quite extreme which makes it hard to say which season is the best time to stay in China. The climate is dominated by the dry and wet monsoon wind. In summer, the moist and warm wind comes from the ocean, from the south to the north, which makes the country warm (or even hot) and wet. However, in winter, the winds come from the higher latitudes and are cold and dry.

In general, the weather in the south and the southeast is better, as the temperature is less extreme and the season changes are never too sudden. It can be very hot in the summer, up to 38°C (100°F), but this is relatively mild compared to some other parts of the country. Summer is also the rain and storm season. Rainfall can be over 400mm in June, July and August and typhoons are common during these months. Spring is very humid in the south, but autumn is cool and dry. The winter is short and mild. The temperature almost never falls below zero and usually stays above 10°C. The average temperature during autumn is about 15°C to 18°C (59°F -64°F), and the weather is dry.

The north can be very cold between December and March. The temperature in Beijing is usually about -10°C or lower. In the far north, such as Haerbin, it is not unusual to be as cold as -40°C (-5°F) in the winter and snow is common. Sandstorms are another annoying problem during winter in the north and summer is not a very attractive season either. It is very hot and temperatures can be 40°C (104°F).

In the middle of the country, Hubei, Hunan, Chongqing and Sichuan are very hot and wet in the summer and very cold and dry in the winter. The summer is long, running from April to October.

You will experience the most extreme weather of China in the northwest. The temperature in Turpan, 150m below sea level, can reach 47°C (117°F) in summer. It is the hottest place in China while winters are extremely cold with temperatures down to -20°C (7°F). The rainfall is below 40mm all year round in these regions. In Tibet, the southwest of the country, the day and night temperatures often differ by 20°C. Even if it is over 30°C at midday, the temperature can drop below 10°C at night. Strong and cold winds are common during winter but snow is quite rare. The winter is long, from November to March, and the temperature can be as low as -10°C from December to February. Rainfall is scarce and there can be less than 5mm rainfall a day for half of the year. Even in the rainy season in July and August, rainfall does not exceed 150mm.

In the winter, staying in the central region can be more difficult than staying in the far north of China, as no winter heaters are allowed south of the Yangtze River. However, heating is usually found in public buildings in the north.

Useful Website

http://www.travelchinaguide.com/climate/, provides details of temperatures and rainfall in different cities.

Pollution. The problem of pollution has been a big challenge for the government over the last ten years. According to the report of the China Environmental Monitoring Center in 2003, about 40% of the seven major river valleys, including the Yangtze River, the Yellow River, Huaihe, Haihe, Liaohe, Songhuajiang and Pearl River in China are reported to have poor water quality. The Yellow River was even classified as Grade Five, which is the lowest water standard in the world. At the time of writing, the China Environmental Monitoring Center reported that more than one-third of the cities recorded an air quality standard at level Three or lower, indicating that the air quality is in general poor in China. Some environmental protection agencies believe that about 40% of the cities suffer bad air pollution, which include the six biggest cities: Beijing, Shanghai, Shenyang, Chongqing, Xian and Guangzhou. Urban areas in industrial regions such as Liaoning and Shanxi provinces are facing even more serious air and water pollution. Air pollution in urban areas is largely due to the combustion of poor quality coal of high-sulphur content for heat and electricity generation. Inefficient use of energy, lack of emission controls and the discharge of pollutants close to ground level also further degrade the air quality. Industrial development is also the major reason for water pollution in China.

The pollution problem has become a threat to residents' health and it is likely to be a burden to the fast-growing economy. China has introduced a series of policies for improving the pollution problem and aims to have a cleaner and greener China in the near future. In 1999, the government decided to spend nearly US$5 billion to combat pollution in the Three Gorges area, where the world's largest hydroelectric station is underway. After being granted the 2008 Olympic Games, anti-pollution is one of the major development directions for Beijing. In January 2002, another five-year programme was adopted, aiming to clean up the polluted waterways and smoggy skies. It is estimated that this programme will cost about US$84 billion and is going to reduce the pollutants in air and water by 10% by 2005. On 29th June, 2002, the government approved a new law named the Cleaner Production Promotion Law, which has been in full effect from 1st January 2003. The law aims to promote cleaner production, to increase the efficiency of the utilization rate of resources, and so reduce or avoid the generation of pollutants, to protect and improve environments, ensure the health of human beings and promote the sustainable development of the economy and society. There are even more anti-pollution policies set up in Beijing. The Beijing municipal government has said its aim is to hold a 'Green Olympics' and present a new Beijing to other countries. Its anti-pollution plan includes tackling the coal-smoke pollution problem in the city, increasing forest coverage and improving treatment of drainage water. About 20,000 municipal buses were converted to use natural gas while thousands of pollution-free new buses will be purchased in future years, bringing the total number of natural gas buses to 150,000 by 2008. The municipal government is also working on the light rail system between Beijing city centre and the Olympics Park, as well as increasing the length of the subway line by four-fifths of the current one. Both the Chinese government and other countries are positive about the anti-pollution projects in Beijing and look forward to the new face of the city. The huge amount of money being spent on China's pollution problems is indicative of the strength and vibrancy of both the economy and the government's political will.

GETTING THERE

Air

The airport facilities in China have been improving and it is now very easy to fly to Beijing and Shanghai. In the old days direct flights to the mainland were limited and rather expensive. Many people chose to fly to Hong Kong, the gateway to the mainland, and then take another flight or train to mainland China. The Chinese government has been opening up its aviation market, and flying to Beijing or Shanghai now costs about the same as flying to Hong Kong. Flying from London to Beijing takes about eleven hours, and costs about £400 for a return ticket in the low season. However, the price is nearly double or even more during the high seasons like the summer vacation. Flying to Shanghai takes two hours longer and the fare is slightly more expensive. In the low season, it costs about £500 while it costs about £800 to £1,000 in the peak season. Starting your trip from the United States will cost you about US$800 in the low seasons and US$1,100 in the high season. It takes about 13 hours or 11 hours to fly to Beijing from the east coast and west coast respectively. Flying to Shanghai will be one to two hours longer and slightly more expensive. Note that flights operating between Shanghai and other countries are less frequent compared to Beijing. You may be required to take a connecting flight in Beijing or Hong Kong.

Trains

Europeans can choose to go to China by train. It certainly takes much longer but it is a totally different experience. The Siberian Railway connects China to Russia, Kazakhstan and Mongolia. If you start your trip from London, it takes about two weeks to reach Beijing, assuming that you do not stop over in other cities. The service between Moscow and Beijing runs twice a week. *The Man in Seat Sixty-one* website *http://www.seat61.com/Trans-Siberian.htm* provides very useful details about travelling on the Siberian Railway, as well as other relevant information for travelling to China.

Ferry

Even though ferry connections are not available from western countries to China, you may consider flying to Japan and taking the ferry to Shanghai. There are two ferry companies sailing from Kobe and Osaka to Shanghai weekly, year-round. It costs about £100-£110 for a one way economy ticket. 4-berth and 2-berth cabins are available but the tickets are more expensive. You can book tickets via the Shanghai Ferry Company's e-mail address at *pax@shanghai-ferry.co.jp*.

There are also ferry connections between South Korea and China. You can take a ferry to Weihai, Tianjin, Qingdao, Dalin, Shanghai or Dandong from the port of Inch' n in South Korea. Ferries to most of the above cities operate two to three times a week and a one-way ticket costs about US$100 (£57).

Useful Addresses

The Man in Seat Sixty-one, e-mail webmaster@seat61.com;_http:// www.seat61.com/index.html: information about how to travel to China (and other countries) by train and ship from London.

China Travel Net Hong Kong Limited, Room A, 2/F, Tak Bo Building, 62-74 Sai Yee Street, Mongkok, Hong Kong; ☎(852) 2789 5401; fax (852) 2789 3498; e-mail enquiry@chinatravel1.com; www.chinatravel1.com.

China International Travel Service, ☎(86) 010 6522 2991/(86) 010 8522 7930; fax (86) 010 6522 2862; e-mail shuyu@cits.com.cn ; www.cits.net.

China Travel Service (Beijing Office), Zidutech Co., Ltd. Beijing; No. 34 Fuwaidajie Ave, Xicheng District, Beijing 100832; ☎(86) 010 6852 4860/ (86) 010 6852 4882; fax (86) 010 6852 4887; e-mail bisc@chinats.com; www.chinats.com.

China Youth Travel Service, 23C Dongjiaominxiang, Beijing 100006; ☎(86) 010 6513 3153; fax (86) 010 6527 7415.

Airline Websites

Air Canada, www.aircanada.ca.

Air France, www.airfrance.com.

Air New Zealand, www.airnz.com.au.

American Airlines, www.aa.com.

Australia Airlines, www.australianairlines.com.au.

British Airways, www.britishairways.com.

Cathay Pacific Airway, www.cathaypacific.com.

China Airlines, www.china-airlines.com.

Delta Airlines, www.delta.com.

Emirates Airlines, www.emirates.com.

EVA Air, www.evaair.com.

Finnair, www.finnair.com.

Singapore Airlines, www.singaporeair.com.

Other Useful Websites

www.priceline.com.

www.expedia.co.uk.

www.onlinetravel.com.

www.statravel.com.

www.traveljungle.co.uk.

www.travelsupermarket.com.

Ferry Companies

Weidong Ferry Company, 1005 Sungji Building, 10th floor, 585 Dohwa-dong, Mapo-gu, Seoul, South Korea; ☎(82) 02 3271 6710; fax (82) 02 3271 6770; www.weidong.com.

Jinchon Ferry Company, ☎(82) 02 517 8671.

International Union Travel Agency, Room 707, 7/F, Daehan Ilbo Building, 340 Taepyonglo 2-ga, Chung-gu, Seoul, South Korea; ☎(82) 02 777 6722. This agency sells ferry tickets to China.

Taeya Travel, ☎(82) 02 514 6226. You can get ferry tickets to Tianjin through this agency.

RESIDENCE & ENTRY REGULATIONS

CHAPTER SUMMARY

- US and UK citizens have to apply for visas regardless of the purpose of their trips.
- A Tibet Travel Bureau Permit (TTP) and other Alien Travel Permits are required to visit Tibet.
- Students who are going to study for more than six months in China should apply for an X visa; students intending to stay for less than six months should apply for an F visa instead.
- Holders of X, Z, J1 and D visas need to go through residential formalities within 30 days of arrival.
- Visa extensions should be applied for at the Public Security Bureau (PSB).
- Macau grants a visa-free stay of 90 days to citizens from the EU and people covered by the Treaty of Schengen (Tratado de Schengen); citizens from the USA can stay in Macau for 30 days without visas.
- After residing in Macau for seven years, permanent residence is granted.
- The legal age for marriage in China for men and women is 22 and 20 years respectively.

OVERVIEW

China is becoming an increasingly attractive place for many foreigners and the government has been trying to make entry easier for visitors. Most visitors will not have much difficulty obtaining a visa. There are eight different types of visa and it takes roughly three to five days for the Chinese Embassy or Consulate-General to issue one. However, during the summer when the country becomes overcrowded with tourists, the Embassy and Consulate-General may apply more stringent standards for visa applications in order to limit the number of tourists. Travelling to Tibet is more complicated. Special travel permits are required in addition to the Chinese visitor's visa; moreover, the regulations are continually changing and you are always advised to check the permit requirements before your trip. China has a population of 1.3 billion and the supply of workers has never been a problem. On the contrary, there is a need to attract foreign investors and professionals and currently, there are about 440,000 foreigners working and living in China. In the past, it was not easy for a foreigner to obtain a permanent residence permit, unless he or she was a close relative of a Chinese citizen. This has recently changed and the government is considering granting permanent residence status to foreigners if they are professionals or investors. In early 2003, 45 three to five year residence permits and multiple entry visas were issued to foreigners. It is believed that the permits and visas serve as a transition towards permanent residence permits.

The validity for a single or double entry visa is 90 days from the date of issue. This means you have to enter China no later than 90 days after the visa has been issued. Often you will be permitted to stay for up to 30 days, this can be extended in some cases. Note that you should apply for your visa extension with the Public Security Bureau (PSB). You are required to have a health check and also an HIV test before entering the country if you intend to stay for over one year.

TYPES OF VISA FOR MAINLAND CHINA

Visit (L Visa)

If you are going to China as a tourist, or to visit family or for other personal reasons, you should apply for an L visa. This will grant you a 30-day stay which you can probably extend twice, for an additional 30 days for each extension. You can also apply for a double or a multiple entry visa if you are a frequent visitor to China. Multiple entry visas are available for six months or twelve months. However, they are usually granted to those who have family members or who own real estate in China. It is not impossible for individual travellers to get multiple entry visas, however this is not very common. If you have family living in China, you should submit proof of relationship or an invitation letter from your family along with your visa application. If you own property in China, you should submit both the original and a photocopy of the property ownership certificate (the original copy will be returned to you). Holders of L visas are not allowed to take up any employment in China during their stay.

Visiting Tibet. An L visa is required for entry to Tibet. Additionally, you are required to apply for a Tibet Tourism Bureau Permit (TTP). Application can be made through travel agencies before you leave your country; alternatively, you can obtain it from the Tibet Tourism Bureau's Shanghai Office if you stop off in Shanghai before visiting Tibet. You will need to provide copies of your visa and passport when applying for the TTP. The TTP grants you the right to visit only some parts of Tibet, which include the towns of Lhasa, Shigatse, Tsetang, and places in the Lhasa region. To visit other regions of Tibet, you will need an Alien Travel Permit for each place you plan to visit. The Public Security Bureau (PSB), which is the police, is responsible for granting these permits. The PSB prefers to deal with travel agencies rather than individuals and many local PSBs, for example that in Lhasa, refuses to issue permits to individual travellers. Many have successfully got their permits at the Shigatse PSB for permits granting access to Sakya, Everest Base Camp, Nangartse, Shalu, Gyantse and anywhere on the Friendship Highway. The permit costs about 50 *yuan* if you apply on-the-spot. The easiest way to get the permit, however, is to join the tours organised by travel agencies but be warned these tours are often quite expensive. It usually takes about 4 working days for the agencies to get a permit. Many travel agencies include the permit applications in a tour package and do not arrange permits separately. You are advised to check the permit requirements and the corresponding application methods as they change frequently.

Useful Addresses

Tibet Tourist Bureau (Head Office), Suite B, 2/F, QiHua Tower 1375 Middle Huaihai Road, Shanghai 200031; ☎(86) 021 6431 1184/(86) 021 6321 1729; fax (86) 021 6323 1016; e-mail ttbshanghai@163.net; www.tibet-tour.com.

China International Travel Services (Head Office), ☎(86) 010 6608 7126/(86) 010 6601 1122-8291; fax (86) 010 6601 2039; e-mail shuyu@cits.com.cn; www.cits.net.

China International Travel Services (Los Angeles Office), 975 East Green Street, Suite 101, Pasadena, CA 91106; ☎(1) 626 568 8993; fax (1) 626 568 9207; e-mail info@citsusa.com; www.citsusa.com.

Business (F Visa)

An F visa is a business visa which also applies to those going to China for research purposes, those giving lectures or those going on scientific, technological and cultural exchanges. Students who go to China for short-term (less than six months) advanced studies or internship should also apply for the F visa, not an X visa. When applying, you are required to provide an invitation letter from the host company or organisation in China. You can apply for a multiple entry visa under the following circumstances:

- The organisation in China, which is mainly responsible for your business visit, specifies that you will need to enter China more than once in a short period. It should be stated in the application in as much detail as possible, how many entries you will need and for each entry how long you will be staying.
- You have investments in China and need to enter the country to manage

them from time to time.

o   You are in a position of management in an foreign company in China; or

o   You need to visit China frequently in order to execute contracts signed with Chinese companies.

o   You have visited China with F visas twice in the last 12 months.

Multiple entry visas for business purposes are available for both 6 months and 12 months. You are required to provide proof, such as a business licence carrying your name and contracts signed with the business partners, to apply for a multiple entry visa.

Employment (Z Visa)

It is necessary to get an employment visa, Z visa, before commencing work in China. After obtaining a Work Permit for Aliens issued by the Chinese Ministry of Labour, or a Foreign Expert's Licence, issued by the Chinese Foreign Expert Bureau, the authorised Chinese unit will provide you with a visa notification. You need this visa notification as well as your original copy of the Work Permit or Foreign Expert's Licence when applying for a Z visa. This visa is valid for one entry only with a duration of three months. You are required to go through residential formalities in the local public security bureau within 30 days when you first enter China. You will then be issued with a Foreigner Residence Certificate as proof of identity for living and working in China.

It is possible to change your visa status inside China, even though it is not encouraged by the Chinese government. If you are offered a job after arriving in China, your employer should apply to the Chinese Foreign Expert Bureau for a change of your visa status. You then have to go through all the formalities to get a Foreign Residence Certificate as mentioned above.

Dependents of the applicant should apply for the same visa if they are going to stay in China with the employed applicant. They will have to provide proof of kinship such as marriage certificates and/or birth certificates to identify their relationship with the employed.

Education (X Visa)

Once you have received an offer from a university or college in China, you must apply for an X visa. For study periods shorter than six months, you should apply for an F visa instead of an X visa. An X visa is for those who intend to study or enrol in advanced studies or internship for six months or more. Apart from the Visa Application Form (Q1) you will need to submit Foreign Student Application Forms (JW201 or JW202), issued by the Ministry of Education, and the enrolment letters from the educational organisation in China. If you intend to stay in China for over a year, you are required to have a medical check-up and attach the Physical Examination Certificate to the application. An X visa is a single entry visa and you, as the holder, should go through residential formalities in the local Public Security Bureau within 30 days of entry into China. Holders of X visas are prohibited from any employment during their stay.

Transit (G Visa)

Under the current regulations, citizens from some countries including the UK are required to hold a transit visa if they are staying in China for any length of time. Many travellers enjoy a visa-free transit if they stay in a transit city for less than 24 hours without leaving the airport. For enjoying this privilege, they have to hold the ticket for the final destination and have booked their seats on international airlines flying directly through China. The rule is more flexible for passengers travelling through Pudong Airport (Shanghai). Citizens of the United States, Canada, Australia, New Zealand, Germany, France, Netherlands, Belgium, Luxemburg, Portugal, Spain, Italy, Austria, Greece and the Republic of Korea do not need a visa if they stay in Shanghai for less than 48 hours. They are not limited to staying in the airport within the limited transit period, so long as they hold valid passports, onward tickets and have booked seats with the airlines. Unfortunately, British citizens are currently excluded from this group and are required to hold transit visas if they travel through Pudong Airport. A transit visa is valid for entry for 90 days and the holder can legally stay for up to a week.

Crew Members (C Visa)

C visas are for crew members on international airlines or shipping or for cross boarder land transport. Family members accompanying the crew members to China should apply for the same visa.

Journalists (J-1 and J-2 Visas)

In China, there are specific visas for visiting journalists. Foreign resident journalists should apply for J-1 visas before entering China. Foreign journalists who are on temporary interview missions in China and will leave the country when the mission is completed should apply for J-2 visas. A letter from the Information Department of the Ministry of Foreign Affairs should be attached to the application. A journalist can also apply for such a letter from the Foreign Affairs Office in Shanghai or Guangdong. In addition, journalists must have a letter from their employers to confirm the purpose of the visit.

Permanent Residence (D Visa)

A D visa is for a someone who is going to reside permanently in China. It is only for people who have already got their application for residence approved by the government of China. You should present a permanent residence confirmation form for the municipality or county where you plan to live, along with your visa application form. You will have to apply for a Foreigner Residence Certificate, which is the actual permit for staying in China for unlimited time, from the local Public Security Bureau within 30 days of your arrival in China. You are required to submit your certificate to the Public Security Bureau for examination once a year.

Application Methods

The application method for all the different types of visa is basically the same. Apart from the specific documents mentioned in each section, there are a few documents which are required with the application for any of the visas. They include:

- ○ Your valid passport (original) which has at least one blank page left inside. Moreover, your passport should be valid for at least a further six months at the time of your visa application.
- ○ Visa Application Form (Q1). The same form is used for application for any of the visas.
- ○ Two passport photos, of which one should be attached to the application form.
- ○ If an applicant was born in China but currently holds a foreign passport, he or she should also submit the original Chinese passport or the last foreign passport held with a Chinese visa in it.

It takes on average three to five days to get a visa in the USA or the UK. If you send the application by mail, it will take two to three weeks for processing. Note that the Embassy and Consulate-General of the People's Republic of China in the USA do not accept applications by mail. If you cannot apply for the visa in person, you have to entrust someone else to do it for you. You may choose to appoint a travel agency to apply for it. Same day and express processing services are available with additional charges. Payments must be settled either by cash or postal order. Personal cheques are not accepted. The embassy and consulate-general in the USA also accept money orders, cashier's cheques and company cheques. If you send your application to the embassy in the UK by mail, you should enclose a self addressed envelope for the embassy to return your passport with your visa enclosed.

You can also apply for your visas to China in Hong Kong. You can apply to the Ministry of Foreign Affairs for your visa, which takes about two days to process. You can also apply through travel agencies such as China Travel Service (CTS) but note that these travel agencies only accept applications for travel visas.

Useful Addresses

Embassy of the People's Republic of China in the United States, Visa Office, 2201

Wisconsin Avenue, NW, Room 110, Washington, DC 20007; tel (1) 202 338 6688; fax (1) 202 588 9760; e-mail chnvisa@bellatlantic.net; www.china-embassy.org.

Consulates General of the People's Republic of China in the United States (New York), Passport and Visa Office, 520 12th Ave. New York, NY 10036; tel (1) 212 868 2078; fax (1) 212 465 1708; e-mail cnconsulate@yahoo.com; www.nyconsulate.prchina.org.

Consulates General of the People's Republic of China in the United States (San Francisco), Visa Office, 1450 Laguna Street, San Francisco CA 94115; ☎(1) 415 674 2940; fax (1) 415 563 4861; www.chinaconsulatesf.org.

Consulates General of the People's Republic of China in the United States (Houston), 3417 Montrose Boulevard, Houston, Texas 77006; ☎(1) 713 524 0780; fax (1) 713 524 7656; e-mail visa@chinahouston.org; www.chinahouston.org.

Consulates General of the People's Republic of China in the United States (Los Angeles), The Passport & Visa Office, 3rd Floor, 500 Shatto Place, Los Angeles, CA 90020; ☎(1) 213 807 8006; e-mail visa@chinaconsulatela.org; losangeles.china-consulate.org.

Embassy of the People's Republic of China in the United Kingdoms, Visa Office, 31 Portland Place, London W1B 1QD; ☎(44) 020 7631 1430; fax (44) 020 7436 9178; www.chinese-embassy.org.uk.

Consulates General of the People's Republic of China in the United Kingdoms (Manchester), *Visa Office,* Denison House, 49 Denison Road, Rusholme, Manchester M14 5RX; ☎(44) 0161 224 8672; fax (44) 0161 257 2672.

Consulates General of the People's Republic of China in the United Kingdoms (Edinburgh), *Visa Office,* 55 Corstorphine Road, Edinburgh EH12 5QG; ☎(44) 0131 337 3220; fax (44) 0131 337 1790.

Ministry of Foreign Affairs of the People's Republic of China (HKSAR Office), Office of the Commissioner, 7th Floor, Lower Block, China Resources Building, 26 Harbour Road, Wanchai, Hong Kong; ☎(852) 3413 2300 (24 hours)/(852) 3413 2424.

Fees

Visa application fees are calculated on the number of entries rather than the type of visa you apply. The following charges are for the Chinese Embassies in the USA and the UK. Note that the application fees for other nationalities in the embassies above are in general lower.

FEES FOR VISAS		
Type of Visa	**US$**	**GBP£**
Single Entry Visas	$50	£30

Double Entry Visas	$75	£45
Multiple entry for 6 months	$100	£60
Multiple entry for 12 months	$150	£90
Express service (same day)	$30	£20
Express service (2 day)	$20	£15
Mail service	-	£20
Application for HK or Macau visa	$50	£30

TYPES OF VISA FOR MACAU

Short-term Stay

Currently, citizens of 53 countries, including the USA, the UK and most European countries do not need a visa if they stay for less than 30 days. Citizens from the EU or members of the Treaty of Schengen (Tratado de Schengen) are allowed to stay for up to 90 days without a visa. Other visitors should apply for a visa through the Embassy or the Consulate General of the People's Republic of China before visiting Macau. Alternatively you can apply for the visa on the spot when you arrive in the city. The charge for obtaining a visa on the spot is MOP$100. Extensions of visas should be made at least ten days before the expiration and the maximum extended period is 90 days.

Students who are going to study in Macau are granted a one year visa which they will have to renew annually throughout their year of studying.

Transit

If you are granted a visa-free stay from the Macau government, there is obviously no need to apply for a transit visa when you stop off in the city. Visitors who arrive in Macau through Macau International Airport are granted a five-day visa-free stay so long as they hold onward tickets and have booked seats with the airlines. If you enter Macau through other immigration ports, you can stay for two days without a visa.

Employment

Employers have to apply to the Labour and Employment Bureau for bringing in employees from other countries. After the application is preliminarily approved, you, the employee, will be issued with an approval letter, which allows you to stay in Macau for 20 days while awaiting a formal approval. After receiving a formal approval, you will need to submit six passport photos and two photocopies of your passport in addition to the letter of approval to apply for an Employment Card (known as the Blue Card).

Useful Addresses
Labour and Employment Bureau, Rotunda de Carlos da Maia, Macao, ☎(853) 564109; fax (853) 550477; e-mail dsteinfo@dste.gov.mo; http://www.dste.gov.mo/.

GETTING MARRIED IN CHINA

If you are marrying a Chinese citizen, you have to make a Statutory Declaration either in front of a registered solicitor or to a Notary Public. You should state in the declaration your name, sex, date of birth, nationality, passport or ID card number, occupation, address and marital status, this declaration then needs to be sent to the Embassy or Consulate-General of the People's Republic of China for authentication. If the document is accepted, your declaration will be legalised. The legalisation is valid for six months. After entering China, you and your fiancée or fiancé must go to the local government office to submit your marriage application. You should also present the legalized declaration you made earlier and you will be required to have your health checked by a designated hospital. You and your partner will go through a marriage registration after the application is approved and the Marriage Certificate will then be issued to you.

Note that there is a minimum age for legal marriage in China. For males it is 22 while for females it is 20. Bigamy is illegal in China. According to the statistics conducted by the Chinese Academy of Social Sciences in Beijing, the male-female ratio is currently 1.2 to 1, which is mainly the result of the One-Child policy of the government. Unfortunately, many Chinese still prefer to have boys for traditional family values and the need for manual labour. Some parents choose to abort when they know that the baby is going to be a girl. The One-Child policy is still running in the country and only people living in some rural areas are allowed to have two children under the system.

CHINESE CITIZENSHIP

Under the current law, foreign nationals or stateless persons may be naturalized as Chinese citizens if they are near relatives of Chinese nationals, or if they have settled in China, or if they have other legitimate reasons. A foreigner should apply to the Public Security Bureau for naturalisation. In the past, most of the approved applicants were close relatives of Chinese nationals; not many foreigners were granted permanent residence for business or other reasons. However, in early 2003, the Chinese government first granted long-term residence permits and multi-entry visas to foreigners who had no relatives in China. The permit allows a foreigner to stay in the country for three to five years and there is no need to renew the permit annually. It is believed that this is the first step towards permanent residence for foreigners.

If you wish to be naturalised and become a Chinese citizen, you should apply to the Ministry of Public Security attaching supporting documents, such as your marriage certificate if applicable and any business certificates. The Ministry will take several factors into consideration for each application. If you have close relatives in China, it is more likely that you will be granted citizenship. Moreover, if you have been an upstanding citizen in your home country and have mastered the Chinese language, your chances of being granted citizenship are greatly increased.

The Chinese government does not allow dual nationality, except for citizens of Hong Kong and Macau who hold British National (Overseas) passports and the Portuguese passport (MSAR); naturalization means you have to give up your original nationality.

Permanent Residence in Macau. You are required to live in Macau for a continuous seven year period in order to get permanent residence. The government issues a Temporary Residence Card (called the 'Yellow Card') to (a) people who have near relatives who are Macau permanent residents and (b) investors or professionals. Currently, successful applicants are initially granted a one year or three year permit as the maximum duration of stay. They can extend their stay but they have to do so at least 30 days before the expiration of their Temporary Residence Card. The government will grant another two years of stay if it is satisfied with the behaviour of the applicant during their initial stay. There is no limit to the number of extensions you can make. After a person has stayed in Macau continuously for seven years, he or she will be granted a Permanent Residence Card (called the 'White Card'). Application for a Temporary Residence Card should be made to the Public Security Forces Bureau. It takes on average 45 days to process an application.

Useful Addresses

Ministry of Public Security, No. 14 East Chang'an Avenue, Beijing 100741; ☎(86) 010 6512 2831; www.PSB.gov.cn.

Ministry of Foreign Affairs, No. 2, Chaoyangmen Nandajie, Chaoyang District, Beijing 100701; ☎(86) 010 6596 1114; www.fmprc.gov.cn/eng/.

Public Security Forces Bureau, Calçada dos Quartéis, Quartel de S. Francisco, Macao; ☎(853) 559999; fax (853) 559998; e-mail info@fsm.gov.mo; www.fsm.gov.mo.

Identification Department, Avenida da Praia Grande, No. 804, Edificia China plaza, 1st, 19th, 20th andar, Macau; ☎(853) 370 777; fax (853) 374 300; e-mail info@dsi.gov.mo; www.dsi.gov.mo.

SETTING UP HOME

CHAPTER SUMMARY

- **Home Ownership.** 80% of urban families own a house or flat.
  - You can buy a property before its construction is completed.
  - Both bought and rented properties are usually unfurnished.
  - More people enjoy decorating their homes; B&Q in Beijing is even bigger than its largest store in the UK home country.
- **Electricity.** The electricity supply is 220 volts (50 Hz).
  - Sockets are designed for plugs with two flat parallel prongs.
- **Water.** Tap water must be boiled before drinking.
- **Telephone.** The International Phone (IP) service is a much cheaper way to make international calls.
- **Car.** The level of car ownership increased by 68% in 2003.
  - The quota for imported cars will be completely removed in 2005.
- **Pets**. You can only bring cats and dogs into China.
  - One family is limited to only one dog and you are required to register your dog with the local police.

HOW THE CHINESE LIVE

Traditionally, owing to family values and the need for manual labour, the Chinese saw having a boy in the family as a necessity. Parents often went on having children until a boy was conceived. However, since the One-Child policy was adopted in 1979, this is no longer legally possible, and Chinese families are thus typically small these days. Instead of staying with their parents in a big family house as in the old days, young couples now usually move away from their families once they get married and quite often the parents will help the young to buy a new house.

Chinese people do not move around that much. One's birthplace is an important part of one's identity. Although young people often have to leave for other provinces for study or work, they usually return to their home towns later in life.

In urban areas, 80% of the people own their houses or flats. This is largely due the housing benefits provided by the state or state-owned enterprises, before the country launched its opening-up and economic reform. Since then, the central government has been reforming the housing system. In the mid 1980s, the government sold luxurious and spacious houses at market prices to the rich in order to compensate for the costs of providing affordable housing for middle and low-income families. Additionally, tax reductions were given to developers who built these more affordable houses.

According to the National Bureau of Statistics of China in November 2003, the average household size was three people, in most provinces in China. The average monthly income per household is 735 *yuan* (US$90/£53). However, the figures vary from province to province and the income in fast developing provinces is usually much higher. The average monthly income per household in Beijing and Shanghai, for instance, was 1,217 *yuan* (US$148/£87) and 1,378 *yuan* (US$168/£98) respectively. However, the average income of Guizhou and Xinjiang was only 540 *yuan* (US$66/£39) and 604 *yuan* (US$74/£43) respectively.

The east is more populated than the west of China, due to geographical, commercial and economic factors. However, the new national construction projects and the discovery of oil fields in the west mean that more people will move there to live and work.

There are mainly two types of housing in China, known as *commodity housing* and *government housing*. *Government housing* is only available for employees of the government and state-owned enterprises. However, owners who have purchased government houses can resell their properties on the market once they have paid the land premium to convert their properties into *commodity housing*. Besides these two types of housing, there is also economic housing provided to lower income families.

Styles of housing, prices and facilities vary from region to region. Both high-rise buildings and houses with gardens are available in big cities like Beijing, Shanghai, Guangdong and Tianjin. Contrary to popular belief, there are more parks or open spaces than might be expected in the big cities. One goal for Beijing, for instance, is to eventually have 50% of its land covered with greenery. However, housing prices are expected to be higher in these areas. For details please refer to the *Property Prices* section later in this chapter.

Newly built flats typically consist of a dining room, a living room, a bathroom with bathtub, a kitchen and two or three bedrooms with one en-suite. Flats these days are usually fully furbished when they are sold. It is expected that in 2005 about 90% of newly launched flats will be fully furbished with gas, electricity and water supplies installed. However, one should note that radiator/heating systems are only available for provinces north of the Yangtze River. Central heating systems are not allowed to be installed in the flats or houses in the south due to the issue of global warming, although portable radiators may be bought by individuals. Land line (telephone) and internet connections are usually pre-installed and services would be made available after subscription. Competition between internet services is so fierce that prices are fairly low these days. Bills may be paid at post offices, convenience stores or banks, where autopay (direct debit) instructions could be set up for the bills.

Macau comprises the peninsula of Macau and the two islands of Taipa and Coloane. Most people used to live on the peninsula of Macau, but thanks to the efficient transport linkage, more people now live on Taipa. In the second quarter of 2003, Macau's population was 444,000. Its population density was over 16,000 per square kilometre.

Useful Addresses and Websites

Ministry of Foreign Affairs, No. 2, Chaoyangmen Nandajie, Chaoyang District, Beijing, 100701; ☎(86) 010 6596 1114; e-mail webmaster@mfa.gov.cn; http://www.fmprc.gov.cn/eng/default.htm.

www.cityweekend.com.cn. A bi-weekly English guide to life in China. It provides information on Shanghai and Beijing.

http://www.thatsmagazines.com/index.asp. Provides classified information on living in Shanghai, Beijing and Guangzhou, including information on accommodation, employment and other services.

http://www.biggles.co.uk/Columbus/CityGuide/cities/sha/CityOverview.htm. An overview of living in Shanghai.

Macao Special Adminstrative Region of The People's Republic of China (MSAR), http://www.macau.gov.mo/.

Macao Trade and Investment Promotion Institute, http://www.ipim.gov.mo/english/E – MainNight.asp. Information on investment, residency, full contacts of official and business bodies.

FINANCE

Mortgages

Home mortgages in China are provided by banks. Usually, developers will nominate at least two partnering banks for a particular project and buyers can choose between them. China Minsheng Banking Corp. Ltd. is the first bank to launch mortgage services that allows borrowers to transfer their mortgages to another bank (non-specific mortgage services), which improves the flexibility to both buyers (borrowers) and the developers. However, at the time of writing, it is still a relatively new idea, which means most mortgages are fixed.

There are three types of home mortgages, namely, a *housing provident fund loan,* a *commercial housing loan* and a *portfolio loan. A housing provident fund loan* caters for staff with a provident (retirement/pension) fund account, which is the source of the loan. For a mortgage on a new property, the maximum loan amount is 100,000 *yuan* (US$12,195/£7,143) but it must not exceed 80% of the property price and the maximum term is 30 years. For a second-hand property, the maximum loan should not exceed 70% of the property price and the maximum term is 15 years. *A commercial housing loan* is usually provided by designated banks chosen by the developers. The maximum loan amount is 500,000 *yuan* (US$60,975/£35,714) with the same limit and terms applied to a housing provident fund loan. *A portfolio loan* is simply the application for both the housing provident fund loan and the commercial housing loan. In early 2004, the interest rate for a housing provident fund loan was 3.6% while that of a commercial housing loan was 4.77%, depending on the term of the loan. Due to fierce competition, banks are constantly trying to design different types of mortgage products to suit the needs of different clients.

In general, it is easy and quick to apply for a home mortgage, so long as you can provide the required documents. You should first submit an application and the relevant information to a bank. If the application is approved, the bank will issue a letter of offer to you. After you sign the letter of offer, the bank will instruct its legal representatives to prepare a mortgage contract and notarisation. The contract has to be sent to government bodies for registration after you have signed it. Finally, the mortgage loan will be released. You will be required to provide your account document, passport, work permit, marriage certificate, title document of the property, proof of income and receipt for the first instalment you have paid for your property to apply for a mortgage.

Various fees are involved in the loan process and they vary from bank to bank. In most banks, you are required to pay an application fee, administration fees such as legal and valuation fees, a mortgage insurance fee and disbursements such as mortgage registration and stamp duty.

People applying for a mortgage in Beijing will need a credit rating report from the Beijing Personal Credit Service Centre. Those with a high rating will be entitled to lower interest rates and higher mortgage loan amounts. Basically, banks will seek ratings from the centre or check if you are on the 'black-list'. Contact DTZ (Debenham Tie Leung, below) for more information about this.

In Macau, various home mortgage products are offered by banks such as HSBC and Bank of China. Home mortgage loans can be up to 90% of the market or evaluated price of the property and repayment periods range from 20 to 30 years.

Bank Addresses

China Minsheng Banking Corporation Limited, No. 4, Zhengyi Road, Dongcheng District, Beijing 100006; e-mail service@cmbc.com.cn; www.cmbc.com.cn.

China Construction Bank, ☎(86) 021 6374 8585; e-mail 95533/zh/ ccb@ccb.com.cn; http://www.ccb.cn/portal/en/home/index.jsp.

Bank of China, 1 Fuxingmen Nei Dajie, Bejing 100818, P.R.China; ☎(86) 010 6659 6688; fax (86) 010 6601 4024; http://www.bank-of-china.com/english/ index.html.

The Hongkong and Shanghai Banking Corporation Limited (HSBC), 36th
   Floor, HSBC Tower, 101 Yin Cheng East Road, Pudong, Shanghai 200120;
   ☎(86) 021 6841 1888; fax (86) 021 6841 2626; e-mail online@hsbc;
   www.hsbc.com.cn.
Standard Chartered Bank Macau, http://www.standardchartered.com/mo/
   index.html.
The Hongkong and Shanghai Banking Corporation Limited (HSBC), 639
   Avenida da Praia Grande, Macau; ☎(853) 553669; fax (853) 322831; http:
   //www.hsbc.com.mo/mo/aboutus/default.htm.

Another Useful Address
DTZ Debenham Tie Leung, ☎(86) 010 6510 1388; e-mail winnie – yip@dtz.bj.cn;
   http://www.dtz.bj.cn/default.htm.

Property Prices

If you are going to stay in China for a short period only, your company
will probably provide you with accommodation as part of your expatriate
remuneration package. Quite often in China companies simply buy the whole
storey of a housing complex to accommodate their staff.

Due to the strong economic boom, property prices have escalated several fold
within years. In one case in Shanghai, 1000 flats from a single housing complex
were sold within a day in 2003. Beijing is going to host the Olympic Games in
2008, and this has attracted a lot of local as well as foreign investors into the real
estate business. Properties with good facilities, and those near the CBD (Central
Business District) are the most popular. All that said, if you are planning to invest
in real estate, do make sure you have a good understanding of how the market
works. Although prices of properties are expected to climb further in 2004, it has
also been suggested that some factors like deflation and tighter control from the
government may cool down the market. Moreover, the conveyancing procedure
can be rather complicated and it may vary in different provinces.

Since the merger of domestic and non-domestic commodity housing markets
in 2002, foreigners are no longer limited to purchasing non-domestic housing. If
you consider buying a property in China, there are many choices available: flats in
high-rise buildings (about 20 storeys); three to four-storey houses; hotel-services
flats (ideal for frequent travellers or those who simply do not want to bother
with housekeeping). Besides traditional marketing methods such as advertising
in newspapers and on television, developers often hold property exhibitions in
big cities like Beijing and Shanghai. The 'China Daily-Biz Events' website *http:
//www.chinadaily.com.cn/english/home/biznews.html* provides information on real
estate exhibitions held in China.

The price of properties varies a lot and depends on location, size and the
facilities available. In Shanghai, a fully furbished flat with club facilities such as

swimming pool, gymnastic room and squash court, etc, can cost up to US$1,705/ £926 per square metre. Some properties in Zhejiang can be more expensive than those in Shanghai, even though the average property price is lower. In general, it is more expensive to buy a house in big cities or the coastal areas, and the price goes down when you move to the north and the west. The following table gives you a general idea of the price of properties in different provinces:

PROPERTY VALUES BY PROVINCE (PER SQUARE METRE)		
	Shanghai	**Beijing**	**Guangzhoou**
Apartment	8,979 *yuan* (US$1095/£595)	7,003 *yuan* (US$854/£500)	7,200 *yuan* (US$878/ £514)
Flat	4,223 *yuan* (US$515/£278)	6,002 *yuan* (US$732/£429)	2,993 *yuan* (US$365/ £242)
Hotel-Flat	17,171 *yuan* (US$2094/£1138)	10,004 *yuan* (US$1220/£714)	N/A
	Zhejiang	**Tianjin**	**Nanjing**
Flat	3,215 *yuan* (US$392/£230)	3,280 *yuan* (US$400/£235)	4,002 *yuan* (US$488/ £2(86))
	Dailin	**Chengzhou**	**Chongqing**
Flat	2,698 *yuan* (US$329/£193)	1,804 *yuan* (US$220/£129)	2,600 *yuan* (US$317/ £1(86))

Parking space may not necessarily come with your flat and sometimes the parking space available may be insufficient for all the households to accommodate their cars. Even if you can obtain a parking space, you will probably need to pay a monthly rental fee of several hundred *yuan*. However, you will be provided with a parking certificate, which is a mandatory document for the annual inspection of the vehicle. You might be able to find cheaper parking if you shop around, but paying slightly more may save you a lot of trouble in the end. Effective from 1st January 2003, indoor car parks sold on the market are required to register with the Real Estate Department. The title document will be issued either separately or together with the associated housing.

The second-hand property market is as vibrant as the new one. A property exhibition held in Beijing in 2003 involved a total of 9,800 housing units, of which 47% were as cheap as 300,000 *yuan* (US$36,585/£21,429) or less. The transaction processes are usually done through agents. However, not all real estate agencies are up to standard and you must choose carefully the ones with good reputations and a good network throughout the country. Please refer to the section on '*Conveyancing*' for more details.

Instead of bringing your own furniture, which is expensive and troublesome, you may consider buying your furniture in China. Furniture and household appliances are much cheaper than those in the USA and Europe. Moreover, there are many one-stop home decoration shops available in China now and it is easy to obtain all the things you need at once. The UK based B&Q owns more than ten stores in major cities like Beijing, Shanghai and Guangzhou, offering all sorts of materials and accessories for home decoration. The Beijing branch is even bigger than the largest branch in the UK. Chinese antiques are of course famous and are popular amongst both locals and foreigners. Good looking Chinese styled furniture often does not cost more than the western styled variety so long as you are not looking for antiques from the Ming or Qing Dynasties.

In Macau, the most expensive region used to be the Macau peninsula. Due to the improvement of transportation, more and more people stay in Taipa nowadays and property there could be as expensive as in the Macau peninsula. It costs about MOP$200,000 to MOP$300,000 (US$26,000/£15,000) to buy a house of about 70 square metres. People normally prefer to appoint real estate agents to purchase a second-hand property. Note that 1% of the property price has to be paid, shared by the buyer and the seller, as commission. There are two kinds of government housing, namely, economic housing and social housing for lower income people. However, they are only for people who have lived in Macau for over five years.

Useful Addresses

DTZ Debenham Tie Leung, ☎(86) 010 6517 1280; e-mail residential@dtz.bj.cn; http://www.dtz.bj.cn/default.htm. The first wholly owned international real estate service provider in mainland China, providing property news, home searching and evaluation services. http://www.shanghaiexpat.com/displayarticle147.html. This link provides you with recommendations of real estate agents in Shanghai.

Talking China, Room 8E, East Tower of Xin'An Building, No. 200 Zhenning Road. Shanghai 200040; ☎(86) 021 6289 4299/(86) 021 6279 4508 /(86) 021 6279 4744/(86) 021 6247 0902(for Japanese); fax (86) 021 6289 4308; e-mail talkingchina@talkingchina.com; http://www.talkingchina.com/english/item – zixun – fangchan.htm. This company provides real estate consultancy, mortgage advice, translation services.

B & Q http://www.bnq.com.cn/website/bnqenglish/default/default.asp. Furniture and household appliances.

Ikea, http://www.ikea.com.cn/. Furniture and households appliances.

366f.com, http://www.365f.com/enindex.asp. Furniture and household appliances.

Kun Cheong Realty Company (Macau), ☎(853) 840444; fax (853) 840413; e-mail kchltd@macau.ctm.net; http://www.kuncheong.com.mo/.

Great International Property Agency (Macau), 3A, Rua Francisco X. Pereira R/C C, Macau; ☎(853) 238399; http://www.homemacau.com/eng/index.asp.

Macau Housing Authority, Travessa Norte do Patane No. 102, Edf. do Centro de Habitação Temporária do Patane, R/C, Macao; ☎(853) 594875; fax (853) 305909; e-mail info@ihm.gov.mo; http://www.ihm.gov.mo/.

PURCHASING AND CONVEYANCE PROCEDURES

Buying a Completed Property

Every property which is approved to be sold on the market must have a title document, which is also called the 'real estate ownership certificate'. The transaction will be void if the title document is missing. Therefore, it is important to ensure that the developers have obtained the title document before buying their properties. After you choose a property, an agreement would then be set up according to the rules pre-defined by the local real estate governing body. An application for registration of the transaction should be made to the local real estate transaction office within 30 days of the signing of the agreement. A receipt of application would then be issued, to indicate that the process is completed and the documents are valid. You will be notified within 15 days if your application is successful. If the transaction is accepted, various fees such as the deed tax and transaction administration fee have to be paid according to the pre-agreed amount, and the new title document, indicating that you are the owner of the property, will be released. For non-local residents, after paying the deed tax and administration fees, a tax clearance document should be obtained and the title document would then be released.

Sometimes, developers make use of various gimmicks such as educational funds and free car-parking spaces which may add up to more than ten thousand *yuan*, to attract customers. However, you should note that developers are not allowed to provide cash-back or other forms of benefits of over 5,000 *yuan* (US$610/£357) to their customers. This is illegal and the promised benefits will not be valid.

In order to encourage foreigners to invest in properties, tax incentives have been offered by the Chinese Government starting from early 2003. Expatriates who hold a DGM (Deputy General Manager) title or above in multinational corporations, such as banks, insurance companies, accountancy firms, investment companies, and research and development centres are eligible to enjoy tax incentives when purchasing cars and properties. However, the total investments of the companies they belong to have to be US$10 million or more. The incentives provided should not exceed 80% of the locally retained portion of their personal income tax paid in the previous year. Implementation guidelines are being drafted and applications can be made starting from May 2003. In addition to the legal and administration fees, the following fees would be involved during purchasing: stamp duty which equals 0.05% of the purchase price; registration fee; fee for issuing a title document; deed duty which is equal to 1.5% of the purchase price but 3% for apartments and property in villages.

Legal documents for buying a property in Macau are in Chinese and Portuguese only. An English version may be available on request but this is not usual. You should consider employing a lawyer to handle the legal documents for you or, at least, find a translator.

Buying a Property Under Construction

Developers in China are allowed to sell their properties before construction is completed. The property markets have now entered a new phase and it is not difficult for you to find 'pre-launch' or 'pre-sale' properties. However, the developers have to obtain a pre-launched certificate from government bodies before putting their uncompleted properties on the market. You could check the pre-launched certificate of the property you are interested in before making a decision. This can be done online at *http://www.xshouse.com/resoult.asp* or you can ask the developers to show you the certificate at their sales counter. Do make sure the name of the developer matches the one on the certificate.

The procedures for buying a property under construction are similar to those for buying a completed property. A pre-sale contract will be drawn up and sent to the real estate governing bodies for registration. This should be done within 5 working days of signing the pre-sale contract, and you will be given a copy of the registration. Payment is usually made by instalments according to the progress of construction. Finally, the title document will be conveyed to you by the developer upon the completion of the project. Should there be any amendment to the pre-sale contract, both parties (developers and buyers) must consent in the form of supplementary contracts and these should be handed to the real estate governing bodies at the time of conveyance.

It used to be a problem in China that, constructors were not able to meet the promised date of completion, and the waiting could be never-ending. Even though this is not common now, you are advised to do some research on the developers and make sure reasonable compensation is covered in the contract if the property cannot be completed on time. Interestingly, a new form of business has developed nowadays where constructors are targeting the building or re-building of those unfinished houses, due to the high competition for land and the shorter time it takes to launch these houses onto the market.

If you do not have permanent residency in China, you have to go through normal procedures as in buying a house such as setting up a contract and registering it with a government body. However, please note that extra fees would have to be paid before selling. In addition, all translation has to be done by real estate governing bodies and you are always welcome to employ your own lawyer or representative throughout the process.

Useful Websites
China Law Database, http://www.chinalaw.gov.cn/indexEN.jsp.
DTZ Debenham Tie Leung, ☎ (86) 010 6517 1280; e-mail residential@dtz.bj.cn; http://www.dtz.bj.cn/default.htm. Provides news on real estate property as well as legal amendments and new regulations relating to the real estate industry.
ShangHome.com, http://www.shanghome.com/website/introduction/ ContractInformation.htm. This real estate agent site provides you with contract information.

Conveyancing

Under the new Property Transfer Regulations that came into effect on 1 December, 2003, owners intending to put their properties on the market for resale are required to submit the original title document and a written sale and purchase agreement. They also have to register with the Land and Real Estate Bureau within 90 days of the transfer of ownership. Pre-sale transactions have to be registered within 30 days of signing the written Pre-sale Agreement, and the transfer has to be registered with the Bureau within 15 days. Besides setting out clearer guidelines on how to settle discrepancies, the Regulations represent a significant policy breakthrough by specifying the standard of service expected of government officials in handling property transfers and the associated liabilities for inadequate performance.

Useful Websites
http://www.eastlaw.net/cnlaw/reference/codes/civil/contract.htm, Contract law including Conveyancing Law in China can be found here.
TransAsia Lawyers, Suite 3718 China World Tower 1, 1 Jianguomenwai Avenue, Beijing 100004; ☎ (86) 010 6505 8188; fax (86) 010 6505 8189; e-mail Beijin g@TransAsiaLawyers.com; http://www.transasialawyers.com/index.htm.

Renting a House

Even though local people do not have to go through estate agents to rent a flat or a house if they can use personal contacts, many people still prefer to do so. In most cases, estate agents do not ask for commission from tenants. You should go for a real estate agent that has a good reputation and ask if you will be charged commission before appointing one. It is best if you have certain criteria in your mind before meeting with your agents, for example, the size, the number of rooms you are looking for, how much rent you can afford and the ideal distance to railway and bus stations. You should plan a site visit and are recommended to take some photos of the house to build up evidence of what is already inside and the condition of the house, etc. The tenant usually has to pay gas, water, electricity and telephone charges even though you may try to negotiate with the landlord.

Expatriates.com offers some information on rental prices though it is advisable to look for other websites of local estate agents for comparison. Many foreigners prefer to live near to the business areas such as the Metropolis and the Pudong areas in Shanghai and the Chaoyang District in Beijing. It costs about $3,000 *yuan* (US$366/£215) to $6,000 *yuan* (US$732/£430) a month for a fully furbished flat with two to three bedrooms in these areas, though there is a wide range of choice available.

It is quite cheap to rent a flat in Macau; about MOP$1,500 (US$195/£114) per month, for a flat with one bedroom.

Before renting a house or flat in China, you should check the title document of the property, and whether it is mortgaged or shared with other legal entities. Consent to lease has to be obtained if there is any other entity involved. The tenancy agreement should then be drawn up stating clearly the rent, payment date and frequency, the period of occupancy, and the rights and responsibilities of both parties. The tenancy agreement has to be registered at the property management body and this should be done by the landlord within 30 days of signing the agreement. A certificate of tenancy would then be released within 5 days after paying an 'evidential fee', which is equal to 2.5% of the annual rental fee. This is shared equally by the landlord and the tenant.

You are usually required to rent a property for a period of 6 months or more. Many landlords do not welcome short-term tenants and will ask for rent of one to three months as a deposit. You do not need a visa or any other identity document to rent an apartment, however, you will need to get the landlord to register you with the local police and you will be asked to provide a copy of your passport at that point. This should be done as soon as you move in, otherwise, you will be fined. You should ask for an ownership certificate if it is government housing. The landlord must own the apartment if it is government housing, and if they don't, complaints from neighbours may result in you getting thrown out. Make sure that you have a clause in the contract which says you get your deposit and unused rent back if something like this happens. In Macau, both the landlord and tenant must pay a commission fee which equals one-month's rent from each party.

Estate Agents

Shanghai Centaline Property Agency LTD, 23-24F.,Pacific Centre, 889 Yan An Xi Road, Shanghai; ☎(86) 021 5240 2808; fax (86) 021 5240 2818; e-mail lili@centaline.com.cn; http://www.shcentaline.com.cn.

Century 21, Rm1725, Hanwei Plaza, No. 7 Guanghua Rd, Chaoyang District, Beijing 100004; ☎(86) 800 810 8821/(86) 010 6561 7788; fax (86) 010 6561 2928; e-mail marketing@century21cn.com; http://www.century21cn.com/en/index.asp.

ShangHome, http://www.shanghome.com/website/default.htm.

Expatriates.com, e-mail contact@expatriates.com; http://www.expatriates.com/.

Phoenix Property Agency, e-mail phoenix@shanghai-realty.com; http://www.shanghai-realty.net/index.htm.

Relocation

The cost of moving your furniture from your home country to China is expensive. It will be cheaper to buy new furniture and household appliances locally for your new home. However, if you are desperate there are overseas relocation companies available to help you to ship your beloved furniture, and even your car, to China. These companies usually take care of the customs documents as well. Some of them are specialized in corporate relocation and provide services such as moving household goods, finding corporate premises, relocating staff and visa application. Some of them even provide support and advice on expatriate staff benefits, personnel management and repatriation.

Useful Websites

The British Association of Removers, 3 Churchill Court, 58 Station Road, North Harrow, Middlesex HA2 7Sa; ☎(44) 020 8861 3331; fax (44) 020 8861 3332; www.removers.org.uk.

Excess Baggage PLC, London Wembley Head Office, 4 Hannah Close Great Central Way, London NW10 0UX; ☎(44) 020 8324 2000; fax (44) 020 8324 2095; e-mail sales@excess-baggage.com; www.excess-baggage.com.

Allied Van Lines, Inc., P.O. Box 4403, Chicago, IL 60680-4403; ☎(1) 800 323 1909; e-mail insurance@alliedintl.com; www.alliedvan.com.

Sterling Corporate Relocation, Hallmark House, Rowdell Road, Northolt, Middlesex, UB5 6AG, England; ☎(44) 020 8841 7000; fax (44) 020 8841 3500; e-mail mail@sterlingrelocation.com; www.sterlingrelocation.com.

Sterling Corporate Relocation (Paris), 116 Avenue Aristide Briand, 93153 Le Blanc-Mesnil Cedex, France; ☎(33) 1 49 39 47 00; fax (33) 1 49 39 47 17; e-mail relocation@sterling-intl.fr; www.sterlingrelocation.com.

Allied International (Corporate Headquarters), 700 Oakmont Lane, Westmont (Chicago), Illinois 60559; ☎(1) 630 570 3500; toll-free (1) 800 323 1909; fax (1) 630 570 3496. *Allied International (UK)*, Heritage House, 345 Southbury Road, Enfield EN1 1UP; ☎(44) 020 8219 8000; fax (44) 020 8219 8321; www.allied-pickfords.co.uk.

Allied International (Australia), 202 Greens Road, Dandenong Victoria 3175; ☎(61) 3 9797 1600; fax (61) 3 9797 1616; e-mail mover@alliedpickfords.com.au; www.allpick.com.au.

Allied International (Vancouver), 819 Cliveden Place, #100 Delta, B.C. V3M 6C7; ☎(1) 604 523 3720; toll-free (1) 800 795 2920; fax (1) 604 523 3722;

e-mail fleal@alliedintl-vancouver.com.

Allied International (Toronto), 190 Duffield Drive, Markham, ON L6G 1B5; ☎(1) 416 940 1720; toll-free (1) 866 267 9106; fax (1) 416 940 1721; e-mail mwatters@alliedintl-toronto.com.

National Moving Network, Inc.; P.O. Box 630850, Miami, Florida 33163; ☎(1) 800 446 0929; fax (1) 305 949 5079; email customerservice@nationalmovi ng.com; http://www.nationalmoving.com/contact/; US movers and provide online fee estimation for international moves.

Monarch-UK & International Movers, ☎(44) 0800 954 6474; e-mail help@theuk movingcompany.co.uk; http://www.theukmovingcompany.co.uk/index.html.

Pacific relocations, Beijing Office, Unit 103, Estoril House, No. 2 Jiangtai Road, Chaoyang District, Beijing 100016; ☎(86) 010 6432 1512/(86) 010 6433 1889; fax (86) 010 6433 1896; e-mail beijing@worthenpacific.com; http://www.worthenpacific.com/company/.

The East Asiatic Company Ltd. A/S, (Sino Santa Fe Beijing); 2/F, Block J, East Lake Villas, 35 Dongzhimenwai Main Street, Beijing 100027; ☎(86) 010 8451 6666; fax (86) 010 8451 8118; e-mail beijing@santafe.com.cn; http://www.eac.com.sg. *Century 21,* Century 21 Corporate Relocation Department, Hanwei Plaza 1725, No.1 Guanghua Road, Chaoyang District, Beijing 100004; ☎(86) 010 6561 7788 ext. 23; fax (86) 010 6561 2928; e-mail relocation@century21cn.com; http://www.century21cn.com/en/relocation/r – service.asp.

Land & Fortune Realty Limited, http://www.shanghai-properties.com/relocation-services.html.

INSURANCE AND WILLS

Insurance

The insurance industry in China is still in its early stages, although it is growing very fast. Due to the increase in income and the entry of foreign insurance companies, people are becoming increasingly aware of the advantages of having a good insurance plan. This is, again, particularly true in big cities. In 2002, AIA (American International Assurance), a leading insurance group from the US, was the first group of foreign insurance companies to be granted a business licence in Beijing where foreign insurance companies were prohibited prior to China's entrance into the World Trade Organisation. Various insurance products are available, such as home, car, travel, life and accident insurance. Online applications are now available on some insurance companies' websites.

Useful Websites

American International Group, Inc. (Shanghai), 7th Floor Novel Plaza 128 Nan Jing Road West, Shanghai, 200003; ☎(86) 021 6350 8180; fax

(86) 021 6350 8182; e-mail ask.aiu@aig.com; http://www.aiush.com.cn/e
– index.htm.

PICC Property and Casualty Company Limited, ☎(86) 010 6315 6688; fax (86)
010 6303 3589; e-mail webmaster@piccnet.com.cn; http://www.picc.com.cn/
en/index.shtml.

AXA Asia Pacific Holdings Ltd, Beijing Representative Office, No. 408 Office
Building, Beijing Hotel, 8 Xinzhong Xi Jie Gongti Bei Lu, Beijing, 100027; ☎
(86) 010 6500 7788 ext 7497/(86) 010 6500 7393; fax
(86) 010 6500 7390; www.axa-chinaregion.com.

Royal & Sun Alliance Insurance (Shanghai) Ltd, 9th floor, HSBC Tower
101 Ying Cheng East Road, Pudong New Area, Shanghai, China 200120; ☎(86)
021 6841 1999; fax (86) 021 6841 2700; e-mail rsashang@uninet.com.cn;
http://www.royalsunalliance.com.cn/.

PICC Property and Casualty Company Limited, 69 Dongheyanjie, Xuanwumen,
Beijing 100052; ☎(86) 010 6315 6688; fax (86) 010 6303 3589; e-mail
webmaster@piccnet.com.cn; http://www.picc.com.cn/en/index.shtml.

ING General Insurance International Limited, 37th Floor, World Trade Tower
No. 25 Tong Xing Street Zhongshan District, Dalian 116001; ☎(86) 0411
2530 881; fax (86) 0411 2530 877; www.ing-cap.com.cn.

New York Life Insurance Worldwide Ltd, No.3601, 36/F Jinmao Building, 88 Shiji
Dadao, New Pudong Area, Shanghai 200121; ☎(86) 800 820 5882; e-mail p
– r@haiernewyorklife.com.cn; www.haiernewyorklife.com.cn.

Wills

If a property owner dies intestate, or if the will is invalid, the person recognised as
the legal inheritor under the Chinese inheritance law will be the lawful recipient of
the property. Under Chinese inheritance laws, primary and secondary inheritance
rights are given to two groups of relatives. Relatives with primary rights include
spouse, children (biological or adopted, born before or after marriage), parents
(biological, adopted or step), and parents-in-law whose livelihood is supported by
the deceased. The order as listed also reflects their priority to claim the inheritance.
Relatives with secondary rights to inherit include siblings (biological or step), who
have priority over grandparents. In addition, according to the inheritance law in
China, if the deceased is a foreigner, the succession of fixed assets has to follow the
rules of local government where the fixed assets are located. For movable assets, it
should follow the rules of the local government where the deceased lived.

You can write a will to indicate one or more relatives to be the lawful inheritors of
your property. Alternatively, you can specify an organisation or private individuals
as the lawful inheritors of your property in China instead of your relatives.

You can also draw up a will regarding your property in China according to the
laws in your home country but you are advised to consult a lawyer and make sure
your will would be valid under the Chinese inheritance laws.

Useful Addresses

China Property, http://www.twlcic.com/cm/icm3/inherit.html. Includes full details of inheritance procedure of property in China.

Masons, 2/F, Room 241, Shanghai Bund No. 12, 12 Zhongshan Dong Yi Road Shanghai 200002; ☎(86) 021 6321 1166; fax (86) 021 6329 2696; www.masons.com. Masons is an international law firm and one of the first foreign law firms to be granted a license to practice in China.

PUBLIC UTILITIES

Electricity and Gas

Several projects have been launched to improve both electricity and gas supplies in the country. For electricity, the West-East electricity transmission project is being carried out; and for gas, the West-to-East natural gas transmission project has been initiated. Some households in provinces like Shaanxi are already benefiting from this natural gas supply.

China broke down the former State Power Corporation into 11 smaller companies in late 2002. In February 2003, the State Electricity Regulatory Commission (SERC), which acts as the watchdog of the industry, started operations. In the same year, China started experimenting with the idea of regional or provincial electricity markets in northeast China. More regional electricity markets are expected to be set up throughout the country due to huge demand for electricity. When the regional electricity markets become mature and the pricing system is revised, they will be fully open to competition. Prices will become market driven instead of government driven.

The electrical supply in China is 220 volts, 50 cycles AC. Sockets accept American-style plugs, with two flat parallel prongs. Appliances with two round prongs may be used as well. You will need an adaptor for using electrical appliances with 3-pin plugs. Due to the voltage difference, you will need a converter to use your electrical appliances purchased in the USA or most of Europe. Most laptop computers and some sophisticated appliances operate equally well on 220 or 110 volts. You are however advised to use a power surge protector for your computer. You may consider buying electrical appliances in China to save the trouble of bringing your own. Electrical appliances are in general cheaper than those in the USA and Europe. In most of the provinces, the electricity supply is stable but, as mentioned before, the electricity network in the west of China is being improved.

Monthly bills for electricity and gas can be paid at banks, or you can set up auto-debit services.

The electricity supply in Macau is the same as that for China. However, as in Hong Kong, sockets accept 3-pin plugs instead of the 2-pin ones. Monthly bills can be settled at banks, at Automated Teller Machines (ATM) or through online services.

Useful Websites

State Grid Corporation of China, http://www.sgcc.com.cn/english/default.htm.
One of the large power transmission enterprises in China, which consists of
institutions and enterprises that were formerly stated owned.

CEM-Companhia de Electricidade de Macau, S.A.R.L., Est. D. Maria II, Ed.
CEM, r/c, Macau; http://www.cem-macau.com/index – e.php.

Water Supply

Water shortage is a serious problem but China aims at solving the water supply
problem completely by the end of 2020. A great deal of money and resources have
been put into related projects for solving these problems. Two of the initiatives
are the South-to-North water diversion project and the 'Three Gorges Project'.
They aim at solving the uneven distribution problem of natural water resources
by re-allocating water to areas of scarcity. All the projects and water supply policy
are monitored by the Ministry of Water Resources.

Similar to the situation of the electricity supply, the water supply is provided by
numerous enterprises. With the aim of introducing competition, foreign-invested
companies are welcome to join the water supply market. The three biggest water
suppliers in the world, Vivendi Group, Thames Water PLC and Suez Lyonnaise
Des Eaux, have made China part of their global market. In addition, Macao
Water Supply Company Limited (Macao Water) is the fourth largest water
supplier in China.

You should boil water before you drink it since it is not advisable to drink tap
water directly. Monthly water bills may also be paid at banks at the rate of about
2 *yuan* per cubic metre for residential use and three *yuan* per cubic metre for
business use.

The Water supply in Macau is provided by the Macao Water Supply Company
Limited (Macao Water). First time users with new meter connections have to
register with the Customer Services counter of the company. You have to present
identification and the title deeds to the property when applying for a meter
connection. You will be charged for the meter connection, a guarantee deposit
and also the government stamp duty. Bi-monthly bills will be sent to your home
and can be settled at post offices, banks, and service counters of Macao Water,
either by cash or cheque.

A joint portal provided by CEM (electricity provider) and Macao Water
provides a variety of online services to enable their customers to view and pay
electricity and water bills through electronic payments. Currently, you can only
pay your bills online by using the e-banking service provided by two banks in
Macau, namely BNU and Bank of China.

Useful Websites

The Ministry of Water Resources, The International Economic & Technical

Cooperation and Exchange Center, Beijing; ☎(86) 010 6320 2557; e-mail webmaster@mwr.gov.cn; http://www.mwr.gov.cn/english/index.htm.

China International Water & Electric Corp, ☎(86) 010 6238 1188; fax (86) 010 6401 3133/(86) 010 6401 4075; http://www.cwe.com.cn/default.asp. State-owned company providing domestic and foreign consultancy services on water and electricity projects.

Macao Water Supply Company Limited (Macao Water), 718, Avenida do Conselheiro Borja, Macao; ☎(853) 220088; fax (853) 234660; e-mail custom er.info@macaowater.com; http://www.macaowater.com/index.htm.

Banco Nacional Ultramarino(BNU), S.A., Av. Almeida Ribeiro 22, P.O. BOX 465, Macau; ☎(853) 335533; e-mail markt@bnu.com.mo; http:// www.bnu.com.mo/en/index.htm.

Bank of China (Macau Branch), http://www.bocmacau.com/eng/its/index.htm.

Telecommunications

The telecommunication industry has been undergoing unprecedented reform by the Chinese government since 2002; the original state-owned China Telecom was split into the north and south sectors in an effort to break up the monopoly in the fixed-line sector and encourage competition. The north sector inherited China Telecom's business (including 30% of the backbone network) in 10 provinces and municipalities, including Beijing, Tianjin, Hebei and Shandong and was merged with China Network, Jitong Network & Telecom forming the new China Network Communication (known as China Netcom). The south sector continued using the name China Telecom with the remaining 70% of the network and includes 21 provinces and municipalities in the southern and northwestern regions.

Up until now, there have been four major telecommunication players in the industry. They are China Telecom, China Network Communication (CNC), China Mobile Communications Corporation (known as CMCC or China Mobile), and China United Telecommunications Corporation (China Unicom). China Telecom still enjoys the biggest share in the telecommunication market, followed by China Mobile. They are all monitored by the Ministry of Information Industries (MII) and provide services such as fixed line telephones, mobile telephone networks, broadband and Virtual Private Network (VPN). Since China entered the WTO, telecommunication services have been opened up to foreign companies.

Local Fixed Telephone Line. A local fixed line is already installed in most newly built houses. To activate the service, you have to fill in a registration form and hand it to the local services provider. The initial installation fee is expensive, at about 800 *yuan* (US$97.56/£57). The monthly rental fee ranges from 15 *yuan* (US$1.8/£1.1) to 25 *yuan* (US$3.4/£1.8), depending on your home location. It is more expensive to install a telephone line in rural areas.

Phone bills can be paid at banks or at convenience stores. Alternatively you can set up a monthly direct debit service with the service provider.

Mobile Phones. The competition is very keen in the mobile phone market, especially in big cities like Shanghai. However, compared with western countries, in which the average penetration is 60%, only about 10% of the population (estimated at 150 million subscribers) are using a mobile phone. It is easy to subscribe to a mobile phone service in China but the network coverage is still needing improvement, even in big cities. GSM and CDMA services are provided in China. The average price of a mobile phone is about 2000 *yuan* (US$244/ £143). People may spend over 100 *yuan* (US$12/£7) a month on their telephone bill, though a typical monthly fee is only about 15 *yuan* (US$1.8/£1.1). Pay-as-you-go mobiles remain popular in China. The UK's biggest company, Vodafone, has already got a minority stake in China Mobile, one of the big mobile phone companies listed above. Nokia, Siemens and Ericsson have also set up manufacturing plants in China, competing with about 20 domestic makers.

International Phone Calls. The introduction of Internet Protocol (IP) phone services in late 1999 has significantly reduced the costs for making international calls. IP phone services allowed you to make telephone calls along Internet cables rather than conventional telephone wires. All of the four major Chinese telecom companies are now offering IP phone services and it is possible to cut the costs of calling overseas by two-thirds with IP services. For example, with the use of IP, calls from the US to China drop from US$0.59 (using fixed line) to US$0.21 a minute. Under the Internet Protocol (IP) service, callers just need to dial 5 digits for the IP servers' access in front of the overseas number you wish to make. There are three main IP services available: IP phone cards (bought on a pre-paid basis), IP phone services (installed to your line) and PC-based Internet phone services. IP cards are the simplest and most convenient way to make cheap calls both domestically and nationally. They are available at hotels, post offices, department stores, convenience stores, telephone shops and small carts selling lottery tickets in big cities. The IP cards can be bought at a cheaper price when they are close to the expiry date, when you can save up to 60% of the printed price. Cards are available from 50 *yuan* (US$6.1/£3.6) to 500 *yuan* (US$61/£36). The larger the value cards are, the more economic, as you lose some units at the end of each card since a minimum of 2.5 *yuan* (US$0.3/£0.2) is required to place an overseas call. You are advised to check the expiry date written on the back of the card (usually valid for 12 months) when you purchase one. It is also worthwhile to compare the different card rates for making calls to different countries and regions, as some cards are better value for certain countries. You can use IP phone cards on your mobile phone, but in general it is only possible if the card is from the same company as your mobile phone provider. The networks can sometimes get congested, so it is best to have a range of cards from different companies.

Arranging an IP phone service connection to your home can be a complicated process. You are not advised to do so if you are not a high usage caller as the monthly fee can be 1000 *yuan* (US$122/£72) far more than a normal fixed line. You are also required to have a residence visa and a local bank account to apply for the IP phone service. The calling fee is about 0.3 *yuan* per minute for calling within mainland China. Calls to the USA and the UK are about 2.4 *yuan* (US$0.29/£0.17) and 3.6 *yuan* (US$0.44/£0.26) per minute respectively.

Internet Phone Services. Internet phone service refers to the use of the Internet, via a computer, to place telephone calls. All you need is a personal computer with an Internet connection, speakers, and a microphone. A headset or a microphone will cost you around 40 *yuan* (US$4.9/£2.9) at computer stores. There are a number of companies offering Internet phone services, and you should compare the services and the prices before chosing one. The procedures for installing an internet phone are simple. You only need to download the software from the service provider and create an account for payment. If you access the Internet through an office server, you may need to check whether your server has 'firewalls' which may prohibit you from using the Internet telephone services. Your software downloading programmes will usually tell you if you have firewalls in place. Internet phone service rates are extremely cheap, with a number of companies even offering free calls to the USA. You can dial from your PC to a normal telephone, or from your PC to another PC if the receiver has the same software. Rates for Internet phone services are approximately 20% of IP phone rates. The sound quality of Internet phone services can be a little patchy with slight delays, but in general it is perfectly audible and of exceptional value.

Macau. Started in the 1990s, telecommunication services in Macau have been greatly developed. Currently, the telecom business of Macau is run solely by Companhia de Telecommunicacoes de Macau S.A.R.L. (Macau Telecommunications Company Ltd.) but the Macau Special Administrative Region Government is planning to open up the telecommunication market. Up to May 2000, Macau had 178,064 regular telephones and 105,034 mobile phones. There were two types of mobile phone system in Macau, analogue and digital, but the analogue network service was terminated on July 1, 2000. There is also a sharp rise in the number of Internet users, from 5,846 by the end of year 1997 to 22,723 by the end of July 2000.

Apart from this, public phones are available on streets and in public areas. There are nearly 3,000 public phones, and all of them take IDD calls. International phone calls can be made via IDD 0050 through a home telephone and cost about MOP$0.99 (US$0.13/£0.07) per minute to make a call to the USA or the UK.

There are many ways to settle your phone bill, such as online electronic payment, direct debit or by telephone, apart from paying at the CTM customer counters. Visit the CTM's website for more information.

Useful Addresses & Websites

China Mobile Communications Corporation (CMCC/China Mobile), http:// www.chinamobile.com/ENGLISH/index.html.

China Telecom: 31, Jinrong Street Xicheng District,Beijing 100032; ☎(86) 010 6602 7217; e-mailcontent@beijingnet.com; http://www.chinatelecom.com.cn/ english/index.html.

China United Telecommunications Corporation, http://www.chinaunicom.com.cn/web/eng/index.htm.

China Network Communications Group Corporation (China Netcom), Block C, 156, Fuxingmennei Street, Beijing, 100031; ☎(86) 010 6611 0006; fax (86) 010 6611 0009; http://www.chinanetcom.com.cn/en/index.asp.

CTM-Companhia de Telecomunicacoes, Rua de Lagos, Telecentro, Taipa, Macau; ☎(853) 8913822; fax (853) 8913813; http://www.ctm.net/.

IP Service Providers

Net2phone, http://www.net2phone.com.

Mediaring, http://www.mediaring.com.

Dialpad, http://www.dialpad.com.

IConnectHere, http://www.iConnectHere.com (formerly deltathree).

CAR OWNERSHIP

Car ownership has been increasing in China. There was a 68.38% increase in 2003 compared to 2002. According to the National Bureau of Statistics in China, Beijing had the highest number of private cars in the country by the end of 2001 with 624,000 vehicles on the road. The number of vehicles in the city further increased and exceeded 800,000 in late 2002. As the infrastructure improves, districts that were originally inaccessible are now attracting house builders and the occupants of the new accommodation all want cars. Since China entered the WTO, the reduction of import duties for foreign cars has attracted European companies such as Audi, Rolls Royce and Mercedes Benz to open showrooms in China to cope with the rising demand. More details about importing a car can be found in the section *Importing Cars* below.

Buying a Car

Buying a new car involves a number of procedures and you may consider paying a service fee to a car dealer to handle most of them for you. If you decide to handle it yourself, first you have to purchase car insurance as third party liability insurance is compulsory in China. This should be completed before getting the licence. In addition, since cars are considered as luxury goods in China, an additional fee of

10% of the nominal price of the car (before value-added tax) has to be paid to the transportation department. After that, you have to show proof of ownership of a car parking space. However, no proof of parking is needed if you buy the car via a company. You are required to send your car for inspection and you will obtain a temporary licence five days after that. You have to wait for another 15 days (for domestic cars) or 30 days (for imported cars) to obtain a formal licence. You should present the temporary licence, a photo of your car, proof of payment of the road maintenance fee and registration information from the safety committee when you collect your formal licence. You are also required to pay the transport tax of 200 *yuan* (US$24/£14) a year to the Inland Revenue in order to complete the whole process.

If you are staying for only a short period, you may prefer to consider renting a car. However, you should note that holders of an International Driving Licence are not permitted to drive between cities in China. They are only allowed to drive within Beijing, Shanghai, Hong Kong and Macau. For more information about driving in China, refer to the next chapter *Daily Life*.

Useful Websites
0755car.com, http://www.0755car.com/buy/.
General Motors, http://www.gmchina.com/english/index.htm.
National Bureau of Statistics of China, http://www.stats.gov.cn/english/.
Huation Auto Commerce Ltd, e-mail huation@vip.163.com; http://www.huation.com/.

Importing a Car
There is a quota system applied to the imported car market in China. However, since China's accession to WTO, import tax is reducing continuously although the quota of imported cars will increase by 15% every year until 2005, when the quota system will be completely abolished. Starting from 2004, import tax for small cars (under 3000cc) is reduced from 38.2% to 34.2% while tax for more powerful cars (over 3000cc) is reduced from 43% to 37.6%. The quota system will be abolished by January 1, 2005 and imported vehicles can enter China freely after that. In 2006, the tax on imported vehicles will be further reduced to only 25%. The current and future tax reductions have attracted many car manufacturers to enter this huge market.

In 2003, there were about 160,000 cars sold, amongst which imported cars accounted for 4% of sales. However, the value of imported cars in monetary terms accounts for 15% of the total. It is expected that the cost of owning an imported car will decrease due to the reduction in import tax and the abolition of import quotas in 2005, and stronger competition between foreign and domestically produced cars, etc.

Import tax, shipping fees and the higher basic price together make foreign cars much more expensive than domestic cars. A domestic car costs you about 120,000 *yuan* (US$14,634/£8,571) while a similar car from Japan will cost you 340,000 *yuan* (US$41,463/£24,286). The quality of domestically manufactured vehicles has been improving and is now comparable to many foreign manufactured vehicles.

To import a car, you will need a quota permit under the current quota system. An application, which is free of charge except for an administration fee of 10 *yuan*, has to be made to the Department of Foreign Economic Cooperation, Ministry of Commerce. However, you are required to appoint a company to handle it for you. Otherwise, you may have to pay a very high price (can be up to 70,000 *yuan*, about US$8,500/£5,000) for buying a quota in the market. In this case, you should consider appointing a car dealer as their negotiating powers and experience in car dealing are much more effective than any individual's. Alternatively, you may delay importing a car until 2005 when the quota system ends.

Useful Websites
China Importing Car Trading Centre, e-mailzjqm@sina.com; http://www.chinaauto.com.cn/ctcai.htm.
Ministry of Commerce, http://english.mofcom.gov.cn/department.shtml.

Car Mortgage
At the time of writing, car mortgage regulation is undergoing consultation. Car mortgages can be divided into private car loans, commercial car loans and fleet loans. The loan for private use (either individual or fleet) should not exceed 80% of the market price of the vehicle while that for commercial use should not exceed 70% of the vehicle's market value. Loans are provided by banks and the maximum loan term is five years. There is the possibility of extending the period once, but you have to negotiate with your bank. It is expected that more types of mortgages will be available for both domestic and imported vehicles.

In December 2003, several foreign-invested companies were allowed to set up car mortgage companies in China. They include Toyota, GE Capital and Volkswagen. Mortgage credit systems were built to improve the quality of the car insurance industry.

Not all banks in Macau offer car mortgages but you can ask for help from the Bank of China, who offer car mortgages up to 80% of the market value of the vehicle. The maximum term of repayment is 60 months.

Useful Websites and Addresses
The People's Bank of China, .32 Chengfang street, Xi Cheng district, Beijing, China PostCode:100800; ☎(86) 010 6619 4114; e-mail master@pbc.gov.cn; http://www.pbc.gov.cn/english/.

Industrial and Commercial Bank of China, e-mail webmaster@icbc.com.cn; http://www.icbc.com.cn/e – index.jsp.

General Electric, Beijing (Amy Zhou) 6/F West Wing, Hanwei Plaza, No. 7 Guang Hua Road, Chaoyang District, Beijing 100004; e-mail amy.zhou@geahk.ge.com; http://www.ge.com.cn/english/index.asp.

Volkswagen, e-mail service@volkswagen.com.cn; http://www.volkswagen.com.cn/en/index.html.

Bank of China (Macau Branch), http://www.bocmacau.com/eng/index.htm.

IMPORTING PETS

If you want to bring your pets (cats and dogs only) with you to China, they will have to be quarantined for at least 15 days. Moreover, each person can only bring one pet in. You should note that birds are not allowed to enter China. Apart from checking the regulations for importing pets in China, you should also check the requirements for taking your pets out of your home country, especially if you want to bring them back some years later. In some cases, you are not allowed to bring them back to your home country after they have left the country. You should also check with the airline for the procedures and costs, if applicable, for bringing a pet with you on the flight.

In general, two certificates are required for bringing pets into China: a Vaccination Certificate and a Health Certificate. The vaccination certificate can be attached to the health certificate and all vaccinations should be done within 30 days prior to departure. You can ask a qualified veterinarian in your home country to issue a health certificate which should be issued within 30 days prior to departure. Copies of the certificate may be required when you leave your country and the airline staff may ask to look at it before allowing your pet to board the plane.

You should also check the regulations for importing pets with the local government authority as the rules vary. For instance, Shanghai is one of the few areas that would allow you to bring a cat into China. Chinese customs offices have the right to deport animals if the vaccination records are not authenticated and notarised by a state notary. Importation of exotic animals may be considered but you must obtain approval from the Chinese customs in advance. You should consider preparing Chinese-translated versions of the documents. This will probably help the customs officers to handle the matter and save your time at immigration. The Chinese embassy in your country should be able to translate the documents, or at least provide useful details about how to get certified documents in Chinese.

You will have to declare your pet at the Customs Department on arrival. Take your pet, fee and certificates to the Customs & Immigration Plant and Quarantine office at the airport, located before the Customs exit. The certificates will be examined and customs officers will give you a stamped document allowing you to bring your pet in. You will have to pay a charge of 150 *yuan* for the examination and the stamped document. Note that there is a mandatory 15- 30 days quarantine period but you can usually keep your pet with you at home for this period. Quarantine officers will come and inspect your pet during the 30-day period, and a small nominal fee will be charged. If visitors do not have their pets with them when entering China, they are advised to phone ahead before departure to ensure there will be staff at the Customs & Immigration Plant and the Quarantine office.

Cats must be vaccinated against Enteritis (E3) within 12 months of arrival in China. You will need a certificate for Feline Panleucopenia and Feline Respiratory Disease Complex Vaccinations. Keeping dogs is not encouraged by the Chinese government. Every family is limited to only one dog and there is also a size limit for dogs in many cities. Moreover, a dog must be registered with the local police station when you move into your apartment. All dogs, whether they are bought locally or imported from outside China, are required to be fully quarantined by law before they are licensed. In some cities, only local Chinese can register dogs and you will need a local resident to act on your behalf. However, many cities allow foreigners who hold a residence visa or a work permit to register their dogs. The cost for a dog licence is expensive and varies from area to area. Even within Shanghai, for example, the city is divided into two areas, the inner ring road and the outer ring road. People living in the inner ring road have to pay 2000 *yuan* (US$244/£143) to register a dog while people in the outer ring road pay 1000 *yuan* (US$122/£72) for doing so. For registering a dog, you have to complete an application form and return it to the local Public Security Bureau (PSB). You have to attach two photos of your dog (face and side) and a passport-sized photo of yourself to the application form. There are some companies that provide a service helping overseas visitors to bring their pets into China. The fee is about 2000 *yuan* (US$244/£143), which includes a collecting fee, administration fee, application fee for importing pets, etc.

In Macau, endangered animal species are banned from importation. A licence of import is required and the imported pet has to be filed with the appropriate Division of Hygiene and Sanidade (DHS) office. You could contact the Macao Customs Service for the further information.

Useful Websites

Ministry of Health, No.1 Xizhimenwai Nanlu, Xicheng District, Beijing 100044; ☎(86) 010 68792114; e-mail manage@moh.gov.cn; http://www.moh.gov.cn/index.htm.

Pudong Airport, ☎(86) 021 3848 4500.

Hong Qiao Airport, ☎(86) 021 6268 8918.

Animal and Plant Quarantine Bureau, 13 Zhongshan Dong Yi Rd, Shanghai; ☎(86) 021 6586 3030; www.shanghaiguide.com.

Customs General Administration (PRC), No. 6 Jianguomennei Dajie, Beijing 100730; ☎(86) 010 6519 4114; http://www.customs.gov.cn/.

Macao Customs Service; Rua S. Tiago da Barra, Doca D. Carlos T, SW, Barra-Macau; ☎(853) 559944; fax (853) 371136; e-mail SA-info@fsm.gov.mo; http://www.sa.gov.mo.

DAILY LIFE

CHAPTER SUMMARY

- **Languages.** Mandarin is the official spoken language and is the mother tongue of 70% of the population.
  - Mainland China is now using the simplified writing system while the traditional system is used in Hong Kong, Macau and Taiwan.
- **Education.** Children in most cities receive nine-years compulsory education, which is supported by the government. It is expected that this will apply to the whole country by 2010.
  - Students need to pass locally organised entrance examinations in order to enter senior high schools.
  - Senior high school graduates need to pass a state organised examination in order to enter universities.
- **Media.** English newspapers and magazines are not common.
  - No licence is required for televisions.
- **Post.** Post offices open seven days a week.
  - Apart from using the mail service, you can also make money transfers in post offices.
  - There is an officially approved way to pack parcels.
  - A PC-Letter allows you to send your letters to the post office through the internet.
- **Telephone.** Internet phone cards are a cheap way to make international calls.
  - Macau uses a separate country code.
- **Driving.** Holders of International Driving Licences are not allowed to drive between cities. They are only allowed to drive in Beijing, Shanghai, Hong Kong and Macau.
- **Banking.** Credit cards are not commonly accepted, even in big cities.
  - Many banks open seven days a week.
- **Health Care.** Hospitals often require you to pay a deposit before providing treatment.

> ○ Fees are charged per treatment or for medicine provided.
> ○ **Crime.** Foreigners who are victims of crime should report to the Foreign Affairs Branch of the Public Security Bureau (PSB).
> ○ PSB is also responsible for handling visa extensions.

THE LANGUAGE

Although written Chinese was standardised across the country over two thousand years ago, there are many different dialects in China. The written language is based on characters but not an alphabet, and there are about 5000 common characters in daily usage. The characters are the smallest linguistic units in the written language, and each of them has a meaning or grammatical function. The form of a character does not determine the pronunciation, and therefore the same words can be pronounced very differently in different dialects, which means learning different dialects is no easy affair.

Mandarin is the official spoken language in China. It is also called *Putonghua* and it is the first language of 70% of the total population. 8.4% of the population speaks *Wu*, which is mainly spoken by people living in Zhejiang, Jiangsu and Anhui. In Hong Kong, Guangdong, Southern Guangxi Zhuang Autonomous Region, parts of Hainan, Macau, and also in many overseas settlements, Cantonese (*Yue*) is the common dialect, which accounts for 5% of the entire population. *Xiang*, also known as Hunanese, is the main language of people in Hunan and other south central regions. Speakers of *Xiang* add up to 5% of the total. 4% of the population speaks *Hakka*, which is popular in a wide range of areas including Guangdong, southwestern Fujian, Jiangxi, Hunan, Yunnan, Guangxi, Guizhou, Sichuan, Hainan, Taiwan, Singapore, Malaysia, Indonesia, and amongst many overseas Chinese communities as well. *Min* speakers account for 4.2% of the population and are common in Fujian, large areas of Taiwan and Hainan, and also parts of eastern Guangdong. Most of the people in Jiangxi, the eastern part of Hunan, and the southeastern corner of Hubei use the *Gan* dialect. About 2.4% of the total population is using this language. Inhabitants who speak other dialects add up to only 1% of the total population. Fortunately, even in the regions where Mandarin is not the first language, you can still just about get by with it as it is a compulsory subject in schools.

Nowadays, Chinese people use *Pinyin* to denote the pronunciation of the Chinese characters in Mandarin, which is a system based on the Roman alphabet. Most of the sounds are similar to English but some particular ones are quite different, for example 'q' (which is pronounced somewhat like 'ch'). Chinese is a tonal language and there are four tones in spoken Mandarin. Many characters share the same Pinyin denotation and are differentiated only by their tones. The four tones include flat, rise, fall-then-rise and fall. If we use numbers to mark the pitch (1 being the lowest and 5 the highest), the four tones can be indicated by the following: flat (55), rise (35), fall-then-rise (214) and fall (51).

Useful Websites

http://www.chinalanguage.com/index.html, includes online dictionaries for Mandarin and some other dialects. It also allows you to input English, Korean and Japanese words to look for the corresponding Chinese characters.

http://acc6.its.brooklyn.cuny.edu/phalsall/texts/chinlng3.html, provide pinyin/Wade-Giles translations of names of places in China.

Simplified Chinese Writing Vs Traditional Chinese Writing

In the 1950s, the Chinese Communist government introduced the simplified writing system with the aim of achieving a higher literacy rate. When compared to traditional writing, the characters of simplified writing have fewer numbers of strokes, which make the words easier to write. Moreover, in the simplified writing system, there are fewer characters in total; some previously different characters now share the same written form. The simplified writing system makes it easier to learn the language. However, it was not introduced in Hong Kong, Macau and Taiwan. In general, people who know one script can read the other, but with some effort. In the 80s and 90s, some people pressed for a return to the traditional writing system in the mainland. To date, although the simplified writing system is still used officially, some schools in Southeast China are teaching students traditional writing as well as the simplified one.

SCHOOLING AND EDUCATION

China introduced a Nine-Year Compulsory Education system in 1986 and children are required to go to school from the age of six. However, the policy is not yet universal over the whole country. In particular, some children in the western provinces are not able to receive free education from the government. Making Nine-Year Compulsory Education universal is currently one of the main projects of the government. Special funds have been set up to help the poor and ethnic minorities. It is expected that all children will be able to receive compulsory education by the year 2010. Nine-Year Compulsory Education includes both primary school education and junior high school education. Primary education starts at the age of six (seven for some areas) and lasts for six years. Primary school graduates should then go to junior high schools, without having to take any examinations. Junior high school education lasts for three years and can be substituted by junior secondary vocational training, which is also open to primary school graduates. Pre-school education is not compulsory but is getting more common. The government reported that over 70% of children attended at least one year of pre-school education by the end of 1998. The government is also trying to accelerate the pace of infrastructure construction, resource construction and talent production for education and is also improving the overall application of IT in the educational system.

Schools and universities in mainland China use Mandarin as the teaching medium. Most reading texts are in Chinese. In Macau, however, most schools teach in Cantonese or English. There are also a small number of schools which conduct lessons in Portuguese. Most students are required to wear school uniform on the mainland and Macau but it is still not very common in rural areas.

Useful Addresses
Ministry of Education (MoE), 37 Mucang Hutong, Xidian Dajie, Beijing 100816; ☎(86) 010 6609 6114; e-mail emic@moe.edu.cn; www.moe.edu.cn.
China education and Research Network: www.edu.cn
Education and Youth Affairs Bureau, Av. Praia Grande, n° 926, Macau; ☎(853) 555533; fax (853) 317307; e-mail webmaster@dsej.gov.mo; www.dsej.gov.mo.

Basic Education
Basic education in China includes pre-school education, primary school education and junior secondary school (high school) education, of which primary and junior secondary education is compulsory under the current system. At the moment, most schools are funded by the government and are free of charge, but parents still need to pay school fees in some schools. School fees are not standardised and are decided by local governments. They range from tens to one or two thousand *yuan* (up to US$240/£140) a year. A 'Single Fee System' will be disseminated nationally in compulsory education within the next five years.

Subjects taken in primary and junior secondary education are divided into state-arranged subjects and locally-arranged subjects. Students are required to take end-of-term examinations or tests and they are also encouraged to take part in after-school activities. These activities include scientific, cultural and recreational activities and are usually organised by children's clubs, scientific and technological centres for teenagers, or other similar institutions.

Moral education plays a very important role in basic education in China. One main focus is the 'Five Loves': love of the motherland, love of the people, love of labour, love of science and love of socialism. Moral education is also important to foster social responsibilities and to consolidate the legal system. Students need to study the cultural traditions and revolutionary history of the Chinese nation, the moral and democratic legal system, modern Chinese history, a general survey of China and policies on current events and to build up a scientific outlook of the world and life. Psychological education is also provided to help the students build up a healthy personality. Labour education and skills training are also included in primary and junior secondary education in order to cultivate a proper attitude towards workers and good working habits. Students are also encouraged to acquire some basic knowledge and skills related to productive labour as well as some basic life skills.

In Macau there is also basic compulsory education but it is slightly different from that of the mainland. Basic education in Macau also consists of six years primary school education and three years junior secondary school education. However, pre-primary education, lasting one year, is also required. Basic education in Macau is free.

The Structure of the Education System

Pre-school Education. Pre-school education is not compulsory in China. Parents can choose to send their children to kindergartens or not. Pre-school education was not common before the 90s, but these days more and more parents send their children to kindergarten if they can afford it. It usually takes three years to finish kindergarten and the entry age is usually three while some kindergartens accept even younger children. In some rural areas where facilities to set up kindergartens are lacking, one-year pre-school classes or seasonal classes for the local children are often organised. Kindergartens can be full-day or half-day, depending on the choice of the parents.

The main purpose for pre-school education is to provide physical, intellectual, aesthetic and moral training to children to prepare them for primary school education. They are also trained to express themselves. Games are an important part of pre-school education. Apart from that, children also start to learn Chinese and basic mathematics. They also have music lessons, art lessons and regular physical education. However, unless the kindergartens are international ones, they usually teach in Mandarin only.

Useful Addresses

The International Children's House, English Montessori Kindergarten, Beijing Lufthansa Center, Unit S 114, 50 Liangmaqiao Road, Chaoyang District, Beijing 100016; ☎(86) 010 6465 1305; fax (86) 010 6465 1802; e-mail info@montessoribeijing.com; www.montessoribeijing.com.

The International Children's House, English Montessori Kindergarten, China World Trade Center, North Lodge, No 1 Jian Guo Men Wai Avenue, Beijing 100004; ☎(86) 010 6505 3(86)9; fax (86) 010 6505 1237; e-mail info@montessoribeijing.com; www.montessoribeijing.com.

Beijing Oxford Little Professor Kindergarten, Asian Games Village North Gate, Building 308, Huizhong District, Beijing; ☎(86) 010 6493 6626.

Beanstalk International School (Kindergarten), 1/F,B Building, No.40 Liangmaqiao Rd Chaoyang District, Beijing; ☎(86) 010 6466 9255/(86) 010 6466 3311 ext.3312/3315; fax (86) 010 8454 3449/(86) 010 8456 6019; e-mail director@bibs.com.cn; www.bibs.com.cn.

JoJo English academy, purple Jade Villas, 1 Purple Jade Dong Lu, Chaoyang District, Beijing; ☎(86) 010 8460 5671.

Eton International School, Room 701, 7/F Lido Office Tower, Lido Place

Jichang Road, Jiang Tai Road, Chaoyang District, Beijing 100004; ☎(86) 010 6430 1590/(86) 010 6430 1591; fax (86) 010 6430 1310; e-mail info@etonkids.com; www.etonkids.com.

Lido Kindergarten, Holiday Inn Lido Beijing, Jichang Road, Jiang Tai Road, Beijing; ☎(86) 010 6437 6688; fax (86) 010 6437 6237; e-mail sybil.wilson@ lidoplace.com; http://www.lidoplace.com/schools/kinder.html.

Shanghai Rainbow Bridge International Kindergarten, 2381 Hong Qiao Road, Shanghai 200335; ☎(86) 021 6268 3121/(86) 021 6268 9773; www.rbik.com.

KinderWorld International Kindergarten, F2, Somerset Grand Shanghai, 8 Jinan Road, Shanghai; ☎(86) 021 6386 7880; fax (86) 021 6387 7131; e-mail kinderworld – sh@yahoo.com; www.kinderworld.net.

Shanghai Montessori Kindergarten, 1481 Haitian Garden, Huqing Ping Highway, Shanghai; ☎(86) 021 5988 5650.

Tiny Tots International Pre-School and Kindergarten, No. 43 West Fuxing Road, Shanghai; ☎(86) 021 6431 3788.

Children's Literature Kindergarten, East Kang Qiao Garden, Lane 2, Kangshi Lu, Shanghai; ☎(86) 021 6812 2658; a Japanese school.

Sunflower International Kindergarten, ☎(86) 021 5030 3681; e-mail sunflowerm@online.sh.cn; www.sunmonte.com.

The Australian International School, No.35 Da Shu Yuan Xiang, Haishu District 315000, Ningbo Zhejiang Province; ☎(86) 0574 8730 6737; fax (86) 0574 8729 6237; www.aussieschool-china.com.

Primary School. Most children enter primary schools at the age of six but schools in some rural areas may postpone the entry age to seven. Primary school education is part of the nine-year compulsory education and usually takes six years (five years if the age for entry is seven) to complete. In general, a school year is divided into two semesters including 38 weeks of teaching, 13 weeks of holidays and an additional week in reserve. The Chinese language and mathematics are compulsory subjects. Even though English is an optional subject, many primary schools include it in the curriculum. Other subjects include physics, biology, chemistry, history, geography and also politics. Unless it is an international school, lessons are conducted in Mandarin except for English Language lessons. After finishing primary school education, all students are eligible for entering secondary schools without taking any examination,.

Secondary School. Secondary school education is divided into two halves, junior high school and senior high school. Junior high school refers to the first three years of secondary school education, which is part of the nine-year compulsory education. A school year consists of 39 weeks of teaching sessions, 12 weeks of holiday and an additional week in reserve. Similarly to primary school education, a school year is usually divided into two semesters. English language is a compulsory subject starting from junior high. Chinese language and mathematics are also compulsory. Other subjects include chemistry, physics, biology, history, geography, another foreign language, etc. Physical Education is not compulsory but is encouraged. Students who want to continue their studies in senior high school have to sit and pass locally organised entrance examinations. Senior high school education lasts for three years and the curriculum is divided into subject courses and activities. Students have to choose their streams, either sciences or humanities, and subject courses are divided into compulsory ones and optional ones. Students are also required to take part in extra-curricular activities. There is one more teaching week in senior high school than junior high school. A school year therefore consists of 10-11 weeks of holiday and another one or two weeks in reserve.

In Macau, senior secondary school usually lasts for two to three years.

International Schools. Since lessons are conducted in Mandarin in local schools, most of the children from foreign families choose to attend international schools. The teaching style in international schools in the mainland is similar to those in other places, such as Hong Kong, which emphasise personal development, creativity and thinking skills. However, international schools can only be found in big and affluent cities like Beijing, Shanghai and Shenzhen. School fees are expensive. In most cases, over US$20,000 (164,000 *yuan*/ £12,000) a year.

Useful Addresses

International School of Beijing, No. 10 An Hua Street, Shunyi District, Beijing 101300; ☎(86) 010 8149 2345 ext 1041 or 1042; fax (86) 010 8046 2003; e-mail admissions@isb.bj.edu.cn; www.isb.bj.edu.cn; it also has a division for kindergarten students.

Western Academy of Beijing, P.O. Box 8547, 10 Lai Guang Ying Dong Lu, Chaoyang District 100103; ☎(86) 010 8456 4155; fax (86) 010 6432 2440; e-mail wabinfo@westernacademy.com; www.wab.edu.

Beijing BISS International School, No. 17, Area 4, An Zhen Xi Li, Chaoyang District, Beijing, 100029, China; ☎(86) 010 6443 3151; fax (86) 010 6443 3156; e-mail daren@biss.com.cn; www.biss.com.cn.

Beijing World Youth academy (WYA), 40 Liangmaqiao Lu,Chaoyang District 100016; ☎(86) 010 6461 7779; fax (86) 010 6461 7717; http://www.chinatefl.com/beijing/teach/beijingsq.htm#3.

Beijing Yew Chung International School, Honglingjin Park, No. 5 Houbalizhuang, Chaoyang District, Beijing 100025; ☎(86) 010 8583 3731; fax (86) 010 8583 2734; www.ycef.com.

Beijing Zongugnacun International School, 14 Taiyangyan, Dazhongsi, Haidian District, Beijing.

International Academy of Beijing (IAB), Lido office tower 3, Lido Place Jichang road,jiangtai road Chaoyang district, Beijing 100004; ☎(86) 010 6430 1600.

Spanish Educational Study Group, Heping Jie Beikou, Huixin Dongjie, Chaoyang District, Beijing.

Swedish School, Legend Garden Villas, 89 Jichang Lu, Chaoyang District, Beijing 101300; ☎(86) 010 6456 0826/(86) 010 6456 0827; fax (86) 010 6456 0824; e-mail swedishschool@netchina.com.cn (during school year)/ kerokina@hotmail.com (all the time); www.swedishschool.org.cn.

Shanghai American School, 258 Jin Feng Lu, Zhudi Town, Minhang District, Shanghai 201107; ☎(86) 021 6221 1445; fax (86) 021 6221 1269; e-mail info@saschina.org; www.saschina.org.

Shanghai Community International Schools, NO.79, Lane 261, Jiangsu Road, Changning, Shanghai 200050; ☎(86) 021 6252 3688; fax (86) 021 6212 2330; e-mail info@scischina.org; www.scischina.org.

Yew Chung International School (Shanghai), 11 Shui Cheng Road, Gubei Campus: 18 Rong Hua Xi Road, Shanghai (Hongqiao Campus)/1983 Hua Mu Road, Shanghai (Pudong Campus); ☎(86) 021 6219 5910; fax (86) 021 6219 0675; e-mail ingridk@sis.ycef.com; www.ycef.com.

Concordia International School (Shanghai), 999 Mingyue Road, Jinqiao, Pudong, Shanghai, 201206; ☎(86) 021 589 90380; fax (86) 021 589 91685; e-mail registrar@ciss.com.cn; www.ciss.com.cn.

German School Shanghai, 437 Jinhui lu, Shanghai 201103; ☎(86) 021 6405 9220; fax (86) 021 6405 9235; e-mail info@ds-shanghai.org.cn; http:// www.ds-shanghai.org.cn.

French School of Shanghai, 437 Jinhui lu, Shanghai; ☎(86) 021 6405 9220; fax (86) 021 6405 9227; e-mail meunier@guomai.sh.cn.

Japanese School, 3185 Hongmei Lu, Shanghai; ☎(86) 021 6406 8027; fax (86) 021 6401 2747; e-mail sjs10@uninet.com.cn; www.sjscn.com.

Teda International School, 9 Xiao Yuan St., Teda, Tianjin, 300457; ☎(86) 022 252 90140; fax (86) 022 252 90631; e-mail tjtis@starinfo.net.cn; www.tedain ternationalschool.net.

Tianjin International School, 1 Meiyuan Rd., Huayuan Industrial Area, Nankai District, Tianjin, 300384; ☎(86) 022 8371 0900 ext. 100; fax (86) 022 8371 0400; e-mail tisadmissions@mtichina.com; www.tiseagles.com.

QSI International School of Shekou, Villa #5, Guishan Villas, Shekou, Guangdong, China; ☎(86) 0755 2667 6031; fax (86) 0755 2667 6030; e-mail shekou@qsi.org; www.qsi.org.

Clifford School, Clifford Estates (Panyu) Ltd., Panyu, Guangdong Province 511495.

QSI International School of Chengdu, 4th Floor, 17th Building, Area A, Phase 1, China Garden, Chengdu, 610041; ☎(86) 028 851 98393; fax (86) 028 851 98393; e-mail chengdu@qsi.org; www.qsi.org.

Guangzhou Nanhu International School, 176,yunxiang road, tonghe street,baiyun district,Guangzhou,Guangdong 510515; ☎(86) 020 8706 0862/(86) 020 8706 0373; fax (86) 020 8706 0330; http://www.GNISChina.com.

American International School of Guangzhou, No. 3, Yan Yu Street South, Er Sha Island, Dong Shan District, Guangzhou, Guangdong, 510105, China; ☎(86) 020 8735 3393; fax (86) 020 8735 3339; e-mail info@aisgz.edu.cn; www.aisgz.edu.cn.

Guangzhou International School, Building No.7, South Area, Zhongshan Dadao, Hua Jing New City, Guangzhou.

Hangzhou International School, 80 Dongxin Street, Binjiang District, Hangzhou, 310053; ☎(86) 0571 8669 0045; fax (86) 0571 8669 0044; e-mail dluebbe@scischina.org; www.scischina.org/hangzhou.

QSI International School of Wuhan, Dong Shun Hua Yuan, Chang Qing Lu, Hankou, Wuhan, Hubei, 430023; ☎(86) 027 8352 5597; fax (86) 027 8352 5597; e-mail jeffabare@qsi.org; www.qsi.org.

QSI International School of Zhuhai, 2 Longxing St.#22 Gongbei Zhuhai, China 519020, ☎(86) 0756 815 6134; fax (86) 0756 889 6758; e-mail zhuhai@qsi.org ; www.qsi.org.

Xiamen International School, Jiu Tian Hu, Xinglin District, Xiamen, Fujian Province, 361022; ☎(86) 0592 625 6581; fax (86) 0592 625 6584; e-mail askxis@hotmail.com; www.xischina.com.

School of the Nations (Macau), Rua Louis G Gomes #136, Edif Lei San, 4 Andar, Macau SAR; ☎(853) 701 759; fax (853) 701 724; e-mail sonmacau@macau.ctm.net; www.schoolofthenations.com.

Vocational Education

Vocational education is divided into three different levels, junior secondary, senior secondary and tertiary, and consists of vocational schools and vocational training.

Junior secondary vocational education is for primary school graduates and is part of the nine-year compulsory education. The aim is to train workers, farmers and employees in other sectors with basic professional knowledge and certain professional skills.

Senior secondary vocational training is another choice for continuing studies for junior high school graduates who cannot continue their studies in senior high schools, or for those who are more interested in learning something different. It is not limited to junior high school graduates only; senior high school graduates can also apply to these vocational schools. Senior secondary vocational training can be offered by specialized secondary schools, skilled workers' schools or vocational high schools. The objective of senior secondary vocational training is to prepare secondary-level practice-oriented talents to work in the forefront of production, service, technology and management. It usually takes four years to finish the training. Some courses are open to senior high school graduates only and these in general last for two years. Students are expected to master the basic knowledge, theory and skills of their speciality after the training. Similarly to senior high schools, cultural knowledge is also part of the studies.

Tertiary vocational training is for graduates from high schools and senior secondary vocational schools. Tertiary vocational training is divided into five categories:

- 30 higher vocational technology colleges.
- 101 short-circle practical vocational universities.
- Five-year higher vocational classes provided in regular specialised secondary schools.
- Tertiary vocational education provided in some regular higher education institutions.
- Reformed regular institutions offering two to three year higher education with emphasis on training technical talents in high-level professionals. The training lasts for two to three years.

Vocational training is mainly conducted and managed by the Department of Education and Labour. However, private enterprises are also encouraged to provide suitable training for their employees.

Universities

Before the education reforms of the 90s, university students were not required to pay tuition fees. However, they were not free to choose their jobs upon graduation. Under the current system, students have to pay a tuition fee of around 5,000 *yuan* (US$600/£360) a year. This may vary from university to university and also from subject to subject. After graduation, most of the students select their jobs freely under the guidance of state policy. There are loans and stipends available for students who have financial difficulties and there is also a part-time job system to help students support themselves. Scholarships are available to reward and help outstanding students.

According to government statistics, there are currently 1984 higher education institutes in China. Senior high school graduates have to sit a national examination to get an offer from universities. The competition for university places is generally quite keen. For most subjects, it takes four years to finish a bachelor's degree. A school year is usually divided into two semesters with the first one from September to January and the second one from February to July. Each semester consists of about 20 weeks. Students can choose their subjects from 12 disciplines including philosophy, economics, law, mathematics, education, literature, history, science, engineering, medicine, management and the military. Teaching is mainly conducted in Mandarin. Foreign students who want to study in universities in China have to pass a language test or study a Mandarin course before starting their studies.

The University of Nottingham is going to open a campus in China in September 2004 named 'University of Nottingham, Ningbo, China' which will be the first joint-venture university in China. The campus will be located in Ningbo of the Zhejiang province and students will graduate with a University of Nottingham degree, the same as that in the UK. Teaching will be in English and staff will be recruited both locally and internationally.

It usually takes three to four years to finish a bachelor's degree in Macau. Teaching is mainly conducted in English. However, courses of the law faculty are conducted in Cantonese and Portuguese, the official languages of Macau. Tuition fees for a bachelor's degree range from MOP$20,000-$25,000 (US$2,500-$3,200/£1,600-£2,000) a year. However, overseas students in general need to pay MOP$6,000-$10,000 (US$800-$1,300/£480-£800) more.

Some Major Universities

Tsinghua University, Foreign Students Office, Tsinghua University 100084; ☎(86) 010 6278 4857/(86) 010 6278 4621; fax (86) 010 6277 1134; e-mail xn-fao@tsinghua.edu.cn; www.tsinghua.edu.cn.

Peking University, Division of General Affairs, Second Floor, South Chamber (Nan Ge), Beijing 100871; ☎(86) 010 6275 1246/(86) 010 6275 1242/ (86) 010 6275 1243; fax (86) 010 6275 1240; e-mail study@pku.edu.cn; www.pku.edu.cn.

Renmin University of China, 59 Zhongguancun Dajie, Haidian District, Beijing 100872; ☎(86) 010 6251 1083/(86) 010 6251 1081; e-mail rmdxxb@ruc.edu.cn; www.ruc.edu.cn.

Tianjin Univeristy, 92 Weijin Lu, Nankai District, Tianjin 300072; ☎(86) 022 2740 6147; fax (86) 022 2740 6209; e-mail iso@tju.edu.cn; www.tju.edu.cn.

Nankai University, 94 Weijin Lu, Nankai District, Tianjin 300071; ☎(86) 022 2350 8825; e-mail admin@nankai.edu.cn; www.nankai.edu.cn.

Fudan University, 220 HandenLu, Shanghai 200433; ☎(86) 021 6564 2222; e-mail webmaster@fudan.edu.cn; www.fudan.edu.cn.

Tongji University, 1239 Siping Road, Shanghai; ☎(86) 021 6598 2200; (86) 021 65983932 (admission office); fax (86) 021 65984158 (admission office); e-mail xshchb@mail.tongji.edu.cn; www.tongji.edu.cn.

Shanghai Jiaotong University, 1954 Huashan Road, Shanghai, 200030; ☎(86) 021 6293 2414; fax (86) 021 6282 9514, e-mail icae@sjtu.edu.cn; www.sjtu.edu.cn.

Xi'an Jiaotong University, Office of International Cooperation and Exchange, 28 Hanningxi Lu, Xi'an, Shannxi, ☎(86) 029 8266 8830/(86) 029 8266 8236; e-mail inte-cao@mail.xjtu.edu.cn; www.xjtu.edu.cn.

Sun Yat-sen University, Office of International Cooperation & Exchange, No. 135

Xingang Xi Rd., Guangzhou 510275; ☎(86) 020 8403 6465; fax (86) 020 8403 6860/(86) 020 8733 3601; e-mail adeao01@zsu.edu.cn; www.zsu.edu.cn.

Wuhan University, The Office of The College of Foreign Students Education, Luojia Hill, Wuhan 430072; ☎(86) 027 8786 3154/(86) 027 8768 2209; fax (86) 027 8786 3154; e-mail fses@whu.edu.cn; www.whu.edu.cn.

University of Macau, Av. Padre Tomás Pereira S.J., Taipa, Macao; ☎(853) 831622; fax (853) 831694; www.umac.mo.

Macao Polytechnic Institute, Rua de Luis Gonzaga Gomes, Macau; ☎(853) 578722; fax (853) 308801; www.ipm.edu.mo.

Macao University of Science and Technology, ☎(853) 881122; fax (853) 880022; e-mail registry@must.edu.mo; www.must.edu.mo.

Useful Address

China Scholarship Council, 160 Fuxingmennei Street Beijing 100031; e-mail webmaster@csc.edu.cn; www.csc.edu.cn.

Useful Websites

China education and Research Network: www.edu.cn.

http://www.index-china.com/index-english/index-china-edumap.html, contains all links to the universities in China.

MEDIA AND COMMUNICATIONS

Newspapers

There are over 2000 national and provincial newspapers in China, of which about 40 are for ethnic minorities. *People's Daily* is the national newspaper and there is an English version as well as a Chinese one. *China Daily* also has an English version. Apart from these, English newspapers are hard to find even in big cities. You may be able to find one or two in newspaper shops at five-star hotels, or in one of the Friendship Stores, which are run by the government. *South China Morning Post*, which is based in Hong Kong, is one of the limited choices of English newspapers. Newspapers like *Asian Wall Street Journal*, *Financial Times* and *International Herald-Tribune* may be found in very high-class hotels, if you are lucky. Online newspapers are better options, if you have access to the internet.

Main Newspapers

People's Daily, Jintaixi Road #2, Chaoyang District, Beijing, 100733; ☎(86) 010 6536 8971; fax (86) 010 6536 8974/(86) 010 6536 8984; e-mail rmrb@peopledaily.com.cn; http://english.peopledaily.com.cn/.

China Daily, China Daily Website, 15, Huixindongjie, Chaoyang District; Beijing 100029; ☎(86) 010 6494 1107; fax (86) 010 6494 1125; www.chinadaily.com.cn.

South China Morning Post, 16/F Somerset House, Taikoo Place, 979 King's
    Road Quarry Bay, Hong Kong; ☎(852) 2565 2222; fax (852) 2811 1048;
    www.scmp.com.
Asian Wall Street Journal, ☎(852) 3105 2555; e-mail awsj.circulation@dowjone
    s.com; www.wsj.com.
Financial Times (Hong Kong Office), ☎(852) 2905 5555; fax (852) 2905 5590;
    e-mail subseasia@ft.com; www.ftasia.net.
The International Herald Tribune, ☎(852) 2922 1171; www.iht.com.

Magazines

As with English newspapers, English magazines are also not easy to find in China.
In big cities like Shanghai and Beijing, you may be able to find *Time*, *Newsweek*,
Far Eastern Economic Review or *The Economist* in five-star hotels and Friendship
Stores. English women's magazines such as *Cosmopolitans*, *Marie Claire* and *Elle*
are very rare, in part because Chinese versions are available.

    In Shanghai, there is a local weekly English newspaper called *Shanghai-Star*. It
is a local guide to a variety of things including travel, life style, food, fashion, etc.
It is published every Thursday and can be found on newspaper stands. It costs
only 2 *yuan* for a copy. There are some other locally published English magazines
which can be useful for expatriates. *That's Magazines* provides local information
about Shanghai, Beijing and Gaungzhou and you can either read it online or
order a copy. *City Weekend* is similar to *That's Magazines* but it is mainly for
Beijing and Shanghai only.

Useful Address

Shanghai-Star, 20F, Huaihai Building, 200 Huaihai Road (Middle), Shanghai
    200021; ☎(86) 021 6387 6060; e-mail shhstar@sh163a.sta.net.cn;
    www.shanghai-star.com.cn.
That's Magazines, www.thatsmagazines.com.
City Weekend, www.cityweekend.com.cn.

Television

Central China Television (CCTV) is the only television station for the whole of
mainland China, and is owned by the government. CCTV provides 11 channels,
nine of which are broadcast in Chinese. CCTV9 and CCTV 4 are the exceptions.
CCTV 9 is an international channel designed for foreigners. There are news
reports, cultural programmes, sports, business-related programmes, travel
programmes, documentaries, etc. In addition, there are sessions for teaching
people to learn basic Chinese. CCTV 4, also broadcasts in English, but is mainly
for news reports. CCTV 8 and CCTV 5 are for music and sports respectively, and
you need not to know much Chinese to enjoy watching these channels.

    Hong Kong Star TV also provides broadcasting services for the mainland via satellites, and you might find it more entertaining. There are nine channels, including movies, sport, documentaries, news, etc.

There is no TV licence requirement in China which means watching TV is free of charge. However, there are advertisements between programmes.

Useful Addresses

CCTV, 11B Fuxing Road, Media Center, Beijing, China 100038; ☎(86) 010 6850 6510; e-mail cctv-international@mail.cctv.com; www.cctv.com.

Star TV (Beijing Office), Unit 5-10, Level 9, Tower E3, The Towers, Oriental Plaza, No.1, East Chang An Ave, Dong Cheng District, Beijing 100738; ☎(86) 010 8518 8500; fax (86) 010 8518 8501; e-mail star@newscorp.com.cn; www.startv.com.

Star TV (Shanghai office), No.186, North Shan Xi Road, Shanghai 200041; ☎(86) 021 6218 3298; fax (86) 021 6218 5208; e-mail sstar@newscorp.com.cn; www.startv.com.

Radio

Central People's Broadcasting Station (CPBS) is responsible for supervising all the radio stations in China. Most of the radio stations broadcast in Mandarin, and some in other Chinese dialects. *China Radio International (CRI)*, a Chinese-run overseas radio service, broadcasts to other countries in about 40 languages including English and it also provides online radio services. If you miss your home radio stations, a short-wave radio receiver enables you to receive some of the overseas channels such as *BBC* (*www.bbc.co.uk/worldservice/tuning/*) and *Voice of America* (*www.voa.gov/*). You can check the broadcasting frequency from their websites.

Useful Address

China Radio International (English Service), China Radio International, Beijing, 100040; ☎(86) 010 6889 1652/(86) 010 6889 1617; fax (86) 010 6889 1582; e-mail crieng@cri.com.cn; http://www.crienglish.com.

Books and Bookshops

Most of the bookstores in mainland China do not sell books in foreign languages. In recent years, the book market has opened to foreign investors and you can now find some bookstores selling English books in big cities. *Foreign Language Bookstore* is one of the most popular amongst foreigners in China. You can also try the bookstores in big hotels and department stores such as *Friendship Stores*. Some of them do have English books and magazines even though the variety is rather limited. Online bookstores maybe more helpful if you are in smaller cities or you are looking for specific books. *Amazon.com* is an obvious choice. Alternatively, you can order books from bookstores in Hong Kong, which might save you some shipping costs.

Bookstore Addresses

Shanghai Foreign Language Bookstore, No.390 Fuzhou Road Shanghai 200001; ☎(86) 021 6322 3200; fax (86) 021 6351 6864; e-mail Cnsbtb@online.sh.cn; www.sbt.com.cn.

Foreign Languages Bookstore (Wangfujing), No.235 Wangfujing Dajie, Beijing; ☎(86) 010 6512 6911.

Foreign Languages Bookstore (Xidan), Xidan Dajie, Beijing.

Foreign Language Bookstore (Dongcheng), #2 Xila Hutong, Dongcheng District, Beijing.

The Foreign Language Bookstore (Guangzhou), Beijing Lu, Guangzhou.

Beijing International Bookstore, #31 Haidian street, Haidian District,Beijing; ☎(86) 010 6255 2499.

Beijing Foreign Language Publications Ltd., No.219 Wangfujing street, Dongcheng District, Beijing; ☎(86) 010 6525 5140.

Lufthansa Centre, 6/F, 50 Liangmaqiao Lu, Beijing; ☎(86) 010 6465 3388.

Haidian Book City, 31 Haidiandajie, Haidian District, Beijing.

Fengrusong Bookstore, 46, Haidian Lu (near south gate of Beijing University), Beijing.

Post

Post offices can usually be found on main streets, at railway stations, at airports and at major scenic spots. They open seven days a week, from 9am-5pm. Local mail within the same province costs 0.6 *yuan* (US$0.07/£0.04), and inter-province mail costs 0.8 *yuan* (US$0.1/£0.06). Sending a letter to the UK or the USA by airmail takes around 10 days and costs 6 *yuan* (US$0.7/£0.4) (weight 20g or less, 1.8 *yuan* (US$0.2/£0.12) for every additional 10g). You can save 0.5 *yuan* (US$0.06/£0.04) by surface mail, but it will be much slower. Express Mail Service (EMS) is available for mail which needs to be delivered in three to seven days (two to four days for the UK or the USA). The charges for EMS are 220 *yuan* (US$27/£16) and 180 *yuan* (US$22/£13) for sending a parcel to the UK and the USA. You can request someone from the post office to collect your parcel at home, by dialling the special number 185 for this service. EMS is also available for domestic mail and costs 20 *yuan* (US$2.5/£1.5). There is also a 'middle-speed' mail service provided by the post offices, which is called First-Priority Mail Service. It takes 5 days to deliver your letter or parcel to other countries under a charge of 40 *yuan* (US$5/£3) (weight 500g or less).

A new service was introduced in late 2002 which is called PC-Letter. PC-Letter allows you to send your mail (in electronic form) to the nearest post office of the receiver and then the letter is printed out on a special printer, which seals your letter immediately after printing. The letter will then be posted through the normal procedure. You need to buy an electronic payment card from post offices in order to use this service. PC-Letter allows you to send your letter without leaving home and it is faster than normal mailing methods as the letter can be sent to the nearest post office of the receiver rather than going through your local post office first. There are limitations on the number of pages and the paper size for the letter. At the moment, only A4 and B5 paper sizes are accepted and you can only send a maximum of four pages. It costs 2 *yuan* (US$0.25/£0.15) for a single-page letter and each additional page costs 0.5 *yuan* (US$0.06/£0.04). You need special software to use the PC-Letter service. For more details and the application method, contact the local post office.

The mail is delivered once every day but it may take longer to deliver letters in rural areas and in the western regions. Mailboxes are green and can be found in main streets and also rail stations. The postal officers usually check the contents of your parcels before posting them for you. You may be required to open your packed parcel for checking, so it is advisable to pack your parcel in the post office, after the staff have checked it and there are materials available for packing parcels in post offices. You are required to bring your identity document to claim a parcel.

Apart from normal mail services, post offices play the role of banks in some respects. You can open a savings account in a post office and you can also make a money transfer there. Every year, there are different stamps issued in China and you can order the forthcoming stamps in advance. The deadline for ordering next year's stamps is November of each year.

Post offices in Macau open 9am-5pm (or 6pm for some bigger post offices) from Monday to Friday, and 9am-1pm on Saturday. Two post offices, at the Macau Jetfoil Terminal and Macau International Airport, have extended opening hours from 10am-8pm Monday to Saturday. In case you cannot get to a post office during normal working hours, you can try these two but they are far away from the city centre. Mailboxes in Macau are red and are located on main streets. There are also some stamp vending machines located on the main roads.

Telephones

Details for installing a telephone and making calls from home are covered in the chapter *Setting Up Home*.

The country code for China is 86 but note that Hong Kong and Macau have separate country codes (852 and 853 representatively). Local telephone numbers consist of eight digits (not including the area code). Apart from the two previously colonised cities, calling China from other countries should involve the following: country code (86) + area code (omit the zero) + the number. You usually need to add '00' in front of '86' when making a call. It is the same to call other countries from China: 00 + country code + area code (omit the zero) + the number. Telephone booths are available in most cities but they are usually not for making international calls, even though you can make domestic long-distance calls. It costs 1 *yuan* (US$0.12/£0.07) for five minutes to make local calls.

You can make international calls from China Telecom offices. By paying a deposit of 200 *yuan*, you are given a card with a number of the phone booth to call from. China Telecom uses computers to time the length of each call and the charges are calculated on a per minute basis. You can also make domestic long-distance calls in the China Telecom offices and the deposit is 50 *yuan* (US$6/£4).

IP (Internet phone) is a more popular way to make international calls since the charge is cheaper. The IP service was introduced in late 1999 and it immediately became a popular option for making international calls. You can buy an IP phone card, which are available in the stored-value of 50 *yuan* (US$6/£4) to 500 *yuan* (US$60/£40), from hotels, post offices, department stores, convenience stores, telephone shops, or small carts selling lottery tickets in major cities or the China Telecom offices. As with making calls with normal phone cards, you can make calls from private telephones by entering the password of the IP card. You can also use your IP card in some of the public telephone booths but you have to pay a service fee of around 0.2 *yuan* (US$0.02/£0.01) per minute. An IP phone card usually expires in 12 months and it is better to check the expiry date before purchase. You can also install an internet phone service if you have a personal computer at home; the charge would then be even cheaper. For details, refer to the chapter *Setting Up Home*. There is another option for making calls home. You can dial the home country direct dial number (108) and then your country code, which puts you through to a local operator. You can either make a collect call or a credit card call. This can be done in China Telecom offices. However, the service is still not widely available and the staff in some offices may not be very helpful with the instructions. Apart from all these, you can always make your calls from hotels but this is the most expensive method of all.

Phone services in Macau are provided by Companhia de Telecomunicacões (CTM). Making local calls from home is free. Making local calls by public telephones cost MOP$1 for five minutes. Coins, phone cards and credit cards are accepted at most of the phone booths but some of them accept coins only. Public telephones also provide an international call service. You can also make Home Country Direct (HCD) calls from some of the public telephones as well, and charges are paid by the receivers (collect calls). The country code for Macau is 853 and there are no area codes in the city. To make a call to Macau, you should dial 853 (with 00 first) + the number. Making an international call from Macau is similar to doing so in mainland China.

There are three emergency numbers for mainland China:

- Police: 110
- Ambulance: 120
- Fire: 119

The emergency services number in Macau is 999.

AREA CODES OF SOME MAJOR CITIES			
City	**Area Code**	**City**	**Area Code**
Beijing	10	Lhasa	891
Changchun	431	Lijiang	888
Changsha	731	Luoyang	379
Chengdu	28	Nanchang	791
Chongqing	23	Nanjing	25
Datong	352	Qingdao	532
Dali	872	Shanghai	21
Dunhuang	937	Shantou	754
Foshan	757	Shenyang	24
Fuzhou	591	Shenzhen	755
Guangzhou	20	Shigatse	892
Guilin	773	Suzhou	512
Guiyang	851	Taiyuan	351
Hangzhou	571	Tianjin	22
Haerbin	451	Turpan	995
Haikou	898	Urumqi	991
Hohhot	471	Wuxi	510
Huangshan	559	Wuhan	27
Jilin	432	Xiamen	592
Jinan	531	Xi'an	29
Kashgar	998	Yangshuo	773
Kunming	871	Yangzhou	514
Lanzhou	931	Zhuhai	756

Other Useful Telephone Numbers

International assistance: 115
Local Directory assistant: 114

Local Long-distance call assistant: 113
Worldwide long-distance call assistant: 173/174
Macau local directory assistant: 185
Directory Enquiries (Chinese/English) (Macau): 181
International Telephone Enquiries (Macau): 101

CARS AND MOTORING

At the moment, there are over 10 million privately owned cars in mainland China and the annual growth rate is about 20% to 30%. There are two million private cars in Beijing alone and congestion is a very serious problem in the city. The same situation also occurs in other big cities like Shanghai, Guangzhou and Chongqing. Consequently riding a bicycle is probably faster than driving a car in Beijing during peak hours. People not holding driving licences issued in China are not allowed to drive between Chinese cities even if they have International Driving Permits. Foreign visitors holding International Driving Permits are allowed to drive within cities but they are limited to Beijing, Shanghai, Macau and Hong Kong.

More and more roads are being built in the big cities and between cities. Tolls are common and drivers need to stop at every toll station to pay. Toll fees are in general below 20 *yuan* (US$2.4/£1.4) for one single use. Roads, except the motorways, are divided into motorcar lanes and non-motorcar lanes and in some cases the boundary between the two is not clearly marked. Non-motorcars include bicycles, animal-towed carts and some electric cars which are under a certain size and which can only run at a limited speed, including electric wheelchairs. Road signs are in Chinese, with the Mandarin *Pinyin* (the Romanised written form of the sound) under the Chinese characters. Parking can be a problem in China. There are never enough parking spaces in big cities and you are prohibited from parking in many areas. Many people prefer to take the risk of a fine (about 5 *yuan*) in addition to a towing fee (about 200 *yuan*), and park on the streets rather than spend time looking for car parks.

Driving Regulations

There is a cumulative points system for regulating driving behaviour. Points are accumulated, usually along with a fine, when a driver breaks particular rules. Drivers who accumulate 12 points, will lose their driving licences and they will need to attend a driving school again and sit a driving examination in order to get their driving licence back. Those who accumulate no points within a year are allowed to renew their driving licences later than the normal period, as an encouragement for good behaviour.

The Chinese, like Americans and most Europeans, drive on the right. Traffic lights consist of red, yellow and green lights. As with other systems, the red light means you have to stop and a green light allows you to go while yellow is the signal for you to get ready. It turns from red to green directly but there is a flashing yellow light in between when it comes back, that is green then yellow then red. Drivers can make right-hand turns even when the red light is on and they are also allowed to start moving under a flashing yellow light, if no pedestrian is crossing the road. Drivers and passengers are required to wear seatbelts, and motorcycle drivers and passengers have to wear helmets. Using mobile phones or checking messages on pagers while driving is strictly prohibited. You are not allowed to overtake the vehicle in front if it is a police car, fire engine or ambulance on urgent service. It is also forbidden to overtake at crossroads, rail crossings, narrow bridges, on steep hills and in tunnels, etc.

The maximum speed on major roads is usually 120km/h and vehicles with a maximum speed of 70km/h or lower are prohibited. Motorcycles should keep to the righthand-lane. For roads with both motorcars and other traffic, the maximum speed is 70km/h if there is a clear separation for the two. Otherwise, it is 60km/h. The government marks the restricted areas by yellow lines. If you find a yellow line on the side of the road, it means you cannot stop your car there.

Penalties for breaking traffic regulations can be in the form of an oral warning, a fine, withdrawal or cancellation of a driving licence and, in more serious cases, arrest. Pedestrians, passengers and non-motorcar drivers usually receive an oral warning or a fine between 5 and 50 *yuan* (US$0.6-$6/£0.35-£35) if they break road regulations. The person will then receive a letter from the officer with details of the offence committed, the penalty, the date, time and location of the incident, and also the signature of the officer. Police officers may collect the fine immediately if the person who breaks the rule agrees that it is his or her fault. He or she will receive an official receipt from the Ministry of Finance after paying. The penalties for motorcars depend on what kind of regulation the drivers break. The fine for illegal parking is from 20 to 200 *yuan* (US$2.4-24/£1.4-14), depending on where you park. And your car may be towed away as well. You are then required to pay the fee for towing. Police usually give an oral warning and ask you to drive the car away immediately if the driver is at the wheel. The exact fine is decided by the local office but it must be within the ranges set by the central government.

Drinking and Driving. According to police statistics, most drink driving cases in China happen between 8pm and 10pm, after the drivers have dined out at restaurants. The drinking limit for a driver in China is relatively low when compared to the UK and the USA. You are considered to be drink-driving if the blood alcohol level exceeds 30mg (per 100ml of blood). The limits in the UK and the USA are both 80mg (per 100ml of blood). Police set up road blocks from time to time and ask suspected drivers to take breath tests. If they find drunk drivers (more than 100mg of alcohol in 100ml of blood), they will send them to hospital for blood tests. A blood test also applies to those drivers who are unwilling or unable to give breath tests.

The penalties for drink-driving depend on the type of car, whether private or public/business, and also the blood alcohol level. A driver is regarded as technically drunk if the blood alcohol level exceeds 100mg (per 100ml of blood), and this is more serious than 'drink-driving'. Drunk drivers face detention for 15 days in addition to fines and suspension of driving licences. The penalty for a private car driver includes a suspension of his driving licence for three to six months, a fine of 500 to 2000 *yuan* (US$61-244/£36-143) and detention for 15 days. A public/business car driver faces the same period of detention, a fine of 2000 *yuan* and also a suspension of his driving licence for 6 months. A drink-driver of a private car will be suspended from driving for one to three months in addition to a fine of 200 to 500 *yuan*. For a public/business driver there is a suspension of his driving licence for three months plus a fine of 500 *yuan*.

Anyone found drunk-driving twice in a year, will have their driving licence cancelled and they will be prohibited from operating public/business vehicles for five years.

Breakdowns and Accidents

There are some government guidelines about what you should do in case of a breakdown or accident on the road. You must turn on the hazard lights. If possible, you should move your car to the side of the road; otherwise, try to put a sign at a certain distance behind your car to warn on-coming cars; you are advised to put a sign at least 150 metres behind your car if it breaks down on a motorway. It is advisable to carry the telephone numbers of companies which can provide towing and repair services.

You should also call the police if your car breaks down on a motorway. Otherwise, if no one is hurt in an accident, you are not required to call the police. The parties involved should move their cars away to keep the road clear, before trying to settle the compensation between themselves. However, if the parties cannot agree about who is responsible, they should call the police. If someone is injured in an accident, you should call the police and an ambulance immediately. Hospitals are required to treat accident casualties immediately, even though they may not be able to pay for the treatment. The charges should be covered by the insurance of the car involved in the accident. If it cannot cover the whole amount, the government has an emergency fund set up specifically for accidents and this can be used to pay for the hospital charges if necessary. The party causing the accident is responsible for paying any treatment charges which exceed the third party insurance cover and the government will ask the person responsible to pay the money back to the fund.

Telephone Numbers for Towing Services:

Dongdan Branch (Dongcheng, Beijing): (86) 010 68399161
Highway Branch (Chaoyang, Beijing): (86) 010 68398140/(86) 010 67320937
Xidan Branch (Xicheng, Beijing): (86) 010 68399221

Driving Licences

Holders of an International Driving Licence can probably skip the driving examination to get a Chinese driving licence, unless their driving licence has been acquired less than three years ago. You should apply to the Traffic Management Bureau office in your city, which is under the Public Security Bureau. You are required to hold a residence permit for at least one year and you must have been staying in China for a continuous period of six months immediately before you hand in your application. Apart from the application form, you are also required to present your passport and your International Driving Licence. You may be asked to have your driving licence translated and stamped officially. Everyone applying for a driving licence needs to provide medical proof from a hospital stating that he or she is physically healthy and is fit to drive. There is no exception for foreigners and you should have a health check in a hospital before you apply for a Chinese driving licence.

For a new application, you have to fill-in the form and bring along the health proof and local identity card or permit to stay for at least one year, to a recognised driving school. After passing the written driving examination and road test, a driving licence will be issued to you. Some people have found that the English in the written examination is incomprehensible and the terms used are not the same as those in other countries. For example, learner drivers may be called 'practitioner drivers'. Questions are mainly in the form of multiple choice but the number of questions can be up to a hundred.

The application fee for a driving licence is 50 *yuan* and the charge for issuing a driving licence is 5 *yuan*.

Car Registration

You must register your vehicle before using it in China. You should fill in a vehicle registration form, which can be found at the local offices of the Traffic Management Bureau. You are also required to supply the following documents: proof of the car owner's identity, proof of the origin of the car (receipt of purchase, import certificate, etc.), certificate issued by the manufacturer proving the safety of the car (for locally manufactured vehicles), other import documents, receipts of tax paid and also photos of the car to be registered. Your car also needs to be examined before getting the registration. It usually takes three to five working days to issue the registration certificate. The fee for registration is 10 *yuan*.

TRANSPORT

Air

In recent years, the government has been improving the facilities of airports and it is now easy and comfortable to travel between cities by air. Airports in Shanghai, Beijing and Hong Kong are the international gateways of China and they are also well connected to other Chinese cities. *The Civil Aviation Administration of China*

(CACC) is responsible for national civil aviation affairs. It publishes timetables for the major airlines of China twice a year (usually in April and November) and these timetables can be purchased from Chinese airports. Beijing is the central connection for many cities. You can fly to almost all internal airports from Beijing via direct flights, including Shanghai, Hong Kong, Guangzhou, Qingdao, Dalian, Shenyang, Haerbin, Hailar, Hohhot, Urumqi, Xining, Kumming, Lanzhou, Chengdu, Xian, Chongqing, Zhengzhou and Wohan. The major airlines include Air China, China Eastern, China Southern, China Northern, China Southwest and China Northwest. It is about 500 to 800 *yuan* for a one-way ticket flying within China and the cost for a return ticket is simply double.

Useful Addresses and Websites

Air China, e-mail master@mail.airchina.com.cn; www.airchina.com.cn.

China Eastern, www.cea.online.sh.cn.

China Southern, ☎(86) 020 8668 2000; e-mail webmaster@cs-air.com; www.cs-air.com.

China Northern, www.cna.ln.cninfo.net.

China Southwest, ☎(86) 028 8666 8080; fax (86) 028 8665 6991; e-mail cturrsz@cswa.com; www.cswa.com.

China Northwest, ☎800 840 2299; fax (86) 029 8426 1622; e-mail belinda917@163.net; www.cnwa.com.

Civil Aviation Administration of China (CAAC), 155 Dongsi Xidajie, Beijing100710; ☎(86) 010 6409 1114; www.caac.gov.cn.

Dragon Air Ticketing Office, Room 4609 – 4611, 46/F., COSCO Tower, 183 Queen's Road Central, Hong Kong; tel(852) 2868 6777; fax (852) 2810 0370; www.dragonair.com.

Air Macau, Novos Aterros do Porto Exterior, Dynasty Plaza, Macau; ☎(853) 396 5555; fax (853) 396 5666; e-mail airmacau@airmacau.com.mo; www.airmacau.com.mo.

Rail

There is a well established and efficient rail network in China and the rail system covers all provinces except Tibet. The first letter of the number of a train indicates the speed of the train: 'T' means special express which is the quickest, most comfortable and also the most expensive; 'K' means fast; 'Y' are tourist trains (connect major tourist cities); those without any letter are normal speed trains. Tickets are not divided into first class and second class. Rather, they are divided into hard seat, hard sleeper, soft seat and soft sleeper. Hard seat is the cheapest ticket, but it can be a very tiring if it takes more than a few hours to reach your destination. Soft seats actually costs about the same as hard seats, but very few trains are equipped with soft seats. For long journeys, people usually prefer sleeper tickets. Travellers with hard sleeper tickets are put into a compartment without doors in which there are six beds. The beds are in two tiers, with three beds in each tier. Pillows, sheets and blankets are provided at no extra charge. Soft sleeper tickets cost about double the price, but give you access to a well decorated, closed compartment with only four beds inside. As with hard sleeper tickets, pillows, sheets and blankets are included in the price.

It is often quite difficult to get tickets for hard seats and hard sleepers. It is almost impossible to purchase a ticket on the same day of travel. You are advised to book in advance and sleeper tickets can be booked five days in advance. If you do not mind paying more, soft sleeper tickets are usually easier to get. Travel agents like China International Travel Service, China Travel and China Youth Travel Service may help you to get train tickets if you fail to get one at the train station. Four-star and Five-star hotels usually help customers to book train tickets, but this may incur service charges. Staff in large train stations can usually speak some English and there are also ticket offices specifically opened for foreigners in some stations such as Beijing. Luggage storage is available in all stations and the charges are from 2 to 4 *yuan*.

If you are travelling from Hong Kong or Macau, China Travel will be able to help you to book the train tickets for entering and travelling within mainland China. Direct trains are available from Hong Kong to Guangzhou.

An underground system has been running in Beijing since 1969, and a similar system started in Shanghai in 2000. The government also launched the CityRail trains in Beijing in early 2003. The CityRail connects the northwestern suburb of Beijing to downtown (from Xizhimen to Dongzhimen) and you can transfer to other rail lines for going to other parts of Beijing. Fares range from 2 to 4 *yuan* (US$0.24-0.48/£0.14-0.28), depending on the distance. The west line which goes from Xizhimen to Huilongguan connects the Olympic Village to the city centre. It is expected to be completed in 2004.

Useful Addresses

Metro and CityRail: http://www.ebeijing.gov.cn/Life/Transportation/t20030927 – 39858.htm.

China Travel Net Hong Kong Limited, Room A, 2/F, Tak Bo Building, 62-74 Sai Yee Street, Mongkok, Hong Kong; ☎(852) 2789 5401; fax (852) 2789 3498; e-mail enquiry@chinatravel1.com ; www.chinatravel1.com.

China International Travel Service, ☎(86) 010 6522 2991/(86) 010 8522 7930; fax (86) 010 6522 2862; e-mail shuyu@cits.com.cn ; www.cits.net.

China Travel Service (Beijing Office), Zidutech Co., Ltd. Beijing; No. 34 Fuwaidajie Ave, Xicheng District, Beijing 100832; ☎(86) 010 6852 4860/ (86) 010 6852 4882; fax (86) 010 6852 4887; e-mail bisc@chinats.com; www.chinats.com.

China Youth Travel Service, 23C Dongjiaominxiang, Beijing 100006; ☎(86) 010 6513 3153; fax (86) 010 6527 7415.

Bus

Long-distance bus is another option for travelling around the country. Routes are extensive, often reaching rural areas which trains do not. Long-distance buses usually have regular stops for toilets and food and they cost about the same as hard seat train tickets. Sleeper buses are available for long-distance travel but there is usually no place to lock your hand luggage. It is advisable to book your bus tickets in advance at the bus stations or through hotels and travel agents. Mini-buses are available on some middle-distance routes. Minibuses are usually privately-owned and the fare is not monitored by the government. Mini-buses are faster than buses and have more flexible timetables. Some of them actually have no timetable at all and leave when the seats are filled up.

Local buses are convenient and cheap. However, the compartments are usually very crowded. It is very difficult to get a seat, even outside rush hours. When buses are packed you must look out for pick-pockets, you should keep an eye on your money and travel documents in these situations. Travel congestion is very serious in some big cities like Beijing and Shanghai, and travelling by bus can be a very uncomfortable experience. Tickets for buses are sold by conductors or drivers.

Buses are the main transport in Macau. All of them travel in circular routes. It costs MOP$2.5-MOP$6 for a trip on a bus and you have to have the exact change. Bus route information is available at airports and ferry ports and all the stops are listed on the route maps. If you are planning to travel from Macau to the mainland, buses No.3, 5 and 9 can take you to the Border Gate (*Portas de Cerco*) and you can walk across to the gate and enter mainland China with your travel documents. You can also take bus No.26 to Zhuhai by crossing the new Lotus Bridge, but this only opens between 9am and 5pm.

Useful Website

http://www.apta.com/links/international/asia/china.cfm, provides links to some bus companies.

Ferry

There are ferry services connecting some cities in China. However, these services may not be available all year round and are mainly available in the cities which are along the main rivers. Ferry services are available in Chongqing, Wuhan, Guilin, Yangshou, Guangzhou, Wuzhou, Leshan, Yibin, etc. It is better to check with the local ferry company for further details well in advance before you plan your travel.

TurboJET, based in Hong Kong, provides ferry services to Macau, Shenzhen and Guangzhou. The fare for going to Macau is MOP$130-$162 and MOP$171-$198 for Shenzhen and Guangzhou. First Ferry operates ferries between Hong Kong and Macau at a price of MOP$123-$131 for a single trip. However, there are only a limited number of ferries every day.

Ferry Companies

TurboJET, Shun Tak – China Travel Ship Management Ltd, 83 Hing Wah Street West, Lai Chi Kok, Kowloon, Hong Kong; ☎(852) 2307 0880/(852) 2859 3333 (enquiry hotline); fax (852) 2786 5125; www.turbojet.com.hk.

Yuet Tung Shipping Company, Av. Almeida Ribeiro, Rua das Lorchas; ☎(853) 574 478.

Taxis

Alex Thomson's thoughts on taxis

Taxi drivers were immediately telling me that the train station was closed and there were no buses to Hangzhou. Whatever seasoning experiences I had gained in my earlier days working in clubs no longer mattered I had Lao Wai (foreigners) written all across my forehead and no matter how hard I tried to present an image that I knew what I was doing I couldn't fake it. They were telling me that it would cost me 900-1200 yuan to get there. I know now that you can rent a driver for an entire day including gas for about 20% of that! My final deal was not too bad though, comparatively. A shuttle bus is 80-100 yuan and I paid something like 260 yuan for the 3 hour drive in a taxi because the driver was a local heading home, and wanted a last fare to bump up the day's take.

Taxis are not expensive in China (about 1 to 2 *yuan* per km). However, not all taxi drivers are honest, particular towards foreigners. The fare is based on the distance travelled but sometimes, especially in smaller cities and rural areas, the driver will propose a rate for the trip instead of following the meter. If you choose to accept the deal, probably after some bargaining, it is best to write the agreed fare down to avoid any 'misunderstanding' when you arrive the destination. It is easy to find a taxi outside hotels and bus stations.

Taxis in Macau are either black or yellow in colour and they charge the same. The first 1.5km costs MOP$10 and MOP$1 for every additional 250m. There is an extra charge of MOP$5 for going to Taipa or Coloane from Macau Peninsula and MOP$2 for travelling between the two islands. It takes MOP$5 more if you take the taxi from the airport.

BANKING AND FINANCE

Bank Accounts

You do not have to be a permanent resident to open a bank account. Foreigners can open bank accounts with the tourist visa or work visa. You can open the account in Chinese or US currencies, and you probably need to put a small deposit into the account when you open one. ATM machines are available in big cities like Beijing, Shanghai, Shenzhen and Guangzhou. However, you can only withdraw Renminbi from a domestic account. Credit card payments are not common in mainland China but you can normally use a credit card in large hotels and department stores. *www.mastercard.com/atmlocator* and *www.international.visa.com/ps* are useful if you are trying to locate an ATM machine in the city where you are staying. Traveller's cheques can be cashed in the Bank of China, CITIC Industrial Bank or hotels. Online banking also brings enormous flexibility to frequent travellers. The following services are usually available: performing transactions of transfer and remittance, obtaining balance enquiries and account transaction histories, using other services like stopping or reporting the loss of a cheque, requesting statements, ordering your cheque book, inquiring on deposits rates, changing of address and sending/receiving secured messages to/from the bank. If your bank at home has branches in China, it may be possible to open an account in advance. It is probably easier to arrange more advanced services like internet banking in your home country. You can also transfer some money to your account in China before you go, reducing the risks entailed with carrying too much cash. Banks, in general, are open seven days a week, from 9am-5pm. However, some banks may close earlier, such as 4pm during weekends.

Despite its relatively small size, more then twenty different banks can be found in Macau. There are two banknotes-issuing banks, namely, Banco Nacional Ultramarino (BNU) and the Bank of China (Macau Branch), whereas coins are issued by the Monetary Authority of Macau. Banks in Macau open 9am-4/4.30pm from Monday to Friday. However, they are closed during lunchtime and on Saturday, which can be quite inconvenient.

Main banks

Bank of China, 1 Fuxingmen Nei Dajie, Bejing 100818; ☎(86) 010 6659 6688; fax (86) 010 6601 4024; www.bank-of-china.com.

The People's Bank of China, No.32 ChengFang Street, XiCheng district, Beijing 100800; ☎(86) 010 6619 4114; e-mail master@pbc.gov.cn; http://www.pbc.gov.cn/.

Bank of Communications, 188 Yin Cheng Road Central, Shanghai 200120; ☎(86) 021 5878 1234; fax (86) 021 5888 0559; e-mail enquiry@bankcomm.com.hk; www.bankcomm.com.hk.

China Minsheng Bank, ☎95568; e-mail service@cmbc.com.cn; www.cmbc.com.cn.

China Construction Bank, 4 Men No.28 West Dajie, Xuanwumen, Beijing 100053; ☎(86) 010 6360 3660; fax (86) 010 6360 3194; www.ccbhk.com.

Hua Xia Bank, 111 Xidianbei Dajie, Beijing; ☎(86) 010 6615 1199; fax (86) 010 6618 8484; e-mail webmaster@hxb.cc; www.hxb.com.cn.

China Merchants Bank, 156 Fuxingmennei Dajie, Xicheng District, Beijing 100036; ☎(86) 010 6642 6868; www.cmbchina.com.

Industrial and Commercial Bank of China, 55# Fuxingmennei Street, Xicheng District, Beijing 100032; ☎95588; e-mail webmaster@icbc.com.cn; www.icbc.com.cn.

Useful Website
Monetary Authority of Maca, http://www.amcm.gov.mo/.
Banco Nacional Ultramarino, http://www.bnu.com.mo/en/.
Bank of China (Macau Branch), http://www.bocmacau.com/eng/index.htm.

International Money Transfer
Foreign currency and travellers cheques can be changed at border crossings, international airports, main branches of the Bank of China and ICBC (not all banks provide this service), large hotels and big department stores. Travellers are advised to get their money exchanged at well-established companies like Thomas Cook. Money transfers can be made in banks and also post offices, but it can take weeks to get your money, unless you are in Beijing, Shanghai, Macau or Hong Kong. Doing it through the internet will probably save you some time, so long as you already have the service set up.

In Macau, there are licenced moneychangers for exchanging travellers cheques. These moneychangers open seven days a week and some even open for 24-hours a day as well. There is one in the basement of the *Hotel Lisboa,* and another is near the bottom of the steps leading up to *São Paulo.*

Money
Renminbi (RMB) literally means 'People's Money' and it uses *yuan* as the unit. You can also see 'RMB' on the price tags sometimes. One *yuan* is divided into ten *jiao* and one *jiao* can be further divided into ten *fen.* Notes are available in the values of 1 *yuan,* 2 *yuan,* 5 *yuan,* 10 *yuan,* 20 *yuan,* 50 *yuan* and 100 *yuan;* there are four different kinds of coins: 1 *yuan,* 5 *jiao,* 1 *jiao* and 5 *fen.*

Macau used *pataca* from the time that it was colonised by Portuguese. As with Hong Kong, Macau also uses the dollar as a unit. People usually denote the price as 'MOP$' or just with the M like 'M$'. There are 5 different denominations of bills including MOP$20, MOP$50, MOP$100, MOP$500 and MOP$1,000. Coins are available with the values of MOP$1, 50 cents, 20 cents and 10 cents. The value of one Macau dollar is very close to one Hong Kong dollar and the Hong Kong dollar is widely accepted in all kinds of businesses.

TAXATION
The Ministry of Finance (MOF) and State Administration of Taxation deal with all tax matters in China. MOF is mainly responsible for making policies

related to taxation and setting the rates for different kinds of taxes. The State Administration of Taxation is involved in some of the policy making but it mainly deals with the administration of taxation like tax returns, tax refunds, etc. The tax year for mainland China is from 1st January to 31st December.

Individual Income Tax

Individual Income Tax (IIT) is charged according to the monthly income of an individual as well as the length of time he or she has been working in China. Foreign employees paid by foreign enterprises and staying in mainland China for fewer than 90 days are exempt from IIT. For those who stay from 90 days to one year, only their income derived in China are subject to IIT. However, directors, general managers or deputy managers of Chinese-based enterprises have to pay tax on foreign-sourced income for services performed outside China as well as the income derived in China. Individuals who have stayed in China for more than one year but less than five years are taxed on both income derived in China and overseas. If you stay beyond five years, all worldwide income, no matter whether it is remitted to China or not, is taxable.

According to the State Administration of Taxation, as well as wages and salaries, bonuses, cash allowances, personal tax paid by an employer and stock options are all taxable. Several allowances, including relocation allowance, child education allowance, business travel allowance, accommodation provided by an employer and company car expenses are exempt from tax. There are monthly deductible allowances of 800 *yuan* and 4,000 *yuan* for local and foreign IIT payers respectively. Tax rates range from 5% to 45%, according to monthly income. Income derived from personal services, royalties, interest and dividends are taxed at a flat rate of 20% if they exceed 4,000 *yuan*, of which 20% is not taxable. If it is less than 4,000 *yuan*, the first 800 *yuan* is not taxable, and the rest is taxed at a flat rate of 20%.

INDIVIDUAL INCOME TAX RATES	
Monthly taxable income	**Rate**
First 5000 yuan	5%
The next 1500 yuan	10%
On the Next 3000	15%
On the Next 15000	20%
On the Next 20000	25%
On the Next 20000	30%
On the Next 20000	35%
On the Next 20000	40%
Remainder	45%

Income tax is called Employment Tax in Macau and taxable income includes wages, salary, bonus, dividends and commissions. The tax year for Macau is the same as mainland China, from 1ˢᵗ January to 31ˢᵗ December. Tax returns should be filed not later than the end of February.

TAX RATES IN MACAU (VALUES IN MOP)	
Annual Taxable Income	**%**
$9500 or less	Exempt
Next $10,500	7%
Next $20,000	8%
Next $40,000	9%
Next $80,000	10%
Next $120,000	11%
Reminding	12%

Other Taxes

For business-related taxes including foreign-invested and foreign enterprise income tax, Value-added tax (VAT), custom duties and consumption tax, please refer to the chapter *Starting a Business*.

Property Tax. Owners of properties have to pay property tax annually. Sometimes, the taxes are paid by the tenants or the agents who manage the properties if there is no clear owner. The tax is calculated according to the value of the property. Taxable value is equal to 70% to 90% of a property and the current tax rate is 1.2%. If the tax is levied on the rent and paid by the tenants, the tax levied is equal to 12% of the rent.

Urban Real Estate Tax. Urban Real Estate Tax was set up in order to make better use of land and to reduce the differences in the incomes from land. The tax is levied annually and is calculated in terms of the area used by enterprises or individuals. The rate is higher in big cities and is 0.5 *yuan* to 10 *yuan* per square metre. In middle sized cities, the tax is 0.4 *yuan* to 8 *yuan* per square metre while that of small cities is 0.3 *yuan* to 6 *yuan* per square metre.

Vehicle Purchase Tax. Owners of new vehicles are subjected to Vehicle Purchase Tax, regardless of whether the vehicles are purchased, imported, awarded or received as a gift. The tax is equal to the taxable value times the tax rate, which is 10% at the time of writing. Taxable value of a newly purchased vehicle is the sum of the selling price (excluding the VAT) plus any other additional charges of the purchase. If the vehicle is imported, the taxable value is equal to the selling price (including the VAT) plus the import tax and consumption tax. The taxable value of a vehicle will be calculated according to the market value of the same type of vehicles in the event that the vehicle is an award or a gift. The tax should be filed within 60 days after the purchase or import. This is a once-off tax and second-hand vehicles are exempted from the Vehicle Purchase Tax. Where the value of a vehicle is calculated in another currency, it will be transferred to Renminbi according to the exchange rate of the People's Bank of China on the day of filing.

Vehicle and Vessel Usage and Licence Plate Tax. Users of vehicles and vessels are subject to this tax. For vessels and trucks, taxes levied are calculated according to tonnage. Otherwise, the amount of tax levied depends on the type of the vehicle. Tax is paid annually and the exact date for paying it is set by local government. Users of motor vessels have to pay 1.2 to 5 *yuan* per tonnage while users of non-motor vessels pay 0.6 to 1.4 *yuan* per tonnage. Trucks are subject to tax of 16 to 60 *yuan* per ton and that for passenger cars is from 60 to 320 *yuan* per car. Motorcycles are levied at from 20 to 80 *yuan*. Users of non-motor vehicles also need to pay the tax, even if the amount is very small, at a rate of 1.2 to 4 *yuan* per vehicle. Note that bicycles are included as non-motor vehicles and pay tax.

Stamp Duty. This applies to contracts, documents for the transfer of property title, business account books, certificates and licences, or documents in the form of a contract. The tax rate varies according to the type of document to be taxed. Extra copies of the taxed documents are exempted from further tax.

Land Transfer Tax. When the ownership of land or property is transferred to another person, the new owner is subject to the Land Transfer Tax. The transfer of ownership can be in the form of a sale, swap or gift. The current tax rate is from 3-5%. The taxable value is equal to the selling price of the land or property, or the market price if the ownership is transferred as a gift. In case of a swap of ownerships between two parties, the tax is levied on the difference in values in the two pieces of land or the properties. The new owner should file the tax within ten days of the transfer of ownership.

Useful Addresses
State Administration of Taxation, 5 Yangfangxi Lu, HaidianDistrict, Beijing 100038; e-mail webmaster@chinatax.gov.cn; www.chinatax.gov.cn.
Finance Service Department (Macau), Av. Da Praia Grande, No. 575, 579 & 585, Macau; ☎(853) 336886; fax (853) 300133; www.dsf.gov.mo.

HEALTH CARE

Hospitals

Almost all hospitals are owned and monitored by the government, even though there are many private hospitals created by joint ventures. There are standard charges for medical treatments but they vary slightly in different provinces. You are required to register at reception before seeing a doctor in a hospital. The charge for making a registration is around 1 *yuan* but you need to pay more if you want to see a specific doctor for consultation. Some hospitals provide phone or online registration services but most of the websites are in Chinese. Consultation and medicines are charged separately. It is hard to predict the exact amount a person will need to pay as treatments and medicines are charged per item. You also need to pay before you receive any treatment. Hospitals usually ask for a deposit before providing services and patients or their family members will be asked to top up the deposit when the money is used up. The consultation fee is around 5 *yuan* and most of the medicine is under 20 *yuan* per box (contains 20-30 doses). However, some particular medicines can be very expensive. For a few imported medicines, the charges can be over 1000 *yuan* (US$120/£70). Staying in a hospital costs 5 to 60 *yuan* a day, depending on the facilities of the room.

Ambulances are available for emergencies. However, unless requested, there will be no medical staff on the ambulance and the personnel present may have little or no medical training. Calling an ambulance costs around 50 *yuan* and there is an extra 40 *yuan* for requesting the presence of medical staff. Except in emergency, foreigners are advised to go to hospitals in big cities, as not all medical staff can speak English. Hospitals in mainland China charge the same for locals and foreigners, but bear in mind that most hospitals do not accept credit card payments and you should have cash available if you or your family members need to go to hospital.

You are required to bring along your DH (Department of Health) Computerized Card when you use the services of hospitals or health centres in Macau. The card can be applied for from the Administrative Service at the hospitals or the Health Centres where you reside. You are asked to present your identity document and also proof of your address (e.g. water, telephone or electricity bill). The general consultation costs MOP$42 for locals, MOP$60 for non-resident workers and MOP$120 for foreigners.

Useful Addresses

Ministry of Health, 1 Xixhimenwai Nanlu, Xicheng District, Beijing 100044; ☎(86) 010 6879 2114; e-mail manage@moh.gov.cn; www.moh.gov.cn.

Guangzhou International SOS Clinic, 2/F, Guangdong Province Hospital of TCM Da Tong Lu, Ersha Island,Guangzhou 510105; ☎(86) 020 8735 1240/(86) 020 8735 1051; fax (86) 020 8735 2045; 24hour Alarm Centre: 852 2528

9900; www.internationalsos.com.

Conde de S. Januário Hospital (Macau), ☎(853) 3906016; fax (853) 346818; e-mail info@ssm.gov.mo.

Useful Websites

China Internet Information Centre, http://www.china.org.cn/english/travel/ 41850.htm; for addresses of all the hospitals in China.

Department of Health (Macau), http://www.ssm.gov.mo/design/guide/e – guide – fs.htm; provides addresses and telephone numbers of hospitals and health centres.

Health Insurance

Under the current legislation, employers and employees are required to contribute to government medical insurance. At the same time, the government encourages residents to have private health insurance as well. The government aims to have an 80% rate of private insurance coverage for the whole population by 2010. Currently, about 50% of people in urban areas are covered by private insurance but the rate is much lower in rural areas, often as low as 10%. You should seek advice from insurance companies before leaving your country, especially if you are going to stay for only a short period and are not going to buy any insurance within China. Some big insurance companies have branches in China and you can look for suitable insurance coverage after you settle in.

Useful Addresses

HTH Worldwide Inc., One Radnor Corporate Center, Suite 100, Radnor, PA 19087 USA; ☎800 242 4178 (inside USA)/(1) 952 903 6418 (outside USA); fax (1) 610 254 8797; e-mail studentinfo@hthworldwide.com ; www.hthstudents.com; special in insurance for students.

American International Assurance Co (Bermuda) Ltd, AIA Building, 17 Zhong Shan Dong Yi Road, Shanghai 200002; ☎(86) 021 6321 6698/(86) 800 820 3588; e-mail AIA – TEC@mail.online.sh.cn; http://www.aigchina.com/aiash/ encontent/aiash – firstpage – en.htm.

AXA Asia Pacific Holdings Ltd, Beijing Representative Office, No. 408 Office Building, Beijing Hotel, 8 Xinzhong Xi Jie Gongti Bei Lu, Beijing, 100027; ☎ (86) 010 6500 7788 ext 7497/(86) 010 6500 7393; fax (86) 010 6500 7390; www.axa-chinaregion.com.

Royal & Sun Alliance Insurance (Shanghai) Ltd, 9th floor, HSBC Tower 101 Ying Cheng East Road, Pudong New Area, Shanghai, China 200120; ☎(86) 021 6841 1999; fax (86) 021 6841 2700; e-mail rsashang@uninet.com.cn; http://www.royalsunalliance.com.cn/.

PICC Property and Casualty Company Limited Address: 69 Dongheyanjie, Xuanwumen, Beijing 100052; ☎(86) 010 6315 6688; fax (86) 010 6303 3589;

e-mail webmaster@piccnet.com.cn; http://www.picc.com.cn/en/index.shtml.

ING General Insurance International Limited, 37th Floor, World Trade Tower No. 25 Tong Xing Street Zhongshan District, Dalian 116001; ☎(86) 0411 2530 881; fax (86) 0411 2530 877; www.ing-cap.com.cn.

New York Life Insurance Worldwide Ltd, No.3601, 36/F Jinmao Building, 88 Shiji Dadao, New Pudong Area, Shanghai 200121; ☎(86) 800 820 5882; e-mail p – r@haiernewyorklife.com.cn; www.haiernewyorklife.com.cn.

AIDS

The problem of AIDS in China has become severe and is accelerating at the rate of 30-40% every year. According to the Chinese government, there are more than 800,000 cases of AIDS and HIV carriers in the country and the UN believes that the number will increase to 10 million or more by the year 2010. In order to prevent AIDS from spreading further the Chinese government set up its first formal research centre in Shanghai in April 2004. Moreover, anyone who is trying to cover-up an outbreak of AIDS will be severely punished. However, some people have criticised public education on the issue and a survey released in 2003 reflected that one in four people in rural areas had never heard of AIDS and only 20% of the population knew HIV could be transmitted through sex.

SOCIAL SECURITY AND BENEFITS

Unemployment

Under current law, men aged 16 to 60 and women aged 16 to 55 are included in the working population. Anyone who is within the above range and is involuntarily not employed is classified as unemployed. Every employed person has to contribute 1% of his or her salary to unemployment insurance and is in return eligible for unemployment subsidy. However, the unemployed must have contributed to the unemployment insurance for at least one year, while employed, to be eligible for the subsidy. In addition, he or she has to register as unemployed and must be actively seeking work. The amount of unemployment pay provided depends on the length of time one has contributed to unemployment insurance during employment. A monthly cash subsidy is provided for a maximum of 12 months to those who have contributed to the insurance for more than one year but less than five years. Those who have contributed to the fund for five years or more but for less than 10 years can receive the cash subsidy for as long as 18 months. Payment for a maximum period of 24 months is provided to someone who has contributed to the fund for more than ten years. The amount of monthly cash payment varies from province to province but it must meet the lowest living standard of the province in which the unemployed person lives. Apart from the monthly cash subsidy, unemployed people can also apply for medical support in case they need medical care during the period of unemployment. If, unfortunately, someone dies while unemployed, the government will provide a sum of money to his or her family as financial help. The government encourages people to attend training during the period of unemployment in order to improve their chance of being employed again in the near future.

Medical Insurance

In mainland China, both employers and employees are required to contribute to medical insurance for employees. In general, employers have to contribute 6% of the salary of their employees while employees themselves contribute 2%. The contributions of employers are divided into two parts, one part is paid to the employees' personal insurance accounts and the other half is used to set up a fund for the general public. Every local government sets a minimum and a maximum level to be paid out through the fund. When the charges are below the minimum level, the amount is paid through the personal insurance accounts of the service users. The charges are paid mainly by the fund if they are within the minimum and maximum levels, while the service users pay a small part of it. The maximum amount the fund will pay is normally equal to four times the average annual salary of employees in the county.

Insurance for Injury at Work

There are three levels of insurance for injury at work according to the perceived risk and employers are required to contribute different rates, from 0.5% to 2% of the total employees' salary. Length of leave due to injury at work is from one month to two years though some seriously injured employees can extend leave up to three years. Compensation for taking care of the injured is provided every month until the end of the leave. The amount of compensation is equal to the average monthly salary in the 12 months before the injury. An additional subsidy is often provided depending on the seriousness of the injury. Disability compensation is provided at different levels, from 75% to 90% of the salary, depending on the seriousness of the injury. Moreover, there is also a one-off compensation of 24 months' salary for the most serious injuries. All the treatment charges will be paid for by the insurance. If an employee dies in the course of work, family members receive compensation from local government every month. The spouse is eligible for 40% of the average salary of the population in the county and each of the other family members receive 30% of that average salary. Moreover, a one-off compensation of 48 to 60 months' average salary will also be provided to the family members.

Child-Bearing Insurance

Child-bearing insurance can be divided into three parts, maternity leave, child-bearing subsidy and medical services. Every female employee is entitled to 90 days of maternity leave, of which 15 days are before confinement and 75 days are after it. At the same time, a child-bearing subsidy is provided to pregnant employees for not less than 90 days. Since child-bearing insurance is not yet universal in the whole of China, for those regions in which the insurance is not available, employers are responsible for paying the child-bearing subsidy for a period of 90 days. The subsidy is a single payment of 400-1000 *yuan*. Pregnant employees may also use hospital services free of charge as long as the services are directly related to their pregnancies.

CRIME AND THE POLICE

In general, foreigners are rarely the targets of violent or other serious crimes. However, many of them experience pickpockets during their visit to China. Buses and trains are common spots for pickpockets. Thieves may work in quiet areas, which you should avoid visiting alone at night. Some provinces are more dangerous than others. They include Guangzhou, Guiyang, Xi'an and some parts of Sichuan. However, it certainly does not mean that you must avoid these areas altogether; just be aware of the surroundings and exercise your commonsense. Big cities like Beijing and Shanghai are safe unless you are alone in some out of the way areas at night. Never exchange Renminbi with locals on the street, even if the exchange rate sounds very attractive. Many foreigners, and even people from Hong Kong, have reported that the stack of money handed over to them is mainly paper with only a few real notes on the top and at the bottom. It may not sound like a very clever scam but surprisingly it works, with a few variations on the same theme.

Beggars are common at train stations and foreigners are particularly targeted as likely generous donors. They can follow you for a long distance even if you refuse to give them anything. Do not give money to any beggar. Once you do so, a group of them will come and follow you for miles until you give money to all of them. Child beggars are especially common and they are usually controlled by adults. The money you give them actually goes into the pockets of these adults, which means you are financing these child-controlling gangs.

Male travellers may come across another annoyance – prostitution. Prostitutes on the streets actively talk to single male travellers or even grab their arms. Some brothels are decorated as hairdressing salons, so be careful, if you only want to have a haircut. Usually the lighting indicates what kind of business they are actually after. Beware of 'nightclubs' as well, as in many regions of the country the word simply means brothels, rather than discos.

Police in mainland China are called *Gongan* and they are under the Public Security Bureau (PSB). Police wear a blue uniform with a hat which is either blue or white. Apart from keeping the country safe, the PSB is also responsible for affairs related to foreigners, for example, extensions of visas. If your belongings are stolen, you should report to the Foreign Affairs Branch of the PSB.

SOCIAL LIFE

Manners and Customs

For addressing someone older than you, or senior to you, you should call them by their surname with the title in front such as 'Mr. Wang', 'Professor Liu', 'Officer Lin' or 'Manager Song'. You should address your Chinese business partners in a formal way, especially the first time you meet them. The younger generation usually introduce themselves with the whole name and it is fine to call them by their first name. Many foreigners are confused by Chinese names. The Chinese put their family names first and given names second. The trouble is, they sometimes try to accommodate you by reversing them, thus making it really confusing. However, most Chinese surnames are monosyllabic and the given names are more often bi-syllabic, so you can do your guesswork accordingly. English names are not common in China, except in Hong Kong. Handshaking is very common, especially at the first meeting. However, hugging or kissing are not common, and if you are male, think twice before initiating such gestures to a woman, unless you know her really well.

The Chinese normally share a number of dishes within a meal. At a family dinner, there is no separate starter and main course. All dishes are presented together and you are free to take whatever you want, in whatever sequence. You can re-visit the same dish as many times as you like and quite often the Chinese use their chopsticks to pick up only a small piece from a dish at a time. Quite often, no serving spoon or chopsticks is provided with the dishes, and everyone just picks the food pieces from the dishes with their own chopsticks. It is perfectly acceptable to hold your bowl in your hand and brush the rice or other food pieces into your mouth directly from the bowl; in fact, leaving the bowl on the table all the time is considered juvenile and improper. Even though there is no starter, it is not unusual to have soup before dinner, and also after dinner. Not many Chinese people go out to drink at pubs but some like to have alcohol during meals. Wine is not very common yet though its popularity is increasing. Beer and Chinese rice wine are more common. For more formal or festival dinners, sometimes brandy is drunk during a meal as well. If you are invited to a friend's place for dinner, the classic gift to bring is fruit, which is often taken as dessert after the meal. You are not supposed to share the bill, if you are invited to eat out at a restaurant, though these things are changing amongst the younger generation.

During a meal, you should always fill others' cups or glasses before your own. Even if you are not having the same kind of drink, you should help others to top up their glasses.

Making Friends

Alex Thomson on making friends

Pretty much anyone with a pulse can make friends in Beijing. If you want to be with international people, there are parties and events almost every night of the week. If you have a hard time dealing with foreigners, there are droves of students and others who want to practice their English or just meet someone outside of their local paradigm.

Chinese people are in general kind and friendly and their shyness is quite often easily explained by the huge language difference. It is not too common for the Chinese to start a conversation with a foreigner, unless they are keen to practise their English, which means knowing how to speak their language definitely helps a great deal.

Unlike in North America, it is unusual for anyone to start a conversation with a stranger in China. Therefore, it is much easier to build up your social network through friends and colleagues that you already know. Universities are one of the easiest places to make local friends, as young people are eager to make the acquaintance of people from different cultures. Joining special interest classes is also a good way to make friends with Chinese people.

Given the size of the country, regional cultural differences are very noticeable. The traditional stereotypes have it that the southerners are talkative and witty, northerners sincere and honest, and westerners stubborn and dedicated. However, demographic factors dominate these days, and thus you are more likely to find young, well-educated middle class people who are eager to make foreign friends in coastal cities, and more sincere and authentic friendships in the rural regions.

The Status of Women

Women were portrayed as the dependents or even possessions of men for a long period in Chinese history. They were asked to stay at home to take care of the children and housework, as well as taking care of the parents of the husbands. A woman going out to work brought shame to the husband as it meant the husband lacked the ability to support his wife. In the old days, a man was allowed to have as many wives as he wanted so long as he was able to support them. Some rich people even bought the women they wanted giving them no choice in the matter.

Even though men and women are becoming more equal nowadays, women are still less favoured in many situations. Many parents prefer boys to girls even nowadays. They believe daughters belong to other families after they get married and they carry their husbands' surnames instead of that of the fathers. On the other hand, sons are supposed to take care of the parents and continue the family business. Many parents will stop a pregnancy if they find out that the baby is a girl, to save the quota for having a boy under the One-Child Policy. Working women account for about 40% of the total workforce but many of them have reported being discriminated against or treated unfairly. Women are also asked to retire at the age of 55, which is five years earlier than men. In rural areas where children do not benefit from free compulsory education, parents prefer the sons to go to school if they cannot afford the school fees for all the children.

Although there is still unfairness between men and women, the gap is actually narrowing. You will find fashionable, well-educated and financially independent women in big cities, where people receive higher education. Many of these women perceive their personal career as being as important as their family and they do not want to be dependents of their husbands. Foreign influence has also changed the view on how Chinese people regard women. The recent Miss World was said to be a great breakthrough for the country. Beauty pageants were banned in China in the past as they were regarded as heretical displays of exploitation and decadence. People in general also regard them as bad-taste events that focus only on outside beauty and ignore inner beauty, which counts for more in Chinese traditions. However, people's views have changed and many reported that they enjoyed watching the show. The hosting of Miss World, along with other western influences such as fashion and the use of make-up, reflects the fact that Chinese women are getting rid of their traditional image and are pursuing equal status with men.

Food and Drink

The Chinese are proud of their food and eating should be a major part of the delight of being in China, for you, and indeed for the locals as well. People roughly divide Chinese cuisine into four schools, according to the geographical locations of the dishes' origins. The Southern school mainly refers to the Guangdong style, where food is often cooked as a stir-fry or by steaming. There is a great variety of fresh materials available in southern China and the cooking methods often capitalise on this, and emphasise freshness instead of strong flavour. Dim-sum, which is very popular amongst locals and foreigners, are small dishes like steamed tapas, often containing meat, especially pork. The southerners often take Dim-sum with tea as brunch or even breakfast. In the southern coastal cities, Chinese seafood is world-famous. Rice is another important element, particularly so for the South, but equally in the whole country; people rarely have a meal without rice, which is often cooked without any seasoning in order to leave room for the flavour of the dishes.

In the northern part, which includes Beijing, Inner Mongolia, Anhui and Shangdong, you will find chunkier and oilier dishes. Mutton is used more commonly than other parts of the country since more farmers keep sheep as livestock. The north is also too cold for much other livestock and poultry. Peking duck, however, is famously tasty. Make sure you do not throw away the skin of the grilled duck, as that is usually the most valued part. Mongolian barbecue, mutton hot pot, and spring rolls are some other famous dishes you can easily find in the north of China. Northerners often eat dumplings or noodles instead of rice. The dumplings can be steamed, served in soups or deep fried.

The eastern part includes Jiangsu, Fujian, Zhejiang, Shanghai and Hangzhou. These places are all along the rivers and there is a great supply of fresh water fish and shrimps. Food is usually fried, stir-fried or stewed. One of the most famous dishes in Hangzhou is '*Longjing* shrimps', which is cooked with the famous *Longjing* green tea leaves. Shanghai dishes deserve a special metion. Located in the eastern part, Shanghai cuisine has its own distinct flavour, and can be spicy, sour and many things else. There are many Shanghainese noodle shops around the whole country.

The Western cuisine may be the most vegetarian friendly of all in China. People there eat a lot of chilli to keep themselves warm, and thus the vegetarian dishes always have plenty of flavour. There are many bamboos in Sichuan and it is a very common ingredient for cooking. Every part of the bamboo can be used: bamboo shoots and the inner parts are for eating; bamboo leaves can be eaten or used as a spice; and the shell can be used to boil soup or for holding the rice when cooking it (so that the rice absorbs the flavour of bamboo). Pork, poultry, legumes and soybeans are also common ingredients in western style dishes, along with chilli and bamboo.

Due to historical factors, there are a lot of Portuguese restaurants in Macau. Many of them serve traditional Portuguese food. If you would like to have a lighter meal as a brunch or afternoon tea, you should try the '*zhupabao*' (pork sandwich), which is very famous in Macau. The desert 'ginger and milk' is worth trying as well.

Tea is the most usual drink amongst the Chinese (some people believe that Chinese people drink more tea than plain water). The Chinese never add sugar or milk to their tea, and putting either of them into a nice cup of green tea is likely to raise eyebrows. Beer is also a relatively common drink during meals. There are many good locally brewed beers and the best-known one must be *Tsingtao*, which is a German-style lager.

Chopsticks are used in most restaurants, except western restaurants and fast food shops. Do not worry if you do not know how to use them. Many places provide forks and spoons to foreign customers, and the Chinese understand that it is a skill that takes a lifetime to truly master.

Shopping

Chinese history goes back several thousand years and its legacy can be seen in its handicrafts, art, antiques and other locally made artefacts. Many of these serve as handy souvenirs and they are often inexpensive. You can choose from a large and expensive Qing vase to a cheap but delicate sandalwood fan. Tea and tea utensils are very popular gifts. Good tea costs a few hundred *yuan* for 50g and there are many interesting varieties to choose from. The best-known one is *Longjing*, of which that produced in Hangzhou is the best. If you are keen to buy the best *Longjing*, tea experts recommend the *yuqian* (before rain) one, which is collected in early April. '*Silver needle tea*' of Hengyang is another famous option. In Yunnan, the tea may taste a bit different from other regions and smoked green tea called *tuocha* deserves at least a try. Good tea should go with good teapots, which are believed to enhance the flavour of the tea. In any case, Chinese teapots are often delicately crafted and really are works of art regardless of their functionality. The most famous teapots are from Yixing County in Jiangsu Province and you can also find other tea utensils there. In Jiangsu, especially in Suzhou, you can find nice embroidery, calligraphy, paintings and sandalwood fans. Silk is particular famous in Suzhou and in the past many rich people travelled all the way from other provinces to buy their cloth there. Ready-made products like scarves. pillowcases and bed linen are more common nowadays but you are still able to select a piece of fabric for tailor-made traditional clothes. Porcelain is particularly famous in Jingdezhen in Jiangxi. Many porcelain factories are open for tourists to visit. In Kuming and Dali of Yunnan, you can get some nice jade and marble. In Wuxi, you can buy pearls and pearl-related products like moisture cream. Many people like to collect antiques all over the world and in China, you can try the antique markets such as Fangbang Lu antique market, Dongtai Lu antique market, Shanghai Antique and Curio Shop (in Duolun Lu) in Shanghai. Apart from arts and handicrafts, antique posters are also worth collecting. There maybe some fake antiques in the markets, so watching out for 'bargains'. In Guilin, you should try the chilli sauce, which is reputedly spicy and good; in Mongolia, inlaid knifes are beautiful souvenirs; religious paintings and embroidery are easy to find and a great variety of bamboo products are famous in Sichuan. People often bring back snacks from visits to Macau as souvenirs.

Cinemas

Cinemas are usually available in cities but they are rare in rural areas. Most of the movies shown in China are in Mandarin. English movies are not usual. Even if you can find an English or American movie, the conversation is probably re-dubbed and translated into Mandarin. In Beijing and Shanghai, you can find some foreign movies but the choices are limited. The cinemas that regularly provide films with English subtitles are *Cheery Lane Movies* (in Beijing), *Golden Cinema Haixing* (in Shangahai) and *Studio City* (in Shanghai). And there is one French cinema in Beijing specialising in French movies. IMAX opened a cinema in Shanghai in 2004 that frequently shows foreign movies.

Useful Addresses
Da Guang Ming Cinema, 290 Xizang Zhong Lu, Shanghai 200001; www.shdgm.com.

Lycee Francais de Pekin, 13 Dongsi Jie, Beijing; ☎(86) 010 6532 3498.

Cheery Lane Movies, Sino-Japanese Youth Exchange Centre, 40 Liangmaqiao Lu, Beijing; ☎(86) 010 6461 5318; www.cherrylanemovies.com.cn; movies with English substitles.

Golden Cinema Haixing, Haixing Plaza 1, Ruijin Nanlu, Shanghai; ☎(86) 021 6418 7034.

Studio City, Westgate Mall, 10th Floor, 1038 Nanjing Xilu, Shanghai; ☎(86) 021 6218 2173.

Gambling

Although Macau is a small city, its gambling business is famous in Asia. Casinos are the landmarks of Macau. There are many large and small ones and the most famous is the *Lisboa Casino*. Its hotel is one of the most expensive in Macau and there are also dance shows available every night inside the casino. *The Macau Jockey Club* organises horse races on every Wednesday and Sunday, which usually attract a lot of Hong Kong people, especially in the summer, when horse racing in Hong Kong is suspended. In addition to horse races, there are also greyhound races in Macau. They are managed by *Canidrome* which is the biggest venue for greyhound racing in Asia.

There is no formal venue for gambling on mainland China. Only recently did the Beijing Jockey Club build a horse racetrack but it is still illegal to bet on horses. Many people enjoy playing Mahjong or card games with relatives and friends, especially during family gatherings such as Chinese New Year. Bets on soccer matches are legal and are welcomed by the Chinese. Even though there is no formal casino, unauthorised casinos on a small scale exist.

Useful Addresses

Lisboa Casino, 2-4 Avenida de Lisboa, Macau Peninsula, Macau; ☎(853) 377 666; fax (853) 567 193; hotel reservations: (853) 375 811; http://www.casinocity.com/mo/macau/maclisbo/.

The Macau Jockey Club, Est.Gov.Albano da Oliveira, Taipa, Macau; ☎(853) 821 188; fax (853) 820 503; www.macauhorse.com.

Canidrome, hotline: (853) 333 399; www.macaudog.com.

Gays and Lesbians

Homosexuality is still a sensitive topic to many Chinese and they regard it as a social disgrace. It was perceived as a mental illness and was only removed from the list of psychiatric disorders in 2001. However, gay marriage is still banned in China. Some homosexuals are brave enough to tell people they are gay but more of them prefer to hide. A hotline for homosexuals receives many calls for counselling and support every day and many callers have claimed they found it difficult to make friends. As the country opens up and it is easier to access to the internet, more people, especially those have received higher education, start to accept gays and lesbians. There are more bars and meeting places for homosexuals and even courses in university which are about homosexuality.

Art and Museums

There are over 1800 museums in China and many of them are worth a whole day's visit. Almost all provinces have a museum concerning the history of the area. Much ancient architecture is also well preserved and turned into museums, which are often very spectacular. They also give you a good picture of the life of the emperors or royal family in the old days. The Forbidden City, the Summer Palace and the Old Summer Palace really must be seen. Other interesting museums include the History Museum, Museum of the Chinese Revolution, the Military Museum of the Chinese People's Revolution and the China Opium War Museum. There are also a great number of art galleries, for example The China Art Gallery. For more specialised topics, there are the China Aviation Museum, the China Geological Museum, the China Coin Museum, the China Printing Museum, etc. The birth places of leaders of China such as Mao Zedong and Deng Xiaoping and other significant people such as Sun Yat-sen, are also very popular.

Most of the museums require an entry fee, which is usually less than 10 *yuan*. Some of them prohibit photography so you should always ask before taking pictures.

PUBLIC HOLIDAYS

1 January	*New Year's Day*
8 March	*International Women's Day (half day off for women)*
1-3 May	*Three days holiday for International Labour Day*
4 May	*Youth Day (half day off for those aged 14-20)*
1 June	*International Children's Day (half day off for those aged 13 or under)*
1 July	*Birthday of the Chinese Communist Party*
1 Aug	*Anniversary of the founding of the PLA (People's Liberation Army, for all armed forces personnel)*
1-3 Oct	*Three days holiday for the National Day*

*Some public holidays are based on the Chinese lunar calendar and therefore do not have a simple fixed date in the western calendar. For instance, Chinese New Year – Late January/February (three days holiday) is an example.

TIME

Even though China is such a big country which geographically covers several time zones, the time is universal and is based on that of Beijing. It is eight hours ahead of Greenwich Mean Time (GMT), which means it is the same as the time in Hong Kong and Macau. China used to have daylight saving time, but this was abolished it in 1992.

RETIREMENT

CHAPTER SUMMARY

- The retirement age for men and women is 60 and 55 respectively.
- Relatives of Chinese citizens, foreign investors and highly-skilled professionals should be able to obtain long-term residence in China.
- It is estimated that 20% of the population will be aged 65 or above by 2050.
- Investors have started to build 'Retirement Zones' in China.
- Pension schemes are currently not universal in the country.
- Pensions are exempted from taxation in China.
- Many local medical staff do not speak English.
- More joint-venture or private hospitals are being set up in big cities.
- Embassies can give you useful guidance if a family member dies in China.

BACKGROUND INFORMATION

Moving to a new country after retirement can be a great challenge. You have to adapt to a different life style, establish a new social network and you may also have to learn a new language. Low living costs are the greatest advantage for retiring in China. The money needed to buy a small flat in Europe or the USA will probably be enough for you to buy a big house in China. Transport, food and daily necessities are all very cheap. However, English is not in common use by locals, which can be a problem. Chinese is the official language, and you will need it for many things from reading menus in restaurants to understanding government notices. Chinese people are kind and polite, but with the language barrier you might find it difficult to make new friends. That said, local people would surely appreciate your efforts if you do try to talk to them in Chinese.

The weather in China can be too hot for Europeans: the average temperature in summer is over 30°C (86°F) and reaches 40°C (104°F) in some areas. The winter in the south and the southeast is relatively mild but it can be very cold in other areas, especially the north and the west. China is far from both the USA and Europe and that may be a problem if you find long-distance flights to visit relatives unbearable.

You are required to hold a visa to visit mainland China and you are only allowed to stay for 30 days unless you have special reasons. However, the good news is that in recent years China has been trying to make it easier for foreigners to visit or even stay permanently in the country. Investors and highly-skilled professionals will not find it too difficult to move to China even though they have no relatives who are Chinese citizens.

Ageing Problem

As mentioned in the chapter *General Introduction*, China is an ageing society. Currently, about 7.5% of the total population is aged 65 or above and it is estimated that this will rise to 20% in 2050. This is in a way a consequence of the One-Child Policy adopted in 1979. Since the population expanded too quickly in the 70s, the government decided to control the natural growth rate. This proved to be successful. However, since too few babies were born, the ratio of the elderly population to the young population has been rising ever since. The elderly in China are mainly supported by three financial sources: their own savings, families or pensions. Under the influence of Confucianism, parents put their greatest effort into nurturing their children and providing them with the best resources available. In turn, children regard supporting their parents as a moral responsibility. These days, due to the low ratio of young to old, it is common for young people to have to support two parents and two grandparents as well as themselves and their own family. This often goes beyond what they can afford. Pension schemes were therefore introduced in the mid-90s but are not yet universal throughout the whole country.

The Decision to Leave

If you have close relatives living in China, this is probably your strongest reason to move there. There are also an increasing number of investors moving to China to take care of their businesses in the country. Although it is easier to get a visa to visit China these days, you are normally limited to a visiting period of 30 days. This is perhaps too short to really look around and decide whether to live there for the rest of your life, and you should consider planning multiple visits to different places, during different seasons of the year.

Useful Address

American Club in Beijing, Lido Holiday Inn, Beijing; ☎(86) 010 6437 6743; http://www.newcomersclub.com/cn.html. This is for foreign newcomers. Apart from organising regular meetings, it also provides useful information for living in Beijing.

RESIDENCE AND ENTRY REGULATIONS

Unlike some other countries such as Canada and Australia, there is no particular immigration or retirement scheme in China. If you have a close relative who is a Chinese citizen, you can apply to move to China. In general, given that you are a good citizen in your home country and you can provide proof of your relationship with a Chinese citizen, it is not too difficult to get accepted as a permanent resident. You are required to contact the local Public Security Bureau for a Foreigner Residence Certificate after you arrive in China with a D visa. The Foreigner Residence Certificate is the actual permit for your long-term residence.

The Chinese government is currently revising its entry policies and considering granting permanent residence to foreign investors who have business or property in China, or to skilled professionals who work on the mainland. The policy is still under discussion but three to five years long-term residence has been granted to foreigners from early 2003. It is believed that this is a transition towards granting permanent residence to foreigners who have no relatives in China. Refer to the chapter *Residence and Entry Regulations* for more information about visas and documents required for applications.

Possible Retirement Areas

Most foreigners, and in fact also the locals, prefer to stay along the coast line. The cities in the south and east are in general more affluent and more developed. Since many of these cities are tourist spots without too many industrial establishments, they are comparatively less polluted than cities further inland. Famous cities like Shanghai and Beijing will probably be the most convenient places to stay. It is easy to get around and it is also easy to travel to and from other countries. As the number of foreigners is increasing in big cities, the availability of imported goods and books is also getting better. It is easy to make friends with other foreigners in these areas.

Some businessmen have started to develop 'retirement zones' in the more rural area of Beijing. They are designated for professionals and investors, and also foreigners who move to China. The first retirement zone was built about three years ago and is about a 40 minute drive from Beijing centre. These retirement zones are usually big avenues with good facilities, located in a scenic environment. There are other similar avenues in Guangdong that are targeted to middle to high-income groups from Hong Kong. You can find some well-developed ones in *Panyu* in Guangdong Province. You may prefer cities in Jiangsu or Zhejiang provinces, if you want to avoid the crowds and enjoy better natural sceneries. The weather in the south and the southeast is mild in the winter but it can be very hot in summer. Living in these areas is slightly cheaper than living in Beijing and Shanghai but more expensive than staying in inland cities, but at any rate they are far cheaper than retiring in the UK or the USA. Kunming in Yunnan Province is also a nice place to live. The weather is Kunming is warm, never too hot or too cold. The place is charming and full of ethnic atmosphere. You can also consider Anhui, Schuan and Chonquing. They are not as affluent as the coastal areas but they are well-developed and easy to get around. It is better to avoid poorer areas including Guangxi, Shanxi and Shannxi, where crime is a more serious problem.

PENSIONS

The pension scheme in China was introduced in 1995. It requires both employers and employees to contribute a certain percentage of the premier base. The premier base is set by local government according to the average salary of the whole working population in the previous year in the province. The total contributed percentage of employer and employee together ranges from 10% to 20%, and the ratio paid by the two is set by the local governments. For example, employers in Shanghai have to contribute 10% of the premier base while the employees contribute 8%. The contribution of an employee is deducted from his or her salary every month. Foreigners holding a work permit or permit of residence and who work in urban areas are also covered by the pension scheme.

The retirement age for men and women is currently 60 and 55 (50 for female blue-collar workers) respectively. Retirees are not allowed to claim a monthly pension payment before retirement age and they must have contributed to the scheme for 15 years or more to claim full benefits. At the moment, the contributions of employees are accumulated in their individual accounts, while that of the employers go into the government fund. The pension benefit for a retiree will be paid by the individual pension account until it runs out, in which case money will be taken from the state pension fund to pay the benefits to the retiree until he or she dies. If a retiree dies before the accumulated pension in his or her account runs out, the rest of the amount will be given to the legal successors, normally the spouse and the children.

The pension scheme has not yet become universal in the whole country. Citizens in rural areas are currently not covered. They are either supported by their families or themselves. Many citizens have to work even after they reach the age for retirement as the low family income cannot support their living costs. The government has set up a particular fund for helping the aged, disabled and young citizens in rural areas. However, the demand for financial help is huge and the fund is sometimes not enough to support everyone in need. According to the statistics in 1998, there were about five million senior citizens in poverty. Introducing the pension scheme in rural areas is more difficult than in urban areas. This is partly due to the low income of rural citizens so that taking away even a small amount of their monthly salaries may make their lives even more difficult. Moreover, it is not easy to collect the pension contribution from citizens in rural areas who are mainly farmers and do not have a stable income. It requires many government officials to calculate the right amount for each person every month, which is difficult and costly in itself. The government is figuring out a more flexible approach in installing the pension scheme in rural areas and aims at making it universal as soon as possible.

The UK and the USA have special pension arrangements with some other countries which allow you to claim your pension payments directly from the country you are staying in. However, China currently does not have such an arrangement with either country. You can receive pension payments from your home country while you are in China but you have to contact your home pension office to apply for this arrangement. Your pension payment will be paid into your Chinese bank account or you can ask the pension office to send you a payable order instead.

Useful Addresses

The International Pension Centre, Tyneview Park, Newcastle Upon Tyne, NE98 1BA, United Kingdom; ☎(44) 0191 218 7777; fax (44) 0 191 218 7293; www.thepensionservice.gov.uk.

Social Security Agency (North Ireland), ☎(44) 0845 601 8821; fax (44) 028 7136 8365; www.ssani.gov.uk.

Social Security Administration, Office of Public Inquiries, Windsor Park Building, 6401 Security Blvd., Baltimore, MD 21235; ☎(1) 800 772 1213; www.ssa.gov/international.

Taxation

Pensions are exempt from taxation in China. However, they may be subject to tax in your home country, in which case your pension may be taxed before it is transferred to your account in China. You are advised to consult the Inland Revenue Department and arrange the payment of your pension before you leave for China. You are subject to property tax and some others taxes, such as use of land and natural resources if you own a business or a property in China. There are also some minor taxes that you are subject to, such as the tax for using a bicycle. For other details about taxation, refer to the chapter *Daily Life*.

MEDICAL CARE

Medical charges in hospital are the same for both locals and foreigners. However, it is difficult to estimate the total cost as treatments and medicines are charged per item. You will be asked to pay a deposit before receiving any treatment. There are few private doctors as the medical services are managed by the government and doctors in the country normally work in hospitals or government clinics. In recent years, there are more joint ventures and private hospitals established in big cities. They are organised by foreign experts and are specially set up for foreigners in China, though locals are also welcome. You can find English-speaking doctors and nurses there, and the hospital is run pretty much in exactly the same way as in western countries. In Macau, the charges for locals and foreigners are slightly different. For more details about medical care, refer to the chapter *Daily Life*.

You are always advised to have personal health insurance. You can either take it out in your home country or after you arrive in China. There are many international insurance companies situated in China now, such as AIA and Prudential.

Wills and Death

You are advised to make a will if you own any property or business in China. If you have not made one, your properties will be allocated according to the Chinese inheritance laws when you die. Your spouse and children will be the primary people to inherit your assets. More details about wills are covered in the chapter *Setting Up Home*.

If a family member dies in China, you should seek help from the embassy of your home country. A death certificate will normally be issued by the hospital. You will need to present identity documents, such as the passports of the deceased, and yourself to obtain a death certificate. If you would like to have a death certificate for your deceased family member from your home country, you can apply to the embassy. You need to present the death certificate issued by the hospital and/or a police report from the local Public Security Bureau (PSB). It will probably be easier to seek advice from the embassy on the costs and procedures for local burial, cremation or the transport of the remains home, especially if you are not familiar with local procedures.

If your family member dies in Macau, you should apply for a death certificate from the Macau Marriage and Death Registry Office. You will be asked to present proof of identity for yourself and the deceased. The Registry Office will also be able to advise you on matters concerning burial, cremation and sending the remains home.

Useful Addresses

Macau Marriage and Death Registry Office, Conservatoria do Registo de Casamentos e Obitos de Macau.

British Embassy (Beijing), 11 Guanghua Lu Jianguomenwai Beijing 100600; ☎ (86) 010 6532 1961; fax (86) 010 6532 1937; e-mail commercialmail@peking.mail.fco.gov.uk; www.britishembassy.org.cn.

British Consulate-General (Shanghai), Suite 301, Shanghai Centre 1376 Nanjing Xi Lu Shanghai 200040; ☎ (86) 021 6279 7650; fax (86) 021 6279 7651; e-mail consulategeneral.shanghai@fco.gov.uk; www.britishembassy.org.cn.

The US Consulate General in Shanghai, 1469 Huai Hai Zhong Lu, Shanghai, P.R.C. 200031; ☎ (86) 021 6433 6880; fax (86) 021 6433 4122; www.usembassy-china.org.cn.

Companies Providing Shipment of Remains

Medex Assistance Beijing, ☎(86) 010 6595 8510; fax (86) 010 6595 8509.

SOS International, ☎(86) 010 6462 9112/(86) 010 6462 9100; fax (86) 010 6464 9111.

World Access, ☎(86) 010 6441 4916; fax (86) 010 6441 4911.

Babaoshan Mortuary Home (embalming/cremation), ☎86 (0)10 6824 3385/ 8825 9786 (Chinese only).

INTERESTS AND HOBBIES

The Chinese government encourages retirees to continue to participate in society. Retirees are encouraged to join special interest classes, such as basic computer skills and Chinese calligraphy. You may consider learning the Chinese language first and it will widen your choices for other special interest classes as many of them are conducted in Chinese. Tai Chi, the famous Chinese martial art, is believed to be very healthy and you can frequently see pensioners practising it in parks early in the mornings There are many museums and exhibitions on Chinese history and culture all over the country. It is easy to spend a whole day in one of these museums. Many of them provide concessionary tickets for people aged 65 or over. Even when there is no concession, the entry fees are very low. There are many mountains in China and people who enjoy hiking should not miss them. Some famous ones include Huang Shan, Wutai Shan, Tai Shan, Song Shan, Emei Shan, Putuoshan and Heng Shan. Many retirees enjoy being volunteers and spending their time helping others in need. There are many global charitable organisations working in China. Some of them aim to fight poverty while some focus on the education of children. There are many charities in Hong Kong that always welcome volunteers and there are also some in mainland China. The China Charity Foundation (CCF), established in 1994, is currently the biggest charity based in mainland China.

Useful Websites

www.thatsmagazines.com, provides directories for events and special interest classes in Beijing, Shanghai and Guangzhou.

www.shanghai-star.com.cn, includes news and information on events in Shanghai.

Charitable Organisation Addresses

China Charity Foundation, 7th Floor, Xinlong Building, 33A Erlong Road,Xicheng District, Beijing,100032; e-mail info@china-charity.org; www.chinacharity.cn.net/ccf.

Friends of the Earth, 2/F, SPA Centre, 53-55 Lockhart Road, Wanchai, Hong Kong; ☎(852) 2528 5588; www.foe.org.hk.

Green Power, Unit A, 7/F, Astoria Building, No.34 Ashley Road, Tsim

Sha Tsui, Kowloon; ☎(852) 23142662; fax (852) 23142661; e-mail info@greenpower.org.hk; www.greenpower.org.hk.

HOPE Worldwide Hong Kong, Room 1910, Fortress Tower, 250 King's Road, North Point, Hong Kong; ☎(852) 2588 1291; fax (852) 2588 1306; e-mail enquiry@hopeww.org.hk; hk.hopeworldwide.org.

Medecins Sans Frontieres, Shop 5B, Laichikok Bay Garden, 272 Lai King Hill Road, Kowloon, Hong Kong; ☎(852) 2338 8277; fax (852) 2304 6081; e-mail office@msf.org.hk; www.msf.org.hk.

Oxfam, 17/F, China United Centre, 28 Marble Road, North Point, Hong Kong; ☎(852) 2520-2525; fax (852) 2527-6307; e-mail info@oxfam.org.hk; www.oxfam.org.hk.

Rotary International (District 3450), 14/F., Capital Commercial Building, 26 Leighton Road, Causeway Bay, Hong Kong; ☎(852) 2576 8882; fax (852) 2895 5926; e-mail ric@rotary3450.org; www.rotary3450.org.

The Community Chest of Hong Kong, Unit 1805 Harcourt House, 39 Gloucester Road, Wanchai, Hong Kong; ☎(852) 2599 6111; fax (852) 2506 1201; e-mail chest@commchest.org; www.commchest.org.

WWF Hong Kong; ☎(852) 2526 1011; fax (852) 2845 2734; e-mail wwf@wwf.org.hk; www.wwf.org.hk.

MAINLAND CHINA

Section II

WORKING IN MAINLAND CHINA

EMPLOYMENT

STARTING A BUSINESS

EMPLOYMENT

CHAPTER SUMMARY

- **Unemployment.** The unemployment rate in China was 4.3% at the end of 2003.
- **Contracts.** An employment contract is compulsory in China.
- **Working Hours and Holidays.** Working hours should not exceed 40 hours a week.
  - Hospitals, post offices and banks usually open seven days a week.
  - Every employee is entitled to at least five days of paid annual leave a year.
  - There are 10 official holidays in China.
- **Insurance.** Employees are entitled to five types of insurance including unemployment insurance, provident fund (pension), work injury insurance, medical insurance and child-bearing insurance.
- **Women at Work.** Women account for 37% of the total labour force.
  - Female workers are entitled to nursing leave in addition to 90-days maternity leave.
  - Sexual discrimination exists and employers in general prefer male workers.
  - In Macau, paid maternity leave for every female worker is limited to a maximum of three deliveries.
- **Retirement.** The retirement age for men and women is 60 and 55 respectively.
- **Teaching English.** You must hold at least a university degree to teach English in China.
  - The Chinese government recruits English teachers from its embassies.
  - The British Council arranges for university students to be teaching assistants in China for a year.

OVERVIEW OF THE EMPLOYMENT MARKET

At the time of writing, the labour market in China is looking promising once again following a downturn in the Chinese economy. China's economy and labour market were seriously affected by SARS (Severe Acute Respiratory Syndrome) for the period between March and July 2003. There was a significant decrease in job vacancies in areas affected by SARS, which included Tianjin and Beijing where a decrease of 26.7% and 17.9% were recorded respectively. However, by the third quarter of 2003, the general economic and employment atmosphere was recovering with a 50.1% increase in job vacancies. More importantly, this figure was in fact 12% higher than the same period in 2002. During the first 6 months of 2003, retailing, catering and manufacturing and social services were the most affected industries. The unemployment rates in these fields were relatively high. However, they were also the three main industries which recovered the quickest in the post-SARS period.

In 2003, the real GDP growth rate in China was 9.1%, which was the fastest in the past six years. It is expected that the GDP in areas around the Yangtze River, including Shanghai, Ningbo and Hangzhou, will continue to grow quickly at a rate of over 7%. However, the fast growing economy also leads to over-production in both the construction and the manufacturing industries. The September 2003 issue of *Beijing Review* and *The Times* pointed out that local bureaucrats regard a high growth rate in the economy as the only key factor to promote businesses. Instead of recognising the actual demand, they keep on pumping funds into the manufacturing and construction sectors. This has resulted in overproduction in over 90% of manufacturing including steel, automobiles, integrated circuits, textiles and electrolytic aluminium. And real estate 'bubbles' can be found in every city as the supply of luxury apartments and tenanted office blocks is way over the actual demand.

It was interesting to discover that towards the end of 2003, there was a high demand for certain types of skills in the labour market. This could probably be related to the fact that after China entered the World Trade Organisation (WTO) in 2001, employers in general wanted to improve the competitiveness of their products. Moreover, high-technology industries are developing rapidly in China and there is a great demand for high-skilled staff. In December 2002, the Chinese leadership outlined the expansionary plans for the next two decades, and attracting long-term foreign investors will be important to secure the long-term economic growth of the country. Although tertiary industries have been developing rapidly in the last two decades, the Chinese economy is currently supported mainly by secondary industries and agriculture.

Unfortunately, a large percentage of the Chinese workforce still lacks the knowledge and skills to develop the tertiary industries such as banking and finance, telecommunications, information technology, etc. Thus, the Chinese government is encouraging more foreign experts and high-skilled workers to come to China. As a result, many big multinational manufacturing companies, biochemical businesses, and high quality technology companies come to the coastal areas to start their businesses. There is no doubt that skilled professionals in these high intellectual and technological industries are in great demand in the current Chinese market. The demand for skilled labour in Shanghai is particularly great and salaries of professionals have been pushed up five-fold since 1994.

The first Shanghai International Forum on Vocational Training, held in December 2003, revealed that the city requires at least 500,000 highly skilled technicians and professionals – the so-called 'Grey Collar' workers – within the next five years. According to the Shanghai Labour and Social Security Bureau, there were 150,000 vacant technical positions available at the end of 2003. The market is badly in need of people who are trained as computerized machine operators, jewellery designers, IT programmers, multi-media programmers and other high-level professionals. As a result, the salaries offered can be very attractive, especially if you take into account the low living costs in China. If you are skilled as mentioned above, you could earn an annual salary of as much as 300,000 *yuan* (US$36,000/£21,400), which is five times the pay of more ordinary positions.

Macau is one of the two duty-free ports in China, which means goods, capital, foreign exchange and people flow freely in and out of the city. It is integrated with the world economy and, due to its historical background, it also has special economic ties with the European Union. The government has planned and launched a series of projects after the hand-over to China in 1999. The first Macau airport, which cost US$11.8 billion, was completed in 1995. Western businessmen and travellers can now avoid the trouble of travelling to Macau through Hong Kong, which has increased Macau's competitiveness as a business centre. Apart from the airport, projects such as the Lotus Bridge project, the construction of a deep-water port on the north-eastern side of Coloane Island, the land reclamation projects along the Praia Grande (Macau's historic waterfront) and the Docas (docks) areas, have also has helped to turn Macau into a business centre and speed up its economic growth. Currently, tourism and gambling are two of the most important industries in Macau.

EMPLOYMENT PROSPECTS FOR FOREIGNERS

One reason why China continues to open its markets is that it provides a chance for industries to absorb the experience and acquire the skills of foreign experts to further speed up economic growth. In general, almost all foreign experts working in China can be categorized as either economic and technological experts, or cultural and educational experts. The economic and technological experts are those working in commerce, finance, industry and foreign enterprises. The cultural and educational experts are those working in higher education, the press and publishing, scientific research and art institutions. According to the State

Statistics Bureau, the number of foreign experts working in China was 440,000 in 2001, of which 250,000 came from foreign countries and the rest from Hong Kong SAR, Macau SAR and Taiwan. Table 1 shows some of the major fields in China which recently employed foreign experts.

THE NUMBER OF FOREIGN EXPERTS IN CHINA	
Types of Jobs	**Number of Foreign Experts (approx.)**
Manufacturing	250,000
Social Services	180,000
Commerce	26,000
Culture/Education/Arts/Media	26,500
Scientific Research and General Technical Services	23,000
Real Estate	14,000
Communication and Telecommunications	11,000
Construction	6,000
Agriculture	4,500
Public Utilities	3,000
Public Health/Sports/Social Welfare	2,000
Mining	1,500
Finance/Insurance	1,250
Prospecting	1,000
Other Organisations	75,000

In February 2004, the Chinese Nation Labour Officials announced the urgency of importing more foreign high-tech and management professionals so as to sharpen the competitiveness of the country in global markets. Apart from senior experts, about 60,000 foreigners from some 90 countries are currently working as secretaries, teachers and chefs in China. Most of these foreign employees come from Japan, the United States, South Korea and Singapore, and some are from Hong Kong, Macau and Taiwan. There are about 50,000 and 30,000 foreign workers in Beijing and Shanghai respectively.

Although the figures might look impressive, the job market for expatriates is actually shrinking. At the moment, a number of foreign experts in China employed as managers, diplomats, and embassy staff are either on megabucks salaries or in very easy jobs. Apart from these, there are drifters, students, English teachers, and foreign experts scraping to make a decent living who are hustling to achieve better career prospects. Realising this, many multi-national companies now prefer to hire Chinese students returning from overseas studies, of which the number is increasing.

Skills and Qualifications

It is difficult to generalise on the skills and qualifications needed to work in China; it varies from industry to industry. As mentioned above, if you possess a certain special skill or are an expert in a particular industry, in general it will not be difficult to find a job in China. A university degree may not be the most important qualification for selection, except for certain academic or teaching posts, but you may get a higher salary if you do have one.

English speakers have a definite advantage when it comes to working in China, as the supply of fluent English speakers in the current labour market is limited but the amount of foreign trade is increasing. Knowing Mandarin is also an advantage as you probably need to work with local clients or suppliers, and also the local government.

Even though the use of computers in China is not yet as popular as in the USA or Europe, the trend is changing quickly and many companies in big cities require their employees to possess basic computer skills.

RESIDENCE AND WORK REGULATIONS IN CHINA

According to the Ministry of Public Security, more than 1.9 million foreigners come to China for business and for conferences; 119,900 people come for employment; and 10,900 people recently came for permanent residence. In order to work in China, you must hold an appropriate type of temporary or permanent residence visa. Visas are issued to foreigners according to the purposes of their visit.

Permanent Residence Visa

In the past, it was not easy to obtain permanent residence in China unless you were a close relative of a Chinese citizen. In 2001, the Chinese Ministry of Public Security launched a reform of the residence policy and mapped out the plan of a 'Green Card'-like system. Under this system, foreigners who do not intend to take up Chinese nationality, but who do plan to stay in China permanently are granted long-term residence (three years or more) and multiple entry visas to China. Under the revised immigration policy in 2003, you are qualified to apply for permanent residence if you:

○ Are invited as a senior advisor by provincial or ministerial level government institutions, or high-tech professionals and senior managerial personnel who come to the country for scientific and technological cooperation projects, key project agreements or for professional personnel exchange programmes in China.
○ Have an outstanding contribution to make to the city, or work for free-aid

protocols for the city or for the central government.

○ Are a scholar who is hired by universities or colleges at the provincial and ministerial level as an associate professor or above.

○ Are hired as senior management staff or technicians, such as president, vice president, vice general manger etc, in a joint venture or foreign-invested company.

○ Have invested a minimum of US$3 million in a Chinese city.

○ Are granted important international awards, are distinguished foreign-born Chinese, and those who studied abroad but work in China for a senior rank management position. This is limited to Chinese people with foreign nationality.

○ Are a dependent of a foreign expert, under the above conditions and who works in China in a senior position.

The policy will be fully implemented in 2004.

Other Visas

F Visa (Business Visa). This visa is for foreigners to come to China for business related purposes or scientific-technological and cultural exchanges. This also applies to short-term advanced studies or intern practice for a period of six months or less. This visa also allows foreigners who are invited to China for a visit, to do research, give a lecture or who need the visa for business purposes.

X Visa (Student Visa). Similar to an F visa, this visa is issued to an applicant who comes to China for the purpose of receiving education, or to pursue advanced studies or an internship for a period for six months or more.

Z Visa (Employment Visa). This is for people who are offered a position by a company in China and for the dependents accompanying the employed. A Z visa is not a formal work permit and you have to contact the local government office to issue the formal permission for staying within 30 days of your arrival in China. After the issue of the formal document, you are granted 2 to 5 years' residence with multiple entry rights, and you must be employed for the duration of your stay. It is possible to change your visa status inside China. If you are holding a visitor's visa but are offered a job in China, your employer should go to the local government offices to apply for a change of visa status for you.

For more details about entry regulations and visa applications for mainland China, refer to the chapter *Residence & Entry Regulations*.

Working in Macau

You will need a work permit for working in Macau. Your employer should arrange it for you before you arrive in the city. If you need to renew your permit, you should go to the Macau Immigration Office in person.

Useful Address

Macau Immigration Office, Ground Floor, Travessa da Amizade (opposite to the Palace Floating Casino near the Macau Ferry terminal), Macau; ☎(853) 725448.

SOURCES OF JOBS

There are only a limited number of English newspapers in China and this may be a problem when you are looking for jobs. Moreover, companies have to get permission before they can place advertisements in the media. Therefore, many companies prefer to use other recruitment methods instead. Overseas publications such as the *Economist*, the *Financial Times* and the *Guardian* may include some vacancies in Chinese companies but the number of jobs you can find there is very limited. If you are looking for a job from abroad, the best and the most convenient resource now is the internet. There are many online newspapers and websites for companies to post recruitment advertisements. There are also a variety of online recruitment agencies, all of which advertise and update the list of vacancies frequently. Most of these websites provide registrations and CV lodgement services. The services are normally free of charge but some of the agencies may require you to pay a membership fee. You can also make an inquiry to these recruitment agencies stating your interests and expectations and they will then search and match the job which is the most suitable for you.

From time to time, there are also job fairs and expos held in China. Many of the cities, especially the bigger ones, hold annual job fairs around the time of university graduations. You can also try writing directly to the company you are interested in joining. Of course there would be no guarantee that there are vacancies, but some students have reported that they have gained intern opportunities through this method.

If you are looking for a teaching job in China, you can put your enquiries to the Chinese embassies abroad. Every year, the Ministry of Foreign Affairs of the People's Republic of China recruits Foreign Teachers (FTs) and Foreign Experts (FEs) through the embassies to teach English in different regions in the country. However, these jobs are not publicised in the media, probably because the supply of teachers is high and it is believed that genuinely interested people will discover the opportunities themselves anyway. More details about FTs and FEs can be found in the section *Teaching* under *Long Term Employment*.

USEFUL RECRUITMENT WEBSITES

○ *China Net for International Talent,* http://www.chinajob.com/En/. This features the latest expert and professional vacancies in teaching, engineering and many highly demanding Hi-Technology jobs, and the latest news of professional jobs in China as well as opportunities for foreign exchanges.

○ *International Manpower Service – China,* http://www.chinesemanpower.com/. This is the largest manpower service in the world. It focuses on recruiting and employing qualified associates in all fields and at all levels for employers. This agency covers most of the top core industries in China, including automobiles, technology and chemistry etc.

○ *JobChina.net,* http://www.jobchina.net/index.php. This is a bulletin board both for employers to post their advertisements and for job seekers to lodge their CV. This website specializes in IT Professional jobs and MBA jobs in China. Currently, the former has over 55,000 candidates and the latter has over 3,000 candidates searching for jobs.

○ *Teach in China,* http://www.teach-in-asia.net/china/. This website will redirect you to another eleven websites for ESL (English as a Second Language) or EFL (English as a Foreign Language) teaching jobs in various parts in China.

○ *Abroad China,* http://www.abroadchina.org/. This is the largest database of language jobs in China. A directory with positions and information on salaries, incentives and workload.

○ *Sinoculture,* http://www.sinoculture.com. This website features English teaching opportunities in schools and universities throughout China.

○ *China Exchange: Teach in China,* http://www.chinaexchange.org/. This is an exchange programme offering opportunities for recent college graduates and seasoned teachers. The programme will subsidize the travelling expenses of successful candidates within China during the employment period.

○ *Wang and Li Asia Resources,* http://www.wang-li.com. This private agency focuses on business and professional management jobs in China, and provides consultation and guidance for individuals to develop and to identify their talents in order to meet the capabilities and qualities that leading multinational companies in China value most.

○ *Talent Consulting Corporation,* http://www.excellent-job.com/indexe.com. A private agency ratified by the Beijing Personnel

Bureau, engaged in talent exchange and consultation. You can fill in an application form to apply for a job through this website.

○ *Portfolio International Recruitment (International site),* http://www. portfoliointernational.com/sect1/subsect2/. An agency specializing in recruitment for hotel, catering, and leisure industries.

○ *Zhaopin.com,* http://english.zhaopin.com/ejobseeker/index.jsp. In the 'citychannel' area, you will be redirected to jobs in some popular regions in China including, Beijing, Xi'an, Dalian, Wuhan and Nanjing. *Zhaopin* is the mainland's leading recruitment job listing and classified website. It offers thousands of jobs from entry level to senior management positions throughout China in multinational, joint-venture and local Chinese companies in all industries and job functions.

Recruitment Agents

Bole Associates, 11th Floor Unit 1101, The Exchange Beijing, No. 2 Dong Huan Nan Lu Chao Yang District, Beijing 100022; ☎(86) 010 6567 6678; fax (86) 010 6567 6538; e-mail bej@bo-le.com; www.bo-le.com. Has five core practices including internet, financial services, consumer products, pharmaceutical and industrial appointments.

Futurestep Corporate USA Headquarter, 1800 Century Park East, Suite 900, Los Angeles, CA 90067, USA; e-mail info@futurestep.com.hk; http://www.futurestep.com.hk.

Futurestep (UK Office), 123 Buckingham Palace Road, London, SW1W 9DZ, UK; ☎(44) 0207 312 3200; info@futurestep.co.uk; http://www.futurestep.com.hk.

Futurestep (Beijing Ofiice), (86) 010 6590 0961; e-mail grace.cheng@kornferry.com.

Futurestep (Shanghai Office), (86) 021 6279 8681; e-mail helen.tantau@kornferry.com.

L&K Consultancy (Shanghai Office): (86) 021 6466 4666; e-mail lkconsuc@online.sh.cn. This is a Singapore consulting firm specializing in Executive search in China. They advertise senior management positions such as General Manager, Deputy General Manager, Financial Controller, Marketing Manager, National Sales Manager etc.

Hudson (Shanghai Office), 11/F, Room 1104, Central Plaza, No.227 Huangpi Bei Lu, Shanghai 200003; ☎(86) 021 6375 8922; fax (86) 021 6375 8211; e-mail shresumé @hudson.com; www.hudson.com/us/.

Hudson (GuangzhouOffice), Room 735, The Garden Hotel, 368 Huanshi Dong Lu, Guangzhou, 510064; ☎(852) 2528 1191; e-mail gzresumé @hudson.com; www.hudson.com/us/.

Hudson (London Office), Chancery House, 53-64 Chancery Lane, London,

WC2A 1QS; ☎(44) 0207 187 6000; fax (44) 0207 187 6001; www.hudson.com/us/.

Stanton Chase International (Baltimore/Washington Office), 100 East Pratt Street, Suite 2530, Baltimore, Maryland 21202 U.S.A; ☎(1) 410 528 8400; fax (1) 410 528 8409; e-mail info@stantonchase.com; www.stantonchase.com.

Stanton Chase International (London Office), 56 Haymarket, London, SW 1Y 4RN, U.K.; ☎(44) 0207 930 6314; fax (44) 0207 930 9539; e-mail london@stantonchase.com; www.stantonchase.com.

Lynton John & Associates (Beijing Office), ☎(86) 010 66526 09614; e-mail lja@ljaconsult.com; http://www.ljaconsult.com.

PriceWaterHouseCoopers (Beijing) Limited, 18/F North Tower, Beijing Kerry Centre, 1 Guang Hua Road, Chaoyang District, Beijing 100020; ☎(86) 010 6561 2233; fax (86) 010 8529 9000; http://www.pwcglobal.com.

PriceWaterHouseCoopers (Shanghai) Limited, 12/F Shui On Plaza, 333 Huai Hai Zhong Road, Shanghai 200021; ☎(86) 021 63(86) 3388/(86) 021 6386 6688; fax (86) 021 6386 3300/(86) 021 6386 2288; http://www.pwcglobal.com.

Euro-group (Beijing), ☎(86) 010 6510 1789; e-mail szhang@euro-group.com.

Recruitment Agencies (Macau)

Agencia Emprego Hong Fu, Ant Basto 2, Macau; ☎(853) 216 679.

Agencia Emprego Son Hou, Ctro Cml Master, Macau; ☎(853) 353 628.

Chong Ou Technical Services Ltd, Ed Nam Kwong; ☎(853) 715 335.

Firma Au Traders, Est Adolfo Lour 18D, Macau; tel: (853) 591 314.

Guang Dong Hoc Shing Labour Managing Group, Chun Pek Gdn bl 1, Macau; ☎ (853) 439 316.

Sociedade Apoio Empresas Macau Lds, ☎(853) 336 936.

Fu Cheong, http://starschool.uhome.net/fucheong.

Successful Consultants (Macau) Ltd., http://www.sclimited.com.

Weng Lei International Company, http://www.wenglei.com.mo.

Online Newspapers

Classified Post, www.classifiedpost.com. This is a supplement of a major Hong Kong based newspaper advertising a lot of jobs in Hong Kong. And there are increasing numbers of good-quality jobs in China advertised there too. The hardcopy of the supplement comes with every Saturday edition of the *South China Morning Post*.

Recruit, http://www.recruit.com.hk/eng/jobseeker/index.jsp?lang=eng. This is a career portal for a wide range of fields from general positions to highly qualified positions for working professionals. Hardcopies can be found on every Tuesday and Thursday in all MTR stations).

JobsDB.com and CJOL.com, http://www.jobsdb.com.cn/main/jobseeker/en/. *China Daily*, http://www.chinadaily.com.cn.

China News Digest, http://my.cnd.org/modules/newbb/viewforum.php?forum=7. A weekly internet news journal with a job advertisement section.

China Economic Review, http://www.chinaeconomicreview.com/. A leading English language business journal about China.

Kidon Media-Link, http://www.kidon.com/media-link/prc.shtml. An independent site providing a complete directory of newspapers and news resources on the internet. This covers the major news and newspaper directories for many parts of China.

That's Magazine, http://www.thatsmagazines.com. This is an online English magazine providing the latest news and vacancies in Beijing, Shanghai and Guangzhou.

USA Today, http://www.usatoday.com.

The Wall Street Journal, http://www.wsj.com.

New York Times, http://www.nytimes.com.

The Global and Mail, http://www.globeandmail.ca. Canada's national newspaper.

The National Post, Canada, http://www.canada.com/national/nationalpost.

The Times, http://www.the-times.co.uk.

The Guardian, http://www.guardian.co.uk.

The Financial Times, http://www.ft.com.

The Independent, http://www.independent.co.uk.

Journal Ou Mum (Macau Daily News), http://www.macaodaily.com.

Jornal Tribuna Macau, http://www.jtm.com.mo.

Semanario Desprtv Macau, http://www.macausports.com.mo.

Other Useful Addresses

British Chamber of Commerce in China, 2/F, 31 Technical Club, 15 Guanghuali, Chaoyang District, Beijing 100020; ☎(86) 010 6593 2150; http://www.britaininchina.com.

British Council China Initiative, Dilbahar Tawakkul, Central Bureau, British Council, 10 Spring Gardens, London SW1A 2BN, UK; ☎(44) 020 7930 8466; http://www.britishcouncil.org.cbiet.

British Council – UK, 10 Spring Gardens, London SW1 2BN, UK; ☎(44) 020 7930 8466; http://www.britishcouncil.org.

China-Britain Business Council, Abford House, 15 Wilton Road, London SW1V 1LT, UK; ☎(44) 020 7828 5176; http://www.cbbc.org.

Global Chinese Resource, http://www.jia-bin.com/. This provides Chinese resources for business, company, travel, job, college, magazine, book and other links.

Vacation Work, www.vacationwork.co.uk. Publishers of a series of publications about working abroad, including hints for looking for jobs and directories for companies in different sectors. Titles including *Summer Jobs Abroad, Work Your Way Around the World* and *The International Directory of Voluntary Work* provide information for short-term employment and voluntary work.

Associaco Commercial de Macau (Macau Business Assocation), Macau's Chammer of Commerce, 175 Rua de Xangai, Macau; tel (853) 576 833; fax (853) 594 513.

Instituto de Promocao do Commercio e do Investimento de Macau (Macau Trade and Investement Promotion Institute), 4th and 5th Floors, World Trade Centre, 918 Avenida da Amizade, Macau; ☎(853) 710 528; fax (853) 590 309.

World Trade Centre Macau, 17th Floor, World Trade Centre, 918 Avenida da Amizda, Macau; ☎(853) 727 666; fax (853) 727 633. This centre offers trade information services and arranges conferences and exhibitions.

Recruitment Procedures for FIEs

A foreign-invested enterprise is a joint venture formed by a foreign and a Chinese partner. Compared to ordinary foreign enterprises, i.e. a business owned solely by foreign investors, foreign-invested enterprises (FIEs) enjoy less flexibility when recruiting employees. Even though foreign enterprises are required to seek permission before posting advertisements in the media in China, the government does not interfere on how they select employees. However, the government has specific rules on recruitment for FIEs. FIEs are required to give priority to candidates from the same province in which the company is located. Also, the Chinese partners in joint ventures are given more authority than the foreign partner when selecting employees. The local labour bureau prefers to have the Chinese partners taking the responsibility for recruiting employees. Only if no suitable candidate fulfils the requirements of a job in the local province can the company recruit people from outside the province, which would include foreigners.

Recruitment of Chinese nationals by FIEs or foreign representative offices are usually done through designated agencies such as the Foreign Enterprises Service Corporation (FESCO) and China International Intellectech Corporation (CIIC). Employers will file the job positions and the requirements to these 'employment centres'. These centres are under the control of labour and social security departments as well as the personnel departments of the government and they keep files of candidates that are looking for jobs. When there is a job vacancy, an employment centre will choose the most suitable candidates for interview. In the past, vacancies were 'appointed' by these government-monitored employment centres and enterprises rarely rejected the candidate appointed. However, the selection process is changing and employers nowadays usually give their opinions on the candidates to the employment centre before someone is finally selected.

Notes on Job Applications

○ You should attach your resumé to your application form or letter when applying for a job. Your resumé should be concise and should pinpoint your relevant strengths such as language ability and computer skills. You should also include details of your education, work experience and contact addresses of referees. You should make your resumé easy to read with suitable headings and neat formatting.

○ You may be asked to fill-in your gender, age, nationality or even weight and height sometimes (the last two are getting rare nowadays, but do not be overly surprised). Some companies may require a passport-size photo as well. In general foreigners need not worry that they will be discriminated against due to their religion, race, disability or gender. The Equal Opportunity Employment laws, which have been effective since January 1995 prohibit all the above discriminations and you can complain to the local labour bureau if you think you are being discriminated against.

○ You should do some research on Chinese culture and business etiquette (see the chapter *Starting A Business*) before an interview. Even when working in multinational organisations, knowing traditional Chinese values and influences will be helpful as they remain the dominant beliefs of society as a whole. And it helps to show that you are genuinely interested in the job and have a commitment to China.

ASPECTS OF EMPLOYMENT

Salaries

China's economic and industrial growth in recent years has driven an increase in the country's salaries. In particular, salaries of middle to high ranking staff working in foreign enterprises have been rising far more rapidly than the Consumer Price Index. The National Bureau of Statistics suggests that in 2003, the per capita income has risen to US$1,090. Nonetheless, salaries paid to talented people in China are generally higher than in other industries as well as their counterparts in ASEAN (Association of South-East Asian Nations), countries such as Singapore and Malaysia. Companies in big cities such as Beijing, Shanghai, Guangzhou and Shenzhen are usually willing to pay even more. A typical worker in the eastern part of China can make a minimum of 1,000 to 1,500 *yuan* per month, while a worker in the western part of China can make very little, at 350 to 400 *yuan* (US$46/£29) or less per month.

According to a recent salary index survey, about 79% of people got a pay rise equivalent to 2.16 times of their original salary through job hopping. The current average annual salary in China in 2002 was, 14.23% higher than in the last survey in 2001.

AVERAGE ANNUAL SALARY OF STAFF AND WORKERS BY SECTOR

Items (by sector)	Average Annual Salary RMB yuan/ US$/GBP£
Farming, Forestry, Animal Husbandry and Fishery	6,938/$846/£496
Mining and Quarrying	11,017/$1,344/£787
Manufacturing	11,001/$1,342/£786
Production and Supply of Electricity Gas and Water	16,440/$2,005/£1,174
Construction	10,279/$1,254/£734
Geological Prospecting and Water Conservancy	12,303/$1,500/£879
Transport, Storage, Post and Telecommunication Services	16,044/$1,957/£1,146
Wholesale and Retail Trade and Catering Services	9,398/$1,146/£671
Finance and Insurance	19,135/$2,334/£1,367
Real Estate	15,501/$1,890/£1,107
Social Services (including recreational services, information and consultative services, and computer application services)	13,499/$1,646/£964
Health Care, Sports and Social Welfare	14,795/$1,804/£1,057
Education, Culture and Arts, Radio, Film and Television	13,290/$1,621/£949
Scientific Research and Polytechnic Services	19,113/$2,330/£1,365
Governmental Agencies, Party Agencies and Social organisations	13,975/$1,704/£998
Others (including Enterprise Management Organisations)	14,215/$1,734/£1,015

The above salary index gives you a general picture of the average salary by sector in China. However, there can be a big difference in the average salary between different areas in China. The western and central part is less developed but there are major development projects being carried out by the central government. However, the average salary in the west and central part is still much lower than that in the coastal cities, which are more developed. In Shanghai and Beijing, the average annual salaries of employees in 2003 were 23,959 *yuan* (US$2,922/ £1,711) and 21,852 *yuan* (US$2,665/£1,561), which was more than double that of central and western regions like Guizhou and Shanxi where employees earned only about 9,000 *yuan* (US$1,100/£640) in the same year. Shanghai, Beijing, Zhejiang, Guangdong and Tianjin were the top five provinces and municipalities paying the highest salaries.

White-Collar Workers. The average annual salary for white-collar workers in general was about 38,450 *yuan* (US$4,630/£2,750) a year in 2003. However, the average salary for university graduates is relatively low. In 2003, there were more than 2.4 million university graduates and this figure is expected to surge to

2.8 million in 2004. Since the current supply of university graduates exceeds the available jobs at the appropriate level, the monthly salaries of graduates majoring in marketing, administration or information technology is only between 1,500 *yuan* (US$180/£110) and 2,500 *yuan* (US$300/£180).

AVERAGE SALARY OF WHITE-COLLAR WORKERS IN DIFFERENT SECTORS	
Items (by sector)	Average Annual Salary (RMB *yuan*/US$/GBP£)
Telecommunications	52,300/$6,380/£3,740
Medical Equipment	48,600/$5,930/£3,470
Consumer Items	46,230/$5,640/£3,300
Medicine, bio-engineering	43,520/$5,300/£3,100
Electrical skills	42,480/$5,180/£3,030
Computer	42,170/$5,140/£3,010
Petroleum, Chemical and Raw Materials	41,990/$5,120/£3000
Finance, Investment, Insurance	41,670/$5,080/£2,980
Consultancy, Specialist's Service	40,280/$4,910/£2,880
Durable Consumer Items	40,210/$4,900/£2,870
Electricity, Energy	39,750/$4,850/£2,840
Internet, Electronic Commerce	39,680/$4,840/£2,830
Mass Media, Film, TV, Culture and Publication	38,870/$4740/£2,780
Car Manufacturing, Maintenance, Accessories and Related Products	38,410/$4,680/£2,740
Transport, Logistics, Courier	38,160/44,650/£2,730
Building, Real Estate, Estate Management, Business Centre	37,820/$4,610/£2,700
Production and Manufacturing	37,440/$4,570/£2,670
Marketing, Advertisement, PR	36,750/$4,480/£2,630
Mechanics, Instruments, Metres	35,460/$4,320/£2,530
Trade, Import and Expert	34,290/$4,180/£2,500

Despite the variability of demand across different industries, foreign language proficiency continues to act as a major factor in salary adjustment. If you have a strong command of a foreign language, especially English, you will probably receive an average annual salary of 54,050 *yuan* (US$6,590/£3,860). If you have an above average command of English, the average annual salary is about 44,000 *yuan* (US$5,370/£3,140). However, the average annual salary of workers with average standard of English is only about 31,440 *yuan* (US$3,830/£2,250).

Educational qualifications are similarly important if you want to negotiate a higher salary. The higher the education level you have obtained, the higher the salary you will probably receive. The average annual salary for university graduates was about 42,830 *yuan* (US$5,220/£3,060) in 2003. However, if you have an MBA qualification, you will receive an average annual salary of about 74,250 *yuan* (US$9,050/£5,300). This reflects the fact that China is urgently in need of experts of higher education level to fill senior managerial positions.

Blue-Collar Workers. In general, blue-collar workers' salaries are lower than those of white-collar workers. This is partly due to the huge supply and partly due to the low qualifications of these workers. In recent years, blue-collar workers' salaries have been rising considerably, due to the high demand for 'skilled' or 'advanced-skilled' workers. However, it is estimated that only 3.7% of the 70 million blue-collar workers are classified as 'advanced skilled workforce'. The supply of skilled workers, although limited, boosts the average salary of the whole group.

The average monthly salary of low level to middle level jobs is 3,000 *yuan* (US$365/£214) while that of a skilled blue-collar worker can be up to 5,000 *yuan* (US$610/£357) a month. It is interesting to note that the salary of a qualified and experienced blue-collar worker or technician is as much as, or even more than a higher degree holder. It has been reported that some enterprises are willing to pay more than 100,000 *yuan* (US$12,195/£7,143) a year for local skilled workers. According to one case reported in the *People's Daily*, an enterprise even paid 700,000 *yuan* (US$86,366/£50,000) annually for a Japanese technical expert. Even though it was an exceptional case, you can see how businesses are actively luring skilled workers into their country. For technicians working in traditional industries, such as skilled locksmiths, pattern makers and oil refiners, the annual salary can be up to 80,000 *yuan* (US$9,760/£5,710) a year. Skilled workers in service sectors, such as hairdressers, chefs, beauticians, can earn up to 50,000 *yuan* (US$6,100/£3,520) a year.

There is a big gap between the salaries of low-skilled and high-skilled workers. Over 70% of Chinese workers are unskilled and have a low educational background. An unskilled labourer in China earns about 750 to 1,000 *yuan* per month (US$90-120/£55-70), which is less than one-fifth of the monthly salary of skilled workers.

Salaries are usually paid monthly, either by cash, cheque or direct to the employees' accounts. Some companies may pay their employees, especially temporary or daily waged workers, through a middleman. However, you should avoid getting your wages through a middleman as there have been complaints that they take the money and disappear. Some companies include an extra monthly payment to employees as a bonus but it depends on the practice of the companies and the profit made that year.

Starting from March 2004, the Regulations on Minimum Wages will protect workers from being exploited. Each local government has its own minimum wage but overtime payments, allowances and any extra payments such as working night shifts or in a dangerous environment are excluded from the minimum wage.

As with Hong Kong, there is no minimum wage in Macau. Wages are set according to the qualifications and experience of employees. There is a great discrepancy between the salaries of different industries. Banking, finance and transport sectors in general enjoy higher salaries when compared to other industries. The average salary of employees in banking and finance is about MOP$12,000 (US$1,500/£950) per month while that in transport is about MOP$9,000 (US$1,125/£720) per month. However, employees in the manufacturing industry, on average, earn only MOP$4,000-$5,000 (US$500-625/£320-400) a month.

Even though tourism is an important industry in Macau, the average incomes of travel agents, restaurant and hotel staff are quite low, just slightly better than that of manufacturing workers. Salaries are usually paid directly to the employees' bank accounts. Even though some companies may still pay their employees in cheques or cash, it is not usual.

Employment Contracts

In China, a written employment contract between the employer and the employee is either in the form of a *collective contract* or an *individual contract*. A *collective contract* is a binding contract between the employer and a trade union, which represents the employees. An *individual contract* is a binding contract between an individual employee and the employer and there is no need to have a trade union as middleman.

According to Chinese Labour Law, collective contracts must be sent to the relevant labour authorities for approval but this is optional for individual contracts. Though it is not compulsory, it is a common practice for the enterprise to submit a draft copy of their employment contract to the local authority for pre-approval. A contract is not valid until it receives certification by the provincial, municipal or autonomous people's government within one month of its execution.

Employers are obliged to address the following issues in the employment contract:

- Job nature.
- Term of probationary period and employment period, if any.
- Dispute resolution.
- Disciplinary action.
- Dismissal and employee resignation.
- Working hours, annual leave and holidays *(optional)*.
- Employee benefits *(optional)*.
- Special training *(optional)*.

- Confidentiality requirement *(optional)*.
- Tort liability *(optional)*.
- Severance pay. *(optional)*.

In addition to the employment contract, Foreign-invested enterprises (FIEs) are required to keep a record for each employee. This record should include the following information about the employee:

- Name, ID number, marital/family status and home address.
- Employment commencement date.
- Probationary period.
- Job title.
- Wages plus bonuses.
- Leave entitlement (annual, sick, holiday and maternity).
- Notice period.
- Date of termination.

The FIEs are also required to give the employee a handbook which clearly outlines the benefits provisions the employee will enjoy and which serves as the employee's code of conduct.

In Macau, an employer should clearly define the job nature and requirements as well as stating the position, length of contract and salary in the employment contract. The contract should also includes holidays and benefits that the employee are entitled to. The probation period, overtime payments, procedures and compensation for ending the contract, bonus (if any), etc, are normally included as well. You should ask your employer to include all these if they are missing in the contract. After signing the contract, your employer should give you a copy of it for reference.

Termination of Employment

The Labour Bureau is very concerned about the laying-off of employees. As a result, the local bureau may sometimes exert pressure on a company not to dismiss their labour unless necessary. The most common method of termination is to give 30 days advance notice to the employee. However, the exact period of notice should be in accordance with the details of the employment contract. The employer also needs to report the dismissal to the local labour bureau.

Employees who are dismissed for disciplinary violations will normally have the opportunity to defend themselves in front of the management of the company. If their defence fails to change the decision, they can appeal against the termination to the labour arbitration commission or before the People's Court if they have strong reasons. The employer must inform the local bureau of pending dismissals due to redundancy or bankruptcy. Companies must seek the support and approval of the labour bureau to terminate a contract with an employee who has not committed any disciplinary violation.

In China, revocation of a contract is permitted under the following conditions:

- Both the employer and employee agree to the termination.
- An employee is found not up to the requirements during the probationary period.
- An employee seriously violates the rules or labour discipline.
- An employee causes serious financial loss through dereliction of duty.
- An employee is investigated for criminal acts.
- An employee does not turn up to work after an illness.
- An employee remains unqualified for a post after training.
- Changes in the 'objective conditions' on which the contract was founded.
- The employer is on the brink of bankruptcy.

If the contract is terminated for any of the above reasons, the severance pay is equal to one-month's salary. If the contract is terminated for other reasons, it must be by mutual consent and further payments could be sought.

You should note that an employer cannot terminate a contract with an employee if the employee has been disabled in an industrial accident or by occupational disease; or a woman is on maternity or nursing leave; or he or she is on non-work-related sick leave within a certain statutorily defined period.

The severance pay should be an 'economical compensation' based on the Labour Law and other regulations. On top of this 'economical compensation', the employee has the right to a further severance pay of three to six months if his or her contract is ended because of non-work-related injury.

In Macau, an employer has to provide prior notice to an employee if he or she wants to end the contract before it expires, and vice versa. An employee who has served the company for three months or more should be given prior notice for ending a contract at least 15 days before the effective date. On the other hand, an employee should tell the employer at least seven days before leaving. Employers have to pay compensation to employees for terminating contracts. The amount of compensation varies from seven to twenty days' salary, depending on the period of service.

Probationary Period

The probationary period in China varies under each city's regulations. It also depends on the length of the contract. If the contract is up to six months, the maximum probationary period is fifteen days. If it is more than six months but less than one year, the maximum probationary period is one month. For more than one year but less than two years, two months is the maximum probationary period. If your contract is more than two years but less than three years, the probationary period can be up to three months. Otherwise, the maximum probationary period is six months.

Working Hours, Overtime and Holidays

According to current Chinese law, excluding meal times, the maximum working hours should not be more than 40 hours a week. For most jobs, you can expect to work for approximately eight hours a day, although some industries like hospitals, post offices and banks are usually open seven days a week and you are required to have greater flexibility if working in these fields. Business hours for many companies are from 9am to 5pm Monday to Friday and some companies may open on Saturday morning as well. Most of the government offices are open on weekdays only and are usually closed after 5pm.

Workers in China are flexible in terms of working hours and are prepared to work extra hours if necessary. In order to protect employees from unreasonable working hours, the Chinese government set up a labour standard system (State Tripartite Conference System of Labour Relations Coordination) in 2001 to protect the rights of both employers and employees. When the employers need to extend the working hours of their employees, they must consult the trade union or the workers. In addition, the extra period of work should not exceed one hour per day. In very special cases, overtime work may be three hours a day, or thirty-six hours in a month. The employer should ensure that all workers enjoy at least one day' holiday per week as well as other legal holidays. More importantly, if you are required to work overtime, under the current labour standard system, you should be paid at 150% of the normal salary for the extra hours. If you are required to work weekends or on legal holidays, you should be paid two or three times your normal pay rate respectively.

Apart from day's off and legal holidays, employees are also entitled to at least five days of paid annual leave. Companies and industries are also required to increase the days of annual leave for employees who serve their companies for a long period. Employees who serve their companies for 15 to 24 years, are entitled to ten days of paid annual leave. Those who serve 25 years or more will receive 14 days of paid leave a year.

Employees can enjoy full pay (monthly base pay, not including bonus or social subsidies) while they have statutory holidays, rest days, annual leave, sick leave, marriage and bereavement leave, unless stated otherwise.

The ten legal holidays include:

- New Year's Day
- Chinese New Year *(3 days holiday, usually in mid-January to early February)*
- International Labour Day *(3 days holiday, 1ˢᵗ May to 3ʳᵈ May)*
- National Day *(3 days holiday, 1st October to 3ʳᵈ October)*

Under the Labour Law in Macau, the working hours of an employee should be within eight hours a day and 48 hours a week. Employers are required to provide at least 30 minutes break for their employees every day. Employees are entitled to a rest day in every seven days, apart from the ten legal holidays. There is no standard overtime rate. It should be according to the contracts between employers and employees. However, if an employee is asked to work on a rest day, the employer has to pay double the normal salary as well as providing the employee another rest day within 30 days. Every employee is entitled to at least five days paid leave a year. Some companies will offer extra annual leave to employees who serve the company for a longer period. If employees do not take all their annual leave before the employment is terminated, employers have to pay for the rest of the annual leave as compensation.

There are ten legal holidays in Macau including:

- New Year's Day
- Chinese New Year *(3 days holiday, usually in mid-January to early February)*
- Ching Ming Festival *(5th April)*
- Labour Holiday *(1st May)*
- The day after the Mid-Autumn Festival *(usually in mid-September to early October)*
- National Day *(1st October)*
- Chung Yang Festival *(in October)*
- Macau Special Administrative Region Establishment Day *(20th December)*

Medical Leave and Sick Pay

The Chinese system of paid medical leave is similar to the system of annual leave. The longer you serve in the company, the longer medical leave you can take. According to the current system, medical leave is divided into 7 levels, ranging from 3 months per year to 24 months in a 30-month period.

LENGTH OF MEDICAL LEAVE	
Condition of Service	**Length of Medical Leave**
Up to 10 years of total working experience and serving in the present company for up to 5 years	3 months continuous or within any 6-month period
Up to 10 years of total working experience and serving in the present company for more than 5 years	6 months medical leave within any 12-month period
10 years or more total working experience and serving in the present company for up to 5 years	6 months medical leave within any 12-month period

10 years or more total working experience and serving in the present company for 6 to 10 years	9 months medical leave within any 15-month period
10 years or more total working experience and serving in the present company for 11 to 15 years	12 months medical leave within 18-month period
Serving in the present company for 16 to 20 years	18 months medical leave within any 24-months period
Serving in the present company for more than 20 years	24 months medical leave within any 30-month period

Apart from medical leave, employees will also receive sick-leave payments. If an employee has to be off for up to six months and he has been working in the company for up to two years, then he will receive 60% of his normal salary. If he has been in the company for eight years or more, he is entitled to 100% of his normal salary. Otherwise, if an employee has to be off for more than six months, and he has been in the company for only two years or less, then he will receive 40% of his normal salary, or 60% of normal salary if he has been working for 3 years or more in the same company.

In the case of work related injury, the employer is also responsible for all medical expenses. The injured employee is also entitled to a disability allowance, which is a single payment of six to 24 months' salary according to the degree of disability. Besides, the employee has the right to be absent from work up to 24 months. For serious injuries, this can be extended to 36 months.

Social Insurances

There are five main kinds of social insurance. Both the employers and employees are required to contribute to three of them: unemployment insurance, the provident fund and medical insurance. The remaining two are the sole responsibility of the employer.

Unemployment Insurance. Both employers and employees are required to contribute to unemployment insurance. Employers have to pay around 2% of the total payroll of the company while employees have to pay about 1% of their wages. However, the actual rate of contribution varies from place to place.

Provident Fund (Pension). As in many other countries, China has a provident fund system for employees. Every employer must register with a local Provident Fund Management Centre within 30 days of the establishment of a company. Both employers and employees are required to contribute to the fund. The rate of contribution is set by local government and varies from place to place but the amount paid by employers will not exceed 20% of the total payroll of the enterprise. Employees have to contribute about 6-8% of their wages to the provident fund.

Work Injury Insurance. The Occupational Safety section of the Labour Law highlights the importance of providing employees with safe work conditions. The employer should provide the employee with at least the minimum safety and hygiene standards based on the national and local regulations. Apart from that, employers are also required to contribute to work injury insurance. The exact amount of contribution, similar to other insurances, is based on the local regulations but in general, employers pay approximately 1% of an employee's salary.

Medical Insurance. Both employers and employees are required to contribute to medical insurance. An employer has to contribute around 6% of an employee's salary for medical insurance while the employee pays 2%, however, there are slight differences between cities.

Child-Bearing Insurance. Female employees are also entitled to child-bearing insurance, which ensures that they receive maternal leave, child-bearing subsidy and other medical care related to their pregnancy. Employers have to contribute about 1% of the employee's salary to this insurance.

Trade Unions

All trade unions in China are under the umbrella of the All-China Federation of Trade Unions (ACFTU). ACFTU is a voluntary organisation of workers and it currently has about 102 million members. The goal of the ACFTU is to safeguard the rights and interests of the workers and it represents them in discussions on different matters related to work with the employers. One of the major functions of trade unions is to assist workers to sign suitable employment contracts with employers. China's Trade Union Law was set up in 1992 and it granted trade unions the authority to sign collective agreements with companies on behalf of the workers. Trade unions act as a representative party to negotiate with the employer on matters relating to remuneration, working hours, vacations, occupational safety and health, insurance and welfare. When trade unions are involved, foreign-invested enterprises normally sign collective contracts instead of individual contracts with their employees. A trade union can also interfere with punishments handed out by employers on workers if the punishments are considered improper or the reasons are not sound. In such cases, an employer has to provide a satisfactory explanation to prevent the trade union from taking the case to court. Trade unions also participate in the investigation of work-related accidents and may ask for compensation on behalf of the injured or deceased. In the case of disputes at work, trade unions will present the demands and opinions of the workers to the employer and negotiate for the benefit of employees.

A basic-level trade union, i.e. one set up within a company, should include at least 25 members. Otherwise, a trade union can be set up jointly with two or more units. All wage-earners in companies, institutions and State organs within China are eligible to join trade unions, regardless of their nationality, race, sex, occupation, religion or educational background. Workers who are members of trade unions are required to contribute 0.5% of their monthly salary into the trade union's fund. Enterprises have to contribute 2% of workers' monthly salaries to the fund as well.

Every employee in Macau is free to join or not to join a trade union and it is illegal for an employer to prohibit the employees from joining, or to force them to join a particular one. Trade unions in Macau are responsible for protecting the rights of employees as well as being their representative in the case of employment disputes. However, some people have reported that trade unions in the city do not have strong bargaining powers and employers may not take the opinions of the trade unions very seriously.

Useful Address

All-China Federation of Trade Unions, 10 Fuxingmenwai Street, Beijing 100865 China; ☎ *(86) 010 6859 2730; fax (86) 010 6856 2031; e-mail* acftuild@publ ic3.bta.net.cn; *www.acftu.org.cn.*

Retirement

In China, the retirement age for men and women is 60 and 55 respectively. However, non-professional female workers are often asked to retire when they reach 50. Since many female workers, especially professionals, prefer to work beyond 55, the government may allow them to extend their retirement age to 60 if they are in good health. Pension schemes were not introduced before the mid-90s. Employees who started working before the launch of the pension scheme have to contribute to the provident fund for ten years to enjoy full benefits. Those who started working after the launch of the scheme, are required to contribute to the fund for at least 15 years to enjoy the same benefits. Employers are also required to contribute to the fund but their contributions will go to the central government provident fund rather than an employee's individual account. More details about pension schemes in China are covered in the chapter *Retirement*.

WOMEN IN WORK

In the old China, the status of women was low and they were mainly restricted to housekeeping and taking care of children. Nowadays, many women have their own career and are financially independent. Currently, female workers make up about 37% of the total workforce. Given that the male to female population is 1.2 to 1, this means that about 50% of the female population is contributing to the economic development of the country. In the old days, women rarely went to work after they married, especially after they had children. However, nowadays many married women work and return to work after they have had children.

Nevertheless, compared to male job-seekers, it is more difficult for female job-seekers to find work. Over 50% of the female population is looking for a job, but only about half of the whole female population is employed. Even though the status of women is rising, sexual inequality at work, and for wages and job opportunities still exists. According to an article in *China Daily*, many female college graduates nowadays attach revealing photographs, such as photos in a mini skirt or even in a bikini, to their resumés in order to increase their chance of getting a job. Some of them also emphasise their ability to sing, dance and drink to show that they are qualified for public relations positions. Some employers do not deny that they prefer male employees to female employees, as women need to take maternity leave and nursing leave. It is not only lower skilled female workers that face unemployment; the situation is the same for highly educated females as well. Many employers prefer not to recruit fresh female university graduates as they believe these mid-to-late twenties women will get married and then maybe pregnant soon after beginning work. Even though the Labour Law clearly states that men and women should be treated equally when they look for jobs, many people believe that there is more to be done to make these regulations work. Many working women also complain that different retirement ages for men and women is also a sexual discrimination, and they are fighting for the same retirement age (60-years-old) as men.

Sexual harassment, sad to say, it quite common in mainland China. According to a survey done in 2003, about 70% of female workers reported that they had experienced sexual harassment at least once. Verbal harassment and physical touching are common, especially from male superiors, or sometimes teachers. However, most of the harassed women do not report these cases. The first court case on sexual harassment in Beijing was not heard until April 2003. Since then, there have been more women complaining about being sexually harassed and the government is considering implementing laws to protect female workers. If you are sexually harassed, you should ask for help from the local labour bureau.

PERCENTAGE OF FEMALE WORKERS IN DIFFERENT SECTORS (2002)

Item (by sector)	National Total in percentage (%)
Farming, Forestry, Animal Husbandry and Fishery	37.1
Mining and Quarrying	25.3
Manufacturing	43.0
Production and Supply of Electricity, Gas and Water	31.6
Construction	17.1
Geological Prospecting and Water Conservancy	27.0
Transport, Storage, Post and Telecommunication Service	28.3

Wholesale, and Retail Trade and Catering Services	44.9
Finance and Insurance	45.9
Real Estate	34.2
Social Services	41.7
Health Care, Sports and Social Welfare	58.0
Education, Culture and Arts, Radio, Film and Television	45.5
Scientific Research and Polytechnic Services	33.5
Government Agencies, Party Agencies, and Social Organisations	25.2
Others	36.2

Maternity Leave and Nursing Leave

According to the Female Worker Labour Protection Provisions, pregnant employees are entitled to 90 days of maternity leave, of which 15 days are before confinement and 75 days are after it. Some cities provide paternity leave as well but the length of leave varies from city to city. Maternity leave can be extended if there are difficulties arising from birth such as miscarriage or multiple offspring. For every extra child born, an extra 15 days maternity leave are granted. 15 to 42 days are granted for employees who miscarry. Employers are also required to provide a nursing period for their employees during work days so that they can feed their babies.

Maternity Benefits

Even though it is not yet a universal policy, some cities require employers to contribute to a local Maternity Insurance Fund. The contribution rate of the fund ranges from 0.5% to 1% of an individual employee's salary. A pregnant employee is expected to receive maternity leave with full pay from her employer. She can also benefit from her local Maternity Social Insurance Fund, which covers all expenses that are associated with her pre- and post- natal care. Hospitalisation, medical expenses and delivery are also covered by the fund in some cities. Moreover, a child-bearing subsidy is provided to pregnant employees for not less than 90 days. The calculation of this subsidy is based on the average salary of the individual employee in the previous year. Employers in regions that do not have the Maternity Insurance Fund still have to pay the maternal subsidy to their pregnant employees, even though they are not required to pay monthly contributions.

DISABLED WORKERS IN CHINA

According to a national survey of people with disabilities conducted by the National Bureau of Statistics in 1987, it was estimated there were about 60 million persons with disabilities in China: among whom 20.57 millions had hearing disabilities; 11.82 million had mental disabilities; there were 8.77 million with physical disabilities; 8.77 million with visual disability; 2.25 million with mental illness and 7.82 million with multi-disabilities. The figures reflect the fact that more attention should be given to disabled groups, especially in the aspect of employment.

The China Disabled Persons' Federation (CDPF) was established in 1988 to protect the rights of people who have disabilities. At the moment, the CDPF has established more than 3,012 employment centres to facilitate persons with different disabilities. These centres offer training to disabled persons and provide recommendations if necessary. CDPF also conducts investigations in the event of discrimination over disabilities during selection. It also helps the disabled to register for labour resources. Its employment quota scheme has helped more than 1.5 million disabled people to obtain a job in both public and private sectors. Below are some key developments about disability in China:

- More than 70,000 placement opportunities were offered by welfare enterprises to people with disabilities.
- Registered disabled people are entitled to the nation's preferential policy of tax reduction or exemption.
- Massage by blind people is a rapidly emerging industry and there are over 5,022 massage institutions in China.
- Over 20,000 trained blind or visually disabled persons are currently employed as masseuses or masseurs in hospitals and clinics. Some of them are engaged in medical treatments or simply health-keeping massage. And nearly one million have obtained jobs with assistance or are self-employed.
- Medium-term and short-tem technical training is also provided for disabled people living in rural areas.
- Production guides, including purchasing materials for farm-use, selling farm commodities and producing other works for sale, are provided to disabled people.

After the CDPF was established in 1988, the employment rate of disabled people in cities and towns was 50% out of the total disability population in the area. This figure has risen to above 80%. Confirmed by the law and ratified by the State Council, the CDPF will continue to act as the unified national organisation of and for persons with various disabilities in China. With support from the central government, CDPF will continue to play an important role in promoting the rights of disabled people and helping them to obtain equal status and opportunities in society.

Useful Website

China Labour Bulletin, http://www.china-labour.org.hk/iso/about – us.adp. This includes current debates on labour rights and labour unions and information on other issues relating to labour and employment. It helps to facilitate workers' collaborative actions and to settle legal and administrative disputes. It also provides forums for workers to express their opinions and discuss labour-related issues.

LONG TERM EMPLOYMENT

Teaching

According to an internet Chinese recruitment agency, *www.chinajob.com,* the demand for English teachers in Chinese schools is very high in both public and private institutions.

As mentioned previously, the Ministry of Foreign Affairs of the Chinese government recruits Foreign Teachers (FTs) and Foreign Experts (FEs) through Chinese embassies every year. You need to hold a master degree or above in the relevant areas, such as English and Linguistics, to be a FE. Moreover, you are also required to have some teaching experience at tertiary level. FTs are mainly university graduates and are not required to have teaching experience. FTs are placed in secondary schools or sometimes primary schools while FEs can choose to work in university level institutes. You should make your application to the Chinese embassy in your home country for teaching in China. You should attach a covering letter, a resumé, a copy of your passport (the page with your personal details), a copy of your education certificate and a passport-size photo to your application. There are also different short-term and long-term programmes held by the China Education Association for International Exchange (CEAIE) for foreigners.

There are plenty of other channels for foreigners to seek for teaching positions in China and one of the best routes is to join a work programme, such as Professional Placement in Chinese Schools organised by China Services International (CSI). CSI only arranges for foreign teachers or experts to go to schools which are assessed by local governments and have fulfilled all criteria. In another words, CSI works closely with local provincial authorities and local schools in order to assure a positive placement experience for potential foreign teachers. International applicants who participate in the CSI teaching placement programme will receive a monthly salary based on contractual agreement.

Salaries for teaching jobs in China are about 2,200 *yuan* per month (US$268/ £157), but the salary varies slightly amongst schools. An interesting point to note is that the salary is open for negotiation and you may ask for a higher salary. Educational level and teaching experience are important factors to determine your salary. The salary of a foreign teacher who has a Bachelor degree is not less than 2,200 *yuan* per month; a master degree holder with five years teaching experience will earn 3,300 *yuan* (US$400/£235) or more per month; and the monthly salary of a doctorate degree holder or an Associate Professor from an overseas institution will be 4,600 *yuan* (US$560/£330) or above. At the end of each academic semester, every foreign teacher will receive 1,000 *yuan* (US$120/£70) as their end-of-term bonus. Other benefits include fully-paid furnished accommodation during the contractual period, and a one-way international travel ticket or an equivalent sum of money in *yuan*. The Council on International Educational Exchange (CIEE) also organises a very similar programmeme to that of CSI. You should bear in mind that you should only apply to schools which have obtained provincial authorisation to hire foreign teachers. Otherwise, you may find that the school cannot afford to provide the above salary payments and benefits.

The British Council also runs a programme arranging university graduates to be English teaching assistants in Chinese secondary schools. Successful candidates will stay in China for about 10 months and they are provided with free accommodation in addition to a salary between 2,500 to 3,500 *yuan* (US$304-427/£180-250). The closing date for this programme is around March every year and you should make your application directly to the British Council. More details can be found at *www.languageassistant.co.uk*.

You can find teaching jobs in China through a number of recruitment websites, such as the China TEFL (Teaching English as a Foreign Language) Network, the Zhejiang Foreign Experts Service and China Education. There are more and more private institutes looking for foreigners to teach English and it is easy to find a huge number of these institutes through a Google or Yahoo search. There are several placement organisations, such as CIEE, who have links with these foreign language institutes and they will be able to arrange a teaching job in China for you.

Teaching English Abroad, published by Vacation Work Publications (www.vacationwork.co.uk) is a very handy directory and provides useful details on teaching English in China.

Useful Addresses & Websites:

China Education Association for International Exchange (CEAIE), 160 Fuxingmen Nei Dajie, Beijing 100031 (mailing address: 37 Damucang Hutong, Beijing 100816; ☎(86) 010 6641 6582; fax (86) 010 6641 6156; e-mail ceaie@ceaie.edu.cn; www.ceaie.edu.cn.

China Services International (CSI), www.chinajob.com/En/.

Council on International Educational Exchange (CIEE), 52 Poland Street, London W1F 7AB, UK: ☎(44) 020 7478 2020; fax (44) 020 7734 7322; e-mail infoUK@councilexchanges.org.uk; www.councilexchanges.org.uk.

The British Council, Language Assistants Team, Education and Training Group, British Council, 10 Spring Gardens, London SW1A 2BN; ☎(44) 020 7389 4596; e-mail assistants@britishcouncil.org; www.languageassistant.co.uk.

China TEFL network, http://www.chinatefl.com/vacancy.html. A China teaching job-listing site.

Zhejiang Foreign Experts Service, http://www.teach-in-zhejiang.com/ywrc/login.asp. Provides the latest ESL/EFL vacancies in schools in China.

China Education, http://www.chinatoday.com/edu/a00.htm. This provides information of vacancies in universities in China.

GAP, 44 Queen's Road Reading Berkshire RG1 4BB; ☎(44) 0118 959 4914; fax (44) 0118 957 6634; e-mail volunteer@gap.org.uk; www.gap.org.uk. A placement organisation arranging teaching jobs for school leavers.

Language Link, 21 Harrington Road, London SW7 3EU; ☎(44) 020 7225 1065; fax (44) 020 7584 3518; e-mail info@languagelink.co.uk; www.languagelink.co.uk.

Preparation for Teaching English in China. There is a special course for those wanting to teach English in China run by the *Boland School TEFL Training Center* (Su Zhou, Jiangsu Province, China; e-mail katie@boland-china.com; www.boland-china.com). The 148-hour course leads to an International TEFL Diploma teaching qualification for teaching English as a foreign language worldwide. The Boland School's China program is designed to prepare those interested in teaching English to live and work in China, Hong Kong, Taiwan, or elsewhere in Asia. In addition to the standard internationally-recognised TEFL Diploma teacher training program, it includes 20 hours of survival language lessons plus coverage of cultural background, etiquette, history,

education, and an introduction to Chinese students and language learning difficulties. The courses are held monthly and consist of a 148 hour graded programme over four and a half weeks. The maximum student/teacher ratio is 8:1 and there are 10 hours peer teaching and minimum of 8 hours observed classroom teaching per trainee. Comprehensive job placement services, job fairs on-site every month. A job guarantee and flight reimbursement guarantee are included. The curriculum includes the optional TEFL-China Certificate. The costs are US$1,395, not including accommodation, or US$1,595 with single room accommodation.

Media

Until mid 2003, the media market faced increasing competition and serious violation of intellectual property. Nevertheless, in the most recent 'China Watch 2004 Annual Country Forecast', the China Watch Forecasting Services predicts a brighter future for this industry in the coming years as a result of the decision to allow greater foreign participation, especially in television production, to boost the revenue of the industry. Currently, foreign experts in the media industry are urgently needed to input new ideas into the industry. As the State Administration for Radio, Film, and Television (SARFT) said in April 2003, most of the current premium contents are foreign made. SAFT also acknowledged the need for deals to exchange content with foreign producers, and then to re-sell them to local cable companies. SARFT's approval for foreign participation and investment in the Chinese entertainment media industry triggers a sudden emergence of multi-national media companies and therefore creates a huge number of jobs in this field.

Besides television production, greater foreign participation can also be found in the cinema industry. There is also a major effort to protect intellectual property and more local incentives are offered to attract foreign investments. At the end of 2003 and the beginning of 2004, there were an increasing number of joint ventures in film production, and a foreign partner can own up to 49% of a joint venture. In addition, more cinemas and production houses in China welcome foreign experts, such as movie producers, to create better prospects and greater profits in the industry.

Banking and Finance

At the end of 2003, Premier Wen Jiabao expressed the view in an interview that financial reform plays a crucial part in economic development. He also said the government has accelerated the reform of the banking system and aims to reduce the risk of doing business in China. In addition, many reports and interviews have mentioned that the Chinese government wants to make Shanghai a major financial centre in Asia, and the world. These statements all reflect the fact that banking and finance plays an important role in Chinese economic development. Foreign banking consultants and financial experts should not find it difficult to find a job in China, especially in Shanghai. Moreover, banks have been extending the scope of their services. Apart from account management and mortgages, many banks provide credit card services, travel insurance and also online banking services. There are also more foreign enterprises using the services of local banks. The expansion of banking business not only creates more job opportunities but actually requires more foreign experts to support the increasing demand in services from foreign enterprises.

Executives

Foreign investment has been increasing at a rate of 20% in recent years and more and more foreign enterprises are tempted to establish branches in China. These enterprises look for experienced executives, especially in human resource management, financial management and marketing, to put the business on the right track and manage the business in this fast-changing economy. Foreign-invested enterprises (FIEs) have to give priority to local candidates under the regulations and you may find it more difficult to obtain a job from them. However, foreign enterprises are not bound by these regulations and some of them are particularly interested in candidates from abroad as their business partners are mainly outside China.

Information Technology

IT is one of the fastest growing industries in China. It is estimated that the industry will grow at a rate of 12% annually in the coming five years. It is believed that there will be enormous business opportunities for IT vendors. Banks and insurance companies in particular look for foreign IT vendors as these foreign experts usually provide all the intellectual solutions, while domestic vendors are mainly responsible for providing hardware and software. Moreover, the education and medical industries, as well as banks and insurance companies, will also demand more IT products in the coming years.

The increase in demand for advanced technology products also stimulates the production of semi-conductors, digital household appliances, medical equipment, etc. In the past, these products were mainly imported from other countries but more domestic products can now be found as the technology and skills for local production are getting better and better. Many locals nowadays actually prefer to buy home grown products instead of imported ones as the quality of the two is similar but it is cheaper to go for local ones. Highly skilled and experienced workers in IT businesses will be very welcome to work in China for the next five to ten years. There is also a demand for product designers to increase the competitiveness of products and to increase the market share. For more details about the development of the industry, refer to the later section *Business Reports*.

Transport

As the country develops rapidly and more foreign traders visit China, the Chinese government has been improving the quality of existing airports as well as opening up its airways to more foreign airlines. At the end of 2003, the Shanghai airport authority announced that it is going to launch an 80 million *yuan* (US$9.67 million/£5.7 million) project to build China's first international airport shopping complex in Pudong. Candidates who can speak fluent English will surely have an advantage in getting a job in this new international complex. As the connections between China and other countries widen, airbuses will become more and more popular in China. Many people are employed to produce airbus parts even though most airbuses are imported.

The Yantai-Dalian Railway Ferry Project, started construction in Yantai in late 2003, and is expected to be in service in 2006. It is only one of a series of new sea transport routes in China and some of the routes, such as the Yuehai Railway Ferry that links South China's Guangdong and Hainan provinces, are already in service. The Chinese government is also extending its rail services and aims to cover more regions in the west of China.

'Go-west' has been an major development project since the late 90s. In order to attract more investors to start their businesses in the west, it is important to improve the transportation connections from east to west. Apart from railways, many highways are being built or will be built to make the transport of materials and finished goods easier. Some existing ones will be extended to provide better connections between cities. More details about transportation development are covered under the *Regional Development* in a later section.

SHORT TERM EMPLOYMENT

In recent years, the short-term or periodic employment pattern has become a new trend in some parts of China. The Beijing Municipal Government has introduced short term and contractual employment to create more job opportunities. Instead of signing a contract that lasts for 10 years with a new employee as in the past, many companies and government institutions prefer short-term contracts, for three to five years, or even periodical contracts. Under this latest employment pattern, many job-seekers prefer to leave their files with employment agencies to search for a better job even when they are employed. Jumping from one job to another new job is more frequent than before.

Summer Training Programmes and Camps

Many local and foreign organisations arrange for foreigners to go to China to lead summer programmes or participate as assistants every year. Most of these are English learning programmes for secondary school students or for English teachers in China. The China Education Association for International Exchange (CEAIE) organises such summer programmes every year and invites foreigners to teach participants English. The programme for secondary teachers lasts for six weeks while an English camp for students is two weeks shorter. There are many organisations that recruit volunteers to teach in China. Educational Services International (ESI), a US Christian group, also organises summer programmes in China but it only recruits English speakers who are Christians. Two-weeks of training will be provided before going to China and the whole programme lasts for about six weeks. You can make your application at anytime of the year but you have to pay about US$3,400 (£1,800) for joining the programme. WorldTeach is a non-profit organisation based at the Centre for International Development at Harvard University. They recruit voluntary English speakers to teach in summer camps in China every year. The whole programme lasts for about two months (from late June to late August) and every volunteer participates in two to three camps in different areas in China. There is a cost of about US$3,900 (£2,160) for joining the programme. Colorado China Council (CCC) includes a great deal of sightseeing out of the teaching time and it sometimes organises additional trips after the programme which you can join by paying extra. You need to hold at least a Bachelor degree to join the programmes of CCC. As with ESI and WorldTeach, participants need to pay for joining the programme.

Useful Addresses

Educational Services International (ESI), 444 E. Huntington Drive Suite 200, Arcadia, CA 91006, USA; ☎(1) 626 294 9400/(1) 800 895 7955 (toll free in USA and Canada); fax (1) 626 821 2022; e-mail teach@esimail.org; www.teachoverseas.org.

WorldTeach, c/o Center for International Development, Harvard University, 79 John F. Kennedy Street, Cambridge MA 02138 USA; ☎(1) 617 495 5527; fax (1) 617 495 1599; e-mail info@worldteach.org; www.worldteach.org.

Colorado China Council, 4556 Apple Way, Boulder, CO 80301, USA; ☎(1) 303 443 1108; fax (1) 303 443 1107; e-mail alice@asiacouncil.org; www.asiacouncil.org.

Hotels

Working in cafes in tourist areas can sometimes be undertaken without a working visa, but you are usually paid at a low rate. Hotels very often employ foreigners to teach their staff English, to write or translate menus, or as receptionists. You can approach a hotel directly and ask if it requires a foreign worker. You will have a greater chance of getting a job if you look into those in the tourist areas. Portfolio International (*http://www.portfoliointernational.com/sect1/*) are professional recruitment experts specialising in the hotel and catering industries. Positions are categorized into hotel general managers, hotel operations, leisure and golf, sales and marketing, corporate, food, drink and entertainment and chefs.

Farming and Horticulture

Agriculture has been an important industry for China. Even though many cities are transforming themselves into industrial and financial bases, agriculture in China is still a major supplier of food to many countries. If you want to experience life in rural areas and are interested in farming and horticulture, the International Farm Experience Programme can arrange a three-month placement on the outskirts of Beijing.

Farmers in China are usually very poor. If you do not mind being a volunteer, you can try to ask the local farmers directly. However, it may be difficult if you do not speak any Mandarin.

Useful Address

International Farm Experience Programme, Young Farmers Centre, National Agriculture Centre, Stoneleigh, Warwickshire CV8 2LG; ☎(44) 024 7685 7204.

Internships

China joined IAESTE (International Association for the Exchange of Students with Technical Experience) in February 2000. IAESTE offers paid course-related work placements for students in science, engineering and technology to provide them with practical experience as well as theoretical knowledge. These placements normally last for 12 weeks in summer but longer placements can be arranged at other times of the year *(http://www.iaeste.org/)*.

The internship is open to students attending courses at universities, institutes of technology and similar institutions of higher education in science, engineering and technology. You must be studying at a university at the time of the internship, which means you cannot join the programme either before your first school term starts in the university, or after you finish your studies. Exceptions can be made for fresh graduates doing their practical training immediately after final examinations. Post-doctorate trainees will normally not be accepted.

You must apply to the IAESTE office in your home country. The application period usually lasts from September to early or mid-January and you are required to pay an application fee of US$50 (£27). You will then be provided with a list of details of all international internships and you have to submit an application update, resumé, transcripts, etc. Successful candidates will be notified by mid-March but placement has to be confirmed by the employer.

Abroad China, based in the USA, organises both exchange studies and placements for university students. It helps to arrange placements in many fields, including accounting, design, business administration, management, communications, computer science, consulting, education, English as a second language, finance, human resources, information systems, international relations, marketing, advertising, public relations, public policy, government, social work, law, hotel/restaurant hospitality and tourism. Short-term interns are usually unpaid but people staying with the organisation for more than six months usually receive a stipend. *Abroad China* will arrange accommodation, usually in universities or host families, for participants.

Useful Addresses

IAESTE United States, 10400 Little Patuxent Parkway, Suite 250, Columbia, MD 21044-3519, USA; ☎(1) 410 997 3069; fax (1) 410 997 5186; e-mail iaeste@aipt.org; http://aipt.org/subpages/iaeste – us/index.php.

Abroad China, Inc., 11250 Roger Bacon Drive, The Atrium Business Center, Unit 6, Reston, VA 20190 USA; ☎(1) 703 834 1118; fax (1) 703 834 7277; e-mail info@abroadchina.net; www.abroadchina.net.

VOLUNTARY WORK

Many local and overseas charitable organisations recruit volunteers to help people in need in China every year. China Charity Federation (CCF) is the largest China-based charitable organisation in China and it has a wide range of programmes to help victims of natural disasters, the elderly, orphanages, etc. Christian Salvation Service, a US-based group, currently operates an after-school study centre for elementary school children in Anhui province in China. It recruits volunteers to help these children with their homework, and you are also welcome to be a helper to build a small library for the study centre. Many Hong Kong and overseas charitable organisations send volunteers to mainland China to help people in need, as well as raising funds overseas. There are also some overseas organisations, such as the Red Cross and the Rotary Club, which have branches in China; you can contact them directly to be a volunteer.

Pollution is a serious problem in China and many environmental protection groups conduct projects or surveys about the situation and aim to arouse the people's concern. These non-profit organisations such as Earthwatch, World Wide Fund for Nature in Hong Kong, and Asia Soil Conservation Network (ASOCON), require many volunteers to carry out these projects and surveys in different parts of China and they welcome your participation.

Useful Addresses

China Charity Federation (CCF), No.9 South Street West, Huangchenggen, Beijing 100032; ☎(86) 010 6601 2629; fax (86) 010 6602 0903; http://www.chinacharity.cn.net/ccf/projects/index.html.

Christian Salvation Service, Programme Coordinator, 4390 Lindell Blvd. Suite 200, Sst Louis, Mo 63108-2735, USA; ☎(1) 314 535 5919.

Red Cross China, 8 Beixinqiao Santiao, Dongcheng District, Beijing 100007; ☎(86) 010 8402 5890; fax (86) 010 6406 0566; e-mail redcross@chineseredcross.org.cn; http://www.chineseredcross.org.cn/english/.

China Environmental Protection Foundation, No.1 Yuhuinanlu,Chaoyang District, Beijing 100029; ☎(86) 010 6494 7722 ext. 5111; fax (86) 010 6493 1438; e-mail cepfpound@public3.bta.net.cn; www.cepf.org.cn.

Rotary Club of Shanghai(Provisional), Shanghai P. O. Box # 03 – 05 D, 200003; e-mail shanghai@rotary3450.org; www.rotaryshanghai.org.

Earth Watch International, 3 Clock Tower Place, Suite 100, Box 75, Maynard, MA 01754 USA; ☎(1) 978 461 0081; fax (1) 978 461 2332; e-mail info@earthwatch.org; www.earthwatch.org.

Asia Soil Conservation Network (ASOCON), Department of Water and Soil Conservation, Minstry of Water Resources, Beijing 100053; ☎(86) 010 6320 2840; fax (86) 010 6320 2846; www.asocon.org.

Friends of the Earth, 2/F, SPA Centre, 53-55 Lockhart Road, Wanchai, Hong Kong; ☎(852) 2528 5588; www.foe.org.hk.

Green Power, Unit A, 7/F, Astoria Building, No.34 Ashley Road, Tsim Sha Tsui, Kowloon; ☎(852) 23142662; fax (852) 23142661; e-mail info@greenpower.org.hk; www.greenpower.org.hk.

HOPE Worldwide Hong Kong, Room 1910, Fortress Tower, 250 King's Road, North Point, Hong Kong; ☎(852) 2588 1291; fax (852) 2588 1306; e-mail enquiry@hopeww.org.hk; hk.hopeworldwide.org.

Medecins Sans Frontieres, Shop 5B, Laichikok Bay Garden, 272 Lai King Hill Road, Kowloon, Hong Kong; ☎(852) 2338 8277; fax (852) 2304 6081; e-mail office@msf.org.hk; www.msf.org.hk.

Oxfam, 17/F, China United Centre, 28 Marble Road, North Point, Hong Kong; ☎(852) 2520 2525; fax (852) 2527 6307; e-mail info@oxfam.org.hk; www.oxfam.org.hk.

The Community Chest of Hong Kong, Unit 1805 Harcourt House, 39 Gloucester Road, Wanchai, Hong Kong; ☎(852) 2599 6111; fax (852) 2506 1201; e-mail chest@commchest.org; www.commchest.org.

WWF Hong Kong, ☎(852) 2526 1011; fax (852) 2845 2734; e-mail wwf@wwf.org.hk; www.wwf.org.hk.

BUSINESS REPORTS ON MAJOR INDUSTRIES

Manufacturing

Manufacturing has always been the key industrial backbone in China and makes up 35% of GDP. Major manufacturing products include steel, automobiles, machinery, petrochemicals, home electrical appliances and computers. At the moment, 50% of the world's best known companies have set up joint ventures or foreign enterprises in China. Since China entered the World Trade Organisation (WTO) in 2001, manufacturing industry has continued to flourish and China is expected to become a major manufacturing centre within 5 to 10 years. In the past, manufacturers focused more on the practical aspect of their products, and the designs might not have been as attractive as those of other countries. Manufacturers nowadays understand that design is another important factor for increasing the competitiveness of products in the market and it is expected that future products will be well designed as well as practical.

The Automobile Industry. The automobile industry in China is looking good. Production of joint ventures accounts for 65% of the whole industry. Many of these joint ventures are formed by world-famous automobile companies. Some famous Chinese brands include: Santana, Jetta, Auti, Polo (partly owned by Volkswagen), Buick, Sail (partly owned by GM), Fukang (partly owned by Sitielong), Accord (partly owned by Honda) and Bluebird (partly owned by Nissan). Wholly domestically developed automobiles account for 25% of automobile production in China while imported automobiles account for only 10% of the market.

The number of automobiles sold in China in 2001 was 800,000, and it is predicted that the number of sales will double by 2005, and will even reach 3.2 million by 2010. As the automobile market is looking so strong, it is believed that more famous manufacturers will set up joint ventures in China. The scale of local automobile manufacturing will grow quickly and domestically made automobiles will be exported to other countries in the near future. In other words, manufacturing industries in China will no longer be restricted to the domestic market but will also penetrate the international market.

Machinery. Much of the lower-level and middle-level machinery and machine tools are produced in China. Domestic production of machinery accounts for 30% of the output of the industry while machine tools, manufactured by both domestic enterprises and joint ventures, was about 25%. Imported tools have a market share of 25% in the industry. More sophisticated machines are mainly imported from abroad and account for 20% of the market. In the next few years, Chinese enterprises will focus on the development of middle-level to high-level machinery. There will be more middle-level machines exported overseas whereas the export and production of low-level machines will be reduced.

Domestic Electrical Appliances. Importing home electrical appliances from abroad is not common in China as domestic products are in general much cheaper, but the quality is good. About 85% of home electrical appliances are made by local enterprises or joint ventures (they account for 40% and 45% respectively). Many of these home electrical appliances are exported to more than 50 countries and have a major market share overseas.

Communications and Telecom

In 2003, there was an imbalance between supply and demand for many telecom products, and it is expected that the growth in consumption will slow down. However, the expenditure on telecommunication products and digital cameras is now accelerating and these two will be the hot products of 2004. China has the largest telecom market in the world. The Ministry of Information Industry (MII) reported there were 421 million telephone users at the end of 2002, and this figure continued to climb in 2003 and early 2004. It is predicted that the fixed line telephone market will continue to expand and the growth will extend to the use of broadband services. Broadband customers will expand from big cities to the less wealthy northwest regions. The goal of the State's telecom development is to merge all national operators into Chinese Satellite, which holds satellite and internet licences. Currently, apart from Chinese Satellite, China Telecom, China Netcom, China Mobile and China Unicom are the four multi-functional operators.

Motorola and Nokia are still the leaders in the handset market. However, a serious oversupply problem will lead to sluggish growth in the sales of traditional handsets and will trigger a technological change in the market. The introduction of new cellular technology, for example, the third generation mobile, is likely to be the future direction in China. The $2.8 billion partnership agreement between the British giant, Vodafone, and China Mobile is an example of building a strategic partnership in this competitive market. The foreign partner contributes more advanced technology while the Chinese partner helps it to expand the business inside China. In order to secure their market share in this large market, many foreign companies are looking for strategic planners and it is believed that they will play an important role in the Chinese telecom industry.

Information Technology

In the foreseeable future, the production of computers, semiconductors and software components will play an important role in the Chinese economy. Besides, massive investment in domestic chip plants will continue to develop in China and large-scale imports of foreign chips will persist in the medium-term only.

Production of Computer Hardware. In order to attain the WTO requirements, China has signed the Information Technology Agreement (ITA), outlawing quotas for chips, computers and other high technology projects. It has also agreed to reduce tariffs on these products to zero by 2005. In the past few years, local computer makers have improved in many ways and they are now very competitive in the market. The number of imported computer products has fallen significantly and local products now occupy a larger market share.

Semiconductors. In recent years, foreign investment in the semiconductor industry has been increasing. Many multinational companies not only invest in computers but also in consumer electronics. Foreign and multinational investments are still the leaders in the semiconductor industry. Local companies are facing more difficulties, such as infrastructure constraints and lack of clean water, in developing the industry. The lack of technological research has also limited the development of the industry. For these reasons, local companies often have to seek foreign advice and investment to further develop their business. The National Labour Department encourages more foreign-technology experts to come to China to conduct research and to provide advice and professional training for local companies.

Electronic Parts in Vehicles. In 1980, the electronic parts used in vehicles in the global market was worth only US$4 billion. However, this figure exceeded US$100 billion in 2003. China sold over 3 million cars and became the fastest expanding market in 2003. It was also the fifth largest automobile manufacturer in the world, competing with industry giants such as Ford, General Motors and Volkswagen. Currently, the use of electronic parts in cars is also on the rise and it is predicted that in future 70% of car innovations will be in electronics. The China Centre for Information Industry Development (CCID) predicts that the industry will grow at a rate of 40% in 2004 and 2005.

Electronic Medical Equipment. The use of electronic medical equipment in China has been growing at a rate of about 30%. About 15% of the 175,000 items of equipment in use in the country date back to the 1970s and need to be replaced and updated. The demand for more advanced equipment has increased in recent years, especially after the SARS outbreak in 2003. It is estimated that the total investment in the market will expand from 27 billion *yuan* to 75 billion *yuan* in a few years.

Electronic Toys. The manufacturing of toys is growing rapidly in China. In order to improve the quality of products and increase their competitiveness in the market, information technology is used in this industry. There are more advanced video games and intelligent toys, such as electronic pets on the market and this will be the main development direction in the world's toy industry. It is expected that the growth of electronic toys will be at a rate of 40%.

Digital TV. It is believed that digitalisation of TV broadcasting will be the main trend throughout the world's broadcasting business. This trend will boost a rapid development of relevant software and information industries. The China Centre for Information Industry Development (CCID) estimates that this will generate a growth of over 1,000 billion *yuan* in the broadcasting industry and will become a major money spinner in China's future economy.

Import/Export

Imports and exports have been an important part of industry since the early 80s and they have further flourished since China entered the WTO in 2001. In 2003, foreign trade recorded the fastest percentage growth ever. The total import and export value was US$851.21 billion, an increase of 37.1% when compared to the previous year. Total exports increased by 34.6% and reached US$438.37 billion; total imports were US$412.84 billion, an increase of 39.9%. Even during the SARS outbreak, imports and exports continued to grow steadily and became an important support for the Chinese economy while many tertiary industries suffered losses. Japan, the United States and the EU are the three major trading partners of China and each exceeded US$100 billion in terms of trade volume. There was over 30% growth in trade volume with both Japan and the USA in 2003, and the growth in trading with the EU even reached 44%. Apart from the above three, Hong Kong, the Republic of Korea, ASEAN (Association of Southeast Asian Nations), Taiwan, Russia, Australia and Canada are also major trading partners.

Machinery and electronic products are major export items. They alone accounted for 51.9% of the total exports of the country and achieved 64.3% growth in 2003. Other export items include garments and accessories, textile yarn, fabrics and textile products, plastic products, shoes, furniture and toys. The import of primary goods showed a significant growth of 47.7% in the same year. Major imported items include iron ore, crude oil, soyabean, timber, machinery and equipment, chemical and chemical-related products, steel and motor vehicles. The import of steel and motor vehicles increased by 51.8% and 35.3% respectively in 2003 when compared with the previous year.

REGIONAL DEVELOPMENT

Southern China

Southern China refers to four areas: *Guangdong, Fujian, Hainan* provinces and *Guangxi* autonomous region. Lying along the coast, the southern part of China enjoys a good supply of natural resources and also warmer weather. Since these regions are along the coastline, easy transportation is an advantage for trading with foreign partners. Moreover, the government has set up many Special Economical Zones (SEZs), particularly in Guangdong province, to further boost the economic development of this area. The southern part is, on average, richer than other areas of China.

In this region, petrochemical, electronics and machinery industries, apart from imports and exports, contribute a great deal to economic development. In Fujian, apart from the above-mentioned industries, construction, forestry, fisheries and aquiculture and textiles are also the pillar industries. The Guangxi government focuses on the development of heavy industries such as hydropower, metal and building materials. In recent years, the Hainan government, in contrast, has focused more on light industry such as electronics and information technology. It has also become a popular tourist destination in the last decade, especially among Asians.

Guangdong is one of the most important business areas in China. Economic development in Guangdong mainly depends on the Special Economic Zones (SEZs), which includes Shantou, Guangzhou, Shenzhen, Chuanzhan and Dongguan. The Guangdong area benefits from its geographical proximity to the Pearl River Delta, which is an important connection to Hong Kong and Macau. In past decades, the development of this region has relied heavily on imports and exports, which account for 74% of the total GDP in this area. However, Guangdong region has been overshadowed by the eastern coastal regions, especially Shanghai over the past five years. Many foreign investors have started their businesses in Shanghai or moved their base there in the last decade. In order to encourage more foreign investors to develop their business to maintain an impressive economic growth in this area, the Chinese government offers more investment incentives to promote the development of small and medium-sized enterprises (SMEs). These now significantly help to support the economy in the Guangdong area. According to statistics from the local industrial and commercial department, there has been an significant increase in the number of privately-owned enterprises since 2002.

The GDP in Guangdong scored over a trillion *yuan* (US$122 billion/£71 billion) in 2003, increasing by 13.6% when compared to that of 2002, and was the highest in the last eight years. The Guangdong area is once again attracting a lot of foreign investment, in particular in the industrial sector which contributed 61.7% to the GDP of the province. Many factories, both locally or foreign owned, have grown rapidly since China joined the World Trade Organisation (WTO) in 2001.

Currently, skilled people who specialize in hi-technology management, software development, electronic, chemical, pharmacy, trade, textile, audio-visual products and toys are highly sought after in this area.

Useful Websites

Job168.com, http://www.job168.com/index.asp or http://www.job168.com/hunternew/aboutusenglish.asp. This website provides the latest information on job vacancies in the Guangdong area. Some of the jobs offered are from big companies such as Coca Cola, Philips, Nokia, Media, Matel, Newell Rubbermaid. It also specializes in searching senior management vacancies for their clients.

Eastern China

Eastern China, including *Shangdong, Jiangsu* and *Zhejiang* provinces has developed rapidly in the last two decades. Areas along the Yangtze River delta, including Nanjing, Ningbo and Shanghai, are important for the economic development of

China. The Chinese government provides a number of investment incentives in order to attract more foreign companies to these areas. As with the southern part, eastern China is particularly desirable for trading because it is along the coastline and has many ports, which make it convenient for trading with other countries.

Eastern China is probably the most important region for industrial development in the whole country. Jiangsu, Shangdong and Zhejiang were the second, third and fourth largest industrial production bases in China in 2002, just after Guangdong. It is interesting that eastern China was mainly engaged in light industries in the 80s and early 90s. However, heavy industries such as automobiles, machinery, petroleum and chemical industries have started to dominate the market and have become a major support for the local economies. They were estimated to account for 60% of the total income of the region. Foreign investment in these regions increased by more than 30% in 2003. Jiangsu is particularly favoured by Taiwanese investors while many Hong Kong investors set up their businesses in Zhejiang. The regions have become important IT, telecommunication and electronics manufacturing bases in recent years. Kunshan and Wujiang in Jiangsu and the Hangzhou Bay area in Zhejiang are major manufacturing areas for the above-mentioned industries. These areas are near to Shanghai but the labour costs are comparatively lower. Eastern China is also famous for beautiful scenery. Cities such as Hangzhou, Suzhou, Jinan and Qingdao are popular destinations for tourists. Income from tourism and souvenirs, such as handicrafts and silk, is also important to local economic development.

Western China

Western China includes *Yunnan, Guizhou, Sichuan, Shannxi, Gansu* and *Qinghai* provinces as well as three autonomous regions, *Tibet, Xinjiang* and *Ningxia*. The implementation of the 'Go West' policy by the Chinese government at the beginning of the 21st century underlines the intensification of its efforts to accelerate the development of the western part of China. Under this strategic development, an increase of capital investment in infrastructure, the provision of favourable investment incentives, widened scope for foreign investment and investment in human capital (labour) are being adopted to create a more conducive investment environment in western cities, such as Urumqi, Chengdu and Xi'an. Currently, over 80 of the world's top 500 companies such as Motorola, Microsoft, Compaq, Itochu, Walmart and Enron have already invested or decided to invest in western China. Moreover, the region is rich in energy and mineral resources that are the backbone of industrial development. Sichuan, Shannxi and Xinjiang have the three largest natural gas fields in China, amounting to 61% of the country's total. The west also has abundant hydropower resources to generate electricity to support domestic consumption as well as satisfying the demands of the coastal areas. The 'west-to-east' natural gas transmission and the 'west-to-east' electricity transmission are two major projects being carried out now and will provide major income for the west in the coming decades. The exploration and development of the western region, apart from economic benefits to the country itself, also implies more employment opportunities in the region. There will be more important positions for foreign technological experts to provide advice and support for the western development projects.

The building of major roads is one of the biggest projects sponsored by the Chinese government in the region. The highway network will connect the west and major cities in the east. 47 roads and bridges will be built in or around Chongqing involving a total investment of 200 billion *yuan* (US$24 billion/£14 billion). The construction of a complete new highway network will connect Chongqing to Guizhou, Ghongqing to Changsha, Chongqing to Wanzhou, Changshou to Fuling, and Chongqing to Hechuan. At the same time, a new 1700km long highway will be constructed in Shaanxi, which will connect Baotou to Beihai, Xi'an to Hefei, and Yinchuan to Wuhan National Trunks. In addition to the above two projects, the current Sichuan highway will be extended from 1000 km to 2000 km by 2005. It is estimated that the total cost for the highway network project will be around 700 to 800 billion *yuan*.

Apart from the highway network project, rail transportation also plays an important role in the development of the west. The Chinese government is currently constructing a railway to connect the east and the west as well as improving the connections between the western regions, such as Tibet and Qinghai. Rail engineers who are specialized in modernising rail networks and high-speed rail are very much in demand.

Apart from the governmental projects, there is also a considerable increase in private projects in the west. Many of these private projects are connected to agriculture, medicine and environmental protection, and employment opportunities in these areas are wide open.

Tourism is going to be another important industry in western China. The State Development Planning Commission, National Tourism Administration and Western Region Development Office of the State Council have decided to explore and to develop several plans in northwestern and southwestern China in 2002 and 2003. Some tourism plans are currently under discussion and areas such as Shannxi, Qinghai, Gansu, Inner Mongolia, Ningxia, and Xinjiang would benefit from this. It is agreed that key areas to be developed should all be around the Silk Road. Some of the potential routes are:

- The north and the south flanks of the Silk Road between Xi'an and Baoji.
- The Tianshui – Lanzhou – Wuwei – Zhangye route.
- The Hulun Buri – Heilongjiang – Jilian route and Zhangjiakou – Chengde – Chifeng – Hohhot route.
- The Urumqi – Korla – Kaxgar route.
- The Baoji – Pingliang – Liupanshan – Yinchuan route.

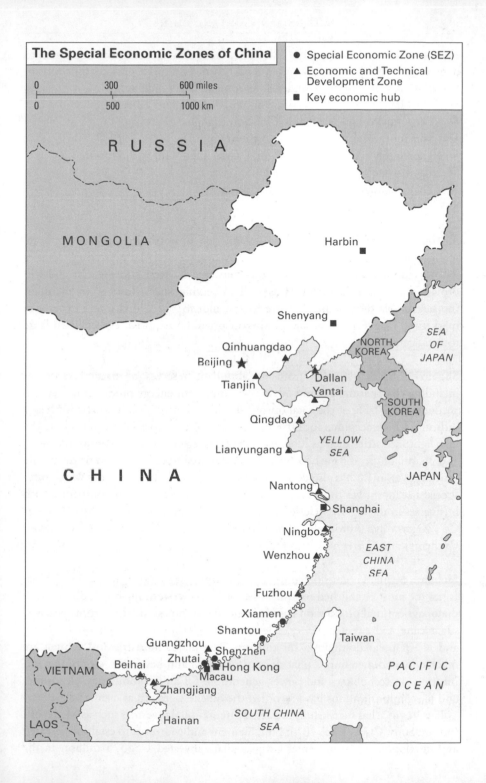

The Special Economic Zones of China

- ● Special Economic Zone (SEZ)
- ▲ Economic and Technical Development Zone
- ■ Key economic hub

0   300   600 miles
0   500   1000 km

RUSSIA

MONGOLIA

Harbin

Shenyang

Qinhuangdao
Beijing
Tianjin
Dallan
Yantai
Qingdao
Lianyungang

CHINA

NORTH KOREA

SEA OF JAPAN

SOUTH KOREA

YELLOW SEA

JAPAN

Nantong
Shanghai
Ningbo
Wenzhou

EAST CHINA SEA

Fuzhou
Xiamen
Shantou
Guangzhou
Zhutai
Beihai
Macau
Zhangjiang
Hainan
Shenzhen
Hong Kong

VIETNAM

LAOS

Taiwan

PACIFIC OCEAN

SOUTH CHINA SEA

Apart from the areas around the Silk Road, the southwest is another key region to benefit from the current government and private enterprise projects for tourism. Seven projects are currently under development. They include:

- ○ The Shangri-la route covering Yunnan, Sichuan and Tibet.
- ○ The Chongqing – Sichuan – Guizhou triangle.
- ○ The Southeastern Guizhou – northern Guilin.
- ○ The Guilin – Yangsuo – Wuzhou – Zhaoqing – Guangzhou route.
- ○ The Lancang – Mekong River route.
- ○ The Fenghuang City in western Hunan.
- ○ The Three Gorges project.

As tourism develops in the region, many job opportunities related to hotel management and catering are created. Moreover, better daily catering facilities will be required on long train journeys between the west and the east and will provide opportunities for chefs as well as serving staff. Besides, to maintain the sustainable development of the tourist industry in China, more experts in marketing, management and administration will be required, especially in large tourist agencies.

Shaanxi. Shaanxi benefits from its abundant reserves of natural resources including coal, natural gas and oil. It is an important energy production base and accounts for 20.4% of the total output. Besides, Shaanxi is also a base for heavy industry, which accounts for 60% of Shaanxi's total industrial output. None the less, light industries such as food and beverages, electronics, telecommunications and pharmaceuticals have become more and more important in recent years. The central government has also developed economic and industrial zones which offer special tax incentives to encourage foreign investment. Famous companies with businesses in the region include Xi'an-Janssen Pharmaceutical Ltd, Xi'an Aircraft Co., Xi'an-Volvo Automobiles, Shaanxi Changling Refrigeration, Metro (from Germany) and Carrefour (from France).

Sichuan. Sichuan is considered to have the strongest economy in western China. It has the most established industrial sector in the western region, and is also the major agricultural production base for rice, wheat, rapeseed, citrus fruit, peaches, sugar cane and sweet potatoes. Moreover, it is famous for its natural scenery and is a popular destination for tourism. The major industries in Sichuan are machinery and metallurgy, pharmaceuticals, food and beverages, electronics and information technology and power generation. Of all the industries, electronics and telecommunications have recorded the quickest growth at over 27.8%.

The province has successfully attracted international investors such as Microsoft, Onsun, Sony, Cisco, Intel, IBM, Fuji, Siemens and Motorola to establish research and development centres. Intel Chipset Plant invested US$375 million in the province at the end of 2003 and became the biggest investor in Chengdu.

Yunnan. Tourism is the most important industry in Yunnan which is one of the most popular tourist centres in western China. There are many hotels with a good reputation and the gross income of the tourism industry reached 29 billion *yuan* in 2002, accounting for 13% of the province's total GDP. Tobacco is an important crop in Yunnan, and accounted for 36.7% of the province's total output in 2002.

Tibet Autonomous Region. The strong cultural and religious atmosphere has made Tibet into a popular tourist destination in China. The total income from tourism is expected to reach 1.55 billion *yuan* in 2005 and accounts for 10% of the total GDP of the region. In order to strengthen tourism in Tibet, some new routes and destinations will be opened to tourists. These new destinations include six different parts of Tibet and five neighbouring provinces in Nepal. There will also be three overland circular routes, namely the Lhasa-Nyingchi-Shannon-Lhasa circuit, the Lhasa-Ngari-Nagqu-Lhasa circuit and the Lhasa-Nagqu-Qamdo-Nyingchi-Lhasa circuit. Apart from tourism, Tibetan medicine, biological products and health food, farm and animal produce processing and traditional handicrafts, mining and building materials are other important industries.

Xinjiang Uygur Autonomous Region. Similar to Shaanxi, Xinjiang is also rich in energy resources. It has the largest reserves of oil, natural gas and coal in the country. Its coal and oil reserves reach 27 million tons (40% of the country's total) and 30 billion tons respectively. Crude oil output reached 20.2 million tons in 2002 which was the third highest in the country. Tarim, Junggar, and Turpan-Hami basins are the major sources for oil and gas supplies.

Oil and petrochemicals, food and beverages, textiles, metallurgy, building materials, and electric power are the six pillar industries of Xinjiang, which account for 85.2% of the total output of the region with the petroleum industry alone accounting for 63.9%. Light industries, such as textiles and garments (especially wool and cashmere), leather processing, papermaking, sugar refining and carpet weaving, are getting more popular. As stated in the 10th Five-year plan, the Xinjiang government will accelerate the development of information, biotech, energy and environmental protection industries in the coming years. Foreign investors are encouraged to participate in the development of agriculture, food processing, textiles, petrochemicals, mining, building materials and environmental protection.

Useful Website
China Xi'an Talent, http://www.zxrs.com/ (Chinese only).

Central China

Central China includes *Shanxi, Henan, Hebei, Anhui, Hunan* and *Hubei* provinces. This region borders the Yellow River which is famous for its rich cultural heritage. The central part, when compared to other regions of China, has less investment incentives and it is not usually the first choice for investors to start their business in.

The central region actually has many social-economic advantages making it a desirable development area. The area is rich in natural resources, which is good for agriculture and industrial development. Moreover, being centrally located, it is well connected to all other areas giving it logistic advantages. The large population of the area also provides enough manpower and low wages. However, since workers, in general, receive very little or even no education, they do not have the knowledge and experience to qualify for important management roles. Consequently, expertise in management, finance and marketing will be major advantages when looking for jobs in this area.

Useful Website

China Career, http://www.chinacareer.com. The website offers a job listing database in both Chinese and English.

Northeast and the North

The northeast region comprises *Heilongjiang, Jilin* and *Liaoning* provinces and the north region consists of Inner Mongolia. In northeast China, half of the region is covered by forest and the timber industry is the backbone of the local economy. It is said that there are 'three treasures' in northeast China, namely milk, pilose deer antlers and ginseng, and they also play important roles in the local economies. In order to avoid further excessive exploitation, in 2003 the Chinese government announced plans to revitalize the region and build up an 'eco-economic'. The idea of 'eco-economic' is to satisfy current demand without threatening the supplies of future generations. It is no longer permitted to cut large amounts of timber and forestry and timber companies are asked to shift their sources of timber regularly to provide time for the trees to regenerate.

Apart from timber, the northeast region is also rich in coal, iron ore, boron, magnesite, diamonds and jade. Primary industry accounts for about 10% of the total income of the region. As with many other regions, secondary industry is the major source of income. Petrochemical and metallurgical and machinery and electronics are the chief industries in the region, particular in Liaoning province. Tobacco processing has recorded a rapid growth of over 15% in recent years. Other industries such as beverages, garments and textiles, furniture, smelting and pressing of ferrous metals, transport equipment, etc, also recorded a desirable growth in 2003.

Inner Mongolia. This autonomous region is located in the north of China and is reported to be the poorest region of all. However, the secondary and tertiary industries in Inner Mongolia are actually growing. There was a 66% growth in foreign investment in 2001and the annual GDP growth was about 10% in the last few years. Farm production and processing, electricity, animal husbandry, and metallurgy and chemicals are the major industries to support the local economy.

MUNICIPALITIES

The four municipalities, include *Shanghai*, *Beijing*, *Tianjin* and *Chongqing*, and are directly under the control of the central government and enjoy privileges in economic development which may not be found in other provinces. The idea of setting up municipalities is to help these regions grow rapidly and hence stimulate the development of the surrounding areas and improve the economic development of the whole country.

SHANGHAI
Population: 13.2 million
Area: 6,340 square kilometres
GDP (per capita): 40, 6678 *yuan*
Growth in GDP (2003): 12%
Shanghai has probably been the fastest growing region over the last decade, especially in commercial development. Foreign investment in Shanghai increased rapidly in the last decade as more tax incentives were provided to investors for setting up their enterprises, especially in the New Pudong Area. Even though tertiary industry accounts for about half of the GDP, industry still plays an important part of the economic development. Major industries in Shanghai include automobiles, petrochemicals and fine chemicals, fine steel and iron, equipment complexes, biomedicine, and electronic information, in which automobiles, equipment complexes and electronic information are growing at rapid rates. They will dominate the GDP in a few years time.

   In Shanghai, expertise in finance, management and marketing will give advantages when looking for jobs. Many companies also seek native English speakers to improve the English standards of staff. It is not difficult to get a teaching job in the the area. Some people may even approach you on the street or at train stations asking you to teach English in their organisations.

Useful Websites
Government Office of Shanghai Municipality, 19 Gao an Road, Shanghai; ☎(86) 021 63212810; http://www.shanghai.gov.cn.
Pudong Human Resources, http://www.pdhr.com/asp/default.asp.
Shanghai Human Resources Market, http://www.hr.net.cn/index.jsp.
Talent Shanghai Co.Ltd., http://www.talentshanghai.com/. This website specializes

in the recruitment of middle to high ranking managerial officers in fields of consumer goods, IT, telecommunications, hi-technology, manufacturing, logistics, finance and insurance, construction and real estates.
Shanghai Job Bank, http://www.shanghaijob.com/.

BEIJING
Population: 13.8 million
Area: 16,800 square kilometres
GDP (per capita): 28,449 *yuan*
Growth in GDP (2003): 10%
Being the capital of the country, Beijing has always been a first choice for investment. Its tertiary sector is the largest in the whole country and accounts for more than 60% of the GDP. It is believed that the tertiary sector will further expand in the future as many international enterprises in finance, IT and telecommunication show their interest in expanding their businesses in Beijing, especially after it was named as the host for the Olympic Games 2008. In recent years, Beijing has undergone a series of reconstructions and developments to prepare itself for the 2008 event and the improvements, such as better transport, makes it a more desirable place for doing business and a significant increase foreign investment has been recorded. Industry also contributes a great deal to the economy. Heavy industries dominate and account for over 70% in the secondary sector and major industries in Beijing include electronics and telecommunications equipment, chemicals, automobiles, machinery, metallurgy and food making. The future focus of development in this area is on hi- tech industries such as electronics, information technology, biological engineering, pharmaceuticals and new materials. Currently, Beijing's gross output value in the technical market makes up nearly 15% of the national total. Retailing is developing fast in Beijing with many international enterprises such as B&Q, Walmart, Ikea, Metro and 7-11 setting up branches in the area. The B&Q in Beijing is even bigger than the largest branch in the UK, its home country.

Useful Address
Government Office of Beijing Municipality, 2 Zhengyi Road, Dongcheng District, Beijing, 10001; ☎(86) 010 6519 2233/(86) 010 6512 8080/(86) 010 6308 8467; e-mail szfbgt@bjgov.gov.cn; http://www.beijing.gov.cn.

TIANJIN
Population: 10.4 million
Area: 11,300 square kilometres
GDP (per capita): 22,380 *yuan*
Growth in GDP (2003): 13%
Tianjin is the biggest mobile phone manufacturing base in China. It has been estimated that four out of every ten cell phones used in the country

are manufactured in Tianjin. This has been the result of investment by large international telecommunication enterprises such as Motorola, Samsung and Sanyo. Apart from telecommunications, Tianjin is also a popular centre for industrial development. Its gross industrial output, of State-owned enterprises and private enterprises together, contributed 332 billion *yuan* in 2002, the third largest among all provincial capitals and other cities, after Shanghai and Shenzhen. The four major industries include electronics, automobiles, metallurgy and petrochemicals. Its tertiary sector is expanding rapidly as well. Transportation and storage, trades and catering services, banking and insurance, and real estate are the four fastest growing service industries. Exports from Tianjin were declining over the last few years, which is unusual in China. However, imports grew at a rate of 37% in the same period. Over the past five years, imports from Korea, Taiwan, Germany and France have had the fastest growth.

Useful Address

Government Office of Tianjin Municipality, #123 29th Fl., Jin Rong Da Xia, Wei Di Dao, Hexi Qu, Tianjin City; ☎(86) 022 2330 5555/(86) 022 2840 1558; e-mail webmaster@tianjin.gov.cn; http://www.tianjin.gov.cn.

CHONGQING
Population: 32.5 million
Area: 82,400 square kilometre
GDP (per capita): 6,347 *yuan;*
Growth in GDP (2003): 11%

Chongqing is the youngest but also the largest amongst the four municipalities. It is one of the most important industrial bases in China, especially in the automobile industry. Other major industries include iron and steel, military production, transport equipment, metallurgical products and chemicals, of which transport equipment accounts for more than 37% of the total industrial output. Many international companies have set up their businesses in Chongqing in recent years. Big names include Nokia, Ericsson, American Standard, Honda, Suzuki, Isuzu, Yamaha, Mobil, Hutchison Whampao and Samsung. Unlike the other three municipalities, where the tertiary sector is the main focus for development, the government plans to further boost Chongqing's secondary development as well as encouraging steady growth in the tertiary sector. The government aims to attract more foreign investment in automobiles, hydropower stations and construction and real estate, in the next few years.

Useful Address

Government Office of Chongqing Municipality, Renmin Road, Yuzhong District, Chongqing; ☎(86) 023 6385 4444; e-mail cqgov@cq.gov.cn; http://www.cq.gov.cn.

Other Useful Websites

http://www.china.org.cn/; includes a brief introduction to each province, autonomous region and municipality (under 'Province Wide').

MAJOR EMPLOYERS

Accounting

Ernst & Young (Beijing), Level 16, Tower E3, The Towers, Oriental Plaza, No.1 East Chang An Ave. Dong Cheng District, Beijing 100738; ☎(86) 010 6524 6688; fax (86) 010 8518 8298; www.ey.com.

Ernst & Young (Shanghai), 12/F Shartex Plaza, 88 Zun Yi Road South, Shanghai 20036; ☎(86) 021 6219 1219; fax (86) 021 6219 3219; www.ey.com.

Ernst & Young (Guangzhou), Room 1103, Main Office Tower Guangdong, International Building, 339 Huan Shi Dong Road, Guangzhou 510098; ☎(86) 020 8331 2788; fax (86) 020 8337 2(86)8; www.ey.com.

Ernst & Young (Chengdu), Chengdu: Suit 1203, 56 Du Yuan Street, Chengdu 610016; ☎(86) 028 8660 6111; fax (86)028 8660 6100; www.ey.com.

KPMG (Beijing), 8/F, Office Tower E2, Oriental Plaza, 1 East Chang An Avenue, Dong Cheng District, Beijing 100738; ☎(86) 010 8518 5000; fax (86) 010 8518 5111; http://www.kpmg.com.cn/.

KPMG (Shanghai), 50/F, Plaza 66, 1266 Nanjing West Road, Shanghai 200040; ☎(86) 021 5359 4666; fax (86) 021 6288 1889; http://www.kpmg.com.cn/.

KPMG (Guangzhou), Room 2907 Guangzhou International Electronics Tower, 403 Huan Shi Dong Road, Guangzhou 510095; ☎(86) 020 8732 2832; fax (86) 020 8732 2883; http://www.kpmg.com.cn/.

KPMG (Shenzhen), Room 1007, Shung Hing Square, Di Wang Commercial Centre, 5002 Shennan Road East, Shenzhen 518008; ☎(86) 0755 8246 3398; fax (86) 0755 8246 2896; http://www.kpmg.com.cn/.

PricewaterhouseCoopers (Beijing), 18/F North Tower, Beijing Kerry Center, 1 Guang Hua Road, Chaoyang District, Beijing 100020; ☎(86) 010 6561 2233; fax (86) 010 8529 9000; http://www.pwccn.com/home/eng/.

PricewaterhouseCoopers (Shanghai), 12/F Shui On Plaza, 333 Huai Hai Zhong Road, Shanghai 200021; ☎(86) 021 6386 3388; fax (86) 021 6386 3300; http://www.pwccn.com/home/eng/.

PricewaterhouseCoopers (Tianjin), 17th Floor, The Exchange Tower One, 189 Nanjing Road, Heping District, Tianjin 300051; ☎(86) 022 2330 6789; fax (86) 022 2339 3662; http://www.pwccn.com/home/eng/.

Deloitte, 11 Deloitte Tower, Sun Dong An Plaza, 138 Wangfujing Dajie, Beijing 100006; ☎(86) 010 6528 1599; fax (86) 010 6528 1598; www.deloitte.com.

Ernst &Young, Rua de Xangai, no. 175, Edificio da Associacao Comercial de Macau, 14 andar F, Macau; ☎852 2629 3882; eee.ey.com.

KPMG (Macau), 23/F D, Bank of China Building, Avenida Doutor Mario

Soares, Caixa Postal 701, Macau; ☎(853) 781 092; fax (853) 781 096; www.kpmg.com.cn.

PricewaterhouseCoopers (Macau), Avenida Doutor Mario Soares, Bank of China Building, 28/F Unit C, Macau; tel (853) 7995 111; fax (853) 7995 222; www.pwccn.com.

Airlines

Air China, e-mail master@mail.airchina.com.cn; www.airchina.com.cn.

China Eastern, www.cea.online.sh.cn.

China Southern, ☎(86) 020 8668 2000; e-mail webmaster@cs-air.com; www.cs-air.com.

China Northern, www.cna.ln.cninfo.net.

China Southwest, ☎(86) 028 8666 8080; fax (86) 028 8665 6991; e-mail cturrsz@cswa.com; www.cswa.com.

China Northwest, ☎800 840 2299; fax (86) 029 8426 1622; e-mail belinda917@163.net; www.cnwa.com.

Civil Aviation Administration of China (CAAC), 155 Dongsi Xidajie, Beijing100710; ☎(86) 010 6409 1114; www.caac.gov.cn.

Dragon Air Ticketing Office, Room 4609 – 4611, 46/F., COSCO Tower, 183 Queen's Road Central, Hong Kong; ☎(852) 2868 6777; fax (852) 2810 0370; www.dragonair.com.

Air Macau, Novos Aterros do Porto Exterior, Dynasty Plaza, Macau; ☎(853) 396 5555; fax (853) 396 5666; e-mail airmacau@airmacau.com.mo; www.airmacau.com.mo.

Banks

Bank of China, 1 Fuxingmen Nei Dajie, Bejing 100818; ☎(86) 010 6659 6688; fax (86) 010 6601 4024; www.bank-of-china.com.

The People's Bank of China, No.32 ChengFang Street, XiCheng district, Beijing 100800; ☎(86)-010 6619 4114; e-mail master@pbc.gov.cn; http://www.pbc.gov.cn/.

Bank of Communications, 188 Yin Cheng Road Central, Shanghai 200120; ☎(86) 021 5878 1234; fax (86) 021 5888 0559; e-mail enquiry@bankcomm.com.hk; www.bankcomm.com.hk.

China Minsheng Bank, ☎95568; e-mail service@cmbc.com.cn; www.cmbc.com.cn.

China Construction Bank, 4 Men No.28 West Dajie, Xuanwumen, Beijing 100053; ☎(86) 010 6360 3660; fax (86) 010 6360 3194; www.ccbhk.com.

Hua Xia Bank, 111 Xidianbei Dajie, Beijing; ☎(86) 010 6615 1199; fax (86) 010 6618 8484; e-mail webmaster@hxb.cc; www.hxb.com.cn.

China Merchants Bank, 156 Fuxingmennei Dajie, Xicheng District, Beijing 100036; ☎(86) 010 6642 6868; www.cmbchina.com.

Industrial and Commercial Bank of China, 55# Fuxingmennei Street, Xicheng District, Beijing 100032; ☎95588; e-mail webmaster@icbc.com.cn; www.icbc.com.cn.

Construction

ARUP (Beijing), Rm 3610, 36/F Jing Quang, Centre Hu, Jia Lou Chao Yang Qu, Beijing 100020; ☎(86) 010 6597 3788; fax (86) 010 6597 3738; e-mail webmail@arup.com.

ARUP (Shanghai), Unit 01-07, 38F Lippo Plaza, 222 Huai Hai Road (M), Shanghai 200021; ☎(86) 021 5396 6633; fax: (86) 021 5396 5578; e-mail webmail@arup.com.

ARUP (Shenzhen), 34th Floor, Development Centre Building, Renminnan Road, Shenzhen; ☎(86) 0755 519 8187; fax (86) 0755 225 5168; e-mail webmail@arup.com.

Atkins Faithful & Gould Ltd (Shanghai), Unit 607, Shanghai Overseas Chinese Mansion, No.129 Yan An West Road, Shanghai 20004; ☎(86) 021 6249 1498/ (86) 021 6249 1499; fax (86) 021 6249 0806; e-mail barry.piper@fgould.com.hk.

Atkins Faithful & Gould Ltd (Beijing), Unit1105, The Exchange Bejing of China Merchants Centre, No.118 Jian Guo Lu Yi, Chao Yang District, Beijing 100022; ☎(86) 010 6567 7933; fax (86) 010 6567 7930; e-mail beijing@atkins.com.cn.

Atkins Faithful & Gould Ltd (Shenzhen), Unit 8-16, 53/F Shun Hing Square, Di Wang Commercial Center, Shenzhen; ☎(86) 0755 8246 2109; fax (86) 0755 2588 2563; e-mail shenzhen@atkins.com.cn.

Industrial Consultancy Services

Watson Wyatt (Beijing), 1 Guanghua Road, 22/F North Tower Beijing Kerry Centre, Chaoyang District, Beijing 100020 PRC; ☎(86) 010 8529 9071; fax (86) 010 8529 9070, e-mail david.cheng@watsonwyatt.com.

Watson Wyatt (Shanghai), 1515 Nanjing West Road, 11th Floor Kerry Centre, Shanghai 200040; ☎(86) 021 5298 6888; fax (86) 021 5298 6889; e-mail Michele.Lee@watsonwyatt.com.

Watson Wyatt (Shenzhen), Rm1821, Kerry centre, 2008 Ren Min Nan Road, Shenzhen 518001; ☎(86) 0755 8236 4888; fax (86) 0755 8236 4668; e-mail Michele.Lee@watsonwyatt.com.

McKinsey, http://www.mckinsey.com/locations/greaterchina/opportunities/.

Information Technology

IBM, http://www-900.ibm.com/cn/employment/index.shtml.

Dell, http://www1.ap.dell.com/content/topics/topic.aspx/ap/topics/careers/cn/ encn?c=cn&l=en&s=gen.

HP, http://www.jobs.hp.com/content/search/search.asp?Lang=ENen&Region=

AP&area=CN.

Insurance

American International Assurance Co (Bermuda) Ltd, AIA Building, 17 Zhong Shan Dong Yi Road, Shanghai 200002; ☎(86) 021 6321 6698/(86) 800 820 3588; e-mail AIA – TEC@mail.online.sh.cn; http://www.aigchina.com/aiash/ encontent/aiash – firstpage – en.htm.

AXA Asia Pacific Holdings Ltd, Beijing Representative Office, No. 408 Office Building, Beijing Hotel, 8 Xinzhong Xi Jie Gongti Bei Lu, Beijing, 100027; ☎(86) 010 6500 7788 ext 7497/(86) 010 6500 7393; fax (86) 010 6500 7390; www.axa-chinaregion.com.

Royal & Sun Alliance Insurance (Shanghai) Ltd, 9th floor, HSBC Tower, 101 Ying Cheng East Road, Pudong New Area, Shanghai, China 200120; ☎(86) 021 6841 1999; fax (86) 021 6841 2700; e-mail rsashang@uninet.com.cn; http://www.royalsunalliance.com.cn/.

ING General Insurance International Limited, 37th Floor, World Trade Tower No. 25 Tong Xing Street Zhongshan District, Dalian 116001; ☎(86) 0411 2530 881; fax (86) 0411 2530 877; www.ing-cap.com.cn.

New York Life Insurance Worldwide Ltd, No.3601, 36/F Jinmao Building, 88 Shiji Dadao, New Pudong Area, Shanghai 200121; ☎800 820 5882; e-mail p – r@haiernewyorklife.com.cn; www.haiernewyorklife.com.cn.

Law

Allen & Overy (Beijing), Suite 522, China World Tower 2, No.1 Jian Guo Men Wai Avenue, Beijing 10004; ☎(86) 010 6505 8800; fax (86) 010 6505 6677; http://www.allenovery.com/asp/careers.asp?officeID=3314&languageID=0.

Allen & Overy (Shanghai), Plaza 66 Suite 5810, 1266 Nanjing Xi Road, Shanghai 200040; ☎(86) 021 6288 3099; fax (86) 021 6288 2099; http://www.allenovery.com/asp/careers.asp?officeID=3314&languageID=0.

Claydon, Gescher Associates, 12-1 CITIC Building, 19 Jiangguomenwai Dajie, Beijing 100004; ☎(86) 010 6500 6552; fax (86) 010 6592 2053; e-mail: cgaltd@public.bta.net.cn; http://www.cgaprc.com.

Baker & McKenzie, Suite 3401, China World Tower 2, China World Trade Centre, 1 Jianguomenwai Dajie, Beijing 10004; ☎(86) 010 6505 0591; fax (86) 010 6505 2309; http://www.bakernet.com/BakerNet/Careers/Current+Openings/ default.htm.

Barlow Lyde & Gilbert, Heida Donegan, Beijing; ☎852 2840 2618; e-mail hdonegan@blg.com.hk; http://www.blg.co.uk/careers/default.asp

Cameron McKenna, China World Tower 2, No1. Jianguomenwai Road, Chaoyang District, Beijing 100004; ☎(86) 010 6289 6363; fax (86) 010 6505 5593; http:www.law-now.com.

Clifford Chance, Room 3326, China World Tower 1, No 1 Jianguomenwai

Dajie, Beijing 100004; ☎(86) 010 6505 9018; fax (86) 010 6505 9028; http://www.cliffordchance.com.

Freshfields Bruckhaus Deringer, 3705 China World Tower Two, 1 Jianguomenwai Avenue, Beijing 100004; ☎(86) 010 6505 3448; fax (86) 010 6505 7783; http://www.freshfields.com/en.asp.

Herbert Smith, Units 1410-1415. China World Tower, 1 Jianguomenwai Ave, Beijing 100004; ☎(86) 010 6505 6512; fax (86) 010 6505 6516; http://www.herbertsmith.com/.

Lovell White Durrant, Units 3-4, Level 3, Office Tower W3, The Towers, Oriental Plaza, No1 East Chang An Avenue, Dongcheng District, Beijing, 100738; ☎(86) 010 8518 4000; fax (86) 010 8518 1656; http://www.lovells.com/home.jsp.

Simmons & Simmons, 33F, Plaza 66, 1266 Nanjing Road West, Shanghai 200040; ☎(86) 021 6249 0700; fax (86) 021 6249 0706; http://www.simmons-simmons.com.

Manufacturing

Texas Instruments China Inc., http://www.ti.com.cn/job/.

Shanghai Apollo-Fudan High-Tech Industry Company Limited, 335 Guo Ding Road, Shanghai 200433; ☎(86) 021 6564 8661; http://www.apollo-fudan.com/.

China Display Company Limited, 11F, Shanghai Tech-Innovation Centre. No.168 Qinzhou Road, Shanghai 200233; ☎(86) 021 6484 9898; e-mail chinadisplay@online.sh.cn; http://www.cn-display.com.

Media.

CCTV, 11B Fuxing Road, Media Center, Beijing, China 100038; ☎(86) 010 6850 6510; e-mail cctv-international@mail.cctv.com; www.cctv.com.

Star TV (Beijing Office), Unit 5-10, Level 9, Tower E3, The Towers, Oriental Plaza, No.1, East Chang An Ave, Dong Cheng District, Beijing 100738; ☎(86) 010 8518 8500; fax (86) 010 8518 8501; e-mail star@newscorp.com.cn; www.startv.com.

Star TV (Shanghai office), No.186, North Shan Xi Road, Shanghai 200041; ☎(86) 021 6218 3298; fax (86) 021 6218 5208; e-mail sstar@newscorp.com.cn; www.startv.com.

China Radio International (English Service), China Radio International, Beijing, 100040; ☎(86) 010 6889 1652/(86) 010 6889 1617; fax (86) 010 6889 1582; e-mail crieng@cri.com.cn; http://www.crienglish.com.

Creative Interface (Beijing), Bldg 7 Bei Li, North San Li Tun, Chao Yang District, Beijing 100027; ☎(86) 010 6416 9388; fax (86) 010 6416 9400; e-mail production@creativeinterface.com; http://www.creativeinterface.com/.

Creative Interface (Shanghai), No72 Fu Xing Xi Road, Xu Hui District, Shanghai 200031; ☎(86) 021 6437 0376; fax (86) 021 6437 1905; e-mail sally@creativ einterface.com; http://www.creativeinterface.com/.

China Star International Advertising Company Limited, PO Box 100600-6612, Beijing 100600; ☎(86) 010 5100 1451; fax (86) 010 5100 1452; e-mail cstar@chinastaradv.com.

BBDO CNUAC (Beijing), Room 1216, Tower B, Cofco Plaza, 8 Jiang Guo Men Nei Avenue, Beijing 100005; ☎(86) 010 6526 3961; fax (86) 010 6526 3962; http://www.bbdo.com.

Optimum Media Direction (Beijing), Rm 1201, North Tower Beijing Kerry Centre, No.1 Guanghua Road, Beijng 100020; ☎(86) 010 8529 9088; fax (86) 010 8529 90(86).

Optimum Media Direction (Shanghai), Room 1004, 227 Huang Pi North Road, Shanghai 200003;.☎(86) 021 6375 8885; fax (86) 021 6375 8750.

Oil Companies

Shell, Human Resource Department, Shell (China) Ltd. 33/F, China World Tower 2, No 1 Jian Guo Men Wai Avenue, Beijing 100004; ☎(86) 010 6505 4501; fax (86) 010 6505 2640; http://www.shell.com.

China National Petrolum Company, 6 Liupukang Jie, Xicheng District, Beijing, 100724; ☎(86) 010 6209 4114; e-mail master@hq.cnpc.com.cn; http://www.cnpc.com.cn.

Pharmaceutical

Dow Chemical (China) Limited (Beijing), Room 1102, Tower W3, Oriental Plaza, No.1 East Chang An Avenue, Dong Cheng District, Beijing, 100738; ☎(86) 020 8752 0380.

Dow Chemical (China) Limited (Guangzhou), CITIC Plaza, Room 3605, Tien He Road North, Tien He, Guangzhou 510613; ☎(86) 020 8752 0380.

Glaxosmithkline, 8/F North Tower, Kerry Centre, 1 Guang Hua Rd, Chao Yang District, Beijing 100020; ☎(86) 010 8529 6868; fax (86) 010 8529 6767.

Johnson & Johnson, http://www.jnj.com/careers/index.htm.

Procter & Gamble (China) Limited, http://www.pg.com.cn/job/index.htm.

Telecommunications

Motorola China Electronics Limited, 12/F, Tower 3, Onward Science & Trade centre, No.2 Dong San Huan South Road, Jian Guo Men Wai, Chaiyang District, Beijing 100022; ☎(86) 010 6564 2288; fax (86) 010 6564 2299; www.motorola.com.cn.

Siemens Ltd China, 7, Wangjing Zhonghuan Nan Lu, Chaoyang District, Beijing 100102; ☎(86) 010 6472 1888; fax (86) 010 6472 1333; http://www.siemens.com/index.jsp?sdc – p=t4c34s3uo1015386pn1015386flm &sdc – sid=6858736745&.

STARTING A BUSINESS

CHAPTER SUMMARY

- China attracted a 20% increase in foreign investment in 2003.
- Foreign investors who want to set up a business in China can either form a joint venture with a local company or start a company independently, i.e. a wholly foreign-owned enterprise.
- **Investment Incentives.** You will normally need to stay in China for several months before you can apply for any business loan.
    - The corporate income tax rate in the special economic zones, technological development zones and the Pudong New Area (Shanghai) is only 15% (instead of 33%).
    - Tax refunds are available for enterprises who re-invest their profits in China.
    - The development of central and western regions is currently one of the highest priorities for the Chinese government.
    - There are now major development projects for the western and central regions with many tax concessions
    - Many banks in Hong Kong provide loans for investors to start businesses in China.
- **Employing Staff.** You might be required to appoint an employment agency for staff recruitment.
    - Prior permission has to be obtained for posting recruitment advertisements in the mass media.
- **Taxation.** Corporate tax for foreign-invested enterprises (joint ventures) and wholly foreign-owned enterprises with establishments in China is 33%, levied on both income derived inside and outside China.
    - Wholly foreign-owned enterprises who have no establishment in China are subject to a corporate tax rate of 20%, which is only levied on income derived within China.
    - The current average import tariff is 11% and there is no export tariff on most commodities.
    - All commodities are subject to value-added tax (VAT) at the current rate of 17%.

ADVANTAGES FOR STARTING A BUSINESS IN CHINA

With good reason, many foreign investors are keen to start their business on mainland China. Some business experts believe that by 2050, the economy of this country of 1.3 billion people will be equal to that of the USA. While the world growth rate was only 2.5% in 2003, and many countries experienced a serious economic downturn, there was 9% growth in China. It is safe to say that China is, at the moment, the fastest growing economy in the world and the rapid increase in foreign investment contributes to this phenomenal growth rate. In 2003 there was a 20.22% increase in foreign investments and it is believed that the rate will continue to rise in the next couple of years.

Apart from the huge market, cheap labour and raw materials are also reasons for foreign investment in China. The average salary in big cities like Beijing and Shanghai is less than 2000 *yuan* (US$240/£140) per month and can be as low as 400 *yuan* (US$50/£28) per month in western regions. The government is also actively attracting more foreign investors to start their business in China by offering various investment incentives. For instance, tax concessions are available in special economic zones and high technology development zones. The tax arrangements are especially attractive for investors who want to start businesses in the western and central regions.

There is no export tariff on most commodities. The average import tariff is currently 11%, but the government has indicated that it will be lowered to 10% by 2005. As a member of the World Trade Organisation (WTO), China also provides preferential tariffs or quota removals to other WTO members.

PROCEDURES INVOLVED IN STARTING A NEW BUSINESS

Preparation from Scratch

As with investing in other countries, some research has to be done before you start. In particular, you may want to pay extra attention to the laws and regulations in China concerning the operation of a business. Take a look at the books and websites about doing business in China to get a rough idea about the business environment and the prospects for different businesses. Consider contacting consultant companies, as it may save you some time in the end. Business regulations, and also investment incentives offered by the government, differ across regions and this may affect the choice of your business location. Sometimes, substantial amounts can be saved with tax concessions. China has also delineated some development zones and companies are usually offered benefits if they establish their businesses in these areas. Many people find it easier to start a joint venture with a local partner. If there is someone you can trust, it may well save you quite a lot of time researching from scratch.

Useful Addresses

Ministry of Commerce of the People's Republic of China (MOFCOM), 2 Dong Chang'an Avenue,Beijing China, 100731; ☎(86) 010 6512 1919; fax (86) 010 6519 8173; http://english.mofcom.gov.cn/.

Ministry of Foreign Trade and Economic Cooperation (MOFTEC), No.2 Dong Chang'an Avenue,Beijing China, 100731; ☎(86) 010 6519 8114; fax (86) 010 6519 8039; e-mailmoftec@moftec.gov.cn; www1.moftec.gov.cn/moftec – en/.

Hong Kong Trade Development Council, 38th Floor, Office Tower, Convention Plaza 1 Harbour Road, Wanchai, Hong Kong; ☎(852) 2584 4333; fax (852) 2824 0249; e-mail hktdc@tdc.org.hk; www.tdctrade.com.

China Council for the Promotion of International Trade (CCPIT), 1 Fuxingmenwai Dajie, Beijing 100860; ☎(86) 010 6802 0229/86 (0)10 6803 4823; fax (86) 010 6803 0747/(86) 010 6801 1370; e-mailinfo@ccpit.org; www.ccpit.org.

China-Britain Business Council (head office), Abford House, 15 Wilton Road, London SW1V 1LT; ☎(44) 020 7828 5176; fax (44) 020 7630 5780; e-mail Bernadette.Rosario@cbbc.org; www.cbbc.org.

US Commercial Service, 31st Floor, North Tower, Beijing Kerry Center, No. 1 Guanghua Lu, Beijing 100020, China; ☎ (86) 010 8529 6655; fax (86) 010 8529 6558; e-mail Beijing.Office.Box@mail.doc.gov; www.buyusa.gov/china/en/.

China Online Inc., Chicago, IL 60611, USA; ☎(1) 312 664 8880; fax (1) 312 664 6469; e-mail cxu@chinaonline.com; www.chinaonline.com.

Business Consultants

East Asia Business, 8 Knoll Drive, London, N14 5LT, UK; ☎(44) 020 8361 5152; fax (44) 020 8361 9777; e-mail info@east-asia-business.com; www.east-asia-business.com.

B.R Cohen & Associates, 1824 Phelps Pl WN, Washington, DC 20008, USA; ☎(1) 877 810 1574; e-mail info@brcohen.com; www.brcohen.com.

Acorn Greater China Market Research(Shanghai) Co.Ltd, Room 1501, 15/F Mingshen Center, No. 3131 Kaixuan Road, Shanghai 200031, PRC; ☎(86) 021 5407 1566; fax (86) 021 5407 1586; e-mail china@acornasia.com; www.acornasia.com.

Synovate Americas (Washington DC), 1650 Tysons Blvd Suite 110, McLean, VA 22102, ☎1 703 790 9099 ext. 104; fax (1) 703 790 9181; e-mail dc.us@synovate.com; www.synovate.com.

Synovate–Europe, Middle East, Africa (London), 3/F, The Glasshouse, 26-28 Glasshouse Yard, London, EC1A 4JU; ☎(44) 020 7017 2400; fax (44) 020 7017 2401; e-mail uk@synovate.com; www.synovate.com.

China Strategy (Shanghai Head Office), Suite 335, Shanghai Center , 1376 Nanjing Xi Lu, Shanghai 200040; ☎(86) 021 6279 7330; fax (86) 021 6279

8659; e-mail Parker@chinastrategic.com; www.chinastrategic.com.

Useful Websites
US Commercial Service, tic@ita.doc.gov; www.export.gov.
The Internationalist, www.internationalist.com/business/China.php.
China Update, www.chinaupdate.net.
China Expat, www.chinaexpat.com.

Accountants
Apart from auditing, many accounting companies also provide business advice and help their clients with business research. Some big accounting companies have regular publications on various issues concerning doing business in China. Accounting firms are familiar with the laws and regulations, which can be very helpful if you are new to the Chinese environment. They can also provide you with the most up-to-date information and professional opinions, which are useful for reducing the risks in this competitive market.

Useful Addresses
Contact the individual companies for branch information
Deloitte Touche Tohmatsu (Beijing), 11/F Deloitte Tower, Sun Dong An Plaza, 138 Wangfujing Dajie, Beijing; ☎(86) 010 6528 1599; fax (86) 010 6528 1598; www.deloitte.com.
Ernst& young (Beijing), Level 16, Tower E3, The Towers, Oriental Plaza, 1 East Chang An Avenue, Dong Cheng District, Beijing, 100738; ☎(86) 010 6524 6688; fax (86) 010 8518 8298; www.ey.com.
KPMG (Beijing), 8/F, Office Tower E2, Oriental Plaza, 1 East Chang An Avenue, Dong Cheng District, Beijing 100738; ☎(86) 010 8518 5000; fax (86) 010 8518 5111; e-mail jane.yang@kpmg.com.cn; www.kpmg.com.hk.
PricewaterhouseCoopers (Beijing), 18/F North Tower, Beijing Kerry Center, 1 Guang Hua Road, Chaoyang District, Beijing 100020; ☎(86) 010 6561 2233; fax (86) 010 8529 9000; www.pwchk.com.
Dezan Shira & Associates Ltd. (Beijing), Suite 1007a, China Resources Building, 8 Jianguomenbei Avenue, Beijing 100005; ☎(86) 010 8519 2001; fax (86) 010 8519 2005; e-mail chris@dezshire.com.

Choosing an Area
Your choice of location should depend on what business you are going to establish, who your target customers are and what budget you can afford. Most of the financial businesses are based in Shanghai, Beijing or Guangdong Province. Many industrial enterprises set up their sites in inner areas such as Sichuan or Shaanxi Provinces, as land and labour are cheaper there than in the coastal cities. In recent years, the government has been trying to attract foreign investment

by setting up many new policies. For example, the corporate tax rate is reduced to 15% from 33% for setting up a company in special economic zones, high technology development zones or the Pudong New Area in Shanghai. In these regions, as with other regions, enterprises are also eligible for a tax refund if they re-invest their profits within China. In addition, the government and provinces usually provide more help in these development zones. Some other provinces are keen to attract particular groups of investors as well. For example, in Guizhou, 13 sectors were opened to foreign investment in July 2003. They include grain, road construction, new electronic components, Chinese medicinal herbs and tourism.

Currently, the government is putting in a lot of effort to develop the western and central areas of the country. It is now improving the transport system, electricity supply etc, to make these areas more accessible and suitable for business. Many investment incentives are available for foreign investment in regions like Gansu, Sichuan, Yunnan, Guizhou, Shanxi, Ningxia, Qinghai, etc. The Hong Kong Trade and Development Council has a complete illustration of the development of the western and central regions, which includes the most updated preferential policies launched by the government.

Depending on the type of business, other factors to consider include the buying power of the local market, which can vary a lot across regions. Even if you are not aiming to sell products to the local market, the standard of living of a region also predicts the quality of staff you can hire locally and their salaries. In the inner parts of China, it is more difficult to find local employees who can speak fluent English or hold university degrees, but the labour costs can be much lower compared to coastal cities. Transport and energy supply are also important issues, especially for factories.

Useful Websites
Chinese Government Wbsite, www.chinainvest.gov.cn. Provides details about investment news and recent projects.

Hong Kong Trade and Development Council ('Go-West'), www.tdctrade.com/gowest/investment/index.htm. It is a particular section for the development of the western provinces.

Hong Kong Trade and Development Council (Western and Central China), www.tdctrade.com/gowest/index.htm. An overview of the development of western and central China.

Hong Kong Trade and Industry Department, www.tid.gov.hk/english/trade – relations/topicalissues/developwest.html.

Business Structures
Foreign investors starting a business on mainland China, can either start an enterprise independently or form a joint venture with a Chinese partner.

Wholly Foreign-owned Enterprises (WFOE). Wholly foreign-owned enterprises are limited liability companies solely owned by foreign investors. They should be primarily engaged in export business and China should not be their primary market. If you intend to sell your products to the local market, the government will generally recommend that you start a joint venture with a local partner instead. Under the government laws, WFOEs have to employ some local labour and they may have to recruit staff through government employment agencies as well. Even though it is not clearly stated what the appropriate ratio of capital contribution for machinery to cash investment should be, business consultancies usually suggest the cash investment should constitute 30% or more of the total investment. WFOEs are subject to a lesser degree of interference from the government compared to joint ventures. However, they are also excluded from some business concessions which joint ventures enjoy. You should consult agencies which are familiar with the business environment and also check the regulations before starting a WFOE.

Joint Ventures. A joint venture refers to a business formed by two or more parties who are from different regions or countries. At least one party must be local. The parties have to come up with an agreement on the details, such as how to run the business, share of responsibilities, profits and capital contributions, etc. The major advantage of forming a joint venture is the sharing of costs, risks and responsibilities. It is also the easiest and officially recommended way to access the Chinese market, since there is a local party who is familiar with the market and the regulations.

There are two types of joint venture in mainland China, *equity joint venture* and *contractual joint venture*. In a *contractual joint venture*, there is no restriction on how much the foreign investor has to contribute. But in an *equity joint venture*, the foreign investor has to contribute at least 25% of the total capital. Investors can contribute to the enterprise in cash, buildings, equipment, materials, intellectual property rights and land use rights. For *contractual joint ventures*, labour, resources and services are also accepted forms of contribution. One other distinctive difference between the two forms of joint ventures is whether investors can withdraw registered capital or not. Investors in *equity joint ventures* are restricted from withdrawing the registered capital during the term of the contract but those of *contractual joint ventures* are not prohibited from doing so. *Contractual joint ventures* also enjoy greater flexibility in management but they are required to have trade unions. Profit and risk sharing in *equity joint ventures* are proportionate to the capital contributions of the parties while they are decided by contractual terms in *contractual joint ventures*. Long term businesses typically take the form of *equity joint ventures*, whereas *contractual joint ventures* are more common in small and medium enterprises.

Raising Finance

Personal savings and contributions of capital from business partners should probably be your primary financial sources, but it is also common for investors to seek help from banks. If possible, you should try the banks in your own country first. Since you have transaction records there, it is easier for the bank to assess your ability to payback the loan. Many Chinese banks do lend money to foreign investors, and interestingly it is sometimes easier for a foreigner than for a local investor to borrow money from them. The terms and interest rates vary from bank to bank so you should contact different banks before making a decision. Some banks only provide loans to established enterprises but not to individuals who are new to the market. And in any case, a few months' local transaction records would be necessary, which means it would not be very easy to borrow money after you enter the country. In addition to that, you have to present documents such as business licences, tax registration certificates and maybe financial statements as well. You may also consider banks in Hong Kong when you look for loans, as many provide loans for investors to start businesses in China.

You have to prepare a business plan to outline the details of the business you want to start and how are you going to run the business. In the business plan, you should include the market research you have done and your vision for the development of the business. A detailed financial plan is also a very important part of your business plan. You should set out the start up cost, daily running cost, salaries, cash flow plan, expected income and when the expected profit can be generated. It would be good to have your CV and that of your business partners in your business plan as well. You should also be familiar with the laws and regulations of running a business in China before going to present your business plan.

There are many government investment incentives available for foreign investment but most of them are tax concessions rather than cash loans. However, do familiarize yourself with these as it will help you to estimate the size of loan you need.

Useful Addresses

Bank of China, 1 Fuxingmen Nei Dajie, Bejing 100818; ☎ (86) 010 6659 6688; fax (86) 010 6601 4024; www.bank-of-china.com.

Industrial and Commercial Bank of China, 55# Fuxingmenmei Street, Xicheng District, Beijing, 100032; e-mail webmaster@icbc.com.cn; http://www.icbc.com.cn/e – index.jsp.

Industrial and Commercial Bank of China (New York Representative Office), 375 Park Avenue, Suite 3508, New York , NY. 10152, U.S.A.; ☎ (1) 212 838 7799; fax (1) 212 838 5770; e-mail icbcusa@yahoo.com.

Industrial and Commercial Bank of China (London Branch), ☎ (44) 020 7397 8888; fax (44) 020 7397 8899.

China Construction Bank (Beijing Branch), 4 Men No.28 West Dajie, Xuanwumen, Beijing, 100053; ☎(86) 010 6360 3660; fax (86) 010 6360 3194; www.ccbhk.com.

Hua Xia Bank, No.111, Xidan Beidajie, Beijing; ☎(86) 010 6615 1199; fax (86) 010 6618 8484; e-mail webmaster@hxb.cc.

China Merchants Bank, China Merchants Bank Tower No.7088, Shennan Boulevard, Shenzhen 518040; ☎(86) 0755 8319 8888; fax (86) 0755 8319 5555/(86) 0755 8319 5777.

China Everbright Bank, Guang Dai Daixia, No.6 Fuxingmenwai Dajie, Beijing 100045; ☎(86) 010 6856 0469.

China Construction Bank, 95533/zh/ccb@ccb.com.cn.; www.ccb.cn

Agricultural Bank of China, e-mail ebmaster@abchina.com.

Bank of China (Hong Kong) Limited, Bank of China Tower 1 Garden Road, Central, Hong Kong; ☎(852) 2826 6888; fax (852) 2810 5963; www.bochk.com.

The Bank of East Asia, Limited, 10 Des Voeux Road Central, Hong Kong; ☎(852) 2842 3200; fax (852) 2845 9333; www.hkbea.com.

Citibank, N.A., 39/F-40/F., 43/F-50/F., Citibank Tower Citibank Plaza, 3 Garden Road, Hong Kong, ☎(852) 2868 8888: fax (852) 2306 8111; www.citibank.com.hk.

Hang Seng Bank Ltd., 83 Des Voeux Road Central, Central Hong Kong; ☎(852) 2198 1111; fax (852) 2845 9301/ (852) 2868 4047; www.hangseng.com.

The Hongkong and Shanghai Banking Corporation Limited, 1 Queen's Road Central, Central, Hong Kong; ☎(852) 2822 1111; fax (852) 2810 1112; www.hsbc.com.hk.

Standard Chartered Bank, 4-4A Des Voeux Road Central, Central, Hong Kong; ☎(852) 2820 3333; fax (852) 2856 9129; www.standardchartered.com.hk.

Investment Incentives

The Chinese market was opened to foreign investment in the 70s and since then, it has grown steadily. In the last decade, the government has been actively seeking foreign investment by developing many new policies, and this is a major reason for the recent phenomenal growth of foreign investment in China.

Tax reduction is granted to foreign-invested enterprises (joint ventures) and foreign enterprises (wholly foreign-owned enterprises) if they start their businesses with establishments or venues in special economic zones including Shenzhen, Zuhai, Shantou, Xiamen and Hainan. The corporate income tax in the special economic zones is 15% rather than 33%. The reduced tax rate also applies to foreign-invested enterprises established in economic and technological development zones and Pudong New Area (Shanghai); or those who are engaged in energy, transportation, port construction projects, and export processing in bonded areas. In some cases, technology-intensive and knowledge-intensive projects launched by foreign-invested enterprises are also taxed at 15% if the total investment exceeds US$30 million (246 million *yuan*/£18 million). Some enterprises may enjoy a reduced tax rate at 24% even though they do not fit into the above categories, for example, enterprises in coastal cities which are open for investment or state-class resorts.

In order to attract enterprises for developing long-term projects in China, some enterprises are granted exemption from income tax for the first few profit-making years. Foreign-invested enterprises with an operation in production for over ten years are allowed to be exempted from corporate income tax in the first two profit-making years. Sino-foreign joint ventures engaged in port and wharf construction and with an operation period of over 15 years can apply for corporate income tax exemption in the first five profit-making years as well. They are also granted a reduction of tax by half in the following five years. The same is offered to infrastructure projects which are to be carried out for 15 or more years and are related to airports, ports, wharfs, railways, highways, power stations, coal mines, water conservancy facilities and agricultural development in Hainan Special Economic Zone and also Pudong New Area.

Owners of foreign-invested enterprises are eligible for a 40% tax refund if they re-invest the profit they obtained in the same enterprises or establish other enterprises locally. If the foreign investor re-invests profits directly in establishing or expanding an export-oriented or high-tech enterprise in China, they can even get a 100% refund for the amount of tax levied on the re-invested amount.

The development of central and western regions is one of the highest priorities for the Chinese government at the moment. Foreign-invested enterprises who develop their businesses in these regions can enjoy exemption of tax for two years and a tax reduction by half in the following three years. They are also offered a reduced tax rate of 15% for another three years after the above tax reduction expires. High-tech or export-oriented enterprises are offered a 50% reduction in corporate income tax for three years, if exports account for 70% or more of their annual output value.

Do not be disappointed if your enterprise does not fit into any of the above categories. The government updates these investment incentives from time to time. For more information, the Hong Kong Trade and Development Council has a very good webpage in English: *www.tdctrade.com/chinaguide*.

Procedures for Establishment and Business Registration

Unfortunately setting up a business in mainland China can be complicated. An application has to go through several different departments at different levels for approval. It usually takes months to get all the necessary approvals.

Joint Ventures. These might be one way to speed up that process. In this case, the Chinese party (i.e. your partner) will be responsible for most of the application procedures. For a new application, the Chinese party has to submit the project proposal to the local development planning commission or economic and trade commission. The business partners then work together to compile a feasibility study report to the commissions stated above for approval after the project proposal is approved. The parties can only sign the contract, the articles of association and other relevant legal documents after the feasibility study is approved. The Chinese party should then submit the documents to the local foreign trade and economic cooperation department where the joint venture is located for examination and approval. After all these are approved, the Chinese party is responsible for applying for an approval certificate from the provincial or municipal foreign trade and economic cooperation department. The department will then issue an approval certificate and the joint venture should then apply for a business licence from the provincial or municipal administration for industry and commerce within 30 days. After registration, however, the joint venture still has to go through some other procedures. These include applying for an official seal and enterprise code, opening a bank account, and registering for tax payment and customs declaration with the local public security. Technical supervision, taxation, customs, finance, foreign exchange administration, banking, insurance and commodity inspection departments will also be required.

Foreign Enterprises. To set up a foreign enterprise, a foreign investor has to first submit a preliminary application, by submitting a report to the foreign and economic cooperation department at county level or above at the place where the proposed enterprise is located. The report should include details of business objectives, business scope, scale of operation, products to be produced. In addition, it should also include details of technology and equipment to be used, land area required, conditions and quantities of water, electricity, gas and other forms of energy resources required, and requirements for public facilities. After receiving a written reply from the relevant government authorities, the investor should then hand in a formal application along with all the required documents to the local foreign trade and economic cooperation department at county, municipal or provincial level. The investor has to apply for an approval certificate to the foreign trade and economic cooperation department after getting the approval for the formal application. Finally, you must apply for a business licence from the provincial or municipal administration for industry and commerce within 30 days of the collection of the approval certificate. Similarly with a joint venture, after registration a foreign enterprise must go through other procedures such as applying for an official seal and enterprise code, before running the business.

Foreign-invested enterprises are also required to make financial registration with the financial authority within 30 days of submiting the applications for business registrations.

Useful Addresses

Ministry of Foreign Trade and Economic Cooperation (MOFTEC), No.2 Dong Chang'an Avenue,Beijing China, 100731; ☎(86) 010 6519 8114; fax (86) 010 6519 8039; e-mailmoftec@moftec.gov.cn; www1.moftec.gov.cn/moftec – en/.

Ministry of Commerce of the People's Republic of China (MOFCOM), 2 Dong Chang'an Avenue,Beijing China, 100731; ☎(86) 010 6512 1919; fax (86) 010 6519 8173; http://english.mofcom.gov.cn/.

Chinese Embassy in the United States (Commercial Office), 2133 Wisconsin Ave., NW, Washington, DC 20007; ☎(1) 202 625 3350; fax (1) 202 337 5845; e-mail chinaembassy – us@fmprc.gov.cn; www.china-embassy.org.

Chinese Embassy in the United Kingdom (Commercial Office), 1-3 Leinster Gardens, London W2 6DP; ☎(44) 020 7723 8923; Fax (44) 020 706 2777; e-mail press@chinese-embassy.org.uk; www.chinese-embassy.org.uk.

Hong Kong Trade and Development Council (Customer Service Centre), HongKongConvention&ExhibitionCentre,1ExpoDrive,Wanchai,HongKong; ☎(852) 1830 668; fax (852) 2248 4888; e-mail hktdc@tdc.org.hk; www.tdctrade.com.

Ministry of Finance (MOF), 3 Nansangxiang, Sanlihe, Xicheng Qu, Beijing, 100820; ☎(86) 010 6855 1114/(86) 010 6855 1118/(86) 010 6855 2237/(86) 010 6855 1888/(86) 010 6855 2128; fax (86) 010 6853 3635/(86) 010 6855 1125/(86) 010 6853 6985/(86) 010 6851 3428; e-mail webmaster@mof.gov.cn; http://www.mof.gov.cn/.

Trademark Registration

There are several departments that are responsible for handling trademarks, and there may be confusion over their responsibilities. All the departments related to trademarks are under the supervision of the State Administration for Industry and Commerce (SAIC). The Trademark Office is the government authority for the registration of trademarks in China; the Trademark Management Office is the administrative unit for managing all trademark-related matters; Trademark Affairs Offices, located in major cities, are trademark agents set up by the state; the Trademark Review and Adjudication Board is responsible for handling disputes related to trademarks.

Enterprises should make their applications to the Trademark Office for the registration of trademarks. Foreign-invested enterprises may apply directly to the Trademark Office or through trademark agents. However, foreign enterprises have to appoint trademark agents for doing so. Note that an application for trademark registration and the supporting documents should be in Chinese; if any of the documents is in a foreign language you should also provide a translated version. If you have registered your trademark in another country within the last three months, you will be given priority for your registration. Under the regulations of SAIC, it is only possible for someone to post an objection to the use of a trademark within the first three months from the date of publication. If this happens, the Trademark Office will make a decision based on the reasons for objection. If there is no opposition or the opposition is not justified, a trademark will be granted a formal approval, and a certificate of registration will then be issued. A registered trademark is valid for ten years and it will be granted validity for another ten years each time it is renewed.

Useful Addresses

Trademark Office (CTMO), No.8 Sanlihedonglu, Xicheng District, Beijing, 100820; ☎(86) 010 6802 7820/(86) 010 6805 2266; fax (86) 010 6801 3623; www.ctmo.gov.cn.

State Administration for Industry and Commerce (SAIC), 8 Sanlihe Donglu, Western District, Beijing, 100820; ☎(86) 010 6803 2233/(86) 010 6852 2771/(86) 010 6853 1133/(86) 010 6801 0463; fax (86) 010 6857 0848; www.saic.gov.cn.

State Intellectual Property Office of PRC, 6 Xituchenglu Haidian, Beijing 100088; http://www.cpo.cn.net/.

Import/Export

Enterprises or individuals need to obtain permission for the right to import or export in advance if they want to engage in the import/export business. Almost all commodities are open to import and export rights, except 16 crucial ones which are currently under state monopoly. Most commodities are subject to import tariffs. The average import tariff is 11%. Tariffs for raw materials and industrial supplies are less than 20% in most cases. Tariffs for consumer goods range from 20% to 50%, except for a few selected luxury items like pearls and tobacco, which will be taxed at 100% or more. The government expects the average import tariff to be lowered to 10% by the year 2005. All commodities are also subjected to Value-Added Tax (VAT), which is calculated on top of the import tariffs. The average VAT rate is 17% at the moment. There is no export tariff on most commodities. However, licences may be required for some of them. You should note that some countries may impose 'safeguard' tariffs on Chinese exports, which is permitted under the terms of China's accession to the World Trade Organisation (WTO) and is valid until 2014.

Useful Addresses

Ministry of Commerce of the People's Republic of China (MOFCOM), 2 Dong Chang'an Avenue,Beijing China, 100731; ☎(86) 010 6512 1919; fax (86) 010 6519 8173; http://english.mofcom.gov.cn/.

General Administration of Customs of the PRC, 6 Jianguomennei Dajie, Beijing 100730; ☎(86) 010 6519 4114; fax (86) 010 6519 4004; http:

//www.customs.gov.cn/

State Import and Export Commodities Inspection Bureau, A10 Chaowai Dajie, Beijing 100020; ☎ (86) 010 6599 4600; fax (86) 010 6599 3846.

State Intellectual Property Office of PRC, 6 Xituchenglu Haidian, Beijing 100088; www.sipo.gov.cn.

IDEAS FOR A NEW BUSINESS

Import/Export

Import and export businesses have been one of the most important industries in China, and are probably the most common business for foreign investors. If you check the origins of the products you use everyday, you will find that many of the things you bought in the USA or Europe are now made in China. These include semi-finished products and also completed products. The USA is one of many countries that import a great deal of Chinese products. China's trade surplus with America was US$103 billion (840 million *yuan*/£65 billion) in 2002. Raw materials and labour in China are cheap, and this is one of the reasons their export business flourishes. In addition, there is no export tariff on most of the goods produced. After entering the WTO in 2002, China has been on tariff agreements with other members of the WTO and thus import tariffs are reducing. At the same time, many of the import and export quotas have been removed. This makes it cheaper to import goods from other WTO countries to China and vice-versa.

Motor Cars

China has been the fastest expanding automotive market in the world in the last few years. It is now the second largest vehicle market in the world, second only to the USA. There was a 70% increase in production of vehicles in September 2003 when compared to the same time a year earlier. Since the technology in car making has been improving, many of the American and European automotive manufacturers have set up joint ventures with Chinese partners to produce cars in China. The low production cost allows the vehicles to be sold at a lower price and this stimulates sales in the western markets as well as in the local market. Moreover, by the year 2005, the quota for imported cars will be removed and it is believed this will boost the sales of imported vehicles in China.

Home Improvement Stores

The concept of 'home' is an important one for the Chinese, and many of them are keen to have their own property. According to government statistics, the home ownership rate is increasing throughout the entire country. In some big cities, the increase in the home ownership rate is up to 75%. Moreover, many Hong Kong people are going to the Mainland to buy houses due to the difference in land prices. Many of these new home owners are willing to spend money to make their home look stylish and modern. Western home designs and furniture are popular. B&Q is one of the successful examples of home improvement stores; its branch in Beijing is even bigger than their largest shop in the UK!

Travel Agencies

The number of Chinese tourists travelling outside of Asia has been increasing. A lot of them are fairly well-off and do not mind spending money abroad. Some young people do enjoy travelling by themselves but most people prefer to join guided tours and travel packages.

On the other hand, local tours in China are mainly organised by Chinese travel agents. Local tours that are conducted in English should be able to attract foreign visitors.

English Learning Centres

The Chinese language is not based on an alphabet, and it is thus not surprising that many Chinese people have a hard time learning English. As international business becomes more and more important, learning English is high up on many job seekers' priority lists. Many of them find that oral English is particularly difficult to learn from books or local Chinese teachers. There are many native English speakers who are willing to travel to China for a gap year, and setting up a business to organise teaching could be very successful. The government also gives great support to importing foreign English teachers. It is easy to get work permits for your foreign staff to work as English teachers.

Restaurants and Pubs

Even though there are many good restaurants in China, the majority of them only serve Chinese cuisine. As the number of foreign visitors keeps rising and Chinese citizens increasingly travel abroad, the demand for restaurants of different styles must increase. In cities, young locals are keen to try anything new, so you should not worry too much about being authentic. To avoid head-on price competition with small family-run restaurants, you should probably target the high-income groups and business visitors looking for a posh night out. Fast food restaurants might be an alternative. Although the traditional food culture is strong in China, hostility towards western fast food outlets is unheard of. Young people see fast food as an interesting and cheap alternative to traditional meals. Similarly, many youngsters in big cities like Shanghai and Beijing are fascinated by the idea of western pubs and clubs.

RUNNING A BUSINESS

Employing Staff

Unlike many other countries, employment through government employment agencies is the main way to employ staff in mainland China. These employment agencies are usually called 'employment centres' or 'human resources markets', and they are under the control of labour and social security departments as well as personnel departments. Apart from the recruitment of staff, employment agencies also provide services like file management and handling matters related to social insurance. In fact, in some situations, you may not be allowed to employ staff on your own, for example, when employing a person who currently works for a State-Owned Enterprise (SOE). In this case, you will need an employment agency to negotiate with the SOE to get the employee released, and also to recover the employee's personnel file. If you want to post an advertisement in the mass media, such as newspapers, magazines, television or radio, you must apply for prior approval from the local labour and social security department. 'Head-hunters' or recruitment consultants are also available and they are becoming increasingly popular, especially amongst foreign enterprises and foreign-invested enterprises.

Before engaging an employment agency, you should ask them to provide proof of legal status, i.e. the approval certificate issued by the labour department. You should have a clear idea about the scope of services, charges, names and telephone numbers of its supervisory authorities before entering into any commitment. Employment agencies, at the same time, will ask you for documents about your enterprise. You should present a letter of introduction, a copy of the business licence and other proof of registration as a legal entity. You should also provide an identification document for the person who is in charge of the recruitment process. You should prepare a profile for recruitment requirements and the employment agency will find the right person for you according to that profile. In the profile, you should include: an introduction to the enterprise; the number of staff to be recruited; the nature of the job, terms of employment and the remuneration of each position; fringe benefits; and labour protection.

Check the validity of the documents provided before signing a contract with any proposed employees. The Labour Law requires that there is a contract between an employer and an employee. You should refer to the Labour Handbook for making mandatory terms and conditions to be included in a contract. After being signed, the contract has to be sent to the labour administrative department for examination for authentication within 30 days of the employee starting work. You should consider appointing a service agency specialising in human resources employment to manage personal files of your Chinese staff. These service agencies provide services including verification of the identity of staff, salary track record and political reports. They also provide services like preparing assessments of technical qualifications, contract authentication and matters related to social insurance.

Employers are required to contribute to social insurance for their employees. There are five types of social insurance including provident fund (pension), medical, unemployment, work-related injury and child-bearing insurances. Both employers and employees have to contribute to the first three, and the last two are the sole responsibility of employers. The rate of contribution varies with the type of risk and type of injury. Refer to the chapter *Daily Life* for more information on social insurance.

There are some important points to bear in mind when you are recruiting for staff

O Do not rely too much on 'personal recommendations' as the recommender may favour his or her relatives or close friends instead of recommending a really suitable candidate.

O Avoid paying wages through employment agencies or middlemen. There have been complaints that employees have not actually received wages from such agencies.

O Try to provide good fringe benefits to attract the best candidates.

O Consider providing training (for instance, language skills) for your staff.

O Avoid discrimination against age or gender. It is illegal.

O Consider employing a reliable personal assistant for hiring, especially if you do not speak the Chinese language.

Ministry of Labour and Social Securities, No.12 Hepingli Zhongjie, Beijing 100716; ☎(86) 010 8420 1114; e-mail webmaster@mail.molss.gov.cn; www.molss.gov.cn.

Centre for International Exchanges, No.12 Hepingli Zhongjie, Beijing 100716; ☎(86) 010 8421 6690/(86) 010 8421 6674; fax (86) 010 8421 6687; e-mail yujingjing@mail.molss.gov.cn

China Employment Training Technical Instruction Center, No.3 Yuhuilu, Beijing 100101; ☎(86) 010 8463 1199 (ext. 8101-8108); fax (86) 010 6493 5483 e-mail master@osta.org.cn; www.osta.org.cn.

Taxation

Foreign-invested enterprises and foreign enterprises are liable for the following taxes:

Foreign-invested Enterprise & Foreign Enterprise Income Tax. There are two tax rates for foreign enterprise income tax, depending on whether an enterprise has establishments or venues within mainland China. Foreign enterprises with establishments in China are subject to the same tax system as a foreign-invested enterprise. They are liable for 30% corporation tax and another 3% local income tax, which is calculated on the income derived from both inside and outside China. For foreign enterprises with no establishments in China, or no proof that the income generated is effectively connected with the establishments, the tax rate is 20% and it is only levied on income derived inside China. For both foreign-invested enterprises and foreign enterprises, the income tax is levied on an annual basis and paid in advance in quarterly instalments. The owners have to file an annual tax return along with final account statements within four months of the end of a tax year and the tax should be paid within five months, from the end of the tax year.

Profit tax in Macau is currently 2%-15%, depending on the level of net income.

Value Added Tax (VAT). All enterprises and individuals engaged in the sale or import of goods or the provision of processing, repair or maintenance services in China have to pay VAT. Taxpayers are divided into two groups, small-scale taxpayers and general taxpayers. Enterprises or individuals whose taxable value of sales is below 1 million *yuan* (US$120,000/£70,000) for production of goods or services and 1.8 million *yuan* (US$220,000/£120,000) for those engaged in wholesaling or retailing are classified as small-scale taxpayers. General taxpayers are those who do not fall into the category of small-scale taxpayer. There is no VAT on exported goods. The following items are taxed at the rate of 13% when imported: grains, edible vegetable oil, drinking water, heating, air-conditioning, hot water, coal gas, liquefied petroleum gas, natural gas, methane, coal products for domestic use; books, newspapers and magazines, feedstuffs, chemical fertilisers, pesticides, agricultural machinery, agricultural plastic sheeting, and other commodities as specified by the state. Other than these commodities, the VAT on imports is 17%.

Customs Duties. There are two tariff rates for custom duties in China, the general tariff rate and the preferential tariff rate. Some countries and regions have signed a reciprocal tariff agreement with China. Goods from these countries and regions are taxed at the preferential tariff, which is lower. Goods from other countries and regions will be taxed at the general tariff rate instead. The average import tariff rate is 11% while the export tariff rates are between 20% and 50%.

Consumption Tax. Consumption tax applies to eleven categories of goods, including cigarettes, alcoholic drinks and alcohol, cosmetics, skin-care and hair-care products, fine jewellery and precious stones, firecrackers and fireworks, gasoline, diesel oil, motor vehicle tyres, motorcycles, and small motor cars. If your enterprise engages in the production, subcontracted processing or importation of any of the above goods, it is subjected to consumption tax. Consumption tax is levied on top of VAT and the tax rates vary from 3% to 45%. With the exception of yellow spirits, beer, gasoline and diesel oil, which are taxed by volume, other goods are taxed by value at the production stage.

Useful Addresses

State Administration of Taxation (Beijing Municipal Office), No.133 Dongsilishi Hutong Dongcheng, Beijing 100010; ☎(86) 010 6513 3585; e-mail dongcheng@bjsat.gov.cn; www.bjsat.gov.cn.

Macau Trade and Investment Promotion Institute, Morada: Avenida da Amizade, 918, Edif. World Trade Centre, 4 andar, Macau; ☎(853) 710300; fax (853) 590309; e-mail ipim@ipim.gov.mo; www.ipim.gov.mo/english/E – Mainday.asp.

BUSINESS ETIQUETTE

Hierarchy

Chinese people in general take business hierarchy quite seriously. People in higher positions expect to earn more and they are usually more experienced, which means they are typically older too. Some Chinese who are in higher positions prefer to keep their distance from their subordinates and may not accept being called by their first names. Sometimes employees would not have the courage to point out the mistakes of their bosses. If you would like to create a friendly and less hierarchical atmosphere inside your company, you have to take a leading role and encourage your Chinese staff to express their opinions. You should also make them understand that promotion or salary is based on performance rather than seniority.

When sending gifts to staff in a company, you should be aware that people in higher positions expect to receive nicer (and more expensive) gifts than their subordinates.

Politeness

It is not usual for Chinese people to point out other's mistakes bluntly, especially in front of other people, and they will expect you to behave the same way. An employer should give advice to an employee individually, especially if he or she is not performing very well. Business partners, also, do not comment on the performance of their companies in social situations, especially when their employees are present. Advice is more easily accepted in a private conversation, and a healthy dose of 'beating around the bush' may help sometimes.

You are expected to reciprocate when someone invites you for dinner or sends you an expensive gift. You should return a meal or gift of some kind. If eating in a restaurant, ask your guests what they like for dinner before suggesting anything from the menu. In the end, they will usually let you make the decision anyway!

Sending the Right Gifts

Some Chinese people are quite superstitious, for example, they do not visit relatives on the third day of the Chinese New Year, as they believe it will lead to quarrels; they do not like the number 'four', and in general prefer the number 'eight' etc. Therefore, you have to be careful when choosing gifts if you do not want to upset your friends. In general, Chinese people prefer practical gifts to decorative gifts, unless it is something really expensive or stylish. As a rule you should avoid sending clocks to Chinese people, as sending clocks implies going to their funerals. Also, never send a Chinese person a green hat, especially to men, as 'wearing a green hat' means one's wife is committing adultery. Fruit is welcome on most occasions but no pears should be sent to couples who are getting married or are newly married as 'pears' sounds like 'separation'. In Cantonese, watermelon, melon, papaya or any other similar shaped fruits and vegetables are all called 'gwa', which sounds the same as 'dying' in informal speech, so you should avoid sending them as gifts too.

The colour of the wrapping is also important. Never wrap your gifts in black or white as both colours are related to death or funerals. Red is particularly good for weddings and Chinese New Year. Gold has also become popular for these situations. Even though red is generally welcome in all situations, you should never wear red clothes at a funeral as this means you are happy to see the person dead; black clothes, or more traditional white ones, have to be worn.

HONG KONG

Section I

LIVING IN HONG KONG

GENERAL INTRODUCTION

RESIDENCE AND ENTRY REGULATIONS

SETTING UP HOME

DAILY LIFE

RETIREMENT

GENERAL
INTRODUCTION

CHAPTER SUMMARY

- **Political.** Hong Kong was a British colony until 1st July 1997.
  - The Hong Kong Special Administrative Region (HKSAR) Government was set up on 1st July 1997 and has been running Hong Kong according to the Basic Law.
- **Economic.** It has been claimed that Hong Kong is the World's freest economy.
  - Finance and banking, tourism and import/export are the major industries.
  - The Closer Economic Partnership Arrangement (CEPA) grants Hong Kong products duty-free access to the mainland and additional market access for Hong Kong companies to the mainland.
- **Area.** Hong Kong is divided into three regions: Hong Kong Island, Kowloon, the New Territories and outlying islands.
- **Population.** The average population density is 6,300 per square kilometre but it is as high as 43,200 per square kilometre in Kowloon.
  - More than 90% of the population is Chinese.
- It takes 12 hours to fly from the UK; 14 hours from the West coast of the USA and 20 hours from the East coast.

PROS AND CONS OF MOVING TO HONG KONG

It is not surprising that Hong Kong is popular amongst foreigners for travelling, working, or even settling down even though it is just a small city in Asia. Skyscrapers, the Big Buddha, the mesmerising city lights by the harbour at night and an almost unlimited choice of food and fashion are all very impressive to foreigners. The good infrastructure makes it easy to travel around the city, and access to mainland China is excellent. Since English is one of the official languages (the other is Chinese), it is easy to get by and travel around the city. Many locals have been taught English at school and are in general friendly and helpful. People are accustomed to the mixed culture, and racial discrimination is rare and is almost never against westerners.

Pros
- very low tax rates
- good infrastructure
- warm weather
- cosmopolitan culture
- no significant racial tension
- reasonable living costs
- very low crime rate
- English is one of the official languages
- easy access to mainland China
- high standard of living

Cons
- no governmental pension
- expensive housing
- overcrowded
- air-pollution
- far away from the USA and Europe
- long working hours

Since the city is already very overcrowded, buying or renting a house or flat can be very expensive. However, apart from that, living costs in Hong Kong are not high when compared to the USA and the UK. The extremely low tax rate and simple tax regime are also very attractive reasons for moving to Hong Kong. There is no sales tax and many industries import cheap raw materials from China, which helps them to maintain their competitiveness. Although it is a busy city, the crime rate is extremely low. Not only is Hong Kong one of the cities with the lowest crime rate (it was recorded as 1.1% in 2003), violent crimes are particularly rare. The weather is never too cold in Hong Kong but it can be unpleasantly hot and humid in the summer. However, almost all restaurants, shopping centres, shops, cinemas and even public transport are air-conditioned. Poor air quality might however be a problem to foreigners. Due to the large number of vehicles in the city, the problem of air-pollution is serious. It may take some time to get used to it and if you end up staying, be warned that some foreigners develop mild respiratory problems. The strong work ethic of the local labour force ensures that the economy is robust, but it could be difficult for foreigners to cope with.

It is common to work for over ten hours a day, and working overtime is so common that in some cases you do not even get paid for it. Hong Kong is also not a popular place for retirement as there is no government pension but only occupational ones.

POLITICAL AND ECONOMIC STRUCTURE

History

Human activity on Hong Kong island dates back to 3000BC. The discovery of a brick tomb in Lei Cheng Uk suggests that people from the mainland came and settled in Hong Kong in the Han Dynasty (206BC-AD220) and it is clear that a significant number of people migrated from mainland China to Hong Kong in the Song Dynasty (960-1279AD), as coins, fishing and farming utensils that are characteristic of that period have been found. Trade between China and the West probably began in the 16th century. Even though the Portuguese were the first to reach China, it was the British who dominated foreign trade in the southern region of Guangzhou. Many of the British trade companies developed very rapidly and the British East India Company, the biggest company trading with southern regions at that time, started to sell opium in Guangzhou to further increase its profits in the beginning of the 19th century. The opium business was very successful (in monetary terms) and the result was that the health of Chinese people in Guangzhou was severely damaged. Seeing this, the government banned the drug trade in 1799 but this was not successful as demand for the drug was huge and smuggling was rife. The British continued to enjoy huge profits from the sale of opium until the government official Lin Zexu was appointed by the emperor to stop the trade in Guangzhou in 1839. Lin and his troops used force to compel the foreign factories to surrender the stocks of opium, and in one historic scene he burned all the collected opium in front of the public to show the determination of the emperor to ban the opium trade. The British were not impressed, and this led to the First Opium War (1839-1842), which resulted in a century-long colonial period for Hong Kong.

Hong Kong Island was occupied by the British in January 1841, whilst China was in a very unfavourable position in the war. After negotiations between the British captain and the Governor of Guangdong Province, Hong Kong was awarded to the British under the Convention of Chuen Pi. Hong Kong was officially ceded to the British in 1842 after the two governments signed the Treaty of Nanjing, and it then became a colony. A series of conflicts between China and the British followed after the First Opium War. The British were backed by the French, the Russians and the Americans. A combined force of the British and the French invaded China in 1859, forcing the emperor to agree to the Convention of Beijing which conceded the Kowloon Peninsula and nearby Stonecutters Island to the British. The Kowloon Peninsula was granted to the British in 1860 under the Convention of Beijing after the Second Opium War (1856-1858). The British were concerned that Hong Kong could not be defended unless the surrounding area was also under its control, and so asked for a lease of the New Territories for a period of 99 years in 1898.

Despite its turbulent and dishonourable beginning during colonial times, Hong Kong developed rapidly in industry and commerce. One exceptional period was the Japanese occupation during the Second World War, which lasted for three years and eight months (1941-1945). There was also a serious labour movement in 1967 (during the Cultural Revolution in China), in which a great number of militant workers went on strike for fair treatment, but it turned out to be more a riot than a protest. Apart from these events, Hong Kong has been a peaceful place. It developed as a warehouse and distribution centre for trade between the British and southern China in the 19th and 20th centuries. Industrialization initially involved the production of cotton textiles, but gradually diversified to include woollen goods and, in the late 1960s, man-made fibres and complete garments. Hong Kong has become a major exporter of high technology goods and since the late 1980s, Hong Kong has been transformed into one of the world's leading economies.

In December 1984, the People's Republic of China (PRC) and the British government signed the Sino-British Joint Declaration, in which the British government agreed to hand over the entire colony when the lease on the New Territories ended in 1997. The first wave of emigration then took place even though PRC agreed Hong Kong would be allowed to retain its pre-1997 social, economic and legal systems for at least 50 years after 1997. Then there was a second and larger wave of emigration after the suppression of the Tiananmen Square protest on 4th June 1989, which affected many Hong Kong people deeply. The emigrants consisted mostly of middle-class people, and their destinations were western countries like Canada, Australia, or the UK. However, many of them returned to Hong Kong after some years. The Basic Law was accepted in 1990 as the mini-constitution of the Hong Kong Special Administrative Region (HKSAR) after the handover. The British colonial period ended on 1st July 1997 and Hong Kong was handed over to the PRC. Tung Chee-hau was the first Chief Executive of the Hong Kong Special Administrative Region government.

One thing that makes Hong Kong significantly different from other Chinese provinces or cities is that it has its own independent judiciary system. Since Hong Kong was returned to China in 1997, the city is running in a 'One Country, Two Systems' mode, which means it runs according its own Basic Law, which was set out by the Sino-British Government and the Central People's Government before the return of Hong Kong, even though it is part of the People's Republic of China.

The government of the Hong Kong Special Administrative Region (HKSAR) is headed by the Chief Executive, who is elected by a broadly representative

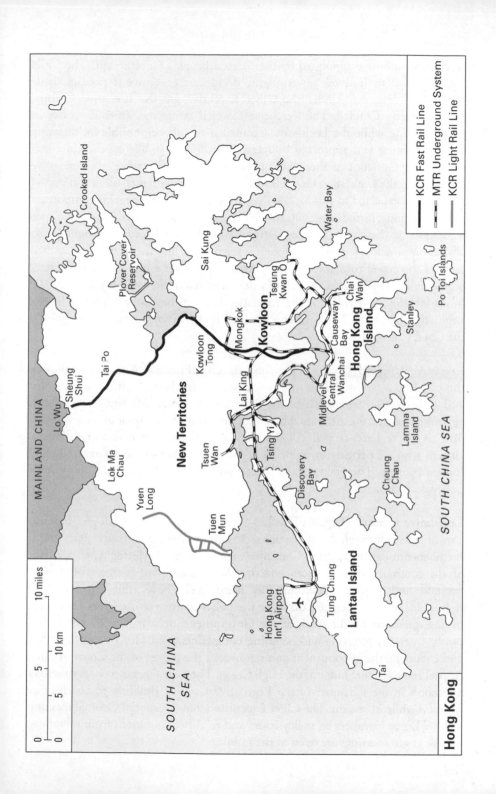

Hong Kong

—		KCR Fast Rail Line
■■		MTR Underground System
—		KCR Light Rail Line

MAINLAND CHINA

Lo Wu

Sheung Shui

Crooked Island

Plover Cover Reservoir

Tai Po

Lok Ma Chau

Yuen Long

Tuen Mun

New Territories

Tsuen Wan

Sai Kung

Kowloon Tong

Lai King

Tsing Yi

Discovery Bay

Cheung Chau

Hong Kong Int'l Airport

Tung Chung

Lantau Island

Tai

Mongkok

Kowloon

Tseung Kwan O

Water Bay

Midlevels
Central
Wanchai

Causeway Bay

Chai Wan

Hong Kong Island

Lamma Island

Stanley

Po Toi Islands

SOUTH CHINA SEA

SOUTH CHINA SEA

10 miles
5

10 km
5

0
0

Election Committee appointed by the Central People's Government. The Chief Executive has to lead the government, decide on government policies, issue executive orders, etc. Under the Chief Executive are the Executive Council and Legislative Council. The Executive Council assists the Chief Executive in policy-making while the Legislative Council is mainly responsible for enacting laws, examining and approving budgets, taxation and public expenditure, and monitoring the work of the government. The Chief Executive, the Executive Council and the Legislation Council work very closely with each other. The Chief Executive is expected to consult the Executive Council before making important policy decisions, introducing bills to the Legislative Council, making subordinate legislation or dissolving the Legislative Council. The Executive Council also advises on principal legislation before it is introduced into the Legislative Council and has the power to make subsidiary legislation under a number of ordinances passed by the Legislative Council. On the other hand, the expenditure of public funds for policies decided by the Executive Council has to be approved by the Legislative Council. The Legislative Council is also given the power to impeach the Chief Executive.

Executive Council (Exco). This comprises 14 Principal Officials, including the Chief Secretary of Administration, Secretary for Justice, Financial Secretary and 11 secretaries (the heads of the departments) from different departments, appointed under the Accountability System. And there are another five non-officials in the Exco as well. All the members of the Exco have to be Chinese citizens who are permanent residents of HKSAR with no right of abode in any foreign country. The Exco usually meets once a week for discussing important policy decisions.

Legislative Council (Legco). This has 60 members, with 24 from geographical constituencies through direct elections, 30 from functional constituencies and 6 members through an Election Committee comprising 800 elected representatives of the community. Apart from enacting laws, examining budgets, approving taxation and public expenditure, as mentioned above, the Legco is also responsible for receiving and debating the policy address of the Chief Executive, raising questions on the work of the Government, debating issues concerning public interests, receiving and handling complaints from Hong Kong residents and endorsing the appointment and removal of the judges of the Court of Final Appeal and the Chief Judge of the High Court. The Legco meets every Wednesday afternoon in the Chamber of the Legislative Council Building to conduct its business while in session. The Chief Executive attends a special Council meeting to brief Legco members on policy issues and to answer questions from members. All the Legco meetings are open to the public.

Political Parties

The history of political parties in Hong Kong is very short, as political parties were illegal before 1990. There were no direct elections for Legco before 1990. Members were either appointed by the governor or selected by functional constituencies at that time.

Political parties in Hong Kong are mainly divided into either pro-democracy or pro-China (mainland) groups. *Hong Kong Democratic Party (DP)* is the most popular political party in Hong Kong. It is a pro-democracy party and has the greatest number of members in the Legco. The *DP* has made strong criticisms to the HKSAR government and is not much favoured by the PRC government. Some of the *DP* members has been branded as 'subversive' and are not welcome to visit mainland China. *The Frontier*, established in 1996, is another pro-democracy party and has been getting more popular in Hong Kong. Its major principle is that Hong Kong people should have the right to elect their own government, which is not the case at present. Other pro-democracy parties include *Association for Democracy and the People's Livelihood* and *Citizens Party*. The basic principle of all the pro-democracy parties is to have the direct election of Chief Executive and members for Exco and Legco. They are all fighting for 'a high degree of autonomy' and 'Hong Kong people ruling Hong Kong', which they believe are implied by the notion of 'One Country, Two Systems'.

The Democratic Alliance for the Betterment of Hong Kong (DAB), formed in 1992, is the leading pro-China group in Hong Kong. It explicitly opposes the direction of the pro-democracy parties. In one dramatic case, for example, after the pro-democracy parties announced that a demonstration against a government proposal would start at the Victory Park, the *DAB* decided to have a party at exactly the same place to celebrate the Special Administrative Region Establishment Day. Other pro-China parties include the *New Century Forum*, the *Hong Kong Progressive Alliance* and the *Liberty Party*. Some people take the *Liberty Party* and the *Hong Kong Progressive Alliance* as pro-business parties rather than pro-China groups as their common and main principle is to ensure 'stability and prosperity', but this also implies avoidance of upsetting the main Chinese government as Hong Kong does a lot of business with mainland China. That is why they are also usually classified as pro-China.

Websites of Political Parties:

The Democratic Party (DP), www.dphk.org.
Democratic Alliance for Betterment of Hong Kong (DAB), www.dab.org.hk.
Citizen Party, www.citizensparty.org.
Liberty Party, www.liberal.org.hk.
The Frontier, www.frontier.org.hk.
The Hong Kong Progressive Alliance, www.hkpa.org.hk.
Association for Democracy and People's Livelihood, www.adpl.org.hk.

Economy

During the 1940s, before the Communists took control of China in 1949 and ended the civil war, many wealthy and skilled people went to Hong Kong to avoid becoming victims of the war. Since then Hong Kong has been getting more and more economically important and it is now one of the world's major financial centres. Since 2000, Canada's Fraser Institute has named Hong Kong as the World's most open economy. The Heritage Foundation has also given the same honour to Hong Kong. In 2001, Hong Kong was the world's second highest per capita holder of foreign currency. The GDP from 2000 to 2002 was around US$160 billion each year, with a steady growth even after the global downturn and the events of 9-11 in 2001.

In the 1950s, Hong Kong developed into a manufacturing centre with new immigrants bringing skills, capital and labour to the city. At that time, Hong Kong was focused on heavy manufacturing, such as ship building. Plastics, textile and toys replaced the heavy manufacturing in the 1960s. Many of these goods were exported to other countries, as they were of high quality and low price. The textile industry was still important in the 70s but there were also some new industries such as electronics, clocks and watches. Starting from the 80s Hong Kong has been changing to a tertiary industry society. Tourism, banking and cargo services have been major contributors to the economy. One of the reasons for Hong Kong changing from a manufacturing society to a commercial centre was the high cost of land and labour for manufacturing. Many of the factory owners chose to move their premises to mainland China to reduce costs. The 90s was a golden time for Hong Kong. It was prosperous with a low unemployment rate (around 2% on average in the early 90s) and there was a great deal of investment from foreign countries, establishing Hong Kong as an important bridge between mainland China and the West. Since then, import/export businesses have grown rapidly. Hong Kong and three other regions in Asia (Singapore, South Korea and Taiwan) were called the Four Little Dragons in the early 90s as they grew rapidly economically and became more and more important globally.

Not long after its return to China, Hong Kong experienced an economic downturn as did many other countries at that time. The real estate market and the stock market collapsed and many property owners experienced financial difficulties for years to come. The unemployment rate in 1998 doubled from that of 1997, from 2.2% to 4.7%. The economy recovered a little in 2000 and 2001 but it then slowed again after the 9-11 attack in the US. Since the Hong Kong currency is tied to the US currency at a fixed rate, the US economy has a big impact on the financial markets in Hong Kong. The unemployment rate has been rising since then and it reached its highest after the SARS (Severe Acute Respiratory Syndrome) outbreak in mid-March 2003. Unemployment increased to a record breaking 8.7% in July 2003. SARS is a fatal, flu-like infectious disease. It killed 300 people, hit the economy badly and many small companies closed down. The catering, retail trade and airline companies suffered the most, since tourists would not take the risk of visiting Hong Kong during the outbreak. The number of tourists dropped by over 50%. Even local people avoided visiting restaurants and other public areas like cinemas and boutiques. Fortunately, Hong Kong has been recovering faster than expected since then. According to the latest government statistics in Oct 2003, the unemployment rate dropped to 8.3% in September and the number of mainland visitors are increasing, this has led to a growth of 8.3% in retail sales volume in the third quarter of the year.

Even though Hong Kong is still recovering from the big blow from SARS, the government is positive about the future economy. The Closer Economic Partnership Arrangement (CEPA) between China and Hong Kong was concluded in late June 2003, which grants Hong Kong products duty-free access to the mainland and additional market access for Hong Kong companies to the mainland. CEPA is believed to be beneficial both to the mainland and to Hong Kong. The Capital Investment Entrant Scheme, launched on 27th October 2003, will attract investment from other countries to Hong Kong. In addition, the low tax rate and government policy of non-interference are still very attractive to foreign companies for investment and trade. The government allows market forces to set wages and prices, and does not restrict foreign capital or investment. It does not impose export performance or local content requirements, and allows free repatriation of profits. Hong Kong is a duty-free port, with very few barriers to trade in goods and services. Moreover, merchandise exports have been growing solidly, even during the outbreak of SARS, which has helped Hong Kong recover from the SARS attack. At the moment, mainland China, the USA, the EU and Japan are the major export markets for Hong Kong.

The Chief Executive emphasized in his Policy Address in January 2003 that financial services, logistics, tourism and producer services have been contributing significantly to the Hong Kong economy and should be reinforced and further strengthened in the future. The Government aims at elevating Hong Kong from its traditional intermediary role, to becoming an active major hub connecting China and international markets. Strengthening the tie with the Pearl River Delta will be essential for the Hong Kong economy as well. The Hong Kong Disneyland project, to be finished by 2005, is expected to be a major project promoting economic recovery.

Here are some highlights of the Hong Kong economy in the past few years:

- World's freest economy
- World's second highest per capita holder of foreign currency
- The second largest source of outward foreign direct investment (FDI) in Asia and tenth in the world
- World's fifth largest holder of foreign exchange reserves
- The tenth largest exporter of commercial services in the world

- The tenth largest trading economy in the world
- World's busiest container port
- World's busiest airport for international cargoes
- The largest venture capital centre in Asia
- The second largest stock market in Asia (after Japan) and the ninth largest in the world
- The third largest foreign exchange market in Asia and seventh in the world

GEOGRAPHICAL INFORMATION

Area

Hong Kong is situated in the south-eastern tip of mainland China, facing the South China Sea. It is a very condensed city with an area of only 1,105 square kilometres, which is about the same size as the City of Los Angeles, two-thirds that of London and half that of Milan.

Regional Divisions

Hong Kong is divided into three regions: Hong Kong Island, Kowloon and the New Territories and outlying islands. Hong Kong Island is the main financial district of the city and is also the earliest developed area in Hong Kong. Many banks and companies are located in *Central*, *Wanchai* and *Causeway Bay*. There are many shopping centres and restaurants on Hong Kong Island and it is usually where the tourists first set foot. Hong Kong Island is separated from the New Territories and Kowloon. However, a good transport system links the areas very well. Kowloon lies to the south of the New Territories and consists of the smallest area (46.89 square kilometres) of the three regions but the population density is the highest. The crowded *Mongkok* is popular with teenagers as there are a lot of trendy shops and a great number of people go to *Wong Tai Sin* to make a wish on Chinese New Year. The New Territories and outlying islands occupy around 80% of the area of Hong Kong (around 970 square kilometres). The New Territories are situated in the middle to northern part of Hong Kong, and consist of many new towns and some old villages. The main connections between mainland China and Hong Kong, Lo Wu and Lok Ma Chau, are located in the New Territories. The three largest outlying islands are Lantau Island, Cheung Chau and Lamma Island, and they all lie to in the south or southwest of Hong Kong. Hong Kong International Airport is located on Lantau Island.

Useful Interactive Map

Centamap, www.centamap.com.

Population

According to government statistics conducted in 2003, there are 6,803,100 people living in Hong Kong with an average population density of 6,300 per square kilometre. The population density can be up to 43,220 per square kilometre in Kowloon. The population growth rate is quite stable at around 1% per year. The female population comprises around 52%. The bulk of the population (72%) is aged between 15 and 64, and the elderly (aged 65 or above) make up about 11% of the population. More than 90% of the population is Chinese and around 2% is Filipino. The rest mainly come from other Asian countries while westerners are a minority in Hong Kong accounting for around 1% of the total population.

Climate

Hong Kong is quite hot in summer and the temperature can be above 30°C (86°F) in July and August. However, air conditioning is very common (even on public transport) so that it will not be too uncomfortable unless you stay outdoors most of the time. Winter falls between December and February with an average temperature of 13-15°C (55-59°F). You may experience a few colder days during the winter but the temperature rarely falls below 5°C (41°F). Temperatures range from 15-25°C (59-77°F) in other months throughout the year. Since Hong Kong is a peninsula, the humidity is quite high with an average of 70%. Summer is the rainy season, which starts in June or July. Summer is also the typhoon season when the weather can be very bad. Since Hong Kong lies near the Equator, sunrise and sun-set times do not vary much throughout the year, and hence there is no daylight-saving season in Hong Kong.

Air pollution in Hong Kong is quite serious due to the large number of vehicles and the emission from factories. Many foreigners take a long time to get used to the poor air quality. Air pollution is particularly serious in *Causeway Bay, Wanchai, Mongkok, Sham Shui Po* and the factory areas. The Environment Protection Department takes the Air Pollution Index everyday and you can find the index in weather forecasts and also newspapers. It is advisable not to go to crowded areas, for examples *Causeway Bay* and *Mongkok*, if the Air Pollution Index is over 100, which means the quality of air is very poor.

GETTING THERE

The cost of flying to Hong Kong varies from low season to peak season. Flying from London to Hong Kong takes 12 to 13 hours and costs around $5,000 (US$640/£400) for a one-way ticket in high season or $3,000 or below in low season. The cost of flying from the East coast of America is around $8,000 (US$1,000/£640) in high season and $6000 (US$800/£500) in low season. Flights fly towards the East and it takes around 20 hours to fly from New York to Hong Kong. It is quicker to fly from the West coast, which takes 14 to 15 hours, since flights go westwards instead. The prices for tickets in high season and low season for flying from the West coast are around $7,000 (US$900/£550) and $5,500 (US$700/£440). The peak season runs from mid-June to September (and also over Christmas). You will get the cheapest tickets in October, November and March. In general, the earlier you book, the cheaper the fare. Indirect flights stopping in Singapore or Taiwan are usually cheaper. There are also some online search engines specifically for air tickets and they usually provide better offers than booking directly from airlines.

It is easy to go to the city centre from Hong Kong International Airport. You can take buses or the Airport Express (operated by MTR, one of the major railways in Hong Kong). You can take a taxi if you do not mind paying more. It costs about $300 to go to Central from the airport by taxi.

Airline Websites

Air Canada, www.aircanada.ca.
Air France, www.airfrance.com.
Air New Zealand, www.airnz.com.au.
American Airlines, www.aa.com.
Australia Airlines, www.australianairlines.com.au.
British Airways, www.britishairways.com.
Cathay Pacific Airway, www.cathaypacific.com.
China Airlines, www.china-airlines.com.
Delta Airlines, www.delta.com.
Emirates Airlines, www.emirates.com.
EVA Air, www.evaair.com.
Finnair, www.finnair.com.
Singapore Airlines, www.singaporeair.com.

Other Useful Websites

www.expedia.co.uk.
www.priceline.com.
www.onlinetravel.com.
www.statravel.com.
www.traveljungle.co.uk.
www.travelsupermarket.com.

Useful addresses

Hong Kong Tourism Board(Head Office), 9-11/F Citicorp Centre, 18 Whitfield Road, North Point, Hong Kong; ☎(852) 2807 6543; fax (852) 2806 0303; e-mail info@www.hktb.com; www.discoverhongkong.com.
Hong Kong Tourism Board (London Office), 6 Grafton Street, London W1S 4EQ, United Kingdom; ☎(44) 20 7533 7100; fax (44) 20 7533 7111; e-mail lonwwo@hktb.com.
Hong Kong Tourism Board (New York Office), 115 East 54th Street, Second Floor, New York, NY 10022-4512, USA; ☎(1) 212 421 3382; fax (1) 212 421 8428;

e-mail nycwwo@hktb.com.

Hong Kong Tourism Board (Toronto Office), Ground Floor, 9 Temperance Street, Toronto, Ontario M5H 1Y6, Canada; ☎(1) 416 366 2389; fax (1) 416 366 1098; e-mail yyzwwo@hktb.com.

The Travel Industry Council of Hong Kong (TIC), Rooms 1706-09, Fortress Tower, 250 King's Road, North Point, Hong Kong; ☎(852) 2807 1199; fax (852) 2510 9907; www.tichk.org.

The Association of British Travel Agents (A.B.T.A.), 68-71 Newman St., London W1T 3AH; ☎(44) 020 7637 2444; fax (44) 020 7637 0713; e-mail corporate@abta.co.uk; www.abta.com.

American Society of Travel Agents (ASTA), 1101 King Street, Ste. 200, Alexandria, VA 22314; tel (1) 703 739 2782; fax (1) 703 684 8319; e-mail askasta@astahq.com; www.astanet.com.

STA Travel (UK), Customer Relations Manager, STA Travel, 6 Wrights Lane, London, W8 6TA; ☎(44) 0870 1 600 599; fax 44 (0)207 938 4755; www.statravel.co.uk.

STA Travel (USA), Customer Services, BerkelyCare, P.O. Box 9366, Garden City, NY 11530; ☎(1) 800-781-4040; www.statravel.com.

STA Travel (Hong Kong), Suite 1703, 17/F Tower One, Silvercord Centre, 30 Canton Road, Tsim Sha Tsui, Kowloon, Hong Kong; ☎(852) 2736 1618; fax (852) 2736 1698; www.statravel.com.hk.

Registrar of Travel Agents, 4901, 49/F., Hopewell Centre, 183 Queen's Road East, Wanchai, Hong Kong; ☎(852) 3151 7945; e-mail targr@edlb.gov.hk.

RESIDENCE & ENTRY REGULATIONS

CHAPTER SUMMARY

○ Citizens of more than 170 countries may visit Hong Kong without a visa for seven days to six months.

○ British Nationals can stay as visitors for up to six months; US and many European citizens are allowed to visit without a visa for 90 days.

○ Visas for employment as professionals and imported workers are only issued to applicants with special skills or knowledge or who have experience of value to Hong Kong which is not readily available locally.

○ You need to have net assets or net equity with a market value of HK$6.5 million or more to enrol into the Capital Investment Entrant scheme.

○ There is a minimum wage for overseas domestic helpers even though there is none for other industries.

○ Foreign children can only be admitted to private schools, unless for tertiary education.

○ The Working Holiday Scheme is open to Australian and New Zealand citizens.

○ **Citizenship**. You must live in Hong Kong for a continuous period of seven years to become a permanent resident.

BACKGROUND

Due to over-crowding, Hong Kong has never been very keen to attract permanent immigrants. In fact, the government has been busy preventing illegal immigrants from entering Hong Kong, especially during the 80s and the early 90s. There were mass influxes of illegal immigrants from mainland China in the early 60s and 70s and they were allowed to stay in Hong Kong and became legal residents. But since October 1980 the government has prohibited illegal immigrants from the Mainland from remaining in the city. However, a great number of illegal immigrants continue to take the risk and enter Hong Kong to take up employment. The government has spent many years fighting illegal employment and introduced several laws in the 90s to prohibit employers from hiring the illegal immigrants. Apart from those from the Mainland, there were also a great number of Vietnamese refugees seeking shelter in the 80s and 90s. Many of them came to Hong Kong to ask the authorities to help them to settle in other countries. Around 140,000 Vietnamese have been settled overseas with the help of the Hong Kong government between 1975 and 2000. However, it has been getting more and more difficult to convince other countries to accept the refugees permanently, and many of those who came in the 90s were not actually qualified as refugees in the first place. The number of Vietnamese arrivals did not decrease until the Hong Kong Government abolished the 'Port of First Asylum' Policy in1998.

It is not easy to obtain long-term residence in Hong Kong. Some professionals are allowed to work and thus stay during their working period in Hong Kong. Alternatively, you could be a dependent of a permanent resident or of a professional who is allowed to work in Hong Kong. If you have enough financial assets you can also consider the *Capital Investment Entrant Scheme*.

Foreigners are always welcomed to enter Hong Kong for short-term visits. Tourism has been an important industry for the city since the early 80s and attracted more than 16 million visitors in 2003. The government has granted visa-free visits to nationals of about 170 countries and territories to make it easy to travel to Hong Kong. Most of the foreigners enjoy a visa-free period from seven days to three months. British Nationals can stay without a visa for six months.

The Immigration Department processed over 107,000 visa applications in 2003, among which more than 10% were issued to professionals to work in Hong Kong. Following the hand-over in 1997, the Hong Kong and Mainland governments have been working on simplifying the immigration procedures between the two. Visiting quotas for Chinese citizens have been removed to make travelling to Hong Kong easier, and the government has been looking for more professionals from mainland China and launched the *Admission Scheme for Mainland Talents and Professionals* in July 2003. In October the same year, the government launched another scheme to attract capital investors. Even though the scheme is not limited to Chinese citizens, it is believed that most potential applicants will be from mainland China.

VISAS

Visit, Transit or Business Visit

Many foreigners enjoy a visa free period, for travel to Hong Kong and as long as you hold a valid passport during your stay, you can buy a flight ticket and visit Hong Kong at anytime. Americans, Australians and most Europeans can stay in Hong Kong without a visa for up to 90 days while British citizens enjoy a longer visa-free stay for up to 180 days. Visitors are not allowed to engage in any employment or become a student at a school, university or other educational institute during their stay.

Business visit refers to a visit related to business but does not entail employment. Staff of multi-national corporations and joint-venture companies going to Hong Kong for orientation, product update or an exchange programme can apply for a business visit visa instead of a training or employment visa.

An onward ticket with a clear destination is required for application for a transit visa. However, no onward ticket is required if the destination of the onward trip is Mainland China or Macau.

Required documents:

- ID936 form with parts A, B, C and D completed.
- A photocopy of your travel document, the page with personal particulars, date of issue and expiry date.
- Evidence of employment (if any) and financial standing.
- Copy of identity card for the reference/sponsor (if any), or copy of the Business Registration Certificate of the company if it is a business visit.

Employment for Professionals or Entry for Investment Purpose

An application for an imported worker or domestic helper is not covered in this section. Please see relevant parts later in this chapter.

Hong Kong issued 16,929 visas for employment and investment purposes in 2002. Applicants for an employment or investment visa are supposed to possess a special skill or knowledge or have experience of value to Hong Kong which is not readily available locally. The applicant is supposed to be in a position to make a substantial contribution to the local economy. Before issuing a visa, the Immigration Department considers whether the applicant is suitably qualified with the relevant experience for the job, whether the terms and conditions of employment are comparable to those in the local market, and whether the job can be filled locally.

These entry arrangements do not apply to nationals from Afghanistan, Albania, Bulgaria, Cambodia, Cuba, Laos, Mongolia, Democratic People's Republic of Korea, Romania and Vietnam. Chinese nationals holding PRC passports can apply only if the applicant has been residing overseas for at least one year immediately before submission of the application.

Required documents for Employment:

- ID936 form with parts A, B, E, F and G completed.

O Photocopies of travel document, the page with personal particulars, date of issue and expiry date.
O Proof of academic qualifications and experience relevant to the post.
O A copy of the service contract or letter of appointment with details of the post, salaries and benefits and employment period.

Required documents for Investment:

O Documents listed under *Supporting documents for Employment* (complete part J instead of part G in the ID936 form).
O Business registration certificate.
O Business registration particulars.
O Partnership agreement.
O Certificate of Incorporation.
O Memorandum and Articles of Association.
O Returns on directors.
O Allotment of all shares.
O Returns on shareholders.
O Office purchase/tenancy agreement and the size.
O Current staff list.
O Company profile.
O Proof of business activities/transactions.
O Import and export customs declaration.
O Current financial standing and source of finance of both the company and the applicant.
O Trading profit and loss account.
O Trial balance sheet up to last month and projected turnover in the coming year.
O A full resume of applicant.
O A full job description of the post that the applicant will take up.
O Provision of housing for the applicant and the remuneration/honorarium the applicant will receive.
O Actual monetary investment of the applicant in the company.
O A detailed business plan.

Capital Investment Entrant Scheme

Some terms specific to the Scheme will come up in this section. Here are some notes for your reference:

Terms relating to the Capital Investment Entrant Scheme

Approval-in-Principle: a preliminary and provisional grant of approval in writing given by the director to the applicant to enter and/or remain in Hong Kong pursuant to the scheme

Director: director of the Immigration Department

Entrant: an individual who has been granted Formal Approval by the director

Formal Approval: a confirmed grant of approval in writing given by the director to the Applicant to enter and/or remain in Hong Kong pursuant to the Scheme

Market Value: the best price obtainable for the exchange of assets or property between a willing buyer and a willing seller in a transaction

Net assets/net equity: the two terms are interchangeable, meaning any asset, property or equity after deducting the amount of lien and encumbrance secured on or attached to it

Premissible investment assets: real estate and specified financial assets, including equities, debt securities, certificates of deposits, subordinated debt, Eligible Collective Investment Scheme

Date of completion: the date of payment on completion, or the last instalment if payment is made by more than one instalment.

Since October 2003 foreigners have been permitted to enter and stay in Hong Kong as a Capital Investment Entrant. 'Investments' here only refer to investments in real estate or specified financial assets (equities, debt securities, certificates of deposits, subordinated debt, Eligible Collective Investment Scheme); other forms of investments do not count under this scheme. In addition, the entrants of the scheme are not allowed to engage in running any business. Up to 31st December, 2003, there were 150 applications with 35 and 19 of them granted Approval-in-Principle and Formal Approval respectively. The total amount of money attracted was around HK$144 million (US$18 million/£12 million).

To be a Capital Investment Entrant, you must be 18 or above, and have net assets or net equity with a market value of not less than HK$6.5 million (US$800,000/£500,000) throughout the two years before you lodge an application. Moreover, you should have started investing within the six months before submission of your application, or will invest within six months after the granting of Approval-in-Principle. A three-month stay as a visitor will be granted after obtaining the Approval-in-Principle, and it can be extended for another three months if evidence of active progress in investment is shown. When the entrant has provided proof that the requisite level of investment has been made, a Formal Approval will be granted and he or she can stay for two years. A further extension of two years will be granted if the entrant can demonstrate further evidence for the continuation of investments. Further extensions, in units of two years, will be granted on the same principle. After the entrant has stayed in Hong

Kong continually for seven years, he or she becomes a permanent resident.

Entrants are allowed to bring their spouse and children under the age of 18 with them to Hong Kong, as long as he or she is capable of supporting their dependents without relying on any return from the Permissible investment assets, from employment in or carried out in Hong Kong, or from any public assistance. Dependents of entrants are prohibited from taking up employment until they become permanent residents but children are allowed to study in local schools.

Entrants are not required to top-up the value of investments even if the market value of the assets falls below HK$6.5 million. However, even if the market value of the investments rises above HK$6.5 million, the entrants are not allowed to withdraw or remove any appreciation from the investment assets without sacrificing the right to stay under the scheme.

Apart from the application form ID967, you should also provide any document, for example transaction records, related to your investment to the Immigration Department when you apply to be an entrant. Moreover, you also need to keep the records of your investment and provide written materials to the Director for assessing your eligibility and entitlement under the scheme. The Immigration Department usually takes four to six weeks to process an application.

Employment as Imported Worker

The Supplementary Labour Scheme (SLS) allows employers to import workers from outside Hong Kong if the employer experiences genuine difficulties in filling the vacancies locally. Workers imported under the SLS are restricted to those at the technician, craftsman, supervisor and experienced operative levels. SLS does not apply to some categories of jobs for which the supply in the local market is plentiful. For further details of the excluded categories, please visit the Immigration Department website. Employers have to apply directly to the Labour Department for approval-in-principle before they make the visa arrangements for their imported workers. The visa application has to be made within three months after the approval-in-principle is obtained.

Required documents:

- ID936 form with parts A, B, E, F, H and I completed;
- Photocopies of travel document, the page with personal particulars, date of issue and expiry date;
- A set of standard employment contracts signed between the applicant and employer;
- Academic qualifications and experience relevant to the post;
- Proof showing the applicant is physically fit for the job.

Employment as Domestic Helper

Domestic helpers in Hong Kong are mainly from the Philippines, Thailand, or Indonesia. The employer has to provide a document stating the salary offered when applying for a visa for a domestic helper, as the Hong Kong Government has set a minimum wage to protect them. The applicant should have more than two years' working experience as a domestic helper and must be physically fit for the job. The employer has to be financially capable of providing accommodation and guaranteeing the applicant's maintenance and repatriation upon the termination of the contract.

Required documents:

- ID936 form with parts A, B, E and F completed
- Photocopies of travel document, the page with personal particulars, date of issue and expiry date;
- Standard employment contracts signed by both employer and applicant;
- A testimonial of previous working experience;
- Proof showing the applicant is physically fit for the job.

Training

If you want to acquire special skills or knowledge not available in your home country, you may apply for a training visa to Hong Kong. A visa for entering Hong Kong for the purpose of training is usually limited to a period 12 months. The applicant should receive training at the company's premises until the end of the agreed period and the trainee will return to his/her home country after that. It will be easier to get the visa if there is a contract between the sponsor and the trainee, and if the sponsor is a well-known company.

Entry arrangements do not apply to nationals from Afghanistan, Albania, Bulgaria, Cambodia, Cuba, Laos, Mongolia, Democratic People's Republic of Korea, Romania, Vietnam, and mainland China.

Required documents: as for an Employment visa.

Education

There are over 1,500 foreign students (not including those from mainland China and dependants of other visa holders) coming to study in Hong Kong every year. One must apply for a student visa before coming to Hong Kong unless one is a Chinese resident of the mainland or Taiwan. Except for tertiary education, foreign students can only be admitted to private schools but not public or suppported schools. Children going to pursue primary education in Hong Kong must be between the ages of 6 and 11. Applicants who are below the age of 20 can be admitted to secondary schools in Hong Kong. The applicant must hold a letter of acceptance from the school before applying for the student visa. Moreover, the applicant has to name a local sponsor who agrees to support and provide accommodation for the student.

Required documents:

- ID936 form with parts A, B and E completed;
- Photocopies of travel document, the page with personal particulars, date of issue and expiry date;
- A letter of acceptance from the school;
- A letter of consent from one of the applicant's parents, if the applicant is under the age of 18;
- A copy of the sponsor's Hong Kong identity card and/or travel document;
- Evidence of the sponsor's financial standing;
- An undertaking that the sponsor is prepared to act as the guardian in Hong Kong and that the applicant will be staying with him, or evidence that a place has been provided in a recognised boarding school.

Working Holiday Scheme

At the moment, this scheme only accepts applications from Australian and New Zealand citizens and there is a quota of 200 for each country every year. The aim of the scheme is to facilitate cultural and educational exchange between Hong Kong and the participating countries. The applicant must be aged between 18 and 30 and the main intention must be for holiday not work. Applicants have to show that they are financially capable of supporting themselves during their stay in Hong Kong and to purchase a return ticket at the end of the stay. Successful applicants are allowed to stay for a period of not more than 12 months. They may take up short-term employment but they are not allowed to work for the same employer for more than three months. They are allowed to enrol in study or training course(s) of not more than three months (New Zealand citizens can only enrol in one course while there is no limit for Australia citizens). A person can only apply for the scheme once and an extension of stay will not normally be considered. It usually takes two weeks to process the application.

Required documents:

- Completed application form ID940.
- A photocopy of travel document, the page with personal particulars, date of issue and expiry date.
- Financial proof of a sufficient amount for maintenance during the stay in Hong Kong, e.g. bank statement, saving accounts passbooks, etc.
- A photocopy of your return ticket or financial proof of having an amount

equivalent to the return air fare.

○ A cashier order/bank draft for payment of the visa fee (which will be returned to the applicant if the application is unsuccessful).

Residence as Dependant

Dependent can be the spouse, unmarried children (aged below 18) and parents (60 or above) of a Hong Kong resident (the sponsor). Widows and widowers can apply as a dependant for joining their relatives in Hong Kong when they reach the age of 60. The applicant has to show a satisfactory relationship with the sponsor. The sponsor must have the right of abode in Hong Kong and be able to support the dependant at a reasonable living standard and provide him/her with suitable accommodation in Hong Kong. Successful visa applicants of Employment as Capital Investment Entrants, professionals entitled to work in Hong Kong, and visa holders for entry for investment, training, study as a full-time undergraduate and post-graduate can also bring their spouses and unmarried dependent children under the age of 18 (but not parents) to Hong Kong. The dependants are not permitted to take up employment during their stay in Hong Kong. Imported workers, domestic helpers and successfully applicants for the Working Holiday Scheme are not allowed to bring in their dependants.

Required documents:

○ ID936 form with parts A, B and I completed;
○ Photocopies of travel document, the page with personal particulars, date of issue and expiry date;
○ A copy of sponsor's Hong Kong identity card;
○ Evidence of the sponsor's financial standing;
○ Evidence of the applicant's relationship with the applicant;
○ Evidence of sponsor's accommodation.

Application Methods

For visa application for employment, investment (Capital Investment Entrant Scheme is not included), education, visit, training and residence, one has to fill-in the relevant parts_of application form ID936 with a photograph affixed to it. The size of the photograph must not larger than 55mm x 45mm and not smaller than 50mm x 40mm. The photograph must be taken full face and without a hat against a plain background of mid-range colours (white, pink or light blue are the most common). Supporting documents should be presented along with application. See supporting documents under each visa section. An application form can be downloaded from the Immigration Department's website: *http://www.immd.gov.hk/*. It usually takes four to six weeks to process an entry visa. Applications for transit or a visit should be sent to the Hong Kong Immigration

Department, Visitors Section, 6/F, Immigration Tower, 7 Gloucester Road, Wan Chai, Hong Kong. For application of Capital Investment Entrant Scheme, send your application to Other Visas & Permits Section, Immigration Department, 7/F, Immigration Tower, 7 Gloucester Road, Wan Chai, Hong Kong. Any other applications should be sent to Hong Kong Immigration Department, Receipt and Despatch Unit, 2/F, Immigration Tower, 7 Gloucester Road, Wan Chai, Hong Kong. Applicants can also hand in the application form in person to the nearest Chinese diplomatic and consular missions in their place of domicile.

Fees

Ordinary Visa	$135
Transit Visa	$70
Working Holiday Scheme	$135
Capital Investment Entrant Scheme	$135
Change of conditions of stay or extension of limit of stay	$135
Declaration of nationality change	$145
Naturalisation as a Chinese National	$2,730

HONG KONG CITIZENSHIP

Unlike Canada and Australia, there is no points system for migrating to Hong Kong. To become a Hong Kong citizen, you have to enter Hong Kong with valid travel documents, and have to reside in Hong Kong for a continuous period of not less than seven years. You will need to apply for the Hong Kong Identity Card and make a declaration adopting Hong Kong as your permanent place of residence. After becoming a permanent resident, you are entitled to vote and receive social security. You can also apply for a HKSAR passport while keeping your original foreign passport. Contact the Immigration Department for further enquiries on Hong Kong citizenship.

SETTING UP HOME

CHAPTER SUMMARY

- **Home Ownership**. 50% of households are owner-occupied.
- The government provides public housing for low-income households.
- Flats and houses are very small and expensive when compared to those in the USA and Europe.
- Buying a property before its construction is completed is common.
- **Electricity.** The electricity supply is 220 volts (50 Hz).
  - Shops are prohibited from selling electrical appliances or components with 2-pin plugs.
- **Telephone**. There is no per-minute charge for making local calls but there is a basic monthly fee.

OVERVIEW

Hong Kong people spend a rather large proportion of their salary on mortgage repayments or rent. According to statistics conducted by the government, the median mortgage payment and loan repayment to income ratio is 28% while median rent to income ratio is 14%. About half the population own their own houses or apartments.

Hong Kong is an extremely crowded area with a population of around 6,800,000 living in an area less than 1105 square kilometres, which is about two-thirds the size of London (1572 square kilometres). What makes the overcrowding worse is the fact that the distribution of this high density is not even. The population density in the Kowloon area, for instance, is as high as 43,200 people per square kilometre. The only way to accommodate all of the people in such a small area is to exploit the three-dimensional space by putting people into very tall buildings. Residential buildings are usually about 30-storeys tall, or higher, and all of them are equipped with elevators. In general, people prefer to live on higher floors, so the higher you live, the more expensive is the price of the apartment. The major determinant of the price or the rent, however, is location. Districts like Mid-Level and Discovery Bay, which are more scenic, are very expensive. Apartments in Causeway Bay and Central are also quite expensive as they are close to the business centre. You will probably find cheaper apartments in the New Territories and outlying islands than in Hong Kong Island or Kowloon, although they are still far from cheap by any standard. Therefore many local people choose to live in public rental apartments, which are managed by the government to provide cheap accommodation for low-income households.

It is quite common to buy an apartment before the construction is finished. The builders advertise when there are going to be new residential avenues and set out dates for purchasing. You can see long queues outside the building sites on the dates for selling. For details please see *Buying Property under Construction* later in this chapter.

About 50% of the people actually own the property they live in. The Hong Kong Government has different policies to help middle and low-income households to purchase their own property to fulfil the goal of 70% home ownership by the year 2007. The Home Ownership Scheme, launched in 1978, assists middle- and low-income households to buy apartments at discounted prices. These flats can be re-sold in the open market starting from the sixth year after purchase. The Home Ownership Scheme is now suspended but it is possible that the government will re-launch the scheme in the future. At the moment, however, the government still provides loans for households to purchase their property. For people living in public housing, the Hong Kong Government has launched another scheme, the Tenants Purchase Scheme, which was designed to help public housing residents to buy the rented apartments. The tenants of public residential complexes can buy the flats they are currently occupying at very affordable prices; the scheme is expected to continue to run until 2007.

If you want to buy or rent an apartment, it is probably easier to do so through real estate agents, especially if you are not familiar with the local legal procedures. All the real estate agents are licensed and you can ask them to show you their licence before engaging them as your representative.

How Do Hong Kong People Live?

Hong Kong people are not a mobile group like Americans and Europeans. They usually spend a very long time in the same place and hence buying an apartment or a house and living there for over 30 years is very common. Apartments in Hong Kong are typically small. It is common to find a family of four or five living in a small apartment of around 300-500 square feet (approximately 28-46 square metres). They usually have a living room, one or two bedrooms, a kitchen and a bathroom. Some bigger and more luxurious houses may have three bedrooms, with one of them en-suite, but it is not common among middle or low income groups. It is considered a real luxury for people to have a house with a backyard, as everyone does in some western countries. If you are really rich, you can look for proper houses in Mid-Level, Stanley, Sai Kung or Tai Po. They do exist, though they usually come at an incredibly high price. The price for a flat of 3000 square feet (280 square metres) is around $28 million, which is around $9500 per square foot (US$1200/£760 per one square foot or US$12,800/£8000 per square metre).

Although the transport system is good, many people still prefer to have a car. The population to car ratio is 15:1, which is on average one car in every five families. Electrical appliances like refrigerators, air-conditioners, washing machines, televisions and microwave ovens are a basic necessity for any household. Computer and broadband network connections are becoming increasingly common in many households as well.

MORTGAGES

In Hong Kong, banks are the main providers of mortgage services. In general, a buyer can borrow around 70% of the value of the apartment from banks and some provide mortgages up to 90%. There are several types of mortgage provided by the banks including Floating Rate Mortgages, Fixed Adjustable Rate Mortgages and Mortgage Insurance Programmes. Fixed Adjustable Rate Mortgages are mortgages originated at a fixed gross mortgage rate, which is fixed for the first year or up to three years. After the end of the fixed term, the borrowers can choose to continue another fixed term under the gross mortgage rate at that time, or change to Floating Rate Mortgage, where the mortgage rate can be adjusted from time to time according to the market rate. The Mortgage Insurance Programme was launched in 1999, with the Hong Kong Mortgage Corporation Limited (a government authority established in 1997) providing the mortgage insurance. Under this programme the banks can provide a mortgage of up to 90% to the borrowers. However, the Mortgage Insurance Programme only applies to borrowers who buy properties for self-occupying purposes but not for investment purposes. Some of the buyers will choose to have a second mortgage, which in general provides a further 15%-20% loan on the value of the property, if the first mortgage is 70% or less of the property value.

The interest rate and repayment period are the two major factors to consider when choosing a mortgage provider. Banks provide different types of mortgages to fit the needs of borrowers and the repayment period can be up to 30-years long. In general, the more you can borrow, the higher the interest rate. And you should bear in mind that there is usually a minimum repayment period, and extra costs may be incurred if you repay all the mortgage before the minimum repayment period expires. Some builders have agreements with specific banks to provide mortgages to buyers at a better rate, but it may not necessarily be the best deal available. It is better to go through the different mortgage plans of different banks before choosing the one that suits your needs. There is a list of mortgage providers in the Hong Kong Mortgage Corporation Limited website and you can also visit the banks' websites (listed under *Banking* in the chapter *Daily Life*) for information about different mortgage plans.

Useful Website

Hong Kong Mortgage Corporation Limited, www.hkmc.com.hk. With information of different kinds of mortgages and a list of mortgage providers.

BUYING A PROPERTY

Buying a Property under Construction

Buying a property before its construction is completed is quite common in Hong Kong. It is called buying *Lou Fa* ('house flowers'), presumably analogous to buying flowers and waiting for them to blossom later on. When a new, residential building under construction is up for sale, interested buyers have to register with the builder and present a cheque for 5% of the average selling price of the apartments in the building. The builder will then arrange a date for the registered buyers to select their desired apartments. The buyers have to sign a temporary contract with the builder after they have selected the apartments. The cheque they have handed in earlier will be used as part of the deposit for the apartments they buy. If the buyers fail to find a desired apartment or they are absent on the date for selecting an apartment, the cheque they have handed in during registration will be returned to them. Otherwise, the buyers will have to sign a standard contract with the builder within three days. In general, the builder will cancel the temporary contract if the buyers do not sign the standard contract within three days and the cheques in this case will not be refunded. The contract is drawn up by a lawyer for the builder and is approved by the Land Department, which should clearly state the selling price, date for the apartment to be finished, payment method, compensation if the apartment is not finished on time, etc. The contract will then be sent to the lawyers of the buyers before the buyers sign it. The apartments are technically owned by the builders until the construction is finished and is approved by the government. The builder has to notify the buyers to take possession of their apartments within a month and the buyers, in general, have to complete all the transaction procedures 14 days after the builder sends the letters.

Buying a Completed Property

The procedures for buying a completed property are simpler than buying a property under construction. At least you do not need to register and sign a temporary contract with the builder. However, most of the new apartments are sold while they are still under construction and hence most completed properties you can find are not new but second-hand ones. Most owners sell their properties through real estate agents, which means the buyers and the owners do not usually negotiate directly over the selling price. It is important to check with the real estate agents to see if the furniture, electrical appliances, etc are included in the selling price. Do also take a careful look at the property before signing the contract, as both the seller and agents will tend to only show you the best aspects of the property.

Finding a Property

> ### Jennifer Atkinson on finding a property
>
> If you want the standard ex-pat package, stay in the Midlevels, but I particularly enjoyed living away from that scene where the majority of your neighbours are not ex-pats.

The most convenient way to find a property is through real estate agents. You can either visit or call them or visit their websites for enquiries. There are also advertisements in newspapers and magazines, with dates for registration, when there are new residential sites for sale. See below for a list of major agents.

Checking the Property

No one wants to pay for an apartment with cracks in the walls or a bathtub that leaks. It is very important to check everything in your new home carefully. Check the sink and bathtub to see if the draining system is working properly. Is there any gap between the door and door frame? Are the keys well-fitted to the doors? Are the electrical appliances supplied working properly and are they exactly the make which the builder or the owner promised to offer (some builders supply electrical appliances as an offer to buyers)? Mark down the readings of electricity and water used during your tests, to see if the meters are working. If there is anything wrong with the property, you should ask the builder or the owner to fix the problems as soon as possible.

Insurance

It is expensive to buy a house or an apartment, and everyone wants to keep his or her home in good shape to minimize any chance of possible loss. Therefore, many people prefer to have a home insurance plan to reduce the loss in case of accidents such as fire. Both insurance companies and banks provide different kinds of home insurance policies. Some cover a single event like fire protection, and there is also a combined one which covers different kinds of losses like burglary, fire, damage to home decoration and even medical expenses for domestic helpers.

Useful Addresses

The Bank of East Asia, Limited, 10 Des Voeux Road Central, Hong Kong; ☎ (852) 2842 3200; fax (852) 2845 9333; www.hkbea.com.
Hang Seng Bank Ltd., 83 Des Voeux Road Central, Central Hong Kong; ☎ (852)

2198 1111; fax (852) 2845 9301/2868 4047; www.hangseng.com.

The Hongkong and Shanghai Banking Corporation Limited, 1 Queen's Road Central, Central, Hong Kong; ☎(852) 2822 1111; fax (852) 2810 1112; www.hsbc.com.hk.

Standard Chartered Bank, 4-4A Des Voeux Road Central, Central, Hong Kong; ☎(852) 2820 3333; fax (852) 2856 9129; www.standardchartered.com.hk.

American International Assurance Co (Bermuda) Ltd, AIA Tower, North Point; ☎(852) 2232 8888; www.aia.com.hk.

Blue Cross (Asia-Pacific) Insurance Ltd, 22/F., Cosco Tower, 183 Queen's Road Central, Hong Kong; ☎(852) 2163 1000; fax (852) 2808 1300; www.bluecross.com.hk.

ING General Insurance International, 7/F ING Tower, 308 Des Voeux Road Central, Hong Kong; ☎(852) 2850 3030; www.ing.com.hk/gi.

Prudential Assurance Co Ltd, The Cityplaza Taikoo Shing, Shau Kei Wan.

RENTING A PROPERTY

It is more usual for a foreigner to rent an apartment or house, rather than buying one immediately, when he or she first arrives. Moreover, it is usually cheaper, if you do not plan to stay for a long period, or if you are not yet sure of what you want. You can find both furnished and unfurnished flats in Hong Kong. It is easiest to look for a flat or house through real estate agents. Many real estate agents put the details of vacant flats or houses on their websites and you can have a look at these websites before contacting the agents. Some owners prefer to put an advertisement in newspapers instead, but it is not very common these days. You may find some on-street advertisements as well, which is more common around rural villages in the New Territories or some older districts. Be careful when dealing with these owners, particularly if you are looking for a flat in older Kowloon districts like Yau Ma Tei and Shum Shui Po. There have been complaints that some advertisements were merely posted to lure people to a place where they can easily be robbed. Universities usually have a notice board for leasing and it would be easier to check up there, instead of with real estate agents, if you are looking for a room or a flat to share. Some of them may be offered to students only, but you can always ask and try.

Tenancy Agreement

It is important to read the tenancy agreement carefully before signing as the law in Hong Kong tends to favour the landlord rather than the tenant, which may sound a bit unusual. It is normal for the landlord to collect a month's rent in advance on top of the first month's rental payment, as deposit. The landlord will hold the deposit until you move out. Bills are usually not included. It would be wise to make sure to what extent you are responsible for damaged furniture during your rental period and make it a written statement on the tenancy agreement. The tenancy agreement may not state the exact rental period but it is important to discuss this with the landlord. You should make sure that the period of notification required in case either side wants to end the tenancy is written in the tenancy agreement. You will probably have to inform the landlord at least a month before you are moving out but it all depends on the agreement between you and the landlord. The landlord should inform you if there is an increase in rent at least a month in advance before the end of the tenancy agreement or the commencing date of the new rent. If a tenant fails to pay the rent within 15 days after the rent is due, the landlord can apply to the court for an order for eviction of the tenants.

Rental Cost

Like many other cities, rental costs are mainly determined by the location and size of the apartment or house. In general, renting an apartment in Hong Kong Island is more expensive than most parts of Kowloon and the New Territories. An apartment in Causeway Bay or Wanchai, at the heart of Hong Kong Island, costs around $8,000 (US$1000/£650) for an apartment of 500 square feet (47 square metres). Expect to pay $10,000 (US$1300/£800) a month for an apartment of 800 square feet (75 square metres) in these busy areas. West Hong Kong Island is a good option if you prefer to live in Hong Kong Island. For apartments of about the same size, the monthly rent is $2000-$3000 cheaper if you are living in Sheung Wan or Kennedy Town instead of Causeway Bay. There is also some cheaper housing in the New Territories and the outlying islands. It is possible to rent a house of 700 square feet for $3000-$4000 (US$400/£250) in rural villages, like those in Yuen Long, Tai Po or Sheung Shui. However, you must pay extra attention to checking the facilities before signing the tenancy agreement as these houses are usually very old. You will find quiet houses facing the sea in Sai Kung, but prices vary a lot depending on the location, size and distance from the beaches, etc. If you are looking for deluxe apartments or houses, the Peak and the surrounding region will be your focus. Alternatively, Discovery Bay, located in Lantau Island and 30 minutes by ferry from Central, has been getting more and more popular amongst the high-income group.

Tenants usually need to pay a maintenance fee for buildings with security guards at the lobby. The fee varies from hundreds to thousands of Hong Kong dollars, depending on how expensive the basic rent is.

Real Estate Agents

Centanet, e-mail info@centaline.com.hk; www.centanet.com.

Century 21 Hong Kong Limited, Units 1609-12, 16/F Nan Fung Tower, 173 Des Voeux Road C., Central, Hong Kong; ☎(852) 2869 7221; fax (852) 2509 3156; www.century21-hk.com.

Hutchison Whampoa Properties Limited, 3/F, One Harbourfront, 18 Tak Fung
   Street, Hunghom, Kowloon, Hong Kong; ☎(852) 2128 7500; fax (852) 2128
   7888; e-mailhk@hwpg.com; www.hwpg.com.
Karlson Property Consultants Ltd., Room 1606A, Nanyang Plaza, 57 Hung To
   Road, Kwun Tong, Kowloon, Hong Kong; ☎(852) 2342 2261; fax (852) 2790
   7099; www.karlson.com.hk.
Sun Hung Kai Properties Limited, 45th Floor, Sun Hung Kai Centre, 30 Harbour
   Road, Wanchai, Hong Kong; ☎(852) 2827 8111; fax (852) 2827 2862; e-mail
   shkp@shkp.com; www.shkp.com.hk.
Evergreen Management Co. Ltd, www.homehksar.com. Specialized in housing in
   Mid Level and the Peak.

UTILITIES

Utility companies provide good services even though there is not much
competition. Electricity and gas bills come every two months while telephone
bills and water bills come every three months and four months respectively. You
can pay most of the bills through PPS, a 24-hour bill payment service which
allows you to settle over 150 bills by a tone phone or the internet at anytime.
Funds will be automatically transferred from your bank account to the merchant's
account upon your transaction. Some banks also provide bill payment services
through the electronic banking system.

Useful Address

PPS, Customer Services Department, EPS Company (Hong Kong) Limited,
12/F, 82-84 Nathan Road, Tsim Sha Tsui, Kowloon; ☎(852) 2311 9876; e-mail
hotline@eps.com.hk; www.ppshk.com.

Electricity

The electricity supply in Hong Kong is 220 volts (50 Hz) and is provided
by two companies, The Hongkong Electric Company, Ltd. (HEC) and CLP
Power Hong Kong Ltd. (CLP Power). Electricity in Hong Kong Island and
Lamma Island is provided by the HEC while CLP Power is responsible for
providing electricity to Kowloon, the New Territories and other outlying
islands. The charges of the two companies are not the same and HEC is
slightly more expensive than CLP Power. The electricity companies take a
meter reading from households every month and there is a minimum charge
of around $20 a month even when no electricity is consumed in that period.
In general, electricity charges are higher in the summer if you use the air-
conditioner (which everybody does). Electrical appliances with flat 3-pin
plugs are common and recommended. 2-pin plugs are considered to be
unsafe and shops in Hong Kong are prohibited from selling them. Round-pin
sockets are not very common and you may need to use an adaptor. Electrical

appliances are relatively cheap when compared to European or North American countries, due to the low taxation and easily available Asian made products. You might want to buy new electrical appliances instead of bringing them all the way from home.

Electricity Providers

The Hongkong Electric Company, Limited (HEC), G.P.O. Box 915, Hong Kong; ☎(852) 2887 3411; fax (852) 2510 7667; e-mail mail@hec.com.hk; www.hec.com.hk/hec.

CLP Power Hong Kong Limited, 147 Argyle Street, Mongkok, Kowloon, Hong Kong; ☎(852) 2678 8111; fax (852) 2760 4448; e-mail clp – info@clp.com.hk; www.clpgroup.com.

Gas

There are two types of gas supply in Hong Kong, Liquefied Petroleum Gas (LPG) and Towngas. Gas is the main fuel for cooking and can also be used on other appliances such as water heaters and dishwashers. Most households use a piped-in system but a very small number of households are still using bottled gas. Gas bills are sent to piped-in gas users every two months.

Gas Suppliers

Shell Hong Kong Limited, Shell Gas 4/F, Shell Building Sai Tso Wan Road, Tsing Yi Island, N.T.; ☎(852) 2435 8388; fax (852) 2323 2001; www.shellgas.com.hk.

Towngas, ☎(852) 2880 6988; www.hkcg.com.

Water

The water supply in Hong Kong is provided by the Water Supplies Department. Since Hong Kong has such a large population, water stored in the reservoirs is not enough for all households. The government has to import water from Dongjiang, Guangdong. It is advisable not to drink tap water directly in Hong Kong even though the water has undergone a series of treatments before being supplied to households. A small amount of chlorine is added to the water to kill bacteria before it reaches households. Flushing water is sea water and is provided free of charge, unless you specifically request drinking water for flushing. Meters for all households are installed in a certain area of each building, and a water bill is sent to households every four months. For enquiries about water supply, call Water Supplies Department hotline ☎(852) 2824 5000 or visit the website *www.info.gov.hk/wsd*.

Telephones

Home telephones are cheap in Hong Kong. There is no per-minute charge for making local calls but there is a basic monthly fee of about $100. Hong Kong Telephone Company Limited was the only provider for home telephone services before July 1995 but the government is opening the telecom market to other companies now and there are now nine companies licensed to provide a home telephone service. For details of the current service providers, visit the Telecommunications Authority *www.ofta.gov.hk*. The installation fee for a new line is around $400-$500 and you can add another line for an additional $400. It is possible to take the old telephone number with you when you move to a new flat in Hong Kong, with a charge of $300. Call waiting, call forwarding, conference calling, voice mail services, etc. are available with an additional charge of around $15-$20 for each service. The telephone companies quite often give promotional offers to customers, especially to new ones. Be careful with these offers. For example, the company may ask you to pay a lump-sum at the beginning for future reductions of the telephone fee. Take a careful look at the later bills to check if the amount you need to pay is the same as the sales mentioned. There are disappointingly many complaints about 'mis-calculations' of fees, especially for sales plans that spread across a number of months. Call the customer service centres if you have any enquiry about the bills.

There are many options for the international call service, and the rates vary quite a lot. More details about international calls are under *Telephones* in the chapter of *Daily Life*.

Telephone Companies

PCCW Head Office, 39/F, PCCW Tower, TaiKoo Place, 979 King's Road, Quarry Bay, Hong Kong; ☎(852) 2888 2888; fax (852) 2877 8877; e-mail general@pccw.com; www.cwhkt.com.

Hong Kong Broadband Network, ☎(852) 128 100; fax (852) 2199 8181; e-mail hmtelsupport@hkbn.net; www.ctinets.com.

New World Telecommunications Limited, 17/F, Chevalier Commercial Centre, 8 Wang Hoi Road, Kowloon Bay, Hong Kong; ☎(852) 2138 2138; fax (852) 2133 2133; http://www.newworldtel.com.

Wharf T&T Limited, 5/F, Wharf T&T Centre, Harbour City, Kowloon, Hong Kong; ☎(852) 2112 1121; fax (852) 2112 1122; e-mail cc@wharftt.com; www.wharfnewtt.com.

Hutchison Global Communications Limited, 19/F, Two Harbourfront, 22 Tak Fung Street, Hunghom, Kowloon, Hong Kong; ☎(852) 2128 2828; fax (852) 2128 3388; e-mail suggestion@hgc.com.hk; www.hgc.com.hk.

CM ☎ *(HK) Limited*, 20/F, Tower II & III, Enterprise Square, 9 Sheung Yuet Road, Kowloon Bay, Kowloon, Hong Kong; ☎(852) 2209 1709; fax (852) 2245 0752; www.chinaone.com.hk.

Eastar Technology Limited, 17/F. Well Tech Centre, 9 Pat Tat Street, San Po

Kong, Kowloon, Hong Kong; ☎(852) 2908 8086; fax (852) 2868 6806;
www.etns.net.

TraxComm Limited, MTR Tower, Telford Plaza, 33 Wai Yip Street, Kowloon Bay,
Kowloon, Hong Kong; ☎(852) 2993 8333; fax (852) 2993 7781.

HKC Network Limited, Room 3305-3306, Hopewell Centre, 183 Queen's Road
East, Wan Chai, Hong Kong; ☎(852) 2890 7866; fax (852) 2895 1009.

RELOCATING

Even though it is probably cheaper to buy new furniture and electrical appliances
for your new home in Hong Kong, you may want to bring your beloved sofa or
antiques with you. If you are moving from the UK, The British Association of
Removers can provide a list of removers according to your current location. There
are many removers in different parts of the USA and other countries as well.
The cost depends greatly on the distance travelled and the weight/bulk of your
possessions. Many companies also provide services for shipping vehicles.

Useful Addresses

The British Association of Removers, 3 Churchill Court, 58 Station Road, North
Harrow, Middlesex HA2 7Sa; ☎(44) 020 8861 3331; fax (44) 020 8861
3332; www.removers.org.uk.

Excess Baggage PLC, London Wembley Head Office, 4 Hannah Close
Great Central Way, London NW10 0UX; ☎(44) 020 8324 2000; fax (44) 020
8324 2095; e-mail sales@excess-baggage.com; www.excess-baggage.com.

Allied Van Lines, Inc., P.O. Box 4403, Chicago, IL 60680-4403; ☎(1) 800 323
1909; e-mail insurance@alliedintl.com; www.alliedvan.com.

Sterling Corporate Relocation, Hallmark House, Rowdell Road, Northolt,
Middlesex, UB5 6AG, England; ☎(44) 020 8841 7000; fax (44) 020 8841 3500;
e-mail mail@sterlingrelocation.com; www.sterlingrelocation.com.

Sterling Corporate Relocation (Paris), 116 Avenue Aristide Briand, 93153 Le
Blanc-Mesnil Cedex, France; ☎(33) 1 49 39 47 00; fax (33) 1 49 39 47 17;
e-mail relocation@sterling-intl.fr; www.sterlingrelocation.com.

Allied International (Corporate Headquarters), 700 Oakmont Lane, Westmont
(Chicago), Illinois 60559; ☎(1) 630 570 3500; toll-free: (1) 800 323 1909;
fax (1) 630 570 3496.

Allied International (UK), Heritage House, 345 Southbury Road, Enfield
EN1 1UP; ☎(44) 020 8219 8000; fax (44) 020 8219 8321; www.allied-
pickfords.co.uk.

Allied International (Australia), 202 Greens Road, Dandenong Victoria 3175;
☎(61) 3 9797 1600; fax (61) 3 9797 1616; e-mail mover@alliedpickfords.co
m.au; www.allpick.com.au.

Allied International (Vancouver), (1) 819 Cliveden Place, #100 Delta, B.C. V3M
6C7; ☎(1) 604 523 3720; toll-free: 800 795 2920; fax (1) 604 523 3722; e-

mail fleal@alliedintl-vancouver.com.

Allied International (Toronto), 190 Duffield Drive, Markham, ON L6G 1B5; ☎(1) 416 940 1720; toll-free: 866 267 9106; fax (1) 416 940 1721; e-mail mwatters@alliedintl-toronto.com.

Customs

Only a few commodities like liquor, tobacco, hydrocarbon oil and methyl alcohol are taxed when imported into Hong Kong. Bringing your household and personal belongings to Hong Kong is duty free as long as you can show the Customs and Excise Department that they are for personal use instead of trade. It is advisable to have a doctor's letter if you are on prescription drugs.

IMPORTING A CAR

There is no customs tax for imported vehicles from other countries, whether they are for sale or personal use. However, it is generally not permitted to import left-hand-drive vehicles to Hong Kong as the road system is designed for right-hand-drive vehicles. If there is some reason why you have to import your left-hand-drive vehicle, you can apply for the Import Licence from the Left Hand Drive Vehicles or the Outboard Engine Licence Office. Right-hand-drive vehicles are not subjected to any licence when imported in to Hong Kong. You need to make a declaration within 14 days of importation, and are also required to submit an Import Return (CED336) and a Declaration on Particulars of Motor Vehicles Imported for Personal Use (CED336A) to the Customs and Excise Department within 30 days of the importation of a right-hand-drive vehicle. Forms can be obtained from the Custom and Excise Department (Motor Vehicles Valuation Group/Office of Dutiable Commodities Administration), Transport Department and Home Affairs Department.

Because of the potential congestion in such a built up area, having a car on the road in Hong Kong is very expensive and discouraged. Even though there is no customs tax for importing your vehicle, you are required to pay the First Registration Tax, which applies to all motor vehicles for use on the roads in Hong Kong, and also to pay a registration fee. You need to pay vehicle licence fee and levy for Traffic Accident Victim Assistance for licensing your vehicle as well. First Registration Tax is calculated according to the published retail price. For private cars, 35% will be the tax on the first $150,000 (US$19,000/£12,000) of the published retail price, then 65% for the next $150,000, 85% on an additional $200,000 and 100% on the remaining taxable value. The First Registration Tax is a once only charge. If the price of the vehicle is expressed in foreign currency, the foreign currency exchange rate will be taken on the date of importation of the vehicle.

Useful Addresses

Left Hand Drive Vehicles/Outboard Engine Licence Office, Custom and Excise Department, Room 1012, Canton Road Government Offices, 393 Canton Road, Kowloon; ☎(852) 2723 3196; www.info.gov.hk/customs.

Motor Vehicles Valuation Group, Customs and Excise Department, Room 1111, 11/F, North Point Government Offices, 333 Java Road, North Point, Hong Kong; ☎(852) 2231 4391; fax (852) 2598 4975; www.info.gov.hk/customs.

Office of Dutiable Commodities Administration, Customs and Excise Department, 2/F, Harbour Building, 38 Pier Road, Central, Hong Kong; ☎(852) 2852 3049; fax (852) 2541 9827; www.info.gov.hk/customs.

Transport Department, 41/F, Immigration Tower, 7 Gloucester Road, Wan Chai, Hong Kong; ☎(852) 2804 2600; fax (852) 2824 0433; www.info.gov.hk/td.

IMPORTING PETS

You have to apply for a Special Permit if you want to bring your pets with you to Hong Kong. Your pets should be given certain vaccinations like Infectious Canine Hepatitis and Canine Parvovirus for dogs and Feline Panleucopacnia (Infectious Enteritis) and Feline Respiratory Disease Complex (Cat Flu) for cats. Otherwise, the Customs and Excise Department may refuse to let your pets enter Hong Kong.

You have to apply to the Agriculture, Fisheries and Conservation Department with an application form, plus a permit fee of $432 for the first animal and $102 for every additional one. Overseas applicants should submit the fee with a bank draft in Hong Kong currency payable to 'The Government of the Hong Kong Special Administration Region'. It takes about five working days for processing the permit and it will be mailed to your home.

Useful Address

Agriculture, Fisheries and Conservation Department, Cheung Sha Wan Government Offices, 5th to 7th, 8th (part), 9th (part) floors, 303 Cheung Sha Wan Road, Kowloon; ☎(852) 2708 8885; www.afcd.gov.hk..

WILLS

People have been increasingly aware of the importance for making a will over the last 20 years, despite the traditional Chinese view that living people should not talk about death. Making a will does not only make a better arrangement for what you have, it also prevents the unhappy legal fights that may occur between family members. Law firms usually provide a service for making wills, and the minimum cost can be as low as a few hundred Hong Kong dollars.

If someone dies without a will, under the current Intestates' Estates Ordinance in Hong Kong, his or her movable personal property goes to the spouse and the residuary estate (other than movable personal properties) is divided into two halves: one goes to the spouse, and the other half goes to the children. If he or she does not have any children, the second half of the residuary estate goes to the parents, or to the siblings if the parents have already died. For the deceased who has no spouse but children, the residuary estate will be held in statutory trusts for the children. If the deceased is still single when he or she dies, the residuary estate goes in sequence to parents, siblings, grandparents and then uncles and aunts, until one of the groups claim the residuary estate.

DAILY LIFE

CHAPTER SUMMARY

- **Languages.** English and Chinese are the official languages in Hong Kong.
- **Education.** Children enjoy nine years of free compulsory education, from Primary One to Secondary Three.
  - Primary and secondary schools are separated into EMI (English as the medium of instruction) and non-EMI.
- **Media.** Choices for English newspapers are limited.
  - There is no television licence fee in Hong Kong.
- **Post.** Apart from general postal services, post offices also accept payments for government bills.
- **Telephone.** The emergency number in Hong Kong is 999.
- **Driving.** Motorcyclists have to undergo a 12-month probation period before they get their full licences.
- **Transport.** Octopus, a stored value card, can be used on almost all public transport in Hong Kong.
  - There are two types of taxi. The green ones are in service in the New Territories only, and cannot go to Kowloon or Hong Kong Island. The red ones serve customers mainly in Kowloon and Hong Kong Island, but are allowed to go to the New Territories as well.
  - There is a ferry connection between Hong Kong and Macau, which takes about an hour.
- **Tax.** Hong Kong has an extremely low tax rate compared to other countries.
- **Crime.** The crime rate in Hong Kong is very low. The number of homicide cases in New York City a year is 11 times of that in Hong Kong.
- **Public Holidays.** Many public holidays are set according to the lunar calendar, for example, Chinese New Year, Mid-Autumn Festival and the Buddha's Birthday.

THE LANGUAGE

English and Chinese are the official languages in Hong Kong and Cantonese is the most spoken Chinese dialect with more than 90% of the population speaking Cantonese and not English at home. While foreigners coming from America, Europe or Australia usually speak English in Hong Kong, there is also a small proportion of people from India and the Middle East who speak their own languages too. Many Filipino women work in Hong Kong as domestic helpers. You will find thousands of people chatting and singing in Filipino on Sunday in the Statue Square in Central.

The written Chinese language was standardized in the Qin dynasty over two thousand years ago. However, in 1956 the written characters have been simplified by the Communists in mainland China. The result is that Chinese people in Hong Kong, Taiwan, Singapore and many in the West still use the traditional characters, which are more complicated than the ones used in mainland China today. Most Hong Kong people can recognise the simplified characters with some effort, but for foreigners it might be a challenge to translate between the two.

Government documents and official signs are bilingual. Restaurants usually have an English menu and products in shops usually have English descriptions as well as the Chinese ones.

Mandarin versus Cantonese

Even though the official spoken language in the People's Republic of China is Mandarin, people in Hong Kong speak Cantonese, as do people from other regions of the Guangdong province. Since Hong Kong was a British colony before 1997, both the government and public in general did not take Mandarin very seriously. Mandarin might be a subject in some schools but it was about as important as music or physical education, if not merely a hobby. Hong Kong people started to take Mandarin more seriously when the economy of mainland China opened to the West in 1984. It was not easy for a foreign merchant to trade with mainland companies at that time and hence Hong Kong acted as a middleman to facilitate the trading and knowing how to speak Mandarin became very useful. In addition, many factories moved from Hong Kong to mainland China in the 80s and early 90s in order to minimise production costs. Since then, more businessmen travel between mainland China and Hong Kong and Hong Kong people started to realise the importance of learning Mandarin. More people started to learn Mandarin after the handover in 1997, especially after Hong Kong experienced the economic downturn in 1998. Mainland China is a very big market and it has been easier to do business with the motherland since the handover. Many companies started to expand their business to the mainland and it is necessary to send staff to the offices on the mainland to monitor the business and facilitate trade with local companies. The economic downturn hit Hong

Kong businessmen quite hard and many companies closed down in 1998, which reduced local job opportunities. Looking for jobs in mainland China became an alternative. Hence, suddenly, learning Mandarin has become as important as acquiring IT proficiency if you want to be employed. Moreover, the Hong Kong government states that being 'biliterate (Chinese and English) and trilingual (Cantonese, Mandarin and English)' is one of the main directions for education. Mandarin is clearly a language Hong Kong people cannot ignore anymore.

That said, you will find that many Hong Kong people do not speak very fluently yet. Most of them learn and use Mandarin more or less out of necessity, and Cantonese still dominates daily usage. It is uncommon for two people to speak to each other in Mandarin if they both know Cantonese. In Hong Kong, many young Chinese people even prefer to talk in English if they cannot communicate in Cantonese. Government officials make their speeches to the public in Cantonese; news reports are in Cantonese; local movies, TV series and songs are mainly in Cantonese as well. The language also reflects the culture of Hong Kong, for which you may not be able to find an equivalent word in Mandarin. If you want to really understand the lives of Hong Kong people, knowing Cantonese will definitely help a lot.

SCHOOLING AND EDUCATION

Hong Kong's education system is very similar to that of the UK. The Hong Kong Government provides nine years of free education, from Primary One to Secondary Three (ages 6-15), for all Hong Kong children. The academic year starts on 1st September and ends in mid-July for both primary and secondary schools. Primary and secondary school students have 90 days of holiday a year, including the summer holiday.

The Structure of the Education System

Pre-Primary Education. Although it is not compulsory in Hong Kong, most of the children (over 90%) attend child care centres, nurseries or kindergartens. Child care centres and nurseries are for children aged 0-6 and are under the supervision of the Social Welfare Department. The minimum age for entering kindergarten is 3-years-old and all kindergartens are under the supervision of the Education and Manpower Bureau. Every kindergarten, child care centre or nursery has to get a licence before it provides an education service. Syllabus and school fees are set by the organisations themselves. School fees can vary from hundreds to four or five thousand dollars (US$40-$600/£30-£400) a month. Parents can apply for subsidies from the Social Welfare Department and the Education and Manpower Bureau for their children's school fees. Opening hours for these centres and kindergartens can be very different as well. Both half-day and full-time schools are available. Some of them stay open till 6pm for working parents.

There are usually fixed timetables in kindergartens and child care centres. Common knowledge like the weather, shapes, colours, etc, will be taught in pre-school education. Children are encouraged to learn social skills through games, singing and physical exercises. Parents have become more concerned about the development of creativity and thinking skills in recent years, and schools are putting more focus on these aspects as well. Reading and writing of simple words may start as early as the age of four or five.

Primary Schools. Primary education is compulsory for all children. There is a strict minimum age limit for Primary One admission. The child has to be at least 5 years and 8 months-old to enter primary school. Most primary schools require students to wear a school uniform and primary education is more standardised compared to pre-primary education. Children have to acquire language, mathematics, general knowledge and simple science skills during their six years of primary school education. English is a compulsory subject and students in most of the schools take Chinese as well. Some schools provide other languages such as French or Japanese as a second language for non-Chinese students. Subjects like Art, Music, Physical Education and Civil Education are also included in the timetable. Extra-curricular activities are provided as supplementary subjects for children to develop different skills as well as to enjoy themselves.

Most of the schools in Hong Kong are funded by the government. There is no school fee for government-run and government-subsidised schools and their syllabus is set under the supervision of the government. Children studying in Direct Subsidy Scheme (DSS) schools and private schools have to pay school fees even if they are within the age range for free education provided by the Hong Kong Government. DSS schools are non-profit-making and also under the monitoring of the government but they have more freedom when designing their own syllabus and usually they have better school facilities, like computers and swimming pools. Less than 10% of the primary schools are operated by private organisations and they are not under the supervision of the government. School fees are more expensive in private schools, which may reach several thousands a month.

When choosing a primary school, you may want to pay attention to whether the school has any link to a particular secondary school. If a primary school and a secondary school are linked, students can usually get a place at that secondary school more easily. Many parents plan very carefully when choosing a primary school as they want their children to enter the desired linked secondary school, which they believe may provide a better learning environment and better facilities.

Both primary and secondary schools in Hong Kong are separated into EMI (English as the medium of instruction) and non-EMI. Foreign children may find it very difficult to catch up if all subjects except English are taught in Chinese.

Around two-fifths of secondary schools but less than one-fifth of primary schools are EMI. However, secondary schools are allowed to choose the language of instruction starting from Secondary Four. Therefore, the number of schools using English as medium of instruction in senior levels may exceed two-fifths of the total number of secondary schools.

Secondary Education. The first three years, usually called junior levels, of the secondary school education, like primary school education, is compulsory and free of charge. Most students prefer to continue their studies after Secondary Three. Compulsory subjects include two languages, mathematics, elementary sciences, history, geography and public affairs. Art, music, physical education, computer studies, home economics and design and technology are common subjects as well. Students choose their streams of studies starting from Secondary Four (start of senior level). They are mainly divided into two streams, arts and sciences. Arts students usually take humanities and social science subjects like economics, literature and geography while sciences students study advanced levels of mathematics, physics, chemistry, biology, computer studies, etc. English and general mathematics are required in both streams. Art and music are voluntary subjects starting from senior level, which means most students are not examined on these subjects. Secondary Five students are required to sit for a public examination, the Hong Kong Certificate Examination of Education (HKCEE), to see if they are eligible for further studies. HKCEE is similar to GCSE in the UK or SAT in the USA. Students take six to ten subjects in their examination and the best six will be taken as reference for assessment. E is the passing grade and a student should pass all exams if he or she wants to pursue further studies. However, the requirements are usually higher, like two Cs and four Ds, due to limited places for Secondary Six. Secondary Six and Seven are taken as the preparation for tertiary education but not all Secondary Seven students are able to get a place in universities. They will have to sit another examination, Hong Kong Advanced Level Examination (HKALE) to fight for a place.

Starting from Secondary Four, students need to pay school fees. It is usually some hundreds a month for government-funded schools. As in primary schools, most of the secondary schools require students to wear school uniform.

HOMEWORK AND EXAMINATIONS

Many people complain that Hong Kong students are under too much pressure. Apart from public examinations like HKCEE and HKALE, students have to sit internal school examinations every term. Some schools even have additional term tests in the middle of a term. There are usually two to three terms in each academic year, which means some schools have up to six examinations a year, plus quizzes and dictations. Homework is given every day and there may be as many as five to eight pieces of homework a day. Many children find it difficult to adapt to the Hong Kong education system if they are from western countries. International schools, however, have a lighter workload compared to local schools and may be more suitable for foreign children.

International Schools. International schools are more popular among foreign residents. There are not many EMI primary schools and many local schools only provide Chinese as the second language, which is very difficult for a foreign child to learn. Besides, these students are used to western education where more focus is put on personal development, creativity and thinking skills. International schools in Hong Kong are mainly taught by native English speakers and the class size is usually smaller. They have good facilities and learning environments but the school fees are higher than local schools.

Useful Addresses

American International School, 125 Waterloo Road, Kowloon Tong, Kowloon, Hong Kong; ☎(852) 2336-3812; fax (852) 2336-5276; e-mail aisadmin@ais.edu.hk; www.ais.edu.hk.

Christian Alliance, P.C. Lau Memorial, International School, 2 Fu Ning Street, Kowloon City, Hong Kong; ☎(852) 2713 3733; fax (852) 2760 4324; e-mail info.cais.edu.hk; www.cais.edu.hk.

Concordia International School, 68 Begonia Road, Yau Yat Chuen, Kowloon, Hong Kong; tel.: (852) 2397 6576/(852) 2789 9890; fax (852) 2392 8820; e-mail adm@cihs.edu.hk; www.cihs.edu.hk.

Hong Kong International School (Office of Admissions), 23 South Bay Close, Repulse Bay, Hong Kong; ☎(852) 2812-5000; fax (852) 2812-0669; e-mail admiss@hkis.edu.hk; www.hkis.edu.hk.

Hong Lok Yuen International School, Twentieth Street, Hong Lok Yuen, Tai Po, New Territories, Hong Kong; ☎(852) 2658 6935; fax (852) 2651 0836; e-mail info@hlyis.edu.hk; www.hlyis.edu.hk.

German Swiss International School, 11 Guildford Road, The Peak, Hong Kong; ☎(852) 2849-6216; fax (852) 2849-6347; e-mail gsis@gsis.edu.hk; www.gsis.edu.hk.

Kellett School, 2 Wah Lok Path; Wah Fu, Pokfulam; Hong Kong; ☎(852) 2551 8234; fax (852) 2875 0262; e-mail kellett@kellettschool.com; kellettmain.kellettschool.com.

Singapore International School, 23 Nam Long Shan Road, Aberdeen, Hong Kong; tel.: (852) 2872 0266; fax (852) 2872 0431; e-mail secretary@singapore.edu.hk; www.singapore.edu.hk.

Yew Chung Education Foundation (Primary and Secondary Section), 10 Somerset Road, Kowloon Tong, Kowloon, Hong Kong; ☎(852) 2338 7106; fax (852)

2338 4045; e-mail inquiry@ycef.com; www.ycef.com.

Vocational Training. Some students choose to attend vocational training institutes after Secondary Five, especially if they do not do very well in the HKCEE. The aim of the courses provided by the vocational institutes is to help students to develop a technical skill for a future career. Students need to attend pre-employment and also in-service education and training. The Hong Kong Institute of Vocational Education (IVE), the Vocational Training Council (VTC), the School of Business and Information Systems (SBI) and its training and development centres are the recognised institutes providing vocational training at the moment.

Higher Education

Universities. There are eight universities providing around 65,000 (both full-time and part-time education) places for students each year. The universities expect the students to finish their degree in three years in general, except for some courses that require a longer period of study like medicine and dentistry. Apart from the specialised subject (the 'major'), students are required to take classes of different disciplines as well. An academic year is usually divided into two semesters, September to Christmas/January is the first one, and February to June is the second. Students need to take examinations after each semester.

Fees are around $42,000 (US$5,400/£3,360) a year. Students can apply for a government grant and loan for paying the fee if the family income is low.

Other Tertiary Institutes. *Hong Kong Institute of Education (HKIEd)*   This is an institute recognised by the government for providing education and training for those who plan to be primary or secondary teachers after graduation. Students take two major subjects for preparation for future teaching. One can either apply to the institute after Secondary Five with HKCEE results that meet the entry requirements, or apply after passing HKALE. For those who enter the institute after Secondary Five, it will take three years to finish the certificate, while it takes only two years for those who attended HKALE. HKIEd also provides a part-time certificate for current teachers. The institute was approved by the government to offer a degree course, Bachelor in Education for primary and secondary education a few years ago.

Hong Kong Academy for Performing Arts – This is the only tertiary institution in Hong Kong solely for the provision of professional education, training and research facilities for the performing arts, theatre technical arts, and film and television. The Hong Kong Academy for Performing Arts provides both diploma and degree courses in dance, drama, music, technical arts, traditional theatre together with film and television for students. The academy organises performances by their students, which are open to the public and are part of their training.

Useful Addresses

The Chinese University of Hong Kong, Shatin, New Territories, Hong Kong, ☎(852) 2609 7000/(852) 2609 6000; fax (852) 2603 5544; www.cuhk.edu.hk.

City University of Hong Kong, Tat Chee Road Avenue, Hong Kong; ☎(852) 27887654; fax (852) 27881167; www.cityu.edu.hk.

Hong Kong Baptist University, Kowloon Tong, Hong Kong; ☎(852) 3411 7400; www.hkbu.edu.hk.

The Hong Kong Polytechnic University, Hung Hom, Kowloon, Hong Kong; ☎(852) 2766 5111; fax (852) 2764 3374; www.polyu.edu.hk.

Hong Kong University of Science and Technology, Clear Water Bay, Kowloon, Hong Kong; ☎(852) 2358 8888; www.ust.hk.

Lingnan University, Tuen Mun, Hong Kong; ☎(852) 2616 8888; fax (852) 2463 8363; www.ln.edu.hk.

Open University of Hong Kong, 30, Good Shepherd Street, Homantin, Kowloon; ☎(852) 2711 2100; www.ouhk.edu.hk.

The University of Hong Kong, Pokfulam Road, Hong Kong. ☎(852) 2859 2111; fax (852) 2858 2549; www.hku.hk.

The Hong Kong Academy for Performing Arts, 1 Gloucester Road, Wanchai, Hong Kong; ☎(852) 2584 8500; fax (852) 2802 4372; Email: PR@hkapa.edu; www.hkapa.edu.

Hong Kong Institute of Education, 10 Lo Ping Road, Tai Po, N.T., Hong Kong; ☎(852) 2948 8888; fax (852) 29486000; www.ied.edu.hk.

Vocational Training Council, VTC Tower, 27 Wood Road, Wan Chai, Hong Kong; ☎(852) 2836 1000; fax (852) 2838 0667; Email: vtcmailbox@vtc.edu.hk; www.vtc.edu.hk.

MEDIA AND COMMUNICATIONS

Newspapers

There are over ten local newspapers in Hong Kong but only three of them are in English. Among these three, The Standard and Asian Times only cover business news. South China Morning Post is the only local English newspaper that covers all the usual sections. Some of the international newspapers may be found in shops in Central, Admiralty and Tsim Sha Tsui but they are not common in newspaper stands. The Hong Kong government website (*http://www.news.gov.hk/en/index.shtml*), reports some of the top stories in English every day, and may be an alternative to get local news.

Main Newspapers

South China Morning Post, 16/F Somerset House, Taikoo Place, 979 King's Road Quarry Bay, Hong Kong; ☎(852) 2565 2222; fax (852) 2811 1048; www.scmp.com.

The Standard, 3/F Sing Tao Building 1 Wang Kwong Road Kowloon Bay Hong
    Kong; ☎(852) 2798 2798; fax (852) 2795 3009; www.thestandard.com.hk.
Asia Times, 6306 The Center, 99 Queen's Road, Central, Hong Kong; ☎(852)
    2585 7119; e-mail editor@atimes.com; www.atimes.com.

Magazines

As with newspapers, there are not many locally published English magazines
but a wide-rage of international magazines is available here. *HK Magazine*
and *bc Magazine* are published locally. The former is a lifestyle publication for
affluent urban professionals, and the latter is an entertainment guide including
information about gigs, cinema, eating out and sports. International magazines
like *Time, Newsweek, Asiaweek* and *The Economist* are popular among locals.
Women's magazines including *Marie Claire, Cosmopolitan* and *Elle* are very
successful as well. Many different kinds of magazines such as *PC World, Arts
of Asia, Rider Magazine* and *The Voice*, etc. are also available in Hong Kong. In
general, there are more English magazines in big bookstores, such as Page One,
than in the newspaper stands or convenience stores.

Television

Television is a common and cheap entertainment for Hong Kong families as
there is no TV licence fee in Hong Kong. There are four main channels broadcast
by two companies, Television Broadcasts Ltd. (TVB) and Asia Television Ltd
(ATV). All four channels are free of charge but there are advertisements between
programmes. Among the four channels, Pearl and World are broadcast in English.
Popular British and American TV series such as Friends, ER, X-Files, Sex and the
City and Ally McBeal are broadcast in peak hours. Programmes about current
affairs and documentaries are also very popular.

Hong Kong Cable Television Ltd. (Cable TV) is the largest pay-TV company.
There are more than 32 channels including BBC, CNN, National Geographic
Channel and Discovery Channel. Programmes run 24 hours a day and are very
varied. Channels for movies, music, sports, news, children and travel can all be
found on Cable TV. The monthly fee for Cable TV depends on how many channels
are subscribed. For further details, visit the website *www.wharfcable.com*.

TV programme schedules can be found in daily newspapers or on the company
websites. For TVB, it is *www.tvb.com*; and for ATV *www.hkatv.com*.

Radio

There are four radio stations in Hong Kong offering around ten to fifteen
channels. However, most of them are broadcast in Cantonese. There are only
three radio channels that are broadcast in English, which include RTHK (Radio
Television Hong Kong) Radio 3 (AM 567/AM 1584/FM 106.8/FM 97.9), Radio
4 (FM 97.6-98.9), and Metro Broadcast Metro Plus (AM1044). You will find

that RTHK Radio 3 provides a greater variety of information than the other two channels. The programmes cover news, current affairs, music, entertainment, etc. RTHK Radio 4 is mainly a music channel and programmes are bilingually broadcast. The presenter explains the text in Cantonese after presenting it in English. You can find all kinds of music: western classical music, contemporary music, Chinese music, jazz and other kinds of music anytime of the day. Metro Plus is somehow like RTHK Radio 4 in that music is the main focus. However, Metro Plus is aimed at people from other Asian countries. There are programmes broadcast in Mandarin, Filipino, Indonesian and Indian every week.

Books and Bookshops

The prices of books in Hong Kong depend a lot on where they are published. Books from China and Taiwan are usually cheap but are mainly in Chinese. In general, English books are more expensive than Chinese books. A medium length (around 200-300 pages) English novel costs around $80- $160 (around US$10-US$20/£7-13). Dymock's Book Sellers, Swindon Book Co., Bookazine and Page One are the major bookshops selling English books. It is better to go to university bookshops for academic and literary works as these may not be available in ordinary bookshops. Even if they do not have the book you are looking for, it is possible for them to order for you but a surcharge may be added for those who are not university staff or students.

There is a huge book fair in Hong Kong every year in late July to early August, which is held in the Hong Kong Convention and Exhibition Centre. The entry fee is around $20 and books are usually at a discount. Avoid visiting on the first day or the weekends if you do not want to queue for hours before you can get into the exhibition halls.

Bookstore Addresses:

Contact the individual companies for branch details.:

Academic & Professional Book Center, Shop 623, Grand Century Place (Mongkok Railway Station), Mongkok, Kowloon, Hong Kong; ☎(852) 2398 3044; fax (852) 2398 7746.

Bookazine, Shop 309-313A, Prince's Building, Central, Hong Kong; ☎(852) 2522 1785; e-mail shonee@feml.com.hk; www.bookazine.com.hk.

City University Bookshop, Level 4, Academic Block, City University of Hong Kong Tat Chee Ave., Kowloon Tong, Kowloon, Hong Kong; ☎(852) 2777 0122; fax (852) 2777 0378; e-mail apcityu@netvigator.com.

Dymocks Booksellers, Shop 115-116, Prince's Building, 10 Chater Road, Central, Hong Kong; ☎(852) 2826 9248; e-mail erictfho@dymockspb.com.hk; www.dymocks.com

Page One, Basement One, Times Square, 1 Matheson Street, Causeway Bay, Hong Kong; ☎(852) 2506 0383; fax (852) 2506 0380.

Swindon Book Company, 310 & 328 Ocean Centre, Harbour City, Tsim Sha Tsui, Kowloon, Hong Kong; ☎(852) 2730 0183; fax (852) 2735 9881; www.swindonbooks.com.

Post

The Hong Kong postal service is cheap and efficient. It usually takes one working day to deliver local letters and four to seven days to deliver letters to the UK and the USA. Post offices open from 9:30am to 5pm, Monday to Friday, and 9:30am to 1pm on Saturday. In case you need the postal service on a Saturday afternoon or on Sunday, the Central Post Office in Central is in service until 6pm on Saturdays and between 9am to 2pm on Sundays. Local letters cost $1.4 (US$0.18/11 pence) unless they are over 30g. Sending letters to the UK and the USA costs $3 (US$0.38/24 pence) by air mail and $2.9 by surface mail. Parcels usually take seven to ten days to deliver to the UK and the USA by air, and around 45 days by surface mail. The cost for sending parcels to Hawaii is lower than sending to other US states and the size limit for sending parcels to the USA (including Puerto Rico) is different from sending parcels to other countries. Information about postal costs and size/weight limits are available at The Hong Kong Post website *www.hongkongpost.com.* Mail is usually delivered once a day from Monday to Saturday. Stamps can be purchased at convenience stores as well as post offices, the prices are the same. Mailboxes on the street are green and can be found in main streets and most residential complexes. Mailboxes can also be found inside train stations and MTR stations but remember the mailboxes inside MTR stations are behind the station gates. SpeedPost is an alternative to other express delivery companies like UPS and FedEx. It promises overnight delivery to 92 destinations. There is also an express service for local post.

Post offices also have PayThruPost Service, which accepts payments for more than 20 government bills, including tax bills, electricity bills, home telephone (and some mobile phone) bills, gas bill, etc. Payment by cash, cheque, cashier order or EPS are all accepted. For further details of the PayThruPost service, call the Hong Kong Post enquiry hotline on (852) 2921 2222.

There are many limited edition stamps issued for festivals or special events in Hong Kong every year. Long queues are found outside post offices when there is a new stamp issued. The Hong Kong Post provides ordering services for stamp collectors every year. Credit card is the only accepted payment method for this service and the minimum ordering amount is $50. The deadline for ordering next year's stamps is usually around September. Delivery of new stamps is provided at a cost of around $10 per delivery, or you can collect your stamps at a designated post office.

Telephones

Installation of a telephone at home is covered in the chapter *Setting Up Home*.

Making a local call with a fixed line is free of charge. Pay phones are common, apart from the telephone boxes in the street, pay phones can also be found in convenience stores, KCR and MTR stations. Local calls cost $1 for five minutes. $1, $2, $5 and $10 coins are accepted in most telephones but be aware that some of the telephones only accept phone cards or credit cards. Phone cards are available in stored values of $50, $100 and $200 and can be found in telephone company retail shops and convenience stores.

Local numbers consist of eight digits and there is no area code within Hong Kong. Making international calls from Hong Kong is the same as from other countries: country code + area code (omit the zero of the area code) + the number. Cantonese, English, Mandarin and Japanese instructions are available when making international calls using public telephones. Local telephone companies provide a home international calls service as well. These companies are keenly competitive and therefore they always provide promotional calling rates to attract customers. However, these promotion schemes are usually under constraints. Most of them provide low rates only during non-business hours, on Sundays and on public holidays. Prices for calls made during business hours can be multiples of those in non-business hours. You can either use the long-distance telephone service from telephone companies, or use a pre-paid long-distance phone card for making international calls at home. However, these cards have no standard call rates and the rates vary widely, and the expiry date might be another problem. The cards usually expire in three to six months. Check the call rates and expiry date carefully before buying. Purchasing from big telephone companies will usually be safer. The access numbers of these cards are usually free to call and instruction in English is available.

If a public telephone cannot be found nearby but making a local call is necessary, telephones are usually available in Chinese restaurants (places for having dim-sum and Chinese tea). Although these telephones are supposed to be used by customers only, no one really checks.

The emergency number in Hong Kong is 999.

Other Useful Telephone Numbers

Public and company phone number enquiry, (852) 1083.

Weather forecast, (852) 187 8066/ (852) 2926 1133.

Taxi stations, (852) 2760 0455 (Hong Kong Island/Kowloon); (852) 2457 2266 (New Territories); (852) 2984 1328 (Lantau Island).

URBTIX (for reserving cultural programmes tickets): (852) 2926 1133; www.lcsd.gov.hk/CE/Entertainment/Ticket/.

CARS AND MOTORING

The number of vehicles in Hong Kong is just as astonishing as the population. There are over 440,000 vehicles running on the roads every day. This does not include public transportation like buses and taxis. It is estimated that, by 2011, the number of vehicles in Hong Kong will be around 1,000,000! Although the number of vehicles has not yet reached this number, congestion is already a serious problem. During rush hours, it can easily take you an hour to complete what should be a 15 minute ride.

Hong Kong is currently running a Driving-Offence Point System. Points will be incurred when a driver commits driving offences, like speeding or jumping traffic lights. If 13 points or more are incurred within two years, disqualification from holding a driving licence applies. The first disqualification lasts for three months and six months for subsequent convictions.

The Hong Kong driving system is the same as the British and people drive on the left. Traffic light runs turn from red to red-and-yellow, and then to green; and green to yellow and then red. Unlike the UK or other European countries, you are not supposed to put your vehicle in motion when the red-and-yellow is on, even where there is no pedestrian crossing the road, and right-hand/left-hand turns on a red light are not allowed. Road signs in Hong Kong all appear in English and Chinese and are usually up above the road while the speed limit is posted on the side of the road.

Motor cyclists in the first year of obtaining their licence are required by law to undergo a 12-month probation period. They have to put 'P' plates at the front and rear of their motor cycles. They are not allowed to carry passengers on the back, exceed the speed of 70km/h and cannot drive on the off-side lane of expressways when there are three or more lanes. A full driving licence will be granted after a year to those whose performance is satisfactory.

Driving Regulations

Hong Kong's road system is basically a copy of that of the British since Hong Kong was a British colony when the road system was built. People coming from the UK should not have much difficulty driving in Hong Kong, but people from America and other European countries will need some adjustment, the most important of which is probably to learn to drive on the left side. Drivers and passengers are required to wear seat belts while the vehicle is in motion. Using hand-held mobile phones when the vehicle is in motion is an offence and will attract a penalty of up to $2,000. The speed limits on expressways and highways are usually 80km/h to 100km/h and 50km/h to 70km/h in the city area. The lane on the far right-hand side is the fast lane, which is prohibited for lorries. Police have speed cameras to catch speed riders and speeding drivers risk incurring penalty points and a fine.

Parking is often a difficult problem in Hong Kong. There are limited parking areas along the roads in the city area. All parking meters only accept parking cards, which you can buy from convenience stores. The maximum period for parking on a meter is two hours for each payment. Car parks are around $15-$20 per hour but they do not necessarily have parking space in rush hours. Vehicles parking in any prohibited area may be towed away and a fine may be charged to the owner.

Drinking and Driving. Drink driving is strictly prohibited and is a criminal offence in Hong Kong. Ten demerit-offensive points will be incurred for the first conviction. The driver may be disqualified from driving for a period of time. The maximum penalty for drink driving is a fine of $25,000 (US$3,200/£2,000) plus up to three years imprisonment. The police can stop a driver for a breath test if the driver is suspected to be drink driving or has committed a traffic offence. A breath test is also given to drivers who are involved in traffic accidents. Further alcohol tests on blood and urine may be necessary. Failure to do the tests without reasonable excuse will incur penalties. The alcohol limit is 50 milligrams per 100ml of blood, or 22 micrograms per 100ml of breath, or 67 milligrams per 100ml of urine. This limit is lower than that of the UK and the USA (80mg of alcohol per 100ml of blood). You will probably reach the limit after a glass of wine or one pint of beer.

Breakdowns and Accidents

There are emergency telephones on every expressway, highway and inside the tunnels for drivers whose vehicles have broken down. Calling help from a mobile phone maybe a safer and quicker way. If your vehicle breaks down on the expressway or highway, try to move it to the side of the road and put the hazard lights on. If it is not possible to move your vehicle, leave the hazard lights on and get out of your vehicle to a safe place to wait for help. It is a good idea to carry the numbers of companies for vehicle repair services, so that you can call them to tow your vehicle away for repair directly.

When there is a traffic accident, the car owners can settle the loss among themselves if no one is injured in the accident and the private property damage is minor. Car owners have a right to make a report to the police within 72 hours. In any case, you must call the police if someone gets hurt, or if the accident involves more than two vehicles, government properties or a government vehicle.

Useful Addresses

Shun Chong Towing Service Limited, Camy Hse, Kowloon City; Hong Kong; ☎(852) 2338 0982;fax (852) 2338 9391; www.yp.com.hk/shunchong.

Universal Towing Service Company Limited, Block 3, 11/F., 168 Jaffe Road, Wanchai, Hong Kong.; ☎(852) 2519 8731; fax (852) 2507 3463; www.yp.com.hk/universaltowing.

AA Towing Services Company, 110 Nga Tsin Wai Rd, Kowloon City, Hong Kong;
☎ (852) 2382 4444.
Auto Power Towing Company Limited, 36 Ho Sheung Heung Rd, Sheung Shui,
N.T., Hong Kong; ☎ (852) 2668 2999.
Compass Auto Club, Luk Mei Tsuen, Sai Kung, N.T., Hong Kong; ☎ (852) 2234
5999.

Driving Licence

People holding an International Driving Licence issued outside Hong Kong are
allowed to drive in Hong Kong for 12 months starting from the date of arrival.
The Transport Department grants a Temporary Driving Licence to people from
some areas. If you hold a driving licence issued by your country, you should check
up with the Transport Department within three months of your arrival. It is not
possible to apply for the Temporary Driving Licence later than three months after
your arrival. In that case, you have to apply for a full Hong Kong Driving Licence
instead.

Car Registration

All vehicles must register with the Hong Kong Licensing Office of the Transport
Department. You are required to pay First Registration Tax and a registration fee
for your vehicle, and to pay a vehicle licence fee and levy for the Traffic Accident
Victim Assistance Fund. First Registration Tax is a once only charge but it can
add up to nearly half of the value of your car. You should note that registration of
a left hand drive vehicle will normally not be accepted.

For further details about driving licences and vehicle licences, visit the Transport
Department website *www.info.gov.hk/td/*.

Some Useful Telephone Numbers
Transport Department Headquarters, ☎ (852) 2804 2600; fax (852) 2824 0433.
Licensing Information (24-Hour Interactive Voice Hotline), ☎ (852) 2804 2600.
Driving-Offence Points, ☎ (852) 2804 2594; fax (852) 2865 3475.
Driving Test, ☎ (852) 2804 2583; fax (852) 2866 6429.
Police Force hotline, ☎ (852) 2527 7177.

TRANSPORT

Even though Hong Kong is too small in area to compare with other big cities
like New York or London, its transportation is up to international standard
and its quality is even better than many other international cities. According
to the results of Skytrax Research in London, global air travellers have picked
Hong Kong International Airport (HKIA) as the world's best airport for three
consecutive years (2001-2003). And HKIA was also named Cargo Airport of the
Year – 2003 by the air cargo trade publication Air Cargo News. The rail system is

well developed and has a good connection to mainland China. Buses are frequent and cover almost all areas of Hong Kong.

Hong Kong introduced a stored value card, Octopus, in 1997. Octopus can be used on most city transport, except red minibuses, the Peak Trams and taxis. Initial stored value Octopus of $100 is available for adults; $50 for students and $20 for the elderly over 60 and children under 12, in addition to a deposit of $50 when a new card is purchased. Octopus can be recharged when the stored value is used up and the maximum stored value is $1,000 while a minimum stored value is $50. There are machines for recharging the Octopus in all KCR and MTR stations, and it can also be done in some convenience stores (7-11 and Circle K). The deposit will be refunded when you return the Octopus to the company. There is also a personalised Octopus. Unlike normal Octopus, it stores personal data inside the card and can recharge directly from a bank account when the stored value is used up. Octopus can be purchased from KCR and MTR stations.

Air

Flights to mainland China are mainly operated by Chinese airlines, which include Air China and China Southern Airlines. Dragon Air is the only Hong Kong based airline that runs domestic flights to mainland China. Recently, more people are taking flights to mainland China from Shenzhen airport instead of Hong Kong International Airport as it can usually save around $1,000-$3,000 (US$128-384/ £80-240). There are also some special offers from travel agents, especially in low seasons.

Useful Addresses and Websites

China Travel Net Hong Kong Limited, Room A, 2/F, Tak Bo Building, 62-74 Sai Yee Street, Mongkok, Hong Kong; ☎(852) 2789 5401; fax (852) 2789 3498; e-mail enquiry@chinatravel1.com ; www.chinatravel1.com.

Dragon Air Ticketing Office, Room 4609 – 4611, 46/F., COSCO Tower, 183 Queen's Road Central, Hong Kong; tel(852) 2868 6777; fax(852) 2810 0370; www.dragonair.com.

Wing On Travel, Room 1707, 17/F, Lane Crawford House, 70 Queen's Road Central, Central; tel(852) 2189 7689; fax (852) 2189 7686; www.wingontravel.com.

Hong Tai Travel, 5/F, United Centre, Admiralty MTR Station; ☎(852) 2108 8888; fax (852) 2108 8555; www.hongthai.com.

Kwun Kin Tours, Room 407-411, Block B, Hunghom Commercial Centre, 37 Ma Tau Wai Road, Hunghom; ☎(852) 2362 2022; e-mail custom@kwankin.com.hk.

Energy Tours, Room 309-331, 3/F, Bank Centre, 636 Nathan Road, Mongkok, Kowloon; ☎(852) 2782 0380.

Rail

There are two railway companies in Hong Kong, The Kowloon-Canton Railway Corporation (KCR) and the Mass Transit Railway (MTR).

KCR. Currently operates two domestic rail services, the East Rail and the Light Rail. The East Rail is a main link for the New Territories and Kowloon. There are 13 stations along the railway, from Hung Hom to the border at Lo Wu. Stations include 'University', located beside The Hong Kong Chinese University. An East Rail train consists of 12 compartments and can accommodate over 2,000 passengers. A single trip is from $3.5 to $33 for an adult. East Rail also operates intercity passenger services to Guangzhou on its own train, and provides access for other intercity trains running to and from Guangzhou, Shanghai and Beijing. The Beijing-Kowloon Through Train and the Shanghai-Kowloon Through Train operate on alternate days with a total journey time about 26 & 23 hours respectively. Tickets are from $500-$1,200, depending on which class you are travelling. The Guangzhou-Kowloon line is much cheaper. Tickets are from $130-230.

The Light Rail is another rail network of KCR. It provides passenger services for the fast-developing North West New Territories (Yuen Long and Tuen Mun). There are 57 stops in total. The Light Rail is more similar to the underground of European countries. A Light Rail train can accommodate around 200 passengers. The fare depends on the number of zones covered ($4-$6).

The KCR Corporation is currently developing the West Rail which should be in service in 2004. For further information about the KCR, visit the company website *www.kcrc.com*.

MTR. The MTR route covers most parts of Hong Kong Island, Kowloon and south New Territories. Each train consists of eight compartments and has a capacity of 2,500 passengers. The fare is $4-$13. The MTR company also operates the Airport Express running between Hong Kong International Airport and Central. It also provides in-town check-in services to many major airlines up to 100 minutes before the flight take-off. Passengers of some airlines can even check-in and get the boarding pass one day prior to departure. It only takes 23 minutes to go to the airport by MTR from Central. However, it is much more expensive than taking the airport buses. It costs $100 from Central to the airport by MTR but it costs around $30 or less if you take the bus instead. For further information about MTR services, visit the MTR customer website *www.mtr.com.hk*.

The East Rail of KCR and MTR are connected at Kowloon Tong Station.

Bus

Apart from trains, the bus is also a popular and easy way to get around the city. Double-decker buses are very common in Hong Kong due to the high population density. Almost all buses in Hong Kong are air-conditioned. Hong Kong has many mountains so many tunnels are built to make transportation easier. In general, buses passing through tunnels, which carry charges, are more expensive. There are three bus companies in Hong Kong. All three companies provide point-to-point bus route enquiry online. If you tell the web where you want to take the bus from and your destination, the point-to-point enquiry service can provide you with the bus details such as bus numbers, duration of the trip, where the bus stops are and the price, etc.

Long Win Bus Co. Ltd, a wholly owned subsidiary company of Kowloon Motor Bus Group (KMB), and Citybus operate bus routes to and from the airport. Details of Long Win Bus Co. Ltd can be found in the KMB website.

Bus Companies

The Kowloon Motor Bus Company (1933) Limited (KMB), 1 Po Lun Street, Lai Chi Kok, Kowloon, ☎(852) 2786 8888/(852) 2745 4466 (enquiry hotline); fax (852) 2745 0300;; www.kmb.com.hk.

First Bus, Admiralty (East) Bus Terminus, 95 Queensway, Admiralty, Hong Kong; ☎(852) 2136 8888; fax (852) 2136 2136; www.nwfb.com.hk.

Citybus Limited, 13/F, 9 Des Voeux Road West, Hong Kong; ☎(852) 2963 4888/(852) 2873 0818 (enquiry hotline); fax (852) 2857 6179; www.citybus.com.hk.

Minibus

Minibuses are small buses that can accommodate 16 passengers. Destinations are written in Chinese and English on the front panel of the bus. There are two types of minibus in Hong Kong, people call them 'red minibuses' and 'green minibuses'. Green minibuses are green and beige in colour. They have fixed routes and fixed stops. You usually pay, either by Octopus or coins, when you get on the minibus. The drivers will not take your money directly as they are hired by the minibus companies and have a monthly salary. Red minibuses are red and beige in colour. They have fixed routes but the drivers may change the routes slightly according to the traffic situation. There are no fixed stops and a passenger can get off anywhere along the route, except in restricted areas marked by double yellow lines along the road. Passengers pay the driver directly when they get off. Octopus is not accepted at the moment. Unlike the green minibuses, many red minibuses run after midnight. The fares of red minibuses may vary sometimes, especially on festivals or after midnight.

Taxi

Taxis are numerous and readily available. Red taxis serve Hong Kong Island and Kowloon; green ones the New Territories and blue taxis Lantau Island. The rate for red taxis starts at \$15.0 for the first two kilometres plus \$1.40 for every 200 metres after. Waiting time is \$1.40 per minute and the fare is shown on the meter. Additional charges apply to cross-harbour tunnels, Lion Rock Tunnel, Junk Bay Tunnel and Aberdeen Tunnel, and a \$5 charge for each piece of luggage. The rate for green taxis starts at \$12.5 for the first two kilometres plus \$1.2 for every additional 200 metres. Waiting time is \$1.2 per minute. Each piece of luggage costs \$4.0. The drivers normally accept Hong Kong dollars only.

Ferry

Star Ferry, which has connected Hong Kong Island and Kowloon since 1898, runs regularly between 6.30am and 11.30pm. At \$ 2.20 (upper deck), it is one of the cheapest and most scenic ferry rides in the world. Crossing the harbour takes approximately eight minutes.

First Ferry operates services to the outlying islands including Cheung Chau and Lantau Island. Fares are from \$10-\$31. Hong Kong & Kowloon Ferry Ltd also provides regular services between Lamma and Hong Kong Island with a fare of \$10-\$20. First Ferry operates ferries between Hong Kong and Macau at a price of \$123-\$131 for a single trip. However, there are only a limited number of ferries every day. TurboJET provides more frequent ferries to Macau as well as providing connections to Shenzhen and Guangzhou. The fare for going to Macau is \$130-\$162 and \$171-\$198 for Shenzhen and Guangzhou.

Ferry Companies

The Star Ferry Company Ltd, ☎(852) 2367 7065; fax (852) 2118 6028; e-mail sf@starferry.com.hk; www.starferry.com.hk.

Hong Kong & Kowloon Ferry Ltd, GPier 4, New Reclamation, Central District, Hong Kong; ☎(852) 2815 6063; www.hkkf.com.hk.

First Ferry, Central Pier No.6; ☎(852) 2131 8181; fax (852) 2131 8877; www.nwff.com.hk.

TurboJET, Shun Tak – China Travel Ship Management Ltd, 83 Hing Wah Street West, Lai Chi Kok, Kowloon, Hong Kong; ☎(852) 2307 0880/(852) 2859 3333 (enquiry hotline); fax (852) 2786 5125; www.turbojet.com.hk.

Trams

Trams are the cheapest transportation in Hong Kong with a flat fare of \$2 for adults and \$1 for children under 12 and senior citizens aged 65 or above. They have been operating on Hong Kong Island since 1904. Hongkong Tramways Limited operates six overlapping routes on 13 kilometres of double track along the northern shore of Hong Kong Island between Kennedy Town and Shau Kei Wan, and about three kilometres of single track around Happy Valley.

Another Hong Kong tramway is the Peak Tram, operated by Peak Tramways Company Limited since 1888. The 1.4 kilometre line runs between Central and the Peak. A single trip for adults costs $20.

BANKING AND FINANCE

Banking in Hong Kong is efficient and reliable. There are a lot of different services to suit all customers. Banks, in general, open Monday to Friday from 9am – 5pm, and 9am – 1pm on Saturday. Most of the banks are particularly busy during lunchtime and on Saturday mornings. Try to avoid going to the banks at these times or you will need to queue for up to 30 minutes. Many banks provide online banking services and basic transactions can be done online. There is no debit card in Hong Kong but EPS, a similar system, is widely accepted in shops. Credit card is another normal payment method and it is easy to get a credit card in Hong Kong. Cheques are normal when doing business or handling fees, but companies prefer to have salaries paid directly to the employees' accounts. ATM machines are easy to find and some banks are linked. No extra fee is needed if you use the ATM machines of linked banks to withdraw money.

Bank Accounts

It is surprising that Hong Kong has over 130 different banks. You can choose from American banks to Chinese banks, or British banks to Indian banks. However, around five to eight banks have a significant domination in the market. Many companies prefer employees to have an account with specific banks to get their salaries paid. Therefore, opening an account in a main bank may save a lot of trouble. Moreover, these banks usually have a lot of branches, which cover most districts.

Many banks require a minimum opening balance of $100-$200. It is best to check up with the bank for the required documents for opening an account. Basically, a passport or other identification, and maybe a document, like the electric bill, to confirm your mailing address. The banks usually suggest other services when you open an account like credit card, internet banking, phone banking or cheque account. You can apply for those according to your need. Internet banking, phone banking and chequebook are all free of charge. Many banks waive the annual fee for credit cards to attract customers. You may try to get your bank to waive the annual fee for your credit card if you use it frequently. Do it before the next annual fee is due. Many banks require customers to maintain a certain average monthly balance, maybe $3,000-$5,000. You will be charged an additional fee of around $20-$50 per month if your average monthly balance is below the required one. Overdrafts apply to some types of account. However, an additional fee may be required and the interest rate is usually quite high.

It is possible and maybe better to open an account in your own country before you go to Hong Kong. Many banks have branches in Hong Kong and are able to arrange an account in advance. Check it up with your home bank, so that you can have your account in Hong Kong ready before you arrive.

International Money Transfer

Transferring money to and from Hong Kong can be done in two ways, either by going to the bank or through electronic banking. A flat rate is required for both methods regardless of how much is to be transferred. Transferring money electronically is usually faster and cheaper, and may be done within one or two days. A bank draft takes around five days.

Money

The Dollar ($) is the monetary unit in Hong Kong, which is equal to 100 cents. Prices are generally presented with two decimal places, e.g. $2.50 represents two dollars and fifty cents. The smallest coin value is 10 cents. Others are $10, $5, $2, $1, 50 cents and 20 cents. There are six different value notes: $1,000, $500, $100, $50, $20 and $10. The Hong Kong dollar currently has a standard exchange rate with the US dollar at US$1=HK$7.8 (or HK$1=US$0.128).

Main Banks

Bank of China (Hong Kong) Limited, Bank of China Tower 1 Garden Road, Central, Hong Kong; ☎(852) 2826 6888; fax (852) 2810 5963; www.bochk.com.

The Bank of East Asia, Limited, 10 Des Voeux Road Central, Hong Kong; ☎(852) 2842 3200; fax (852) 2845 9333; www.hkbea.com.

Citibank, N.A., 39/F-40/F., 43/F-50/F., Citibank Tower Citibank Plaza, 3 Garden Road, Hong Kong, ☎(852) 2868 8888: fax (852) 2306 8111; www.citibank.com.hk.

Hang Seng Bank Ltd., 83 Des Voeux Road Central, Central Hong Kong; ☎(852) 2198 1111; fax (852) 2845 9301/(852) 2868 4047; www.hangseng.com.

The Hongkong and Shanghai Banking Corporation Limited, 1 Queen's Road Central, Central, Hong Kong; ☎(852) 2822 1111; fax (852) 2810 1112; www.hsbc.com.hk.

Standard Chartered Bank, 4-4A Des Voeux Road Central, Central, Hong Kong; ☎(852) 2820 3333; fax (852) 2856 9129; www.standardchartered.com.hk.

Other Banks

American Express Bank Limited, 36/F One Pacific Place 88 Queensway, Central, Hong Kong; ☎(852) 2844 0688; fax (852) 2845 3637; www.americanexpress.com/hk.

Barclays Bank Plc., 42/F., Citibank Tower, 3 Garden Road, Hong Kong; ☎(852) 2903 2000; fax (852) 2903 2999; www.barclays.com.

Australia & New Zealand Banking Group Ltd., Suite 3101-3105, One Exchange Square 8 Connaught Place, Central, Hong Kong; ☎(852) 2843 7111; fax (852) 2868 0089/(852) 2525 2475; www.anz.com.

TAXATION

Hong Kong has a very low tax rate when compared to most of the countries in the world, and the items that are taxed are limited. This is a very attractive for people moving to Hong Kong. The tax rates for locals and foreigners are the same.

Income Tax

Full-time employees of a company in Hong Kong, no matter if it is a local company or a foreign owned one, have to pay full tax. The amount paid depends on annual income and deductions. Annual income includes salaries, commission, allowances, tips, salary tax paid by employer, value of a place of residence provided by the employer, share option gains, awards and gratuities and payments received from retirement schemes. The annual income is counted from 1st April of the previous year to 31st March of the current year. There are several deductions that can be claimed before tax. These deductions include allowances, concessionary deductions and outgoings and expenses. Approved charitable donations, mandatory contributions (pension contributions) or occupational retirement schemes, home loan interest and elderly residential care expenses can be claimed as concessionary deductions. However, voluntary mandatory contributions are not counted in concessionary deductions. For some employment like insurance representatives, certain types of expenses are necessary in the production of the assessable income. It is possible for them to claim a deduction if they can prove the expenses are wholly, exclusively and necessarily for the employment. And if buying a uniform and joining a professional body is a pre-requisite for the employment, deduction can also be claimed. Self-education and depreciation allowances on plant and machinery, related to producing an income, are also counted as outgoings and expenses. The biggest deduction from annual income is allowances and everyone can claim the types and amount of allowances as shown in the below table. Tax rates are in a graduated system. The higher the net income (annual income minus the deductions), the more tax you pay.

TAX ALLOWANCES	
Year of Assessment 2004/05	Hong Kong $
Basic Allowance	100,000
Married Person's Allowance	200,000
Child Allowance -For each of the first nine children	30,000
Dependent Brother/Sister Allowance -For each qualified brother/sister	30,000

Dependent Parent/Grandparent Allowance	
-For each qualified parent	30,000
Additional dependent parent allowance	
-For each qualified parent	30,000
Single Parent Allowance	100,000
Disabled Dependant Allowance	
-For each qualified dependant	60,000

Year of Assessment 2004/05

	Net Chargeable Income ($)	Rate
On the First	30,000	2%
On the Next	30,000	8%
On the Next	30,000	14%
Remainder		20%

Every taxpayer is responsible for filling in the tax return on time. Failure to do so without good reason will be subject to a penalty. One can also use the Tele Tax, provided by the Inland and Revenue Department, to file the tax return. Tax will not be deducted from your salary directly, but can be paid by telephone, internet, bank ATM machines, by post or in person.

Other Taxes

Property Tax. This tax applies to owners of land or buildings in Hong Kong. Payments received by the owners, which include rent, payment for the right of use of premises under licence, lump sum premiums, service charges and management fees paid to the owner. Property Tax will be imposed on this net assessable value after deducting expenditures. The rate for the tax in 2004/2005 will be 16%.

Profit Tax. Persons or corporations carrying on a trade, profession or business which derives profit from Hong Kong have to pay Profit Tax. It is not limited to local or international corporations. The key point is if the profit is derived from Hong Kong. Profit Tax for corporation businesses and incorporated businesses are 17.5% and 16% respectively.

Stamp Duty. Stamp Duty is imposed on certain types of documents, which are mainly a conveyance on sale, agreement for sale of residential property, lease of immovable property, and transfer of Hong Kong stock.

Business Registration. Every person carrying on any business must register his business. 'Business' means any form of trade, commerce, craftsmanship, profession, calling or other activity carried on for the purpose of gain. Clubs and organisations providing social and recreational activities for members, have to apply for business registration no matter whether it is for making a profit or not.

Hotel Accommodation Tax. 3% of all accommodation charges is for Hotel Accommodation Tax. It is usually included in the listed prices.

Betting Duty. This is charged on horse racing, lotteries and football betting at rates of 12% to 50%.

Estate Duty. One's property is chargeable to Estate Duty on death. This includes everything the deceased owned, the share property jointly owned by the deceased and others, and property that the deceased gave away anytime during the three years before death.

For more information about taxes in Hong Kong, visit this website *www.info.gov.hk/ird.*

HEALTH CARE

Hospitals

All Hong Kong public hospitals are managed by The Hospital Authority (HA). The HA has revised the health care system in the last few years and has made some adjustments to the fees in 2003. The Accident and Emergency (A&E) service was free before April, 2003, but many people chose to use the A&E service even in non-emergency cases and so the demand was huge. There are four levels of emergency in the A&E Unit. A wait of two or three hours for people who are classified as third or fourth emergency levels is usual. The HA introduced the A&E service charge of $100 starting from April, 2003 aiming to reduce the demand for A&E service. If you need to stay in the hospital, unless you are transferred from the A&E Unit, there is an extra $50 for admission in addition to the charge of $100 per day. General out-patient service charges are $45 per attendance and $10 for each drug item. Recipients of Comprehensive Social Security Assistance (CSSA) will be exempt from payment of their medical expenses for public health care services. Non-CSSA recipients who could not afford medical fees can apply for a fee waiver from the Medical Social Workers of public hospitals and clinics.

The above charges are for local residents with a Hong Kong Identity Card. If you do not hold a Hong Kong Identity Card, the charges will be much higher. The A&E service charges foreigners $570 (US$73/£46) per attendance; in-patient service is $3,300 (US$423/£266) per day; general out-patient service is $215 (US$28/£17) per attendance; special intensive care ward/unit charges a very high fee of $18,100 (US$2,320/£1,460) per day. These charges may be even higher in private hospitals.

The demand for public health services is really huge. Prepare to wait for at least two months for arranging a non-urgent operation. Private hospitals are an alternative but the charges may be much higher.

Consulting private clinics costs around $150-$250 (US$19-32/£12-20) per attendance and dental services are from $150-$1,500 depending on what treatments you need.

Useful Address
Hospital Authority, ☎(852) 2882 4866; www.ha.org.hk.

Health Insurance
Even though the charges in Hong Kong hospitals are low if you are a local resident, many people prefer to have personal health insurance. Usually, people buy health insurance through insurance agents, although some companies have health and dental benefit packages for their employees. Big insurance companies like AIA, Blue Cross and AXA are reliable and offer more varied insurance plans.

Useful Addresses
American International Assurance Co (Bermuda) Ltd, AIA Tower, North Point; ☎(852) 2232 8888; www.aia.com.hk.
AXA Asia Pacific Holdings Ltd, AXA Centre, 151 Gloucester Road, Wanchai, Hong Kong; ☎(852) 2519 1111; fax (852) 2598 4965; www.axa-chinaregion.com.
Blue Cross (Asia-Pacific) Insurance Ltd, 22/F., Cosco Tower, 183 Queen's Road Central, Hong Kong; ☎(852) 2163 1000; fax (852) 2808 1300; www.bluecross.com.hk.
Eagle Star Life Assurance Co Ltd, Levels 15-17, Cityplaza 3, 14 Taikoo Wan Road, Hong Kong; ☎(852) 2967 8393; fax (852) 2569 2607; www.eaglestar.com.hk/eng.
ING General Insurance International, 7/F ING Tower, 308 Des Voeux Road Central, Hong Kong; ☎(852) 2850 3030; www.ing.com.hk/gi.
New York Life Insurance Worldwide Ltd, Windsor Hse, Causeway Bay, Hong Kong; ☎(852) 2881 0688; fax2577 0866; www.newyorklife.com.hk.
Prudential Assurance Co Ltd, The Cityplaza Taikoo Shing, Shau Kei Wan; ☎(852) 2977 3888; www.prudential.com.hk.
Royal & Sun Alliance Insurance (HK) Ltd, Dorset Hse, Quarry Bay, Hong Kong; ☎(852) 2968 3000; fax (852) 2915 4370; www.royalsunalliance.com.hk.

Emergencies
999 is the emergency number in Hong Kong. The operator will direct the line to the relevant departments. An ambulance will generally arrive within 10 minutes. Many buildings have a direct connection with fire stations; if the fire alarm is on, the fire station will send firemen to the building even if no one calls 999.

SOCIAL SECURITY AND BENEFITS

Even though the tax rate in Hong Kong is low, social security and benefits are good. Unlike Canada or the USA, Hong Kong does not require citizens to pay additional tax for social security and benefits.

Comprehensive Social Security Assistance (CSSA). This scheme is intended to help low-income individuals or families live up to a prescribed level to meet their basic needs. Applicants must be Hong Kong residents and have resided in Hong Kong for at least a year before applying. The Social Welfare Department will assess the capital assets of the individual or family and then decide if the application is eligible. There is an additional requirement for adults aged 15-59 in normal health. They should be working or actively looking for a paid job if they apply for CSSA. The standard rate for a family with physically healthy parents and two children is about $5,000-6,000 (US$640-770/£400-480) a month. The family can apply for additional grants for rent allowance, water and electrical charges allowances and school fee grants. The assistance is a bit more for those aged over 60, disabled, single parent and those medically certified to be in ill-health.

Social Security Allowance (SSA) Scheme. This scheme is for the elderly who have reached the age of 65 or above and have lived in Hong Kong continuously for five years or more after they are 60. Elderly people who are under the capital asset limit will receive a monthly allowance of $625-$705. For those who have a disability, the allowance will be between $1,120 and $2,240.

Criminal and Law Enforcement Injuries Compensation Scheme (CLEICS). If a person is innocently injured or has died as a result of a crime of violence, or by a law enforcement officer using a weapon in the execution of his duty, he or she can apply for CLEICS. This scheme is not limited to Hong Kong citizens. Victims who are able to show they were legally permitted to stay in Hong Kong at the time of the incident, and have to receive treatment for at least three days can apply for it. It is non-means-tested financial assistance. In the case of death, the compensation will be given to the dependants of the victim.

Traffic Accident Victims Assistance Scheme (TAVAS). This is another financial assistance not solely for Hong Kong citizens. Victims of road accidents, even if they caused the accident, can apply for it. Similar to CLEICS, applicants must show they were legally permitted to stay in Hong Kong when the accident happened, and received treatment for at least three days after the accident. Financial assistance will be provided to dependants of the victims in case of death.

Emergency Relief (ER). In the event of natural and other disasters, the Social and Welfare Department will provide material aid including hot meals, blankets and other essential relief articles. There is also a financial assistance called the Emergency Relief Fund (ERF), providing cash assistance for persons in need of urgent relief as a result of natural or other disasters.

The Social Welfare Department also provides supporting services to single parents, new immigrants, disabled, elderly and young people, and general community service to the public. For further details of these services, visit the Social Welfare Department website at *www.info.gov.hk/swd*.

CRIME AND THE POLICE

The crime rate in Hong Kong is extremely low. In 2001, the crime rate in Hong Kong was 1.1% while the crime rate for London in 2002 was 15.2%.

While violent crime is rare, foreigners should still exercise their commonsense concerning pickpocketing. Be aware of your personal belongings, particularly when you are in a crowded area or public areas like bars and restaurants. Criminals may sometimes work in a group, so that one of them draws your attention while the other takes away your belongings. Complaints concerning deception during retail or other commercial transactions are not unusual as well. Some shops do not show the prices for the products in the display window and then demand a price according to the perceived wealth of the customers. It is not a crime if you and the shop agree on a deal, even if you later found out that you paid a much higher price than the locals. It is only a crime if the shops give you wrong information on what you pay, the model number, the functions of the products and so on. Shops like these are more concentrated in tourist areas like Tsim Sha Tsui and Causeway Bay. You are advised to visit several shops before buying something and it is safer to buy electrical products in big stores like Fortress and Broadway.

There are around 35,000 policemen in Hong Kong, around one per 200 Hong Kong citizens. They are in blue uniform and are armed. It is not difficult to find a police officer on the street and they are generally very helpful. Even if you lose your way, you can ask them to help. You are required to carry your Hong Kong Identity Card with you if you have one. In case a crime happens, the emergency number is 999.

SOCIAL LIFE

Hong Kong is a friendly and easy going place for most foreigners. The people are willing to help and welcome foreigners. Though it is not very common for Hong Kong people to start a conversation with a stranger at the bus stop or on a train, but if you take the initiative, they will usually keep up a conversation with you if there is no language barrier.

Manners and Customs

Even though Hong Kong is a mixed culture of the East and the West, the oriental tradition has a bigger influence. In a casual meeting or at a party, people usually introduce themselves by their first names and expect to be called by that name. Some young people even have English names and it is not rude to call them by that name, if they introduce themselves that way. However, if you meet someone in business and trade at more formal meetings, like an interview, people usually introduce themselves by their surnames and their positions. It is better to call them Mr/Ms X unless they ask to be called by their first names. In universities, students usually call their teachers Prof. X instead of their first names even if they know each other well. Handshaking is common in all situations when you first meet someone. Both men and women welcome someone by handshaking. Hugs and pecks on the cheek are not very common among locals, especially with older people. Young people accept it as a way of showing politeness and friendliness to foreigners but they do not do it much among local friends.

It is not usual for Hong Kong people to have wine during dinner although it is getting more and more popular among middle-class businessmen. It may be a better idea to bring a box of chocolate or desserts if you are invited for a dinner. Traditionally, people tend to share food amongst each other and there are usually a number of dishes served together with no starter. It is also normal to have soup both before and after dinner. Traditionally, Chinese people would not expect to share the bill if you are invited for a dinner in the restaurant. You may consider a reciprocal dinner invitation if you would like to thank your hosts.

Making Friends

The work place or university (if you are a student) is a good place to start making friends. You may find that some of the locals are a bit shy in the beginning but that is probably part of the culture. Most of them are however very friendly to westerners. Bars and pubs are good places for making friends, although Hong Kong people in general do not drink as much as people do in the west. You may want to stay away from Central, and hang out in Kowloon and Wan Chai, if you want to meet the locals in bars and pubs.

Michiel Gen on social life in Hong Kong

My social life was very active. There was a sizable contingent of expats and other exchange students with whom it was easy to make contact. Making friends with Chinese students proved a little more difficult as they seemed rather shy and reluctant to speak English (with the exception of the authors of this book). I decided to choose the more difficult (yet rewarding) path by focusing on meeting local people and spending less time with westerners. One

> of the reasons why I chose to go to HK was to learn about other cultures, after all. Anyway, I made a number of Chinese friends with whom I'm still in regular contact.

Even though Hong Kong people are in general too busy to take part in physical exercise, many of them enjoy watching sports, particularly football and basketball. It can be a good topic to start a conversation with your new friends. There are many sports centres, mainly operated by the government, that provide training courses for different sports at low fees, which is a good chance to make friends as well as learning a new sport. If you are not a big fan of sports, city halls and other cultural organisations also organise regular cultural activities or courses at low prices for the public as well.

Food and Drink

People say that the food in Hong Kong is a genuine comfort when someone misses home. You can find cuisines from most parts of the world in Hong Kong: Italian, French, Spanish, American, Japanese, Korean, Indian, Thai, Malay, Singaporean, Brazilian, Middle-East or Greek, etc. As for Chinese food, you can easily find over 10 different styles in Hong Kong. You will never find it difficult to find a restaurant for your favourite food. Rather, it is often hard to choose from the varied choices. Seafood is a particular highlight. Do not go to those famous seafood restaurants written up in the travel guides. There is no problem with them, but there are many better and cheaper ones in the outlying islands like Cheung Chau. Fast food is very common in Hong Kong too. Apart from McDonald's, KFC or Burger King, you can try the local fast-food restaurants (not those that serve dim-sum, but small restaurants serving quick meals, called *cha-chaan-tang* or Chinese noodle shops, which both serve cheap and good food.) Foreigners may also find *dai-pai-dong* interesting. These restaurants place the tables and chairs in the open areas in front of their kitchens, and are usually located inside those complex public residential estates. There are some good ones in Shatin, Fo Tan and Yau Ma Tei. Table manners are not of much concern in these places, but the dishes are usually cheap and very tasty. The caveat is that there may not be an English menu for foreigners. The waiters or waitresses are usually middle-aged locals who may also not speak English. Therefore, it would be good to learn the names of the dishes you want to try from your local friends, or ask them to go with you – it is well worth it even if you have to pay the bill.

For real local specialties, there are tons of street snacks like fish balls (which do not really taste like fish; *yu-daan*), fake shark fin soup (made with soya beans, cooked with meat and other ingredients like the real shark fin soup; *woon-chai-chi*), rice rolls (*cheung-fan*), etc. They are all very tasty. You can find many small food stalls selling these snacks in Mongkok, Causeway Bay and Wan Chai. They are often very cheap but food cleanliness is sometimes a concern.

Bars and pubs are common in Kowloon and Hong Kong Island particularly Central (Lan Kwai Fong), Wanchai (Jaffe Road) and Tsim Sha Tsui. You may find some small pubs in the New Territories but they are rare. Pubs usually open from 4pm or 5pm until very late, maybe 3 in the morning. Alcohol is only sold to those who are over 18. You will find that drinks, for instance beer, served at bars and pubs are much more expensive than what you can get in supermarkets and convenience stores – sometimes up to ten-fold or more. You can drink outside on the streets as long as you do not disturb others.

You will probably be surprised if you ask a taxi driver to take you to a night club in Hong Kong. 'Night clubs' in Hong Kong refer to the expensive places where you can find prostitutes or the like. Hong Kong people call dancing and drinking places with loud music on all night 'discos'. Many discos can be found in the pub area in Wanchai but there are also some in Tsim Sha Shui and Mongkok.

Coffee shops are popular for those who want to sit down comfortably and chat, which can be a bit difficult given the crowdedness of the city. Apart from those big coffee shops like Pacific Coffee and Starbucks, there are also some small but nice coffee shops in Hankow Road, Tsim Sha Tsui.

Shopping

Many tourists like visiting Hong Kong because they find it a shoppers' heaven. Shops usually open from 11am to 9 or 10pm, seven days a week. There are lots of shopping centres located in different parts of Hong Kong and you can find almost all you need in them. For designer clothing, go to Park Lane in Tsim Sha Tsui. Tailor-made suits are still available in some tailor shops, even though most people prefer ready-made ones at cheaper prices, or designer labels. Kwun Ki is the largest clothing store with branches in different districts. If you are looking for some cheap and hip clothing, visit Fay Yuen Street in Mongkok or Granville Road in Tsim Sha Tsui. You will be surprised by the prices of the clothes. A T-shirt can cost around $10-$50 (US$1.2-$6/80 pence-£4) and a warm jacket can be as cheap as $70 (US$9/£5). Do not expect the quality to be good, but there is a lot of choice.

> ### Jennifer Atkinson on shopping
> I don't think there was anything I could not get in Hong Kong that I needed – either in terms of clothing and footwear, or in terms of food.

You can also find all sorts of interesting local special goods. There is a street which is full of shops selling goldfish near to Fay Yuen Street. You can find lots of sports shops in Sai Yee Street, just next to Fay Yuen Street. The Jade Market is in Yau Ma Tei, behind the Kowloon Central Post Office. You can find good deals for jade, if you are experienced at identifying the best quality. In Sheung Wan in Hong Kong Island, there are many shops selling dried seafoods, which are great for cooking or as presents for the Chinese New Year. Since the competition is keen, the quality is in general very good although the price may not be significantly lower than you may find elsewhere.

Electrical appliances are in general cheaper than in the USA and Europe. It is better to go to the big electrical chain stores like Fortress or Broadway if you are not familiar with the small shops, even if the price is usually more attractive there. Be careful when buying electrical appliances in tourist areas like Tsim Sha Tsui and Causeway Bay as the price is usually marked up for tourists. You can probably get furniture at reasonable prices in Hong Kong. Ikea provides a great selection but small furniture shops can sometimes provide similar choices at a lower price.

Gold and jewellery is a must-buy for visitors from mainland China. The gold sold in Hong Kong is under strict supervision, the guaranteed quality attracts many tourists from mainland China. Moreover, the designs of jewellery are also more fashionable and provide more choice.

Useful Addresses

Broadway, Shop 714, Times Square, Causeway Bay; ☎(852) 2506 1330; www.ibroadway.com.hk (visit the website for more branches information).

Fortress, 1st Floor, Cavendish Centre, 23 Yip Hing Street, Wong Chuk Hang, Hong Kong; ☎(852) 2555 5788; e-mail fortress@asw.com.hk; www.fortress.com.hk (with branches information on the website).

Ikea, ☎(852) 3125 0888; fax (852) 3125 0880; www.ikea.com.hk (visit the website for branches information).

Kwun Ki, No. 1, Yee Wo Street, Causeway Bay, Hong Kong; ☎(852) 2576 2505; customer hotline (for enquiry on addresses and telephone numbers of other branches): (852) 2793 1393.

Cinemas

Movies are a popular entertainment in Hong Kong. You can find Chinese (from mainland China), European, Japanese and Korean movies as well as western and local ones. Hollywood movies are popular. Movies usually have English and Chinese subtitles and you can book the tickets online or by telephone. Tickets are from $40-$70 (US$5-9/£3-5.5) and you can buy three days in advance or sometimes seven days for very popular movies. If you like to stay away from the mainstream movies, try Cine-Art House and Broadway Cinematheque, both show many non-Hollywood and non-local movies.

Useful Addresses

Cine-Art House, 30 Harbour Road, Wanchai, Hong Kong; ☎(852) 2827 4778.

Broadway Cinematheque, Phase 2, Properous Garden, No.3, Public Square's Street, Yau Ma Tei, Kowloon, Hong Kong; ☎(852) 2388 3188.

Broadway cinemas, www.cinema.com.hk.

UA cinemas, www.uacinemas.com.hk.

Cityline (for booking tickets online), www.cityline.com.hk.

Hong Kong Film's Web (for addresses and telephone numbers of all cinemas in Hong Kong), www.hkfilms.com.

Art and Museums

Museums in Hong Kong are not exactly impressive. However, there are many exhibitions about the history and development of Hong Kong, which may interest you. If you are interested in the development of Hong Kong and how Hong Kong looked in the past, The Hong Kong Museum of History is an interesting place with models and photos of old Hong Kong as well as the strange Chinese traditions. And you will find some very venerable collections in the Hong Kong Heritage Museum. Otherwise, the biggest collection of western painting is in the Museum of Art, located in Tsim Sha Tsui. You can spend two to three hours there. Apart from the three mentioned, there are also the Hong Kong Museum of Coastal Defence, Hong Kong Science Museum, Hong Kong Space Museum, Art Museum of the Chinese University of Hong Kong, University Museum and Art Gallery (The University of Hong Kong), Police Museum, The Hong Kong Racing Museum and Tai Po Kau Interactive Nature Centre.

There are many cultural centres or city halls with different performances every night. Some internationally famous productions or dance groups have performances, like *The Phantom of the Opera* and *Chicago*.

Museums

Hong Kong Museum of History, 100 Chatham Road South, Tsim Sha Tsui, Kowloon, Hong Kong (next to the Hong Kong Science Museum); ☎(852) 2724 9042; fax (852) 2724 9090; e-mail hkmh@lcsd.gov.hk; www.lcsd.gov.hk/CE/Museum/History/.

Hong Kong Heritage Museum, 1 Man Lam Road, Sha Tin, Hong Kong; ☎(852) 2180 8188; www.heritagemuseum.gov.hk.

Hong Kong Museum of Art, 10 Salisbury Road, Tsim Sha Tsui, Kowloon, Hong Kong; ☎(852) 2721 0116; fax (852) 2723 7666; E-mail enquiries@lcsd.gov.hk; www.lcsd.gov.hk/CE/Museum/Arts/.

Hong Kong Museum of Coastal Defence, 175 Tung Hei Road, Shau Kei Wan, Hong Kong; ☎(852) 2569 1500; fax (852) 2569 1637; e-mail hkmcd@lcsd.gov.hk; hk.coastaldefence.museum.

Hong Kong Science Museum, 2 Science Museum Road, Tsimshatsui East, Kowloon, Hong Kong, ☎(852) 2732 3232; www.lcsd.gov.hk/CE/Museum/Science/

Hong Kong Space Museum, 10 Salisbury Road, Tsim Sha Tsui, Kowloon, Hong Kong; tel (852) 2721 0226; fax (852) 2311 5804; www.lcsd.gov.hk/CE/Museum/Space/.

Art Museum The Chinese University of Hong Kong, Shatin, N.T. Hong Kong; ☎(852) 2609 7416; fax (852) 2603 5366; www.cuhk.edu.hk/ics/amm/.

University Museum and Art Gallery, The University of Hong Kong 94 Bonham Road, Pokfulam, Hong Kong; ☎(852) 2241 5500 fax: (852) 2546 9659; http://www.hku.hk/hkumag/.

Hong Kong Police Museum, 27 Coombe Road, The Peak, Hong Kong; ☎(852) 2849 7019; fax (852) 2849 4573; www.info.gov.hk/police/.

The Hong Kong Racing museum, 2/F., Happy Valley Stand, Happy Valley, Hong Kong; ☎(852) 2966 8065; fax (852) 2966 7057; e-mail museum@hkjc.org.hk; www.hongkongjockeyclub.com/chinese/school/2002 – museum/mu02 – index.htm.

PUBLIC HOLIDAYS

New Year	*1 January*
Ching Ming Festival	*5 April*
Good Friday	
The day following Good Friday	
Easter Monday	
Labour Day	*1 May*
Hong Kong Special Administrative Region Establishment Day	*1 July*
National Day	*1 Oct*
Christmas Day	*25 Dec*
Boxing Day	*26 Dec*

There are some other public holidays which are based on the Chinese lunar calendar and therefore do not have a simple fixed date in the western calendar.

- Chinese New Year – *Late January/February.* Holiday starts from the day before the New Year to Day 3 of the New Year.
- The Buddha's Birthday – *May.*
- Tuen Ng Festival – *May/June.*
- The day following Mid-Autumn Festival – *September/October.*
- Chung Yueng Festival – *Around October.*

TIME

Hong Kong is eight hours ahead of Greenwich Mean Time and seven hours ahead during Daylight-Saving.

RETIREMENT

CHAPTER SUMMARY

- 65 is the standard retirement age.
- Retired people can immigrate as a dependent or an entrant of the Capital Investment Entrant Scheme.
- British citizens can stay in Hong Kong without a visa for up to 180 days; Americans and Europeans can stay visa-free for 90 days.
- **Pension**. There is no governmental pension scheme.
  - Pension payments are not subjected to taxation.
- **Medical Care**. Public medical services are expensive for non-locals.
  - Private doctors charge the same for locals and non-locals.
- **Death**. Any human death that occurs in Hong Kong must be registered; this registration is free of charge.
  - Before shipping a body to another country a permit must be applied for.

BACKGROUND INFORMATION

Hong Kong is not a popular place for retirement. In fact, many locals prefer to retire elsewhere in countries like Australia, Canada, the UK or mainland China, if they can afford it. Hong Kong is too crowded and noisy to be suitable for retirement and most Europeans find the hot and humid summers unpleasant. The houses are in general small and expensive, and it is not easy to get a house with a scenic view even if you are willing to pay a lot. If you are not a Hong Kong citizen, you will have to pay expensive fees for using public medical services. Even if you become a permanent resident, there is only limited social welfare particularly for the elderly. The government does provide a cash subsidy to those who reach the aged of 65, however, the amount is so little that it is difficult to live on it even humbly in this expensive city. In fact, recipients of this subsidy are encouraged by the government to move to Guangdong where living costs are lower.

The greatest advantage of living in Hong Kong is its simple tax system and low tax rates. Basically, you do not need to pay any tax if you neither work nor own property in Hong Kong. There is no sales tax for items other than liquor, tobacco, hydrocarbon oil and methyl alcohol. The crime rate is very low and the city infrastructure and public transport are good. In general, you can get by with English but it may be a bit difficult to make friends with local pensioners as few of them are educated in English.

The Decision to Leave

Choosing a place for retirement is not a simple decision. The best way to actually assess the pros and cons would be to visit and stay for a short period. The Americans and most Europeans are granted a 90 days visa-free visit period and British citizens can stay for up 180 days without a visa. British citizens may consider spending half a year in Hong Kong and half a year at home instead of moving to Hong Kong completely. The summer in Hong Kong maybe too hot (over 30°C/86°F on average) for the British and Europeans but the winter in Hong Kong is much warmer (around 15°C/59°F) than Europe.

RESIDENCE AND ENTRY REGULATIONS

There is no particular visa for retired people. If you do not get permanent residence in Hong Kong before the age of 60, you can enter Hong Kong as the spouse or parent of a Hong Kong resident, or as the spouse of an overseas professional who is permitted to stay in Hong Kong. Alternatively, you can enter Hong Kong through the Capital Investment Entrant Scheme.

Dependent

The spouse and the parents of a Hong Kong resident, or the spouse of an overseas professional who is permitted to stay in Hong Kong can enter and stay in Hong Kong as a dependent. If you are entering Hong Kong as a dependent, you are not allowed to take up any employment until you become a permanent resident. For more details, refer to the chapter *Residence & Entry Regulations*.

Capital Investment Entrant Scheme

If you have plenty of money, you can consider the Capital Investment Entrant Scheme. You must possess a minimum amount of net assets or net equity with a market value of HK$6.5 million (US$830,000/£500,000) if you want to stay in Hong Kong as a capital investor. You should also have started investing your capital in Hong Kong for at least six months before lodging an application. You have to show the Director of the scheme that you can support yourself and your dependents without relying on the return on your investment or other public assistance in Hong Kong. You will be granted a three-month stay after obtaining an Approval-in-Principle (a temporary approval) and you can extend the stay for another three months if active progress of your investment can be shown. You will be granted a two-year stay as a non-Hong Kong resident if you can show the Director that the purpose of your initial investment scheme has been completed. And the stay can be extended for another two years if you continue to show further investment progress. After a continuous stay in Hong Kong for seven years or more, you will become a permanent resident. For further details of entering into Hong Kong through the Capital Investment Entrant Scheme, refer to the chapter *Residence & Entry Regulations*.

POSSIBLE RETIREMENT AREAS

Choosing the area for retirement is important because many areas of the city are overcrowded and polluted. Some exceptions are Sai Kung and Stanley, where they are away from the busy city centre and are next to the sea, and are thus attractive to those who want a quieter life. The level of rent varies according to the size of the house, transportation in the area and the distance from the beaches. The Outlying Islands are good choices as well since it is cheaper to live there than to live in the city centre. For many of these islands, it takes about 45 minutes to an hour to get to Central, which is actually not bad compared to some other areas in the New Territories. If you do not mind paying more, many people find Discovery Bay a nice place to live too. Discovery Bay has good scenery and unpolluted air, like Sai Kung and Stanley. It is a more recently developed area targeted at middle income to high-income class customers. It takes only 30 minutes to go to Central by ferry. If you are interested in exploring the local culture as well as living a quiet life, you may want to stay in one of the small villages in Yuen Long or Sheung Shui. These villages are usually quite old and some are surrounded with interesting historical buildings. It is usually cheap to rent a house in these villages but the facilities may not be great because of the age of the buildings. Moreover, you may find it hard to make friends with the villagers as they are mainly old locals who do not speak English, and in general they are more conservative when compared to the younger generation who prefer to live in the city centre.

PENSIONS

Surprising as it may sound, there was no pension scheme in Hong Kong before 2000. It is an old Confucius idea that parents should provide the best they could to nurture their children, and when they get old, it is the turn for the children to take care of them. Even nowadays, many married young people still live with their parents out of a sense of moral obligation, and it is in general deemed indecent to fail to support ones parents financially. For these reasons, the social system worked well without a pension scheme until the late 90s, when heated discussions suddenly began in Legco (Legislative Council) meetings. By December 2000, the pension scheme was made compulsory. Under the scheme, both employers and employees have to contribute at least 5% of the employees' salaries, and an employee will receive the whole amount of money when he or she retires. However, there is no government pension scheme like the state pension in the USA and the UK.

Hong Kong does not have a special pension agreement with the UK or the USA. However both UK and US residents, can receive pension payments from home while they are in Hong Kong. It is usually paid to your account in Hong Kong, or you can ask for a payable order to be sent to your home. For details of the arrangement of your pension, contact the local pension offices.

Useful Addresses

The International Pension Centre, Tyneview Park, Newcastle Upon Tyne, NE98 1BA, United Kingdom; ☎(44) 0191 218 7777; fax (44) 0191 218 7293; www.thepensionservice.gov.uk.

Social Security Agency (North Ireland), ☎(44) 0845 601 8821; fax (44) 028 7136 8365; www.ssani.gov.uk.

Social Security Administration, Office of Public Inquiries, Windsor Park Building, 6401 Security Blvd., Baltimore, MD 21235; ☎(1) 800 772 1213; www.ssa.gov/international.

www.ssa.gov/policy/docs/progdesc/ssptw/2002-2003/asia/hongkong.html: summary of social securities of Hong Kong.

Taxation

There is no special taxation for retired people in Hong Kong. If you have never worked in Hong Kong, which means your income was not earned in Hong Kong before retirement, no tax will be charged on the pension you bring with you. Even if you have worked in Hong Kong for some years, unless you still receive a monthly payment on top of pensions from your previous employer(s), you do not need to pay any tax. For other details about taxation, refer to the chapter *Daily Life*.

MEDICAL CARE

As mentioned in last chapter *Daily Life*, the governmental medical services for non-residents are very expensive. However, there is no price difference for locals and non-locals in the private sector, where services considered are to be very good. Consulting a private doctor, including medicines for three days, costs from $150 to $300 (US$19-$38/£12-£24). Permanent residents who have reached the age of 65 are eligible to enjoy the Elderly Health Services provided by the government, for an annual fee of only $110. These services are also available for non-residents who are aged 65 or above but the annual fee will be $770 (US$99/£62). Elderly people enrolled for the Elderly Health Services can enjoy health assessment, physical check ups, counselling, curative treatment and health education in the elderly health centres of the government. And there are visiting health teams to carry out regular vaccination for high-risk groups as well as teaching the elderly how to maintain a healthy life.

Useful Addresses

Elderly Health Services Head Office, Room 3502-4, 35th Floor, Hopewell Centre, 183 Queen's Road East, Wan Chai, Hong Kong; ☎(852) 2121 8621; 24-Hour Health Information Hotline: 2121 8080; e-mail ehsenq@dh.gov.hk; www.info.gov.hk/elderly.

Department of Health, 21/F, Wu Chung House, 213 Queen's Road East, Hong Kong; ☎(852) 2961 8989; fax (852) 2836 0071; e-mail enquiries@dh.gov.hk; www.info.gov.hk/dh/.

WILLS AND DEATH

The details of *Wills* are covered in the chapter *Setting Up Home*.

If someone dies due to old age or sickness, his or her family members or relatives must register the death with the Birth and Death Register Office within 24 hours. The person who is registering the death of the deceased has to bring along a Medical Certificate stating the Cause of Death, signed by the registered medical practitioner who attended the deceased during the last illness. This certificate states clearly the cause and time of the death. Apart from the Medical Certificate, the informant also needs to bring along his or her Hong Kong Identity Card (or travel document) and the deceased's Hong Kong Identity Card (or travel document). The informant also needs to provide personal information of the deceased such as occupation, nationality, marital status, etc.

Cases of unnatural death, for example death from poisoning or accidents, have to been reported to the coroner to determine the cause of death. It normally takes one to six months for the investigation. Death will then be registered within one week by the Birth and Death Register Office after the cause of death is determined, and the Registry will inform the deceased's relatives about the cause of death and let them know that the registration has been done.

The registration for death is free of charge. However, the issue of a certified copy of the certificate will be charged for, according to the number of copies to be made.

Burial spaces are available in Wo Hop Shek Cemetery, Cheung Chau Cemetery, Tai O Cemetery and Lai Chi Yuen Cemetery. However, the deceased has to be an indigenous villager or a local resident of the island concerned for the latter three. There are six government crematoria for the cremation of a dead body, including Cape Collinson crematorium on Hong Kong Island, Diamond Hill Crematorium in Kowloon, Fu Shan Crematorium, Kwai Chung Crematorium and Wo Hop Shek Crematorium in the New Territories, and also Cheung Chau Crematorium. There is an online enquiry service to find out available timeslots for the cremation. Alternatively, you can approach the relevant offices of the Department of Health and the Food and Environment Hygiene Department at the joint office of Birth and Death General Register Office.

The relatives must apply for a Permit for Removal of the Dead Body from

Hong Kong if they want to ship the body home. It is necessary to register the death with the Birth and Death Register Office first before making an application for the permit. There is no fee for the issue of the permit but the shipping cost can be very expensive. For more information about the removal of bodies from Hong Kong, contact the Immigration Department.

Useful Addresses

The Births and Deaths General Register Office (Hong Kong Island Deaths Registry), 18th Floor, Wu Chung House, 213 Queen's Road East, Wan Chai; ☎(852) 2961 8841.

The Births and Deaths General Register Office (Kowloon Deaths Registry), 1st Floor, Cheung Sha Wan Government Offices, 303 Cheung Sha Wan Road, Cheung Sha Wan; ☎(852) 2368 4706.

The Births and Deaths General Register Office (for deaths registration referred by coroner), 3rd Floor, Low Block, Queensway Government Offices, 66 Queensway; ☎(852) 2867 2785.

Food and Environmental Hygiene Department (Headquarters), 44/F Queensway Government Offices, 66 Queensway, Hong Kong.; ☎(852) 2868 0000; fax (852) 2869 0169; e-mail enquiries@fehd.gov.hk; www.fehd.gov.hk.

Offices in Immigration Headquarters, Immigration Tower, 7 Gloucester Road, Wan Chai; ☎(852) 2824 6111; fax (852) 2877 7711; www.immd.gov.hk.

INTERESTS AND HOBBIES

There are various organisations running interesting classes for pensioners. You may start to learn Chinese or other languages, or to explore Chinese culture by learning martial arts like *Tai-chi*, which is very popular amongst retired locals. These days computer classes are welcomed by the elderly too. There are also social centres for pensioners, which organise games, health talks and seasonal activities (for example, Mid-Autumn, New year celebrations) from time to time.

Many pensioners also become volunteers after retirement and help those who are in need. Volunteers can join the Red Cross, Girl Guides and many other charitable organisations. Local community centres also need volunteers of all ages from time to time.

If you are aged 60 or above, you often get concessionary rates when visiting museums, cinemas or joining special interest classes. Some venues may even offer free entry for the elderly.

Useful Addresses

Young Women's Christian Association of Hong Kong, 1 Macdonnell Road, Central, Hong Kong; ☎ (852) 2522 3101; fax (852) 2524 4237; e-mail ywca@ywca.org.hk; www.ywca.org.hk.

Hong Kong Christian Service, 4/F, 33 Granville Road, Tsimshatsui, Kowloon. Hong Kong; ☎(852) 2731 6248/2722 5117; fax: (852) 2724 3593/2781 4951; e-mail: ois@hkcs.org.

Po Leung Kuk, 66 Leighton Road, Hong Kong; ☎(852) 2882 0011; fax (852) 2576 4509; e-mail plkinfo@poleungkuk.org.hk; www.poleungkuk.org.hk.

Hong Kong Red Cross, ☎(852) 2802 0021; e-mail info@redcross.org.hk; www.redcross.org.hk.

Hong Kong Girl Guides Association, 8, Gascoigne Road, Kowloon, Hong Kong; ☎(852) 2332 5523; fax (852) 2782 6466; e-mail hkgga@hkgga.org.hk; www.hkgga.org.hk.

Leisure and Cultural Services Department, www.lcsd.gov.hk. With details of recent leisure and cultural programmes, including information of special interest classes.

HONG KONG

Section II

WORKING IN HONG KONG

EMPLOYMENT

STARTING A BUSINESS

EMPLOYMENT

CHAPTER SUMMARY

- **Unemployment**. The unemployment rate is currently about 7-8%.
- **Job Prospects**. IT, import/export, finance and banking offer good prospects for employment.
- **Salaries**. There is no minimum salary level.
  - Salaries are usually paid at the end of each month.
- **Holidays**. Every employee is granted 12 statutory days holiday every year.
  - There is one rest day in every period of seven days.
  - Female employees are entitled to maternity leave of a continuous period of 10 weeks.
- **Trade Unions**. It is illegal for employers to prevent employees from joining a trade union.
- **Work Practice**. Long working hours are very common.
- **Women in Work**. Women account for 44% of the total labour force.
  - It is illegal to turn down an application based on the gender or family role of an applicant.

THE EMPLOYMENT SCENE

The unemployment rate before 1998 was very low, below 3% of the population. However, it has been rising since 1998, and reached a peak of 8.7% in July 2003, after the outbreak of SARS; the highest recorded rate in Hong Kong history. Airlines, restaurants, hotels and retail shops were hit badly and many of them closed down. The average monthly salary of all industries in June 2003 (up to supervisory levels) dropped by $400 to $600 (2% to 8%), compared to June 2001.

Hong Kong experienced an economic downturn after September-11, and the government decided to cut the salaries of civil servants in April 2002 and announced a suspension of employment for the public sector. This means that a retired or resigned position may not be replaced, and the government is not recruiting new Executive Officers (EO) or Administrative Officers (AO), which was customary every year before 2002. Many companies have cut overtime payments and reduced salaries; they also now prefer contract or part-time employment, which is more flexible and entails fewer fringe benefits. Middle-aged workers and teenagers with low qualifications find it particularly difficult to get a job as more competitive candidates are willing to lower their expected salary and take up less professional jobs.

The import/export trade is recovering well and it is believed that there will be more trade between Hong Kong and mainland China after the Closer Economic Partnership Arrangement (CEPA) which was signed in late June 2003. Tourism, finance and banking are now major areas of development in Hong Kong.

Skills and Qualifications

In general, Hong Kong employers expect to see certificates and proof of your professional qualifications. Degrees and certificates issued by the US and the British universities are usually recognised in Hong Kong. For professions like law, medicine, teaching, etc, you may have to pass the relevant exams or their equivalents and register with the authorities before you can carry out your work. Details about each profession will be discussed later in this chapter.

Since tertiary education has become increasingly common, employers are quite keen to look for university degree holders to fill basic job positions (in some cases including personal secretaries/clerks). Even if you are being interviewed for a position which does not require a university degree, the employer is usually happier to see some certificates or evidence of training related to the job. Although most industries take formal qualifications seriously, there are some exceptions. Experience and other hands-on skills are more important in some jobs like reporters, hairstylists, insurance agents and artists.

Computer skills are welcomed, if not necessary, in almost all industries. It is very difficult to find a clerical job these days without having good computer skills. Many shops use computers for record keeping and shop assistants are thus often required to operate computers. Good language skills are useful for working in Hong Kong as well. Fluent English and Mandarin are particularly important when looking for business related jobs.

Work Regulations

You must get a work permit in order to work in Hong Kong if you are not a resident. Your work permit should be ready before you arrive and you should present it to Immigration when you first enter the city. For imported workers and domestic helpers, the employers are responsible for getting the work permits ready before their employees arrive. Visitors are not allowed to take up any employment during their stay in Hong Kong. Dependents of residents, or those of professionals approved to stay in Hong Kong, cannot take up employment unless they become permanent residents themselves. If you have a Working Holidaymaker Visa, you can work in Hong Kong but you must not work with the same employer for more than three months during your stay. For further details about work regulations, see the chapter *Residence and Entry Regulations.*

SOURCES OF JOBS

Newspapers and Specialist Publications

Many newspapers have a job section printed on particular days of the week. For example, the *South China Morning Post (SCMP)* has a *Classified Post* every Wednesday and Saturday. There is also an online version *www.classifiedpost.com.* *Ming Pao* is a Chinese newspaper, but half of the job advertisements are in English. There is a section on Tuesdays and Thursdays especially for teaching jobs. Specialist publications like *Career Times* and *Recruit* are also available. They are free of charge and are available in all underground (MTR) stations. *Recruit* is issued twice a week, on Tuesdays and Fridays, and you can find the *Career Times* every Wednesday and Saturday. Both *Recruit* and the *Career Times* have online versions (*www.recruit.com.hk* and *www.careertimes.com.hk*). Try *The Guardian*, *Economist* and *Overseas Jobs Express* (UK) if you plan to look for a job before coming to Hong Kong.

   Vacation Work Publications has a series of publications about working abroad, including hints for looking for jobs and directories for companies in different sectors. *Summer Jobs Abroad, Work Your Way Around the World* and *Taking a Gap Year* provide information for short-term employment. If you are interested in working as a volunteer, take a look at *The International Directory of Voluntary Work*. For a whole list of publications for Vacation Work, visit our website at *www.vacationwork.co.uk.*

Employment Agencies

There are many employment agencies in the USA and the UK, which look for overseas employment for their clients. You have to join and pay a membership fee for posting your resumé on an agency's website: the agency will contact the employers you are interested in for you. If you are already in Hong Kong, there are also local employment agencies to help you with job hunting.

Useful Addresses

Beyond Recruitment, www.staffservice.com/eng.
Gemini Personnel Limited, 15/F Silver Fortune Plaza, 1 Wellington Street, Central, Hong Komg, ☎(852) 2525 7283; fax (852) 2810 6467; www.gemini.com.hk.
Expats Direct Limited, Stockton Business Centre, 70 Brunswick Street, Stockton on Tees, TS18 1DW, United Kingdom; ☎(44) 01642 730822; e-mail info@expatsdirect.com; www.expatsdirect.com.

Inter Career Net (New York Office), 420 Lexington Ave. (between 43rd & 44th
St.), Graybar Building Suite 1750, New York, NY 10170, USA; ☎(1) 800
859 8535/212 476 4400; fax (1) 212 476 4240; e-mail admin@rici.com;
www.intercareer.com.

VIP International, VIP House, 17 Charing Cross Road, London, WC2H 0QW,
UK; ☎(44) 020 7930 0541; fax (44) 020 7930 2860; e-mail vip@vipinternati
onal.co.uk; www.vipinternational.

Recruitment Websites

Civil Service Bureau, www.csb.gov.hk. Provides details about government
vacancies.

Interactive Employment Service of the Labour Departmen,: www.jobs.gov.hk.

Classified Post, www.classifiedpost.com.hk.

CareerTimes, www.careertimes.com.hk.

Recruit Online, www.recruit.com.hk.

JobsDB, www.jobsdb.com.

Jobs Financial, www.jobsfinancial.com.

Ambition, www.ambition.biz. Provides details of jobs in finance, accounting and
marketing.

Hong Kong Jobs, www.hkjobs.com.

Best Job Hong Kong, www.bestjobshk.com.

JobOK, www.jobok.com.

APPLICATIONS

Letters Of Application

An employer may not explicitly require a letter of application in the job
advertisement but it is usually better to send one. You should briefly explain your
interest in the position and why you are a suitable candidate. Your letter should
be in a fairly formal tone and should highlight relevant achievements in past jobs.
Commonsense applies. You need to be clear and polite, but not be excessively
modest.

Resumé/Curriculum Vitae

A resumé is the summary of what you have done, usually in a table or as a list
of points. It should provide the details for the employers to decide if you are
the suitable candidate the company is looking for. It is important to make it
easy to read as the Hong Kong labour force is big and mobile and employers
typically receive many applications. You should make the headings prominent
and readable at a glance. Use action words, and focus on relevant experience
rather than putting everything in. Education and working experience should
be in chronological order (or its reverse). Avoid leaving unexplained periods of

unemployment as they may lead to undesirable assumptions. You should also include details of referees in your CV (names, addresses, contact numbers and e-mail addresses).

These days it is usually not necessary to include a photograph in your CV. Similarly you do not need to mention your expected salary unless you are explicitly required to.

Interview

Normally, employers in Hong Kong invite you for interviews only if they think you are reasonably suitable. The employer will be wanting to know more about you than can be shown on the application letter and resumé. You should be familiar with your CV and should do some research on the organisation and the whole field of its operation. Being familiar with current issues related to the business will also be to your advantage. Think about some possible questions that may come up in the interview and practise the answers. You should think of one or two sensible questions to ask them to show your interest in the company – intelligent questions will leave a good impression. If you are not familiar with the location, check it on the map to see how to get there and how long it takes. Punctuality is clearly very important and the traffic in Hong Kong can be tricky. Many employers will ask the opinions of the receptionist after interviews, so you should be polite and pleasant to them also. Employers in general prefer candidates who are positive and confident, who dress smartly and are pleasant.

Companies usually do not pay for travel costs if you are applying for a job overseas. Depending on the post you are applying for, you may ask for a phone interview or a net meeting instead, if you are applying from abroad.

Some common questions in an interview

○ Tell me something about yourself.
○ Why did you, why do you want to, come to Hong Kong?
○ What are your expectations for this job?
○ In what way have you added value to your organisation in your current or past positions?
○ What makes you want to change your job?
○ What do you think are the most important qualities for this job? Do you posses these qualities? Can you give me some examples?
○ Do you have any questions? (you should try not to say 'no'!)

ASPECTS OF EMPLOYMENT

Salaries

The biggest advantage of working in Hong Kong is the low tax rate, which means the amount you earn is almost equal to what you take home. However, there is no legally stipulated minimum level of salary for local employees in Hong Kong, except for imported domestic helpers. Therefore, the salary discrepancy is generally wide. A general clerk in the government earns over $10,000 (US$1300/ £800) per month, while the same position in a small company can receive as little as $6,000 (US$770/£480) per month. The salary of a primary school teacher ($17,100 per month, which is equal to US$2200/£1370) is higher than that of an administrative supervisor of a company ($16,500 per month, which is equal to US$2100/£1330). In general, people working in finance companies, banks, education, and computer-related business enjoy higher salaries than in other fields. Civil servants also enjoy high salaries and extremely good job security. The average monthly salary of all industries (excluding managerial and professional positions) is $10,600 (US$1400/£850). The figure looks quite impressive, especially given the low taxation rate. However, many lower level positions like cleaning workers earn $5,000 (US$640/£400) or less, even though they work for ten hours or more a day.

Salaries are usually paid at the end of each calendar month. Employers, in general, prefer to pay by direct debit through banks than paying by cheque. Pension contributions are automatically deducted from the salary, but income tax is not.

Benefits

Hong Kong companies are not very generous when offering fringe benefits for employees, unless you are working for the government. The legal requirements concerning these are not particularly strong either. Some bigger companies may have deals with insurance companies, banks or shops to provide discounts for employees. Discounted medical or dental care packages are becoming more common, and extra paid holidays are also a common benefit. Cash rewards exist but they are usually under certain specific conditions. Some employers provide an extra month's salary to employees at the end of the year, normally during the month prior to the Chinese New Year. There are also bonus schemes in some companies which reward employees according to their performance at the end of the year. Childcare services or childcare allowances are not common in Hong Kong. It is not usual for a company to provide a car for employees to use unless they work in a very high position in a large company. Travel expenses for business trips are usually covered by companies and employees are usually allowed to use the flyer mileages on private trips.

Working Hours, Overtime and Holidays

For many companies, official working hours are generally from 9am to 5pm/ 6pm, which is around eight to nine hours with an hour lunch break. However, you should be warned that many employers expect employees to work overtime if work has not been finished during working hours. See *Work Practice* below for more details. Some industries require employees, like nurses and security guards, to work shifts and each shift is between eight and twelve hours. Due to the economic downturn in the last few years, many companies have cut overtime payments substantially in order to reduce running costs and hence employees in many cases receive no overtime payment even though they continue work after normal working hours. Even so, not many employees refuse to work overtime as the unemployment rate has been increasing for three consecutive years, and was over 8% after the SARS outbreak in spring 2003; four times that in 1997. It is believed that when the economic situation improves, payments for overtime work will improve.

Under the Employment Ordinance, every employee is granted 12 statutory days holiday every year (see the chart below for details). Employees under continuous contract are also entitled to a rest day in every period of seven days. If the statutory holiday falls on an employee's rest day, the employer should give a rest day on the day following the statutory holiday. It is illegal for the employer to fail to grant rest days to employees or compel employees to work on those days. Failure to grant rest days for employees will attract a fine of $50,000 (US$6500/ £4000). An employee is also entitled to annual leave with pay, if he or she is employed under a continuous contract of 12 months. The number of days leave is dependent on the number of years of service. There should be at least seven days of leave for the first two years of service and the number increases by one day per extra year of service in the company until it reaches the maximum of 14 days. Some companies may offer more annual leave to employees but this is not very common. If an employer requires an employee to work on a statutory holiday or annual leave period with the consent of the employee, the employee should get holiday pay or annual leave pay, which is equal to the average daily wage. However, without the employees' consent employers are prohibited to make any form of payment in place of granting employees holidays.

THE 12 STATUTORY HOLIDAYS

1. New Year (1st January)
2. Lunar New Year's Day (falls in mid-January to mid-February)
3. The second day of Lunar New Year (falls in mid-January to mid-February)

4. The third day of Lunar New Year (falls in mid-January to mid-February)

5. Ching Ming Festival (5th April)

6. Labour Day (1st May)

7. Tuen Ng Festival (June)

8. Hong Kong Special Administrative Region Establishment Day (1st July)

9. The day following Chinese Mid-Autumn Festival (September/October)

10. National Day (1st October)

11. Chung Yeung Festival (October)

12. Chinese Winter Solstice Festival (22nd December) or Christmas Day (25th December) (at the option of the employer)

Maternity Leave and Sick Leave

Every female employee under a continuous contract is entitled to maternity leave. Maternity leave is a continuous period of 10 weeks and the employee can choose to start her leave two to four weeks before the expected date of confinement. If confinement occurs later than the expected date, the employee will enjoy further leave. And she can enjoy another four weeks leave (as maximum) on grounds of illness or disability due to pregnancy or confinement. Employees who work with companies for 40 continuous weeks or more before commencement of maternity leave are entitled to maternity leave pay of 10 weeks. The amount is equal to four-fifths of the normal wages, if proper notice and medical proof are provided to the employer after pregnancy is confirmed. Absence for medical examination in relation to pregnancy, post medical treatment or miscarriage should be counted as sick leave with sick leave allowance equal to four-fifths of normal wages. The Employment Ordinance protects employees from being laid off because of their pregnancy; it is an offence for an employer to dismiss a pregnant employee for her pregnancy and will incur a fine of $100,000 (US$13,000/£8000). The law also requires an employer to remove heavy, hazardous or harmful work, e.g. working in a slippery environment or requiring the pregnant employee to lift heavy objects, if she is working in such situations before pregnancy.

Employees under continuous contracts are also entitled to paid sick leave and sickness allowance. Employees are granted two paid sickness days each month in their first 12 months of employment and then the number of paid sickness days will increase to four each month. Paid sickness days can be accumulated up to 120 days as maximum. You will be paid at the normal rate for taking sick leave so long as you have not used up your paid sickness days. Employers in general do not deduct from the salary of employees if they take one or two days more than the accumulated paid sickness days they have. Sickness allowance is equal to four-fifths of the normal wages and is granted to employees who take sick leave for four or more consecutive days. An employee is able to claim the sickness allowance if he or she can provide a certificate issued by a registered medical practitioner or a registered dentist, and the maximum paid leave for sickness is 36 days. Employers can request an investigation if the amount of sick leave taken is more than 36 days, even if certificates are provided.

Trade Unions

There are around 660 trade unions in Hong Kong and every trade union has to register with the Registry of Trade Unions.

Trade unions in Hong Kong are not as powerful as they are in western countries as Hong Kong trade unions have no right to organise collective bargaining. Employers, in general, refuse to recognise trade unions and there have been cases where staff have been laid off after trade disputes, which is very likely to be related to their roles in the trade unions. Unfortunately, even though employees should be protected from anti-union discrimination under the Employment Ordinance, it can sometimes be tricky to prove that the staff were laid off due to their roles in the unions. Moreover, the ordinance only ensures that a worker has the right to sue the employer for compensation but does not entitle him or her to reinstatement if he or she is dismissed for strike action. It is however illegal for employers to prohibit employees from joining trade unions and taking part in union activities outside working hours. It is legal for employees to attend picket lines in the case of trade disputes.

Even though trade unions today are not as powerful as they were, many employees still join unions to enjoy the benefits provided by them and taking part in activities held by trade unions provides a chance to make new friends.

Employment Contracts

An employment contract is an agreement made between employers and employees and it can be in the form of a written statement or an oral agreement. An employment contract is not required by law but it is recommended, as it protects both employees and employers. An employment contract should include information about wages, working hours, allowances, overtime rates, holidays, sick leave, sick leave allowances and the period of employment. It should also include the length of notice required to terminate the contract and compensation for failure to give such notice. The employer should give a copy of the written contract to the employee for reference. Even in the case of an oral agreement, employers have to provide employees with such information in writing if they are requested to do so. All employees, no matter if they are working full-time or part-time, are covered by the Employment Ordinance. They are entitled to basic protection including statuary holidays, wage protection and protection against anti-union discrimination. Employees who are employed under a continuous contract are further entitled to benefits such as rest days, paid annual leave, sickness allowance, severance payment and long service payments, etc. Employers cannot modify the contents of the employment contract without the consent of the employees. Employers should also provide employees with a copy of the written amendments of the contract after obtaining the consent of employees.

Working Practices

One should try not to over-generalise about work practices in all industries but many of them share some common features that we shall try to discuss here. Hong Kong people are reputedly quick. They walk very quickly, eat quickly and are expected to work quickly as well. Many employers expect employees to finish their work before going home, even when it goes beyond normal working hours. Do not be surprised if a friend in Hong Kong tells you that he or she works in the office until 10pm everyday, as it regularly happens. Being punctual is a general requirement in all disciplines. Some of the companies require employees to sign-in formally every morning. This practice was very common in manufacturing industries in the 80s and some companies still use this system to check employees' punctuality. You are supposed to phone the company with an acceptable reason if you expect to be late by over 30 minutes. If you need to take sick leave, you should give a call to the company in the morning, and you should provide a medical certificate the next day when you are back at work. It is not usual for Hong Kong companies to have regular coffee breaks in the morning, where people gather together socially and chat. However, many companies do have a short tea break at around 3pm and it is common to order food and drinks to be delivered to the offices. More and more offices are smoke-free these days and it is thought to be inconsiderate to smoke in the office, even though it is not explicitly stated that the office is smoke-free.

Usually, a month's notice should be given before resignation. It may take longer, for example, three months, if you are in a higher position, but this all depends on the employment contract.

It is common to use first names amongst colleagues, but to address your clients and bosses by their last names, especially the first time you meet them. Some companies allow employees to dress in casual wear on Fridays but this is by no means universal.

Women in Work

The balance between men and women in work has changed a great deal in the last two decades. Women did work in the 60s and 70s but they were expected to be full-time mothers after they had children. Moreover, girls in many families did not have the opportunity for education, which made it difficult for them to look for a job. More girls received education only after the government introduced the nine years of free education for all children up to the age of 15 in 1978.

Since then, more women have been provided with an increasing number of job opportunities.

About half of the female population work in Hong Kong now, which accounts for 44% of the total labour force. Women nowadays are very competitive and are doing better than men in many aspects. Opportunities provided to men and women have been made more and more equal. Many jobs are open to both sexes now: the fire service is a recent example, and more women take up other 'traditional men's jobs' like helicopter pilots and policemen. The government has been working hard to eliminate sex discrimination in society. The Sex Discrimination Ordinance was set up in 1995 in order to protect women from being deprived of enjoying the same rights as men in society. Job advertisements are not allowed to set gender as a requirement for a post. If anyone, man or woman, is treated unfairly due to his or her gender, the Sex Discrimination Ordinance applies. Another ordinance, the Equal Opportunities Commission, was set up in 1996 to expand this protection to other groups which were treated unfairly in the past. This new law aims to eliminate discrimination for disability, age or the status of the family. The Convention on the Elimination of All Forms of Discrimination Against Women (CEDAW) was established in the same year and women have been provided with stronger protection under these two new laws ever since. Before the introduction of the laws, it was not difficult to find cases where older women or women with children were less favoured by employers, even though this might be difficult to prove. The situation has now improved as employers are in general more concerned about the problem, and women are more willing to speak out with the support of the legal system. After the establishment of the Women's Commission in 2001, women's concerns have been taken into account when the government formulates policies. The Commission was established to promote the well-being and interests of women, and to arouse community concern over perceptions about what women should or should not do.

Sexual harassment does exist in the workplace. Most of the cases of sexual harassment in Hong Kong are related to unwanted touching, making sexual jokes about gender and making remarks about the body or features relating to gender. There are also complaints of receiving unwanted letters, phone calls or photos (through e-mails) of a sexual nature, and of unwanted kissing; but complaints of pressure for sexual activity is rare. Unfortunately, although both the Sexual Discrimination Ordinance and Equal Opportunities Commission protect women from being sexually harassed, not many women report their unpleasant experiences. About half the women ignore harassment and only 40% of them show the harasser how much they object. Only a few percent report the matter to employers or take legal action.

Pensions

The establishment of a pension scheme in Hong Kong was very recent. The

Mandatory Provident Fund (MPF) scheme, a compulsory pension scheme, came into full operation on the 1st December 2000. With the exception of civil servants, judicial officials, and teachers in subsidized or grant schools, statutory pensions or provident funds schemes were not available to the general public before the MPF. Only very few companies had provident funds schemes as a benefit for employees before MPF.

Employees and self-employed people have to join the MPF if they are aged between 18 and 65, and are employed for 60 days or more with the same employer. Both the employee and employer have to make a contribution of 5% of the employee's salary. Additional voluntary contributions are accepted. Under the current system, an employee whose monthly income is $5000 (US$640/£400) or below is exempt from MPF and the mandatory contributions are capped at $1,000 for people whose income is $20,000 (US$2,600/£1,600) or above. The same principle applies to self-employed people as well. These figures are subject to change and it is better to check up with the MPF Schemes Authority (MPFA), the authority set up by the government for regulating, supervising and monitoring the operation of the MPF System, for updated information. MPF funds are managed by Trustees and all Trustees must register with the MPFA. An employee is allowed to transfer the accrued benefits to another scheme when taking up new employment in a different company. The benefits derived from MPF cannot be attained before retirement age of 65, or early retirement at the age of 60 or above. You can attain the benefits before 65 if there is a particular reason like death or permanent departure from Hong Kong.

Employees can claim a tax deduction under Salaries Tax for the mandatory contributions made to the MPF scheme. The maximum deductible amount for each year of assessment is $1,200 (US$150/£95).

Useful Website
MPFA, www.mpfahk.org.

PERMANENT WORK

Civil Servants

Hong Kong people call their jobs a 'rice bowl' and a job as a civil servant is called 'the iron bowl'. An iron bowl is very solid and not easily broken, which means job security is very good. Moreover, a civil servant is eligible for enjoying a great number of allowances and benefits, in addition to having a high salary. Therefore, more than half of university graduates sit for the examination for selecting civil servants every year. Hong Kong has been in economic recession since 1998 but no civil servant has been laid off due to that, even though there were massive lay-offs in many industries. However, it is now getting more difficult to be offered a job by the government. In order to reduce expenditure, the government is reducing the number of new recruits. Moreover, the government is encouraging early retirement and resignation by paying compensation to employees who retire early.

Finance and Banking

Finance and banking is one of the industries with the best prospects in Hong Kong. Hong Kong is one of the most important financial centres in the world and it was second in the World's per capita holding of foreign currency in 2001. There are more than 180 different banks in Hong Kong and banking business has expanded the scope of its services in recent years. Electronic banking is one of the main developments. More and more bank services can be used through the internet, and the banks are putting more effort into making electronic banking safe and quick. The industry requires all sorts of professionals from different areas to ensure that business runs smoothly, which means you can join the industry if you are an expert in accounting, marketing, risk management, advertising or information technology.

Information Technology

Many students in Hong Kong choose to study Computer Science or Information Science at universities because of the career prospects. The general public is positive about the development of information technology and the industry showed that it is doing well even under the economic downturns in the last few years. More and more services are being computerised everyday, and the Hong Kong Identity Card is but one example. Due to the phenomenal growth rate of mainland China, there are also many opportunities for Hong Kong IT professionals to provide their services there or even develop their careers in the mainland.

Law

The legal system in Hong Kong is similar to that of the UK. To practise law in Hong Kong you have to be registered with the Law Society of Hong Kong. Foreign lawyers, who offer their services to the public as a practitioner of foreign law other than solicitors or barristers, are prohibited from practising Hong Kong law. They are also prohibited from joining a partnership with, or being employed by Hong Kong solicitors. Foreign lawyers can be employed as foreign legal consultants by a Hong Kong solicitor. An overseas lawyer, who is entitled to practice law in an overseas jurisdication, may be able to be admitted as a solicitor in Hong Kong. You can check with this link *http://www.hklawsoc.org.hk/pub – e/admission/Foreignlawyers/pdf/oversealawyer.pdf* to see if you are eligible to be a solicitor in Hong Kong. Both foreign and overseas lawyers have to register with The Law Society of Hong Kong before practising or working. For more information about the requirements for being a lawyer in Hong Kong and the registration procedures, visit the website of The Law Society of Hong Kong.

Useful Address

The Law Society of Hong Kong, 3rd Floor, Wing On House, 71 Des Voeux Road, Central, Hong Kong; ☎(852) 2846 0500; fax (852) 2845 0387; e-mail sg@hklawsoc.org.hk; www.hklawsoc.org.hk.

Medicine

Doctors working in public hospitals are very well paid, but they usually work for very long hours as well. Some of them work for 18 hours in one shift and they have to be on-call at night to take care of patients who need urgent treatment. Private doctors, in general, enjoy a higher income than hospital doctors, and their working hours are also more flexible. A qualified doctor from another country has to register with the Registrar of Medical Practitioners, and may be asked to go through some tests, before he or she can be a recognised doctor in Hong Kong. For further details about being a doctor in Hong Kong, refer to the Medical Registration Ordinance (*http://www.mchk.org.hk/ch161/index.htm*).

There are two kinds of nurse in Hong Kong: Registered Nurse (RN) and Enrolled Nurse (EN). Nurses are also paid well in Hong Kong, with a starting salary of $19,000 for a registered nurse. Someone from overseas who is interested in being a nurse in Hong Kong must hold a relevant qualification and must register with the Nursing Council of Hong Kong. If you are interested in working in the hospitals of Hong Kong, as a doctor or nurse, the Hospital Authority (*www.ha.org.hk*) will provide you with more details.

Useful Addresses

The Medical Council of Hong Kong, 4/F, Hong Kong Academy of Medicine Jockey Club Building, 99 Wong Chuk Hang Road, Aberdeen, Hong Kong; ☎(852) 2873 5131; fax (852) 2554 0577; e-mail mc-dc@dh.gov.hk; www.hkam.org.hk.
Hospital Authority, ☎(852) 2882 4866/(852) 2300 6555; www.ha.org.hk.
Nursing Council of Hong Kong, 3/F., Hing Wan Commercial Building, 25-27 Parkes Street, Jordon, Kowloon; ☎(852) 2314 6900; fax (852) 2736 6020; e-mail info@nurse.org.hk; www.nurse.org.hk.

Teaching

The salary starting point is high for a teacher in Hong Kong ($17,000 per month, which is equal to US$2170/£1370). This is not determined according to the supply and demand of the job market, which means the salary in teaching is more stable than many other industries. Therefore, being a teacher is particularly attractive during economic downturns. Moreover, having long vacations is another positive factor.

The government has proposed many policies in order to improve the quality of primary and secondary education in the last decade. It is more difficult to be a teacher nowadays than in the 80s or the early 90s. If you were a university graduate in the 80s, you would not have much difficulty in finding a teaching job. However, now you have to either hold a recognised degree/diploma in Education or a Certificate in Education in addition to a first degree (if your first degree is not in education) to be qualified as a primary or secondary school teacher. Moreover, you have to pass the Language Proficiency Requirement for Teachers if you plan to teach English or Mandarin. The government introduced the mother-tongue (Chinese) as the medium of instruction in 1997. The Native-speaking English Teacher (NET) Scheme was introduced at the same time, as the government wants to keep up the English standard of the students after switching to using Chinese as the medium of instruction. One NET is provided to each primary or secondary school with 40 classes or fewer (two NETs for a school with more than 40 classes) to teach English as well as helping the English panel develop an English curriculum. The NETs are also expected to bring more variety to English teaching in schools. Visit the Education and Manpower Bureau (*www.emb.gov.hk*) for details of duty, qualifications required and application method to be a NET.

The salary of a university lecturer in Hong Kong is one of the highest in the world. The starting salary for a lecturer is over $40,000 per month (US$5,000/£3,000) and the universities generally provide a strong fringe benefit package, usually including housing allowances.

SHORT TERM EMPLOYMENT

Activity Leader/Organisation
Community centres or other organisations have many activities like camping, indoor camping (stay inside a recreational centre with accommodation facilities) and workshops every year, especially during the summer vacation. Activity organisers and leaders are recruited for preparing and running the activities. These kinds of employment are usually project-based and employees are paid after the end of the activity. Keep an eye on the notice boards of city halls and community centres if you are interested in being an activity organiser or leader. This is also a good way to meet young people. Advertisements for programmes held during summer vacations are usually placed around May.

Nanny/Housework Helper
Nannies are not in great demand in Hong Kong as many middle-class or rich people can afford to hire a live-in domestic helper, usually from south-east Asia, to take care of the children as well as handling the housework. Moreover, childcare centres and kindergartens in general open for quite long hours for the convenience of working parents. However, some families prefer a part-time nanny instead of a live-in domestic helper, especially during economic downturns. Some parents require nannies to help their children with homework and revision as well as looking after the children. If you speak English as a native language, you

can capitalise on this as most middle-class parents are quite concerned with the development of their children' language skills.

Part-time housework helpers have become popular with working couples or individuals in the last few years. They usually work a few hours a day, three to five days a week, tidy up the employer's house and do some housework including laundry and cleaning. Some employers require their housework helpers to cook dinner as well. In this case, wages are higher and the cost of buying raw materials can be claimed. The wages for being a housework helper are around $30-$50 per hour.

Seasonal Employment

There are more part-time jobs available before and during festivals like Christmas, Chinese New Year and Valentine's Day. Department stores and shops are busier before these festivals, and extra staff are required for cashier work or for wrapping presents. Restaurants and bars usually need more staff as well, since many of them extend their opening hours during festivals. The wages are usually not high, but there are plenty of job opportunities.

Addresses of Department Stores

Sogo Hong Kong Co. Ltd, 555 Hennessy Rd., Causeway Bay, Hong Kong; ☎(852) 2833 8338; fax (852) 2838 2030; www.sogo.com.hk.

Jusco, AEON Stores (H.K.) Co., Ltd., 3/F, Stanhope House, 738 King's Road, Quarry Bay, Hong Kong; e-mail recruitment@jusco.com.hk; www.jusco.com.hk (visit the website for other branches information).

Sincere Co. Ltd, 173 Des Voeux Road Central, Sheung Wan, Hong Kong; ☎(852) 2544 2688; fax (852) 2541 7977; e-mail mktg@sincere.com.hk; www.sincere.com.hk (visit the website for other branches information).

Mitsukoshi Hong Kong, Hennessy Centre, 500 Hennessy Road; Causeway Bay, Hong Kong; ☎(852) 2576 5222; fax (852) 2890 8972; www.mitsukoshi.com.hk.

Lane Crawford, Pacific Place, 88 Queensway, Admiralty, Hong Kong; ☎(852) 2118 3668; www.lanecrawford.com (visit the website for other branches information). *Seiyu (Shatin) Co., Ltd.*, New Town Plaza Phase III , 2-8 Shatin Centre Street, Shatin, New Territories, Hong Kong; ☎(852) 2694 1111; fax (852) 2603 0454; e-mail cs@seiyu.com.hk; www.seiyu.com.hk.

Citistore, City Landmark II, TWTL 301, Tsuen Wan, N. T., Hong Kong; ☎(852) 2413 8686; fax (852) 2944 8846; www.hld.com/english/associate/citistore/ (visit the website for other branches information).

Wing On Centre, 211 Des Voeux Road Central, Sheung Wan, Hong Kong; tel: (852) 2852 1888; www.wingonet.com (visit the website for other branches information).

Yueh Wa Store, 301-309 Nathan Road, Kowloon, Hong Kong; ☎(852) 2384 0084; www.yuehwa.com (visit the website for other branches information).

Sales

In general, shop assistants change their jobs frequently and shop owners are always looking for new employees to fill positions. Therefore, it is not difficult to get a temporary job as a shop assistant, if you do not mind the low wage.

On-street promotion counters are a common promotion method in Hong Kong particularly for telecommunications and banks. Short-term promoters are employed to set up counters in different districts to persuade people to use particular credit cards or join the internet services of some telecommunication companies. Some of the staff are paid hourly while some are paid with a premium salary plus commission.

Teaching English or Other Foreign Languages

Even though students have English lessons at schools, many parents still prefer to have a private native English teacher for their children. In order to make learning English more interesting, some schools (mainly private schools) employ foreigners to carry out activities conducted in English, so the students can learn English is a non-classroom situation.

There are many foreign language centres in Hong Kong and it is not too difficult to find a job as a foreign language teacher. However, private language teachers (except for English) are not in great demand. French, German, Spanish, Italian and Japanese are the next most popular languages in Hong Kong.

If you are looking for students to teach, you can place an advertisement on the notice boards in universities and interestingly also in supermarkets, which is free of charge.

VOLUNTARY WORK

It is very easy to be a volunteer, except where special qualifications and skills are required. There are many charitable organisations in Hong Kong that provide a wide variety of services. Many organisations like HOPE Worldwide and The Community Chest are very concerned about problems in China, and they organise on site services in some poor regions in China as well as raising funds in Hong Kong. If you are interested in helping the poor people in China, these programmes would probably be what you are looking for. Travel expenses, lodging and meal costs are normally covered by the organisations. Apart from joining the programmes organised by charitable organisations, you can also approach a location where you want to work directly. Small organisations such as orphanages, centres for the elderly and mental disability centres usually welcome volunteers for organising activities for their members or just making regular visits.

Useful Addresses

Friends of the Earth, 2/F, SPA Centre, 53-55 Lockhart Road, Wanchai, Hong Kong; ☎ (852) 2528 5588; www.foe.org.hk.

Green Power, Unit A, 7/F, Astoria Building, No.34 Ashley Road, Tsim Sha Tsui, Kowloon; ☎(852) 23142662; fax (852) 23142661; e-mail info@greenpower.org.hk; www.greenpower.org.hk.

HOPE Worldwide Hong Kong, Room 1910, Fortress Tower, 250 King's Road, North Point, Hong Kong; ☎(852) 2588 1291; fax (852) 2588 1306; e-mail enquiry@hopeww.org.hk; hk.hopeworldwide.org.

Medecins Sans Frontieres, Shop 5B, Laichikok Bay Garden, 272 Lai King Hill Road, Kowloon, Hong Kong; ☎(852) 2338 8277; fax (852) 2304 6081; e-mail office@msf.org.hk; www.msf.org.hk.

Oxfam, 17/F, China United Centre, 28 Marble Road, North Point, Hong Kong; ☎(852) 2520-2525; fax (852) 2527-6307; e-mail info@oxfam.org.hk; www.oxfam.org.hk.

Rotary International (District 3450), 14/F., Capital Commercial Building, 26 Leighton Road, Causeway Bay, Hong Kong; ☎(852) 2576 8882; fax (852) 2895 5926; e-mail ric@rotary3450.org; www.rotary3450.org.

The Community Chest of Hong Kong, Unit 1805 Harcourt House, 39 Gloucester Road, Wanchai, Hong Kong; ☎(852) 2599 6111; fax (852) 2506 1201; e-mail chest@commchest.org; www.commchest.org.

WWF Hong Kong; ☎(852) 2526 1011; fax (852) 2845 2734; e-mail wwf@wwf.org.hk;   www.wwf.org.hk.

BUSINESS AND INDUSTRY REPORT

Finance and Banking

More than 10% of the GDP of Hong Kong comes from Finance and Insurance. There are more than 180 banks in Hong Kong and the number of branches add up to 1,527. Hong Kong is the third largest international banking centre in Asia in terms of the volume of external transactions. It also has the second highest per capita holding of foreign currency in the world. The Hong Kong stock market plays an important role in the world as well. The stock markets in New York, London and Hong Kong open continuously one after another, making a full day's schedule. Hong Kong is the ninth largest stock market and also the seventh largest exchange market in the world.

Apart from ordinary banking services, banks also provide insurance, loans and investment services to customers. Some of the banks in Hong Kong have branches or have arrangements with banks in other countries, to provide overseas banking services at reasonable charges. The banking sector alone provides around 80,000 jobs in Hong Kong.

Import/Export

Import and export trade accounts for 20% of the GDP of Hong Kong. The main trading partners of Hong Kong are mainland China, the USA, Japan and the UK.

Clothing and accessories from Hong Kong are famous for good quality and low prices and the domestic export of these items brought $65 billion (US$8 billion/£5 billion) income to Hong Kong in 2002. Apart from clothing and accessories, electrical machinery, apparatus and appliances, and electrical parts are also major export items, and bring $15.6 billion (US$2 billion/£1.2 billion) in income to Hong Kong. The main import items are raw materials and semi-manufactures goods, which are mostly bought from mainland China.

Many industries experienced a seriously hard time during the outbreak of SARS. However, the amount of import/export trade during the same period did not drop, and in fact even increased. This helped the Hong Kong economy to recover quickly. There was an 8% to 15% increase in the amount of trade from March to June 2003 when compared to the same period in the previous year. Hong Kong and mainland China signed the Closer Economic Partnership Arrangement (CEPA) in late June 2003. CEPA grants Hong Kong products duty-free access to the mainland and additional market access for Hong Kong companies in the mainland. It is believed that the CEPA will further boost the import/export trading between Hong Kong and mainland China.

Restaurants and Hotels

Hong Kong is famous for its variety of different cuisines, and the number of restaurants in total is huge. There were over 17,000 license applications in the year 2001 alone. Restaurants and hotels are responsible for 3% of the GDP. Although the figure in 2002 decreased slightly when compared to that in the previous years, it is believed that it will increase as the Hong Kong government has been starting several projects for the development of tourism.

Restaurants and hotels were two of the badly hit sectors during the SARS outbreak. There were massive dismissals in many restaurants, and some of them even closed down. Hotels required their staff to take unpaid leave in order to save costs. Fortunately, these two sectors are recovering quite well as the number of tourists is now increasing again.

Teaching

Since the handover to mainland China in 1997, the government has been working hard to produce students that are 'biliteral (English and Chinese) and trilingual (English, Cantonese and Mandarin)'. Apart from encouraging primary and secondary schools to include Mandarin as one of the subjects, most of the secondary schools were asked to use Chinese as the medium of instruction (using Chinese books and lessons conducted in Cantonese) in junior levels. Nevertheless, school principles can decide to use English or Chinese, or both, to teach senior students. You may find at senior levels some of the topics of a subject are taught in English and some in Chinese. Many principals, teachers, students and parents found it difficult to adjust to the new system as the change has been too fast. Students in particular found it difficult to switch between the languages for instruction.

Getting a teaching job is more difficult now. All teachers are required to be degree holders and have a certificate for education starting from September 2004. Moreover, graduates who want to teach English or Mandarin have to pass the language proficiency requirement before teaching in primary and secondary schools. The government encourages schools to teach the Chinese language in Mandarin and it is believed that it will become a compulsory policy in a few years' time.

A substantial number of students have moved from mainland China in the last few years, and more schools have changed to a whole-day from a half-day schedule. Since then, the demand for teachers in general increased but the distribution of students is uneven throughout different districts. The number of students in particular districts, like Shatin and Taipo, reduced at a high rate in the last few years and many of the teachers in these districts were laid-off due to the reduction in the number of classes in schools.

Telecommunications

Hong Kong is the second largest telecommunications market in Asia and telecommunications brought revenue of $48,789 million (US$6.2 billion/£3.9 billion) to Hong Kong in the year 2002. However, telecom companies in Hong Kong face keen competition and the telephone markets are quite saturated. According to government statistics conducted in August 2003, the number of mobile service subscribers was around 6.7 million (98% of the population), which is one of the highest penetration rates in the world. International Direct Dialing (IDD) service and residential fixed line telephones also face severe competition. According to the same government statistics, the telephone density was 56 lines per 100 people, which was the highest amongst Asian countries. The telecom companies compete to attract customers from other companies by lowering their rates and improving the quality of services. More staff are then employed to do strategic planning, promotion and systems maintenance and upgrades.

Up to the year 2002, more than half of households had access to the internet at home. Internet service providers are actively seeking potential customers through setting up promotion counters in different districts and sending staff to households for promotion.

Tourism

Tourism is very important to the Hong Kong economy and is one of the main areas of development in the next ten years. There were more than 16 million visitors to Hong Kong in 2002, which was 20% higher than for 2001. There was a continuous increase in the number of visitors before the outbreak of SARS in March 2003, which was a really big blow to tourism and tourism-related businesses, for example, airlines and retail. However, the city is recovering at a faster rate than many expected. The number of tourists visiting Hong Kong in July 2003 was 1.3 million. The government has a number of major projects for developing tourist attractions and facilities in the coming years. Apart from the Hong Kong Disneyland (to be completed in 2005), there will also be the Tung Chung Cable Car, the Hong Kong Wetland Park, Tsim Sha Tsui Promenade, the Stanley Waterfront, etc.

According to the statistics, more than one-third of the visitors to Hong Kong in 2002 were from mainland China. It is believed that there will be more mainland visitors coming to Hong Kong in the coming few years as residents of four Guangdong cities can apply to visit Hong Kong as individual visitors without going through agencies, which was not allowed before July 2003. This scheme will soon be extended to other cities, including Beijing and Shanghai.

There was no specific qualification required to be a tourist guide in the past, but all tourist guides must now go through training and only those who complete the training and pass the examination will be qualified to work as guides.

DIRECTORY OF MAJOR EMPLOYERS

Accounting

Deloitte Touche Tohmatsu, 26/F Wing On Centre, 111 Connaught Road, Central, Hong Kong; ☎(852) 2852 1600; fax (852) 2541 1911; www.deloitte.com.

Ernst& young, 15/F Hutchison House, 10 Harcourt Rood, Central, Hong Kong; ☎(852) 2846 9888; fax (852) 2868 4432; www.ey.com.

KPMG, 8/F Prince's Building, 10 Chater Road, Central, Hong Kong; ☎(852) 2522 6022; fax (852) 2845 2588; www.kpmg.com.hk.

PricewaterhouseCoopers, GPO Box 690, Hong Kong; ☎(852) 2289 8888; fax (852) 2810 9888; www.pwchk.com.

Engineering

Far East Engineering Services Limited, Flat A, 19th Floor, Chai Wan Industrial Centre Bldg, 20 Lee Chung St., Chai Wan, HK; ☎(852) 2898-7331; fax (852) 2558-7280; www.fareast.com.hk.

Gammon Skanska Limited, 28th Floor, Devon House, TaiKoo Place, 979 King's Road, Hong Kong; tel: (852) 2516 8823; fax: (852) 2516 6260; e-mail: hongkong@gammonskanska.com; www.gammonskanska.com/hk.

Jardine Engineering House, 260 King's Rd North Point, Hong Kong; ☎(852) 2807 1717; fax (852) 2887 9090; e-mail jec@jec.com; www.jec.com.

Maunsell Group, 9/F., Grand Central Plaza, Tower 2, 138 Shatin Rural Committee Road, Shatin, N.T., Hong Kong; ☎(852) 2605 6262; fax (852) 2691 2649; e-mail Tony.Shum@maunsell.com.hk; www.maunsell.com.hk.

Ove ARUP, Level 5, Festival Walk, 80 Tat Chee Avenue, Kowloon Tong,

Kowloon, Hong Kong; ☎(852) 2528 3031; fax (852) 2865 6493; e-mail andrew.chan@arup.com; www.arup.com.hk.

Shui On Construction and Materials Limited, 12/F New Kowloon Plaza, 38 Tai Kok Tsui Road, Kowloon, Hong Kong; ☎(852) 2398 4888; fax (852) 2787 3874; e-mail corpcomm@shuion.com.hk; www.shuion.com.

Food and Beverages

Cafe de Coral Holdings Limited, Foo Tan, Sha Tin; tel2693 6218.

Double Rainbow (desert house), Shopping Arcade, Times Square, Causeway Bay; ☎(852) 2506 4278; www.yp.com.hk/doublerainbow.

Double Star Cafe, Shopping Arc, Grand Century Place, Mong Kok; ☎(852) 2628 3126.

Hard Rock Cafe, Silvercord Shopping Centre, Tsim Sha Tsui; ☎(852) 2375 1323.

Maxim's, 13/F., Luk Kwok Centre, 72 Gloucester Road, Wanchai, Hong Kong; (852) 2101 1333; (852) 2216 7883; pr@maxims.com.hk; www.maxims.com.hk.

McDonald's Restaurants (Hong Kong) Limited, Upper Ground Floor, Parkvale 1060 King's Road, Quarry Bay, Hong Kong; tel: (852) 2880 7300; fax: (852) 2563 1284; www.mcdonalds.com.hk.

Pacific Coffee, Pacific Place Mall, Shop 404, Level 4, Admiralty,, Hong Kong; ☎(852) 2536 4860; (852) 2530 4846; www2.netvigator.com/ente/cafe/pacific.

Pokka Corp (HK) Ltd, Paramount Bldg, Chai Wan; ☎(852) 2367 4101.

Swire Coca-Cola HK Ltd, 17 Yuen Shun Circuit, Sha Tin; ☎(852) 2636 7888; fax (852) 2635 1736; www.swirepacific.com.

Tsingtao Beverage Co Ltd, Yardley Coml Bldg, Sheung Wan; ☎(852) 2850 6882; fax (852) 2144 5978.

Vitasoy International Holdings Ltd, 1 Kin Wong St, Tuen Mun; ☎(852) 2466 0333; fax (852) 2456 3441; www.vitasoy.com.hk.

Hotels

Grand Hyatt Hong Kong, 1 Harbour Road, Hong Kong; ☎(852) 2588 1234; fax (852) 2802 0677; e-mail info@grandhyatt.com.hk; hongkong.grand.hyatt.com.

Holiday Inn Hong Kong – Golden Mile, 50 Nathan Road, Tsim Sha Tsui, Kowloon, Hong Kong; ☎(852) 2369 3111; fax (852) 2369 8016; e-mail reserv@goldenmile.com; goldenmile-hk.holiday-inn.com.

Hyatt Regency Hong Kong, 67 Nathan Road, Kowloon, Hong Kong; ☎(852) 2311 1234; fax (852) 2739 8701; e-mail general.hkgrh@hyattintl.com; hongkong.regency.hyatt.com.

Island Shangri-La Hotel Hong Kong, Pacific Place, Supreme Court Road, Central,

Hong Kong; ☎(852) 2877 3838; Fax (852) 2521 8742; e-mail isl@shangri-la.com; www.shangri-la.com.

Kowloon Shangri-La Hotel Hong Kong, 64 Mody Road, Tsimshatsui East, Kowloon, Hong Kong; ☎(852) 2721 2111; fax (852) 2723 8686; e-mail ksl@shangri-la.com; www.shangri-la.com.

Mandarin Oriental Hong Kong, 5 Connaught Road, Central, Hong Kong; ☎(852) 2522 0111; fax (852) 2810 6190; e-mail mohkg-reservations@mohg.com; www.mandarinoriental.com.

The Excelsior Hong Kong, 281 Gloucester Road, Causeway Bay, Hong Kong; ☎(852) 2894 8888; fax (852) 2895 6459; e-mail info-exhkg@mohg.com; www.mandarinoriental.com.

The Marco Polo Hongkong Hotel, Harbour City, Kowloon, Hong Kong; ☎(852) 2113 0088; fax (852) 2113 0011; e-mail hongkong@marcopolohotels.com; www.marcopolohotels.com.

The Peninsula Hong Kong, Salisbury Road, Kowloon, Hong Kong; ☎(852) 2920 2888; fax (852) 2722 4170; e-mail pen@peninsula.com; www.peninsula.com.

Insurance

American International Assurance Co (Bermuda) Ltd, AIA Tower, North Point; ☎(852) 2232 8888; www.aia.com.hk.

AXA Asia Pacific Holdings Ltd, AXA Centre, 151 Gloucester Road, Wanchai, Hong Kong; ☎(852) 2519 1111; fax (852) 2598 4965; www.axa-chinaregion.com.

Blue Cross (Asia-Pacific) Insurance Ltd, 22/F., Cosco Tower, 183 Queen's Road Central, Hong Kong; ☎(852) 2163 1000; fax (852) 2808 1300; www.bluecross.com.hk.

Eagle Star Life Assurance Co Ltd, Levels 15-17, Cityplaza 3, 14 Taikoo Wan Road, Hong Kong; ☎(852) 2967 8393; fax (852) 2569 2607; www.eaglestar.com.hk/eng.

ING General Insurance International, 7/F ING Tower, 308 Des Voeux Road Central, Hong Kong; ☎(852) 2850 3030; www.ing.com.hk/gi.

New York Life Insurance Worldwide Ltd, Windsor Hse, Causeway Bay, Hong Kong; ☎(852) 2881 0688; fax2577 0866; www.newyorklife.com.hk.

Prudential Assurance Co Ltd, The Cityplaza Taikoo Shing, Shau Kei Wan; ☎(852) 2977 3888; www.prudential.com.hk.

Royal & Sun Alliance Insurance (HK) Ltd, Dorset Hse, Quarry Bay, Hong Kong; ☎(852) 2968 3000; fax (852) 2915 4370; www.royalsunalliance.com.hk.

Law

Baker & Mckenzie, 14th Floor, Hutchison House, 10 Harcourt Road, Hong Kong; tel (852) 2846 1888; fax (852) 2845 0476; email: hklaw@bakernet.com; www.bakernet.com.

Deacons, 3rd -7th , 18th & 29th Floors, Alexandar House, Chater Road, Hong

Kong; tel (852) 2825 9211; fax (852) 2810 0431; email: hongkong@deaconsl aw.com; www.deaconslaw.com.

Freshfields Bruckhaus Deringer, 11th Floor, Two Exchange Aquare, Hong Kong; tel (852) 2846 3400; fax (852) 2810 6192; e-mail perry.noble@freshfields.co m; www.freshfields.com.

Herbert Smith, 23rd Floor, Gloucester Tower, 11 Pedder Street, Hong Kong; tel (852) 2845 6639; fax (852) 2845 9099; e-mail contact.asia@herbertsmith .com; www.herbertsmith.com.

Jones Stokee and Master, 18/F Prince's Building, 10 Chater Road, Central, Hong Kong; tel (852) 2843 2211; fax (852) 2810 5562; e-mail jsm@jsm.com.hk; www.jsm-law.com.

Linklaters, 10th Floor, Alexandar House, Chater Road, Hong Kong; tel (852) 2842 4888; fax (852) 2810 8133; e-mail nrees@linklaters.com; www.linklaters.com.

Lovells, 23rd Floor, Cheung Kong Centre, 2 Queen's Road, Central, Hong Kong; tel (852) 2219 0888; fax (852) 2219 0222; e-mail may.law@lovells.com; www.lovells.com.

Simmons and Simmons, 35th Floor, The Cheung Kong Centre, 2 Queens Road, Central, Hong Kong; tel (852) 2868 1131; fax (852) 2810 5040; e-mail tracey.lees@simmons-simmons.com; www.simmons-simmons.com.

Richards Butler, 20th Floor, Alexandar House, 16-20 Chater Road, Hong Kong; tel (852) 2810 8008; fax (852) 2810 0664; e-mail law@richardsbutler.com.hk; www.richardsbutler.com.

Nurseries and Kindergartens

Deborah English Kindergarten (Bauhinia Garden), Kindergarten Block, Bauhinia Garden, Tseung Kwan O; ☎(852) 3403 4393; fax (852) 3403 4320; www.deborah-intl.com.

Deborah International Play School, G/F, Site 9, Whampoa Garden, Hung Hom, Kowloon; ☎(852) 2994 8998; www.deborah-intl.com.

Good Time International Play School, Block C & D, L4, Shatin Plaza, Sha Tin; ☎(852)2601 3278; fax (852)2603 2878.

Good Time International Play School, Shop 79, Ground Floor, Union Plaza, No.9, Wao Muk Road, Luen Wo Market, N.T.; ☎(852) 2682 8001.

Highgate House School, 2/F 100 Peak Road, The Peak, Hong Kong/53 Beach Road, Repulse Bay, Hong Kong; ☎(852) 2849 6336; fax (852) 2849 6332 email: info@highgatehouse.edu.hk; www.highgatehouse.edu.hk.

Olympic International Pre-School, 33 Cambridge Rd, Kowloon Tong; ☎(852) 2338 8175.

Po Leung Kuk Tam Au Yeung Siu Fong Memorial Kindergarten, 11, Tak On Street, Shop No. 1A, G/F., Site 7, Whampoa Garden; ☎(852) 2311 3871/(852) 2367 7248; fax (852) 2366 0971; e-mail plktaysfk@hknet.com; www.kids-club.net/edu/taysfmkg.

Rosaryhill Kindergarten, 41B Stubbs Road, Wan Chai, Hong Kong; ☎(852) 2835 5122; fax (852) 2838 6141; e-mail rhs@rhs.edu.hk; www.rhs.edu.hk/ Kindergarten/kghome.

Small World Christian Kindergarten, 10 Borrett Road, Mid Levels, Hong Kong; ☎(852) 2525-0922; fax (852) 2530-5448; e-mail smallworld@swck.edu.hk; www.swck.edu.hk.

Sun Island, e-mail info@sunisland.com.hk; www.sunisland.com.hk.

The Woodland Group of Pre-School, Suite 2405 Universal Trade Centre, 3-5A Arbuthnot Road, Central, Hong Kong SAR; ☎(852) 2559 4855; fax (852) 2559 7162; e-mail enquiry@woodlandschools.com; www.woodlandschools.com.hk

Victoria (South Horizons) International Nursery, Yee Wan Ct, Ap Lei Chau; ☎(852) 2884 3781.

York English Kindergarten, 14 York Road, Kowloon Tong; ☎(852) 2338 2544.

Teaching

American International School, 125 Waterloo Road, Kowloon Tong, Kowloon, Hong Kong; ☎(852) 2336-3812; fax (852) 2336-5276; e-mail aisadmin@ais.edu.hk; www.ais.edu.hk.

Christian Alliance , P.C. Lau Memorial, International School, 2 Fu Ning Street, Kowloon City, Hong Kong; ☎(852) 2713 3733; fax (852) 2760 4324; e-mail info.cais.edu.hk; www.cais.edu.hk.

Concordia International School, 68 Begonia Road, Yau Yat Chuen, Kowloon, Hong Kong; tel.: (852) 2397 6576/(852) 2789 9890; fax (852) 2392 8820; e-mail adm@cihs.edu.hk; www.cihs.edu.hk.

Hong Kong International School (Office of Admissions), 23 South Bay Close, Repulse Bay, Hong Kong; ☎(852) 2812 5000; fax (852) 2812 0669; e-mail admiss@hkis.edu.hk; www.hkis.edu.hk.

Hong Lok Yuen International School, Twentieth Street, Hong Lok Yuen, Tai Po, New Territories, Hong Kong; ☎(852) 2658 6935; fax (852) 2651 0836; e-mail info@hlyis.edu.hk; www.hlyis.edu.hk.

German Swiss International School, 11 Guildford Road, The Peak, Hong Kong; ☎(852) 2849 6216; fax (852) 2849 6347; e-mail gsis@gsis.edu.hk; www.gsis.edu.hk.

Kellett School, 2 Wah Lok Path; Wah Fu, Pokfulam; Hong Kong; ☎(852) 2551 8234; fax (852) 2875 0262; e-mail kellett@kellettschool.com; kellettmain.kellettschool.com.

Singapore International School, 23 Nam Long Shan Road, Aberdeen, Hong Kong; tel.: (852) 2872 0266; fax (852) 2872 0431; e-mail secretary@singapore.edu.hk; www.singapore.edu.hk.

Yew Chung Education Foundation (Primary and Secondary Section), 10 Somerset Road, Kowloon Tong, Kowloon, Hong Kong; ☎(852) 2338 7106; fax (852)

2338 4045; e-mail inquiry@ycef.com; www.ycef.com.

Telecommunications

City Telecom, Champion Bldg, Sheung Wan; ☎(852) 2854 1268.

Ericsson Limited, 12/F, Devon House, 979 King's Road, Quarry Bay, GPO
  Box 13487, Hong Kong; ☎(852) 2590 2388; fax (852) 2590 9550;
  www.ericsson.com.hk.

Nokia (HK) Ltd, Cityplaza Taikoo Shing, Shau Kei Wan, Hong Kong; ☎(852)
  2597 0100; e-mailcareline.hk@nokia.com; www.nokia.com.hk.

Orange, tel(852)9753 5458; fax(852)9044 7412; e-mail feedback@orangehk.com;
  www.orangehk.com.

Sunday, Warwick Hse, Quarry Bay, ☎(852) 2113 8118; www.sunday.com.

STARTING A BUSINESS

CHAPTER SUMMARY

○ More than 98% of the business establishments in Hong Kong are small or medium size enterprises (SMEs).

○ 60% of the jobs in the private sector are provided by SMEs.

○ A Limited Company is the most popular form of business structure and they are required to be registered with the Company Registry.

○ There is no customs tariff in Hong Kong, except for importing and exporting tobacco, liquor, methyl alcohol and hydrocarbon oil.

○ Under the Equal Opportunity Ordinance, it is illegal to reject a job application due to the age, sex, disability or family role of candidates.

○ Profit tax rates for sole proprietorships and partnerships is 15.5%; and 17% for limited companies.

○ There is no minimum wage in Hong Kong.

ADVANTAGES FOR STARTING A BUSINESS IN HONG KONG

Hong Kong has been a popular city to set up a business in for the last three decades. Many international companies choose to set up their offices in Hong Kong in order to develop their business in Asia. Hong Kong is one of the most important economic centres in the world and is also a gateway to the fast-growing mainland Chinese market, it is also the world's freest economy.

The infrastructure and taxation systems are also very attractive. The tax system in Hong Kong is simple and the corporate tax rate is only 17%, which compares very favourably with other economies. For instance, the corporation tax rates for Japan, South Korea, Singapore and mainland China in 2003 were 42%, 30%, 22% and 33% respectively. In Hong Kong there is also no withholding tax on dividends or interest, nor is there capital gains tax or sales tax.

There are more than 180 banks in Hong Kong. Many of them are internationally renowned and provide worldwide finance services. Also, thanks to the 9-years mandatory free education system and the eight local universities in the region, the workforce in Hong Kong is in general well-educated.

PROCEDURES INVOLVED IN STARTING A NEW BUSINESS

Preparation from Scratch

There are a number of things to consider when you plan to start a business. Obviously, you have to decide what kind of business you want to set up and which is the appropriate form of business ownership. A considerable amount of research has to be done before making a good decision. In doing so, you could consult the statistics conducted by the government, universities and trade associations. If necessary, you may even consult a market research company. If you are short on budget, there are some government loan schemes that you might be able to apply for. On the other hand, if you decide to borrow money from banks, you should get information from different banks and choose the one which suits you best.

The Hong Kong Trade Development Council has a special unit for Small and Medium Enterprises (SMEs). There is a free advisory service, which you can book via the Council's internet website *www.tid.gov.hk*.

The Trade and Industry Department also has a lot of information about setting up a business in Hong Kong, including information for funding schemes and business licences.

Useful Addresses

Hong Kong Trade Development Council, 38th Floor, Office Tower, Convention Plaza 1 Harbour Road, Wanchai, Hong Kong; ☎(852) 2584 4333; fax (852) 2824 0249; e-mail hktdc@tdc.org.hk; www.tdctrade.com/sme/export.htm.

Small and Medium Enterprises (SME) Service Station, Trade and Industry Department Tower, Mezzanine Floor, 700 Nathan Road, Mong Kok, Kowloon, Hong Kong; ☎(852) 1830 668; fax (852) 2787 3092; www.tid.gov.hk.

Census and Statistics Department, www.info.gov.hk/censtatd/.

Market Research Companies

DN Acorn Ltd (Hong Kong Office), Unit 6-9 9/F Island Place Tower 510 King's Road, North Point, Hong Kong; ☎(852) 2881 5250; fax (852) 2890 5496; e-mail hongkong@acornasia.com; www.acornasia.com.

Fusion Consulting, 88 Hing Fat Street, Causeway Bay, Hong Kong; ☎(852) 2107 4299; www.fusionc.com.

Synovate-Asia Pacific Hong Kong, 9/F Leighton Centre, 77 Leighton Road, Causeway Bay, Hong Kong; ☎(852) 2881 5388; fax (852) 2881 5918; e-mail hongkong@synovate.com; www.synovate.com.

Strategic Focus, 2102, Tung Sun Commercial Centre, 194-200 Lockhart Road, Wanchai, Hong Kong, ☎(852) 2832 7861; fax (852) 2832 7189; e-mail davidhui@strategicfocus.com.hk; www.strategicfocus.net.

Accountants

A limited company must appoint an accountant for auditing. Even though sole proprietorships and partnerships are not required to hire an accountant, it may still be beneficial to do so, especially if you are inexperienced in running a business. Apart from doing the auditing, a good accountant can also provide useful advice on how best to manage your money. Some experienced accountants may even help the clients to analyse their business plans and help you to reduce the risks. There are a great number of accountants in Hong Kong and their charges vary quite a lot. Look them up in the Yellow Page to find one which fits your budget.

Useful Addresses

Yellow Page Online, www.yp.com.hk.

Deloitte Touche Tohmatsu, 26/F Wing On Centre, 111 Connaught Road, Central, Hong Kong; ☎(852) 2852 1600; fax (852) 2541 1911; www.deloitte.com.

Ernst& young, 15/F Hutchison House, 10 Harcourt Rood, Central, Hong Kong; ☎(852) 2846 9888; fax (852) 2868 4432; www.ey.com.

KPMG, 8/F Prince's Building, 10 Chater Road, Central, Hong Kong; ☎(852) 2522 6022; fax (852) 2845 2588; www.kpmg.com.hk.

PricewaterhouseCoopers, GPO Box 690, Hong Kong; ☎(852) 2289 8888; fax (852) 2810 9888; www.pwchk.com.

Choosing an Area

A good location probably brings you more business. Unlike starting a business in a big country, weather and geographical factors are not as important when you are selecting a location for your business in Hong Kong. The major factors to consider are your budget, the size and type of office, shop or factory you need, who your targeted customers are and where they are likely to be.

Central, Admiralty, Wanchai and Causeway Bay are particularly popular for setting up an office. International trading, banking and finance providers are active in these areas and you can find the offices of many local and international companies there. Rents in these areas are however very high. If you are looking for a cheaper office, there are more choices in the New Territories like Shatin and Tsuen Wan, or to the east of the Hong Kong Island like Chai Wan.

If you are trying to sell goods to young customers or tourists, you may want to consider setting up in Tsim Sha Tsui, Causeway Bay or Mongkok. Factories can only be set up in certain areas such as Tai Po, Yuen Long, Tseung Kwan O, Tsuen Wan, Cheung Sha Wan and Kwun Tong.

Raising Finance

Apart from personal savings, banks are the main funding providers for starting a business. However, if you have never run a business before or do not have a track record of assets and cash flow for the banks to use as reference, it is not easy to obtain the funding. Obviously, you have to convince the banks that your business will be profitable and you will be able to pay back the loan. You will normally be required to prepare a business plan, in which you should outline the business you want to start, along with the details of the market research you have done, and your views and aspirations about the future of the business. You also have to include a detailed financial budget, in which you have to list the start up costs, daily running cost, salaries, cash flow schedules, expected income, etc. If you have contacted the suppliers and got a quote for the goods, it will be a good idea to include it in the plan. In general, the more details you can provide, the more likely the banks are going to be convinced. You should also include CVs for yourself and other active members in the business. Your experience and skills are things that the bank assesses when considering an application for a business loan. A business plan should be for five years or more, especially if you are applying for a long-term loan. You should be positive when you present the business plan but not unrealistic. Show the bank you understand both your strengths and weaknesses.

Even if you have enough money to start the business yourself, some of the short-term financial schemes provided by banks may help you to maintain a better cash flow. It is good to get as much information about the different kinds of funding you can obtain from the banks even though you may not need it in the end. More information provides you with more flexibility and it is better to be prepared to face financial problems before they occur.

Investment Incentives

More than 98% of the business establishments in Hong Kong are small and medium enterprises (SMEs), which means they have less than a hundred employees. Although each of them hires only a small number of people, together the jobs they provide count for 60% of the private business sector employment. For this reason, the government has some special funding schemes for SMEs.

SME Loan Guarantee Scheme (SGS). There are three types of loans available:

1. *Business Installation and Equipment Loans* could be used for acquiring installations and equipment needed in business operations. The maximum guarantee limit is $2 million (US$260,000/£160,000), or 50% of the loan approved by the participating lending institute concerned, whichever is the less. The maximum guarantee period is five years.
2. *Guarantee for Associated Working Capital Loans* could be used to meet additional operational expenses arising from or in relation to the business installations and equipment acquired, or to be acquired under the SGS. If the applicant has applied for Business Installation and Equipment Loans from a participating lending institute, the Associated Working Capital Loan must

be provided by the same institute. The maximum amount of the loan is 50% of the Guarantee for Business Installations and Equipment Loan, or 50% of the Associated Working Capital Loan approved by the participating lending institute, depends on which is the less. The maximum guarantee period is two years.

3. *Guarantee for Accounts Receivable Loans* should only be used for meeting the working capital needs arising from provision of credit terms to the customers. An applicant is granted a guarantee of $1 million (US$130,000/£80,000) or 50% of the approved loan as maximum, whichever is the less. As with the *Guarantee for Associated Working Capital Loans*, the guarantee period is up to two years as maximum.

SME Export Marketing Fund (EMF). This is set up to help SMEs to expand their businesses through active participation in export promotion activities. SMEs can apply for grants to participate in overseas trade fairs or exhibitions and study missions. This also applies to local trade fairs or exhibitions which are export-oriented. However, the promotion activities must be organised by experienced and reputable export promotion organisations or companies, which are directly relevant to the business of the applicants. There is no limit to the number of applications for a single applicant but the total amount granted is limited to $80,000 (US$10,200/£6500).

SME Training Fund (STF). STF aims to provide grants to encourage SMEs to provide relevant training to their employers and employees. It also aims to assist the SMEs to enhance their human resources and hence improve their capabilities and competitiveness. There are two categories, one is for employers' training and one is for employees' training. The maximum cumulative amount of grant for an SME to support employers' training is $10,000 (US$1300/£800) and $20,000 (US$2600/£1600) for employees. The amount of grant for each successful application will be 70% of the training expenses directly incurred or the balance of the accumulative grant for respective categories, whichever is lower. The training must be given by professional training organisations.

SME Development Fund (SDF). SDF aims to provide support to projects carried out by non-profit-distributing organisations operating as support organisations, trade and industrial organisations, professional bodies or research institutes to enhance the competitiveness of the SMEs in Hong Kong. The total amount of funding for an approved project is up to HK$2 million, or 90% of the total project expenditure as a maximum, whichever is lower. The fund can be spent on manpower, equipment and other direct costs for carrying out the project. In general, the project should be completed in two years even though longer support may be considered if the applicant is able to show that the project cannot be carried on due to the lack of financial support after the cessation of SDF.

In order to apply for SGS, EMF and STF, your company must be registered in Hong Kong and the number of persons employed (including individual proprietors, partners, shareholders actively engaged in the work of the business and employees who get paid), has to be fewer than 50 for non-manufacturing business and 100 for manufacturing business. To apply for SDF, your organisation must be non-profit-distributing (which means profits are not distributed to its directors, shareholders, employees or any person). It can be operating as support organisations, professional bodies or research institutes. For further details of the above funding schemes and their application methods, visit The Trade and Industry Department website *www.smefund.tid.gov.hk.*

Business Registration

Every business or branch of business in Hong Kong must be registered with the Business Registration Office of the Inland Revenue Department. This must be done within one month of the commencement of the business. You will get a Business Registration Certificate after that and it must be displayed in a conspicuous place at the location where the business is carried out. The Business Registration Certificate has to be renewed every year. Business Licence Information Service (*www.licence.tid.gov.hk*), run by the government, is very useful for checking the required licenses, permits, certificates and approvals related to particular businesses.

Useful Addresses

Business Licence Information Service, M/F, Trade and Industry Department Tower, 700 Nathan Road, Kowloon, Hong Kong; ☎(852) 2398 5133; fax (852) 2737 2377; e-mail enq@licence.tid.gcn.gov.hk; www.licence.tid.gov.hk.

Business Registration Office, 4th Floor, Revenue Tower, 5 Gloucester Road, Wan Chai, Hong Kong; ☎(852) 2594 3146; fax (852) 2594 3146; www.info.gov.hk/ird/index.htm.

Company Registration

Not all companies have to be registered with the Companies Registry, which keeps a record of company names and details. Only limited companies are required to be registered. Other business structures such as partnerships, however, can also register their company names if they want. The name of a new company must not be the same as any name registered on the Registrar's Index. You are required to provide the memorandum and Articles of Association of your company; a statutory declaration of compliance; a proforma stating your company's name, the presenter's name, contact telephone number, fax number and address, and also the prescribed fee for the registration. You can also deregister your company or change the company name. Contact the Company Registry for more details.

Useful Address

Companies Registry, Queensway Government Offices, 14/F, 66 Queensway, Hong Kong; ☎(852) 2234 9933; fax (852) 2596 0585; www.info.gov.hk/cr.

Trademark Registration

Even though a trademark registration is not legally required it is strongly recommended if there is a chance that the pirate industry may take advantage of your business. A new design of certain goods, for instance, can be registered. However, the trademark registration does not apply to computer programmes, protected layout designs (topographies), and designs for articles of a literary or artistic character. For more details about trademark registration, contact the Intellectual Property Services Centre of the Hong Kong Productivity Council or Intellectual Property Department.

Useful Address

Intellectual Property Services Centre, Hong Kong Productivity Council Building, 78 Tat Chee Avenue, Kowloon, Hong Kong ☎(852) 2788 5456; fax (852) 2788 5403; e-mail ipsc@hkpc.org; http://www.tdctrade.com/intpro/hk/itbbx – e3.htm.

Intellectual Property Department, 24/F, Wu Chung House, 213 Queen's Road East, Wan Chai, Hong Kong; ☎(852) 2803 5860; fax (852) 2838 6276; e-mail enquiry@ipd.gov.hk; www.info.gov.hk/ipd.

Business Structures

Sole Proprietorship. If you are going to start a small business and you are the only director of the company, sole proprietorship is an easy way to begin. The legal procedure for setting up a sole proprietorship is far easier than setting up a limited company. All you need to do is look for an office and get the business registered.

Sole proprietorship is conducted by one person and this person is also the beneficiary of all profits produced by the business. The profit tax rate for sole proprietorship is 15.5%, which is lower than that for limited companies. Sole proprietorships are not required to prepare audited accounts but are required to keep sufficient records for at least seven years. The biggest disadvantage of sole proprietorship is its unlimited liability. The owner is not legally separated from the company and thus the owner is personally responsible for all the losses of the company. Sole proprietors may also find it difficult to raise capital as banks are very wary of providing loans to sole proprietors.

Partnership. Partnerships are similar to sole proprietorships in many ways but there have to be at least two owners (maximum 20). Partnerships are also easy to set up. The partners have to come up with an agreement on how to run the business, and state clearly the duties and rights of each partner. It is easier to raise funds from banks for starting a partnership compared to starting a sole proprietorship business. Similarly to sole proprietorship, owners of a partnership business have unlimited personal liability and each partner is fully liable for any business debt, even if the debt is incurred by just one of the partners. Therefore, it is very important to find trustworthy partners.

Profits are shared among the partners according to the agreement made and the profit tax rate of partnerships is the same as for sole proprietorships at 15.5%.

Limited Company. There are two types of limited company in Hong Kong, private limited companies and public limited companies. More than 99% of the investors set up business by forming a private limited company. A private limited company has a maximum of 50 shareholders and the right to transfer shares is restricted. There are 50 or more shareholders in a public limited company and there is no restriction on share transfers. Under certain conditions, public limited companies can also invite the public to subscribe the shares.

A limited company is legally separated from the owner(s) and thus the owners are not personally responsible for the debts of the company. Limited companies are comparatively easy to obtain funds for since there can be up to 50 shareholders for a private limited company, and public limited companies can even invite the public to subscribe the shares. Moreover, banks are more willing to issue loans to these companies.

However, limited companies, both private and public, are subjected to a slightly higher profit tax rate of 17.5%. Limited companies are also more complicated to set up. A limited company needs to register the company name, prepare the Memorandum and Articles of Association, prepare and execute a Declaration of Compliance after the Memorandum and Articles of Association has been printed and signed, prepare the company stamp, statutory books, etc. A limited company is also required to summit annual audited accounts and hence it has to appoint auditors. The information of public limited companies (but not private limited companies) will be filed with the Companies Registry and is available for public scrutiny. They are also required to keep minutes of meetings for inspection if necessary.

It is not easy to close down a limited company, which can only be closed down by liquidation. A company has to appoint a liquidator to evaluate the assets of the company and then distribute payments to creditors and shareholders. It often requires a solicitor and an accountancy firm to handle the process, which can be very costly.

Franchising. Franchising maybe a good choice for your first business venture as the franchisors provide a great deal of support to the franchisees. The failure rate of franchising is low when compared to other forms of business. Even though you are not familiar with running a business, an experienced franchisor is able to help as the frame-work is already set up and market research has been done. Moreover, a franchisor is usually well-known to the public and holds a certain market share. A franchisor usually takes care of all the promotions and advertisements, which saves money and time. Franchisors usually have fixed procedures for running a business and require the franchisees to follow the management style. Having specific steps to follow can be extremely valuable if you are not experienced in running a business. On the other hand, there will be much less flexibility and your profit will have to be shared with the franchisor. In Hong Kong, franchising is particularly common in fast-food businesses and convenience stores. Some of the famous franchising businesses are McDonald's, 7-11 and OK (convenience stores).

Useful Addresses
Small and Medium Enterprises (SME) Service Station, Trade and Industry Department Tower, Mezzanine Floor, 700 Nathan Road, Mong Kok, Kowloon, Hong Kong; ☎(852) 1830 668; fax (852) 2787 3092; www.tid.gov.hk.
Hong Kong Trade Development Council, 38th Floor, Office Tower, Convention Plaza 1 Harbour Road, Wanchai, Hong Kong; ☎(852) 2584 4333; fax (852) 2824 0249; e-mail hktdc@tdc.org.hk; www.tdctrade.com/sme/export.htm.

Import/Export
There is no customs tariff in Hong Kong and only a few items, such as tobacco, liquor, methyl alcohol and hydrocarbon oil, are subjected to excise duties. Import and export licences are not common and they are required only to fulfil obligations under international agreements or requirements for importing countries. However, if you import or export prohibited goods, you must of course obtain licences in advance. The Trade and Industry Department will provide you with more details on prohibited goods and the procedures for applying for the appropriate licences. Import and export declarations are required within 14 days from the import or export of all goods. If you plan to run a textile and clothing business, bear in mind that there is a quota for exporting to certain countries.

Useful Address
Trade and Industry Department, Room 908, Trade and Industry Department Tower, 700 Nathan Road, Kowloon, Hong Kong; ☎(852) 2392 2922; fax (852) 2787 7422; e-mail enquiry@tid.gov.hk; www.tid.gov.hk.

IDEAS FOR NEW BUSINESS
Although things are slowly changing, Hong Kong people in general perceive western goods as stylish and of high quality. Apart from a few things like electronic gadgets, many people prefer to buy goods of a western make if they can afford

the price. You will probably have to capitalise on this perceived image of western products to compete with the much lower prices of goods imported from Asia.

Hong Kong people also like new ideas. They are eager to try new and interesting things. For instance, *Tamagotchi*, a Japanese portable digital toy for keeping virtual pets, was very popular amongst all ages a few years ago. However, as trends change quickly, their craze for a particular idea often dies out pretty soon. If you are an owner of a business, especially a trendy one, it is important to keep bringing out new alternatives for your customers from time to time.

Fashion and Clothing

Clothing is one of the things for which people's perception really makes a difference. Mainland Chinese brands are practically unheard of in Hong Kong, although many local companies are basically just selling mainland products with a Hong Kong label attached to them. Expensive as they are, western designer labels are, on the other hand, extremely popular among the young.

Import/Export

Hong Kong has a world reputation for being the gateway to the fast-growing, ever-expanding, billion-people market of mainland China. Although China has now opened its market and joined the World Trade Organisation, a lot of import/export business is still done through Hong Kong, where finance, banking and legal services are excellent. In June 2003, a new Mainland and Hong Kong Closer Economic Partnership Arrangement (CEPA) was signed, which means trading between Hong Kong and mainland China will be even more barrier-free.

Bars/Restaurants

Hong Kong people like dining out. Although you may find Asian food cheap and tasty, there are always middle-class young locals or tourists who fancy sampling western cuisines. In fact, Hong Kong people are so spoiled and obsessed with the variety of food offered by the city that you can see people paying literally ten times the price for an equally filling meal, 'just for a change'. There are lots of opportunities for classy restaurants serving authentic western cuisines.

Similarly for bars and pubs, while beer in supermarkets can be as cheap as a tenth of the price of a pint from the tap, going out is associated with a certain image of being hip and posh. Selecting a good location is however very important, as Hong Kong people do not drink as frequently nor as much as westerners. When they do, they often hang out around Wanchai, Central or Tsim Sha Tsui, where you will also find the tourists.

Guided Tours

Interestingly, Hong Kong people rarely travel on their own. They usually join guided tour packages and have everything taken care of for them, including having someone to show them around in groups. This is especially true for older people, who have the money to spend but not the language ability to get by easily in a foreign country. Just as you might find their city fascinating, they might be equally impressed with your country as well.

RUNNING A BUSINESS

Employing Staff

Due to the Government's policy of non-intervention, there is no minimum wage in Hong Kong and an employer can negotiate the salary with an individual employee. Salaries are usually paid once a month through direct deposit to the employees' bank accounts. Employees, such as construction workers, may be paid weekly or even daily if the number of working days is variable. Apart from the basic salary, employers have to contribute at least 5% of the salaries of the employees to a pension scheme, which is known as the Mandatory Provident Fund (MPF) Scheme. This is a compulsory pension scheme run by the government, and failing to contribute the minimum 5% is illegal. Even though people who earn HK$5000 a month or less are exempt from contributing the employee's part of the MPF, employers still have to contribute their part. The minimum age for work in Hong Kong is 15. However, the MPF Scheme only applies to employees aged 18 to 65 who have worked in a company for 60 days or more.

Under the Equal Opportunity Ordinance, it is illegal to reject a job application due to age, sex, disability or the family role of a candidate. Be careful when placing job advertisements, as the information contained in your ad must not suggest discrimination.

Employees' right to join unions is protected by law. An employer is not allowed to force an employee to join or withdraw from an union, nor can an employer prohibit an employee from joining the activities organised by trade unions outside office hours.

Even though employment training is not compulsory, many companies provide it to help their staff to adapt to the new working environment and help them to develop the skills required for the job. In addition, many people view employment training as a kind of employment benefit and take it into consideration when looking for a job.

Refer to Chapter 6 *Employment* for further details concerning employing staff.

Taxation

The simple taxation system is one of the great advantages of running a business in Hong Kong. Compared to other countries, the tax rates in Hong Kong are very low and there are only a few taxes that have to be paid when running a business. All persons, corporations, partnerships and trustees who carry out trade or business in Hong Kong are subject to Profits Tax. Even if you are running a company whose head office is overseas, you are still liable for Profits Tax if your company's income is earned in Hong Kong. You are required to make a Profits Tax Return every year, usually in April. The tax rates for residents and non-residents are the same. It is 17.5% for limited and 15.5% for unlimited businesses. There is no special tax or licence required unless you are importing or exporting certain specified goods.

Employers are also responsible for providing an annual return of remuneration for employees (for filling-in their personal tax returns) within one month from the date of issue, which is normally in April each year. In addition they are required to notify the Commissioner of the Inland Revenue Department in writing within three months of a new employee starting work, and one month prior to an employee leaving. When an employee is going to leave Hong Kong for over a month and not for business purposes, the employer has to report to the Inland Revenue Department at least one month before the departure of the employee. Moreover, the employer should temporarily withhold the payment of salary and other remuneration to the employee until the Inland Revenue Department issues a 'letter of release'.

There is a more detailed illustration of the taxation system of Hong Kong in the chapter *Daily Life in Hong Kong*. Refer to it for further details.

APPENDIX I

PERSONAL CASE HISTORIES

MAINLAND CHINA

ALEX THOMSON – Teacher at a Chinese School
How did you come to be living and working in China?
In 1988 I was re-examining my slightly eccentric life as a club manager/ bartender and musician, thinking about how I could make a responsible shift into some new career opportunities. The economy in the USA was booming and there was a lot of optimism that you could do business in a non-corporate, creative way so I thought I would go to school to get my MBA. The problem was that just getting an MBA was not really appealing to me at all, but a top rated international MBA programme happened to be right next door. The opportunity to study culture and language while getting a business degree made the transition much easier to accept. Basically, even though I was taking strides toward what I thought was the next stage in mature personal development, I knew I wanted to continue to make my life as unusual and interesting as possible. I truly believe, at least for myself, that a challenging environment is crucial for keeping the mind awake, so China seemed to be the best possible choice for my regional specialization. After I was well into my MBA program, the other students in the programme used to joke that all the Chinese Track students (only 5) were a little crazy, did not fit the MBA profile, and just wanted and excuse to hang out in China.

I can't say that that is the root of my motivation exactly, just the turning point. I grew up in San Jose, California and spent my teen years hanging out around San Francisco where the Chinese ethnic population is something around 30 percent. I was particularly infatuated with the world outside of the US. The Latin American and Chinese communities around me were inspiring in that they had penetrating cultures and histories that I couldn't reconcile with what I saw in my everyday life and on the television of the seventies and eighties. This was really the beginning of my interests as an adult.

I've been in China for around three years. I first spent a couple months in Taiwan, at the time of the 1st inauguration of Chen Shui Bian. Then I started the language phase of my program in Hangzhou, stayed there for about six months and then moved to Beijing in February 2001. After a semester of language and a six month internship at a Chinese software company in Ya Yun Cun, I went back to the States to finish the MBA. Finally, I came back in September 2002 and have been in Beijing ever since.

What was your first impression of China?

I came over from Taiwan, so there was a bit of a transition period. What I remember about Taiwan were the pungent odours, conflictingly wonderful and disgusting at the same time: fresh and not so fresh fish, night markets, smog, musty humidity, *chou dofu* (a deep fried tofu with a strong smell), temple incense. I loved it. Hangzhou had similar sensory impact but I was already acclimated a bit. The distinction was that the aroma of southeastern China was permeated with dust and seemingly unbridled industrial exhaust.

I thought Taiwan was pretty chaotic, but when I stepped out of customs at the grimy architecturally functional international airport in Shanghai (Hongqiao Airport) and set out to find a way to Hangzhou, I knew that I was where I wanted to be. Taxi drivers were immediately telling me that the train station was closed and there were no busses to Hangzhou. Whatever seasoning experiences I had gained in my earlier days working in clubs no longer mattered I had *Lao Wai* (foreigner) written all across my forehead and no matter how hard I tried to present an image that I knew what I was doing I couldn't fake it. They were telling me that it would cost me 900-1200 *yuan* to get there. I know now that you can rent a driver for an entire day including gas for nearly 20% of that! My final deal was not too bad though. Shuttle bus is 80-100 *yuan* and I paid something like 260 *yuan* for the 3 hour drive in a taxi because the driver was a local heading home, and wanted a last fare to bump up the day's take.

Of course, the drive was a teeth-clenching horror story, blazing through abandoned-looking industrial badlands and roadside villages where the chickens and the old folks seemed to instinctively get out of the cab's devastating path at the last second. The driver augmented the effect by driving one-handed while screeching Hangzhou *Hua* (spoken language) into his cell phone. I realized later that the Hangzhou language only *sounds* like all out vicious arguing when the driver told me he had just asked his friend to meet him for beers and dinner after he dropped me off.

Finally at Hangzhou Shang Xue Yuan I knew I had arrived when I got into the elevator, the door closed and a Chinese *tongxue* (schoolmate) lit up a cigarette in the enclosed space. This place was cool.

The secondary impression was that most people were nice, food was great, trying to get extra money out of foreigners was not cheating, but rather an institutionalized form of taking advantage of asymmetries in the marketplace, and that Hangzhou's West Lake was one of the most uniquely romantic places in the world.

What is/was your visa status? Was it difficult to get such a visa?
I have an F visa (business visa) now. It is not at all difficult to get one if you have a couple of thousand *yuan*. I've heard it can be cheaper, but I'm not sure how to go about it. I just call one of the many 'Visa consultants' and they pay a certain 'relationship fee' to the security bureau. They, in turn, send my visa to Guangzhou to be stamped and I'm all set for 6 more months. I don't even have to leave the country if my time has expired. Now that China is supposed to retaliate against the US for Visa restrictions and fingerprinting, however, I'm not sure how easy it will be in the future.

What sort of place do/did you live in? Was it easy to find accommodation?
In Hangzhou I lived in a foreigner dormitory apartment building. Three foreign students each had their own room and shared a living room and bathroom. It was a luxury apartment compared to the Chinese students who lived in bunks, eight to a room with no bathroom. We had a big fight with the administration because they told us we had to be back every night by eleven. We were forced to boost each other up to climb through the first floor bathroom window after a night on the town. It was ultimately necessary to formally take issue with their policy when they started locking the bathroom window in retaliation. My schoolmates and I were graduate students in our late 20's and were dumbfounded that the people we were paying so much money to were telling us when we should go to bed. Their opinion was that we would cause unrest and instability among the regular college students if they knew we were trying to make an exception of ourselves and getting away with it. Ultimately a compromise was reached when we told the chief administrator that we would tell all future potential students from our schools that this school had a problem reconciling the rights of adults with its future revenue and marketing plans. The MBA was more useful than I thought it would be!

I have lived in varied conditions here in Beijing. I started with a new but overpriced apartment for foreign students at Beijing University of International Business and Economics (I think at least 4,800 *yuan* a month). Then I made a move to an apartment behind the east gate at a time when it was still supposedly illegal for foreigners to live in local housing communities. The rent for a really shabby two bedroom apartment was about 2,800 *yuan*, definitely gauged under the auspices of the risk of housing foreign students.

Then I lived in an apartment in Hua Jia Di Xi Li, which was rented by my former boss to my former girlfriend. He made a deal with her that, as a 'friend', he would rent a two bedroom apartment of around 100 square metres to her for the same price plus 1½ hours of free English lessons a week. The market value for private teachers in the area at the time was about 160 *yuan* per hour, so the total cost was 3,760 *yuan* a month. Several months after I had inherited this deal, I realized that I had to talk to this person who said I was his 'close friend' every time he wanted me to translate something for him or help him with his IELTS (International English Language Testing System) studies. Despite insisting that if I ever needed anything for all my help, he was totally insulted when I suggested the arrangement was somewhat unfair. After a tremendous argument and the realization that '*pengyou*' (friends), if someone actually has to say it out loud, is just another term for leverage in a business relationship. I moved out and never spoke with him again.

I now live in Wang Jing in a 90 square metre one bedroom apartment for 2,700 *yuan*. It is modern and clean with relatively high speed internet. I never measured either apartment but they are nearly the same size while the new one has a sizeable sun room. The community is very clean, modern and convenient, and it has one of the largest South Korean populations in China.

Today I am actually looking for a larger apartment, hopefully with satellite TV and a bathtub. I've looked at quite a few this week and it's pretty good fun to watch the landlords factor in the extra charge for being a foreigner. There's a pause, their faces turn a little red, and their eyes turn to the upper right as they try to quickly calculate what can be added without seeming totally ridiculous. Sometimes they succeed and sometimes they don't. To be fair, all this became evident to me when, for my current apartment, I actually found a nice, honest landlord who preferred a stable tenant over an extra 500-1000 *yuan*. I was then able to see through what I call the '*lao wai te jia*' ('discounted' foreigner price) for apartments.

I have quite a few friends here so I am able to compare quality and price relatively well. There's a bit of a gold rush mentality among the landlords because foreigners have tended to move here to Wang Jing over the past six to seven years. The problem is that there are so many new developments around that they can't keep occupancy high enough to warrant the high prices. For bargaining purposes and in the hope that there will be a new sucker just off the plane, they knock the price up anywhere between 500-1,500 *yuan*.

The 2 bedroom apartments I'm looking at here range from 3,300 *yuan* for old looking places with completely un-matching furniture, to 4,500-5,000 *yuan* for anything from the aforementioned to something nice. That is just the offer price though. I will expect to bring it down to between 3,500-4,000 *yuan*, depending on the place. The guy today told me that there's a penthouse near my building where they paid a fortune for the design and remodelling. It has Hong Kong satellite TV, ultra-hip furniture, Japanese imported spa-bath-shower equipment, etc. Originally, they were asking for around 6,000 *yuan* and after a half a year on the market they got 4,000 *yuan*. I'm sure he was asking himself later why he told me this just after taking me to a really ugly old apartment that was also going for 4,000 *yuan*.

What is the social life like? Was it easy to make a new group of local friends?
The social life is exploding in Beijing and it's very easy to make friends. Three

years ago, there were a variety of clubs to go to, but you still didn't have a wide range of environments. Now you have at least the choices you would have in other large international cities, if not more. I like Beijing because it has become an international melting pot while at the same time feeling intimate and relatively safe. This is very conducive to meeting people without having to worry about personal safety or similar concerns.

Most of the action takes place around Dong Zhi Men/ San Li Tun, but places like Hou Hai north of Gu Gong, and some of the college areas like Wu Dao Kou and Bei Da (Peking University) have become well worth the visit.
The music scene is supposed to be the best in China, but I find that, although there are several clubs for live music, there is still not a lot of creativity beyond copying the music of western bands and then adding their own Chinese lyrics. Chinese rock for the most part totally missed out on Motown, and is mostly influenced by commercials and eighties rock.

Pretty much anyone with a pulse can make friends in Beijing. If you want to be with international people, there are parties and events almost every night of the week. If you have a hard time dealing with foreigners, there are droves of students and others who want to practice their English or just meet someone outside of their local paradigm.

What do you like best about China? What do you like least about China?
I must answer both questions at the same time because all I can give you is contradictions, contradictions, and more contradictions. I have heard this view from so many other people who have lived here for a while. People are friendly, but not. Everyone works hard, but doesn't get anything done. And often the best food leaves you with the worst side effects!

Well, of course I like the food! After a brutal Beijing winter, there is nothing better than going to an outside *'dao pai dang'* place to eat *'yang rou chuanr'* (roasted lamb) and drink Yan Jing beer with friends. Or taking said friends to Gui Jie for hot pot on a cold January night. In all my travels in China, the night's meal and the potential to meet come interesting people are always the highlights.
Of course there are a lot of friendly people who have taken me into their homes, and when you have dinner as a guest you always have to say that people are friendly; but I have mixed views on this. First, I am a little uncomfortable at times when people put me in the position that I must say the locals are so friendly for reasons of *'mianzi'* (face), because I have found that when I am invited to a friendly dinner, there are so often aspirations that as a foreigner I will bring some kind of *'guanxi'* (relationship) or opportunity to the table, and the 'let's be friends' thing comes up again. My recent landlord wants me to invest in his wife's Lavender connections, my old landlord wants me to do English translations for him for free and possibly help him start an English school, someone wants me to teach their kids. All of this is a friendly way to do business, but it is not really friendship or real friendliness to me,

and represents a grey area I have found to be frustrating at times.

On the other hand, on the occasions when my relationship fell into situations where there wasn't something to be gained, the environment was truly relaxing and endlessly giving. In the cases of teachers and students who became friends, or the family of my girlfriend, or friends that were made outside of the so-called 'friendly' realms of dinners and karaoke, the words '*women shi pengyou*' (we are friends) are not really said, and the true experience of friendships are very strong. I know, contradictions!

I think that people in cities in China are often not friendly toward each other unless they are from the same '*danwei*' (a working department), family or have other social connections. There's just not much friendliness or consideration for the stranger next to you. In a country of 1.3 billion people, there seems to be a kind of survival myopia where in your everyday activities you just try to pretend like there's no one else in line, or on the road, or trying to buy things, etc. I can't tell you how many ladies and men, young and old, have looked me right in the eye and then pushed me out of the way to cut in a queue. Actually, in the cafeteria where I went to school in Hangzhou, the cutting edge technology of 'lines' had not yet been developed. Every meal was an every-man-or-woman-for-him/herself, as students and professors battled as though the starvations of the Great Leap Forward would return and we would all die of hunger or lack of Coca Cola within minutes.

This ties into the other big problem I have which is not really traffic, per se, but the attitude to traffic. This past week I have had a couple of great conversations with taxi drivers (who doesn't, I know) about the traffic situation. The Beijing taxi drivers are reeling at how many cars and new drivers have been added to the roads over the last two years. According to one taxi driver, driver training consists of something like knowing how to turn on the car, drive forward and pay a fee. It is not uncommon to see a woman with stuffed animals obscuring every inch of the left side, right side, and rear windows to the extent that the only unimpaired vision is directly to the front of the driver. I think this is symbolic in many ways of the myopia that I referred to above and the idea that most people on the streets are just looking out for number one. Concurrently, I am amazed at the amount of people who look truly dumfounded when they walk directly into a busy street without looking to find a screeching car sliding their way. Then they give an angry look to the driver as though he should not be in their path. It's like the tunnel vision of an individual who is working with a total lack of common sense, something that I still haven't really figured out yet.

The final contradiction is the contradiction between working and getting things done. I cannot diminish my respect for the people I see working hard everyday to make their lives better. This is the case all over China, and there is a tremendous amount of entrepreneurial spirit and dedication in the people I meet every day. At the same time, there seems to be a hold-over from the cultural revolution, where common sense and the will to go the extra mile took some devastating blows.

One friend of mine worked previously as an IT director for a large corporation in Shanghai, and now works for an international Chinese company. He says that his greatest problem is getting people to do something beyond the minimum required to keep the job and get a pay check. As I tell my girlfriend's brother, who is a recently graduated Chinese programmer, this friend of mine would give anything for someone who took the initiative to solve problems and 'fix things when they break'.

According to him and others I have spoken with, if something is broken or there is a problem that would require creative thinking, everything shuts down and, most workers are likely to avoid it until management deals with the issue, even if it is inconvenient to them as well. Then, management must solve the problem because no one has memorized the solution during their time at university. I find this situation constantly in my everyday life also, from the waitress who panics if I ask her to leave the cucumbers out of my *'gong bao ji ding'* (a chicken dish), to the police who will only file a report about my girlfriend's stolen cell phone because they will lose face in front of a foreigner if they don't. *'Mei banfa's'* (no way/cannot help) are everywhere…

What advice would you have for anyone thinking of coming to live and work in China?

I must make it clear after saying these few gripes that I truly love China. Everywhere there is the feeling that this is a culture that has survived history in an amazing way. People are fascinating. Places are unimaginably diverse. And this is truly a place where you can feel the remote past and the future of the human race grinding along together as twin behemoths.

I see so many foreigners every weekend who refuse to, at the least, learn a little Chinese. They live in totally isolated and self contained communities, and represent everything that I was dissatisfied with in my own culture. They are here only to make a buck and it is obvious. They make rounds from work to home to Starbucks to the markets to buy the pirated goods that their various companies supposedly battle against. Many people like this that I have met seem to think that China is not much more than a flea market or a larger, cheaper Chinatown where you can find less expensive goods and housemaids, while living in a big house behind a wall. It completely feeds into stereotypes about foreigners and stereotypes about Chinese, and it plays no productive role in bringing our cultures closer together.

This is China. This is the country of the Chinese people and a rich Chinese culture. Don't come here if you don't want to participate. Well… come here if you want, but participate!

SEAN WILLIAMS – Assistant Director for a Study Programme

How did you come to be living and working in China?

I have lived in three parts of greater China, three years in Hong Kong, over a year in Taiwan, and four months in Mainland China. I had a different reason for going to each place. In Hong Kong, where my dad lives, I went first to study the Chinese language and teaching English and later to take a job as a paralegal in 1999 which so alienated me that I decided to go back to school and get a second degree in Psychology at HKU. I went to Taiwan twice, once for 8 months and once for six months, both times to teach English, first for a bushiban, and later for a Zen Buddhist temple. When I went to live in China, I went to act as an assistant director for a study abroad programme in Chongqing at Southwest China Normal University. I was supervising students who had come to visit China for the first time from a Benedictine university in Minnesota (College of St. Benedict/St. John's University).

What was your first impression of China?

The first time I saw China was in 1989, not long after the Beijing Massacre. I went to Guangzhou, which seemed drab and depressing and broken down at that time, and then to Guilin, which was beautiful and stirred some feeling of travelling excitement in me—though at the time I was a self-concerned teenager being taken there by my father, so I didn't pay as much attention to my surroundings as to my inner thoughts, obsessions, resentments, etc.

I really got to look at China with fresh eyes when I went in by myself for the first time in 1995. I took a big backpack and about US$500 and tried to get to as many places as I could in a month and a half. The impression I got from China from that trip was informed by journeys to Xiamen, Shanghai, Qingdao, Beijing, Wuhan, Wudang Mountain, and Yangshuo. Needless to say the impression was rather complex. I guess I saw the spiritual and the natural in tremendous tension with the man-made and material, with there being something to appreciate and to recoil at in each.

What sort of place did you live in? Was it easy to find accommodation?

When living in Chongqing (actually Beipei, a couple of hours out of Chongqing), I stayed in the 'Foreign Experts' quarters. I don't know how much my accommodation cost the university. For me it was part of my payment package. It was a decent-sized place, but pretty Spartan. The carpeting and the wallpaper both looked several decades old. The bathtub did not have hot running water, so I had to heat up water on a stove and then pour it into the bath to wash. One time the *fuwuyuan* (service attendant), who would frequently unlock the door and enter without knocking, came in to find me bathing, looked terribly embarrassed and then scurried out. My window didn't have a view of much other than the courtyard outside, where the students practiced Tai Ch'I, but it was pretty enough.

What was the social life like? Was it easy to make a new group of local friends?

The social life in Beipei was odd, but we did make a few friends, mostly through the university, and I met a couple of interesting characters in the little bars that they had there as well. On a Friday or Saturday night, you could go into one of these nightclubs and only about 30 people would be there, all dancing under a cheap revolving disco ball in front of a big mirror looking at themselves. There were karaokes as well, but I didn't feel so welcome there and they seemed more explicitly connected with prostitution. The local friends I and others on the programme got closest to were students or teachers at the university.

What do you like best about China?

I felt like China was another world, a fascinating and engaging but not a dangerous or threatening one, one that could teach me about who I was and who people are generally, without destroying me. Also, the mountains, the food, the trains, the friendly people, the US$1 haircuts that come with a head wash and backrub, 25 cent beers in big cold bottles with *jiaozi* (Chinese dumplings), hot pot, singing Chinese communist-era songs in bars with strangers, the surprising diversity, the tolerance and openness, the intelligence, curiosity, humour, and optimism. And lest I be dishonest, I found the opposite sex even more charming and enticing than usual while in China, more so than in Hong Kong or Taiwan.

What do you like least about China?

The fear, the indifference to a stranger's suffering, the indifference to animal suffering, the pollution, the incivility in getting on a bus, the spitting, the greed-driven and face-driven dishonesty and corruption, the blaring of dogma, the potential oppression that hangs in the air even when it is not obviously expressed, the ugliness of most cityscapes, the spirit-robbing commercialization of the most compelling and impactful aspects of Chinese landscape and culture.

What advice would you have for anyone thinking of coming to live and work in China?

Open yourself as wide as you can to new people, new landscapes and new experiences without losing sight of who you are, and who you've always wanted to be. Try to give back as much or more than you will inevitably take. Be prepared to learn what it means to have unaccountable power, even after a lifetime of feeling like a victim of unaccountable power yourself. The trouble you make for yourself will likely be easy to bear, easier than it might be at home, in fact probably too easy. That will not be the case for the trouble you make for others. Some of the people you will never see again will face things that you will never have to face.

JOEY ROBERTS – Businessman

Why have you spent a few years in China?
It was not planned at all. I was working in Hong Kong, and my company proposed that I should move to Shanghai. I accepted.

What was your first impression of China?
First impressions were biased by my excitement of discovering this mysterious country. I was amazed by the scale and speed of development in Shanghai. Then, over time, I realized the numerous shortcomings of living in a developing country without knowing the local language. I was amazed by the mix of people in Shanghai: well educated Chinese people living side by side with poor and poorly educated people.

What is your visa status? Was it difficult to get such a visa?
My employer got me an employment visa (Z) with work and residence permit. Not a problem to obtain.

What sort of place do/did you live in? Was it easy to find accommodation?
Town house within the ring road, US$2000/month, in a Chinese community. Accommodation was very easy to find. We worked through one agent only and found one the second day of my visit.

What is the social life like? Was it easy to make a new group of local friends?
Being a non Mandarin speaker, I only made local friends at work; none in the area I am living in. Social life in our Chinese community seems well developed. People share the alleyway together, especially in summer.

What do you like best about China?
The opportunity to learn about the challenges faced by the country and how the economy develops.

What do you like least about China?
The fact that some Chinese people – although a limited number – genuinely dislike foreigners.

What advice would you have for anyone thinking of coming to live and work in China?
Build up a reasonable level of Mandarin first; one that is sufficient to start interacting socially in Chinese in order to learn further through daily-life communication.

KEN SHERMAN – Researcher

How did you come to be living in China?

To conduct fieldwork research for my Ph.D. dissertation. I lived in Shanghai for two years.

What was your first impression about China?

Noisy and busy and exciting. Difficult to get basic things done at first. People were friendly and helpful.

What was your visa status? Was it difficult to get such a visa?

I had an F visa for *fangwen*, essentially for a researcher. It was very easy for me to get, but I had already established institutional affiliation with a major academic institution in Shanghai. They took care of the necessary invitations and paperwork.

What sort of place did you live in? Was it easy to find accommodation?

In the 90s, westerners were still required to choose between living in dormitories or expensive housing designed for expatriates, with little in between. This has since changed. I rented a small apartment in the city centre (in the French Concession, near Huaihai Road). In 2000, the rent was 2,500 *yuan* per month. The apartment was about 20 years old and not at all luxurious, but very adequate for me. It had two large rooms, one of which I used as a lounge/study, the other as a bedroom, plus a small kitchen and bathroom. The apartment was unfurnished when I rented it, but the landlord furnished it well with my rent money, and after 18 months, decreased my rent to 2000 *yuan*. The apartment did not have a washing machine, but I was able to make an arrangement with the landlord. They would have had to raise the rent a few hundred *yuan* per month to recover part of the cost of installing a new washing machine. Instead, they suggested I pay them 100 *yuan* for them to pick up my clothes and wash them for me. Over the course of my stay we both came out ahead.

Friends with business salaries typically lived in nicer apartments, paying 5000 to 6000 *yuan* per month.

I found the apartment through a real estate agent. I consulted many such agents, each showing me about three apartments before giving up on me. Most seemed quite tricky and played a lot of games – I only felt comfortable with two. I found the agents by simply walking around the neighbourhoods I hoped to live in, looking for realtors, and walking in. By law they were only allowed to receive a total commission worth one month's rent, but in practice they tried to receive 1.5 to 2 months commission by overcharging both parties. In my case I paid half a month, and the landlord paid a full month.

What was the social life like in your area? Was it easy to make a new group of local friends?

Shanghai is a very vibrant city with an exciting night life. It may take some time to begin with, but once you have made a few friends it is easy to meet a lot of people. I did make friends and establish long-term relationships, but perhaps not as close and not as easily as in other places. The Shanghainese can be very helpful and friendly, but have a reputation of being more inward looking, not as open to outsiders. I believe it is not as easy to make friends with local Shanghainese as it is in Beijing or Taibei. This is based on my own experience, and anecdotal evidence from friends have lived in these cities.

What do you like best about China?

The people. It takes a long time and a lot of work to get to know people on their own terms, but I find it vastly rewarding. And the food. Where else can you eat such fabulous food on such a low budget?

What do you like least about China?

The difficulty in getting things done. For many things this gets easier with time, but it does take more work to live in China. Of course, this is also becomes one of the rewarding things about living in China, but it can be difficult to see it that way at the beginning.

What advice would you have for anyone thinking of coming to live and work in China?

Patience. Everything will take longer, and seem more complicated, than it should. It is extremely worthwhile to work at getting to know China and the Chinese on their own terms, rather than expecting them to do all the work to understand you on your terms. When you are about to reach boiling point, short trips to get away are most advisable and productive. Rather than avoidance, such trips should be seen as part of the adaptation process. Keep your hobbies or develop new ones, eat good food, and make friends.

More practically, as soon as you arrive, there will be some kind of weekly English language newspaper or magazine advertising local events and the major Western social and business organisations. Also, there are now many websites that offer up-to-the-minute information for people living in or moving to Shanghai – simply enter Shanghai in google.com.

APPENDIX II

PERSONAL CASE HISTORIES

HONG KONG

JENNIFER ATKINSON – Solicitor

How did you come to be living and working in Hong Kong?
I spent a year working in Hong Kong. I was seconded to the Hong Kong office of the firm I worked for at the time, Clifford Chance (solicitors), for my final six months of training, but I arranged to stay for a further few months in order to gain more experience and an extra qualification.

What was your first impression of Hong Kong?
I first visited Hong Kong in February. My first impressions are very memorable: Kai Tak was the only airport in Hong Kong at the time and of course the weather in February was rather miserable – damp and grey with low cloud. As I looked down out of the plane window I was really depressed! Everything looked so dirty and grey. I thought: what have I just flown half the way round the world for if it's a horrible as this?
The friend I was visiting was lucky enough to be staying in the Mandarin Oriental at the time and he sent a hotel car to collect me from the airport. It was a Rolls Royce Silver Shadow! So I had a journey in this car from Kai Tak to the Mandarin with such mixed feelings: the city looked so dirty and miserable and wet, but the car was so luxurious and it was such a treat to be driven around by someone else.

What was your visa status? Was it difficult to get such a visa?
I have a British passport, so this was not a problem for me. I got a year's entitlement to remain with my British passport.

What sort of place did you live in? Was it easy to find accommodation?
I lived in a flat with another trainee solicitor which was rented on our behalf by Clifford Chance, so I'm afraid I don't know what the rental amount was. This flat had been rented by the firm for a number of years, along with several others in the same block, so there was no problem for us finding accommodation. It was a

two-bed apartment in Happy Valley and it was small but comfortable.

What was the social life like? Was it easy to make a new group of local friends?

For us trainee solicitors, the social life revolved around the office and among the trainee solicitors from other firms. I tended to socialise with the other trainee solicitors from my firm who had come out from London at the same time as me, and also with the young local solicitors from Clifford Chance. To this extent, there was a ready-made social group.

I suppose it was a typical ex-pat social scene: we would go out for the evening once or twice a week to Lan Kwai Fong or Wanchai, and one or two weekends per month we would be invited to go out on the firm's junk. We would occasionally go to the cinema at Pacific Place. We would also spend some time entertaining clients of the firm by going for evenings out to restaurants or on the junk.

Whilst this sounds as if I lived quite an ex-pat lifestyle, I spent the majority of my free time alone, exploring the city and the countryside, and spent some time on most weekends walking, alone, in the New Territories, which is fantastic hiking country.

What do you like best about Hong Kong?

I love Hong Kong for its delicately balanced mix of East and West. It is the ideal place for a first-time visitor to Asia from Britain, as, whilst on the one hand it is a Chinese city, on the other, there is enough English spoken and written there to be able to lead the sort of life you would recognise at home. Also, I like the fact that it is so easy to get out of the city and into the countryside, such as the New Territories. This is a lot more difficult in London, for example. Also, Hong Kong is well-placed for getting to other Asian destinations for the weekend or for a holiday – I went to China, Vietnam, Macau and the Philippines during my year in Hong Kong.

What do you like least about Hong Kong?

I suppose there are two things I dislike about Hong Kong. One is the rather limited cultural life. The number of exhibitions or concerts to go to is very small compared to life in London, and because they are less frequent, the tickets sell out very quickly.

The other aspect I dislike is that most of the ex-pats have a very blasé attitude to the place. In a lot of cases, these people only go to the office and the nightclub and do very little else. This must give a very bad and shallow impression, and one that I don't want to associate myself with. In fact, the opposite was true of my local friends in Hong Kong: they were very bright, very interesting people. I expect that both these sets of people are exactly the ones you would expect to come into contact with most frequently as an English professional working in Hong Kong.

What advice would you have for anyone thinking of coming to live and work in Hong Kong?

First, I'd say pay a lot of attention to where you live. If you want the standard ex-pat package, stay in the Midlevels, but I particularly enjoyed living away from that scene where the majority of your neighbours are not ex-pats.

Secondly, don't worry about not being able to get things you rely on at home and having to bring a lot of things with you. I don't think there was anything I could not get in Hong Kong that I needed – either in terms of clothing and footwear, or in terms of food.

Finally, learn a little bit of Cantonese: at the very least learn how to say your address (so you can get home in a taxi from anywhere) and the numbers from nought to nine (so you can understand the prices of things and so you can phone directory enquiries which at the last count only had one English-speaking line and many more Cantonese-speaking lines.

MARK ADAMS – University Lecturer

How did you come to be living and working in Hong Kong?

I found myself 'addicted' to Hong Kong after my first visit in the early 1960's. It has seemed like my adopted home although I never lived continuously here until I arrived in 1991. But I had managed to spend a year here on some 'academic mission' in about every decade over that time and felt a need to experience first hand the historic changeover. I met Joyce here while I was on a sabbatical year and came to know the people at the philosophy department quite well. So when I was offered a job, I was excited to accept it.

What was your first impression of Hong Kong?

It was about as totally 'other' as an impression could be. I arrived here almost directly from my life on the insanely, remote and sparsely populated desert north-slope plateaus of the High Uintah Mountains in eastern Utah. Our nearest neighbours were about three miles away and I would usually visit my neighbour 'friend' on horseback. I arrived in Hong Kong just the day before a visit from some royalty (I think it was Princess Margaret) and the streets were crammed. I remember thinking as I struggled with the crowds on Nathan Road that I was seeing in this hour more people than I had seen in my entire life up to this point.

What is/was your visa status? Was it difficult to get such a visa?

I haven't had too much trouble with visa status except for the time spent in immigration. All of my earlier visits were on full time visas and I was on an employment visa until I got permanent residence.

What sort of place do you live in? Was it easy to find accommodation?

I am still in university accommodation and I pay about HK$8700 per month in rent. There was a regular HKU 'bidding' process for the available flats in operation when I arrived and it was relatively straightforward to get assigned a place. Since then, the system has become much less transparent and we have had trouble moving to more suitable places.

What is the social life like? Was it easy to make a new group of local friends?
The University does have a kind of built in community. We have made friends primarily through work and our child's various school situation and friends.

What do you like best about Hong Kong?
It's hard to say a single thing—it certainly is the package: Chinese people and culture, food, social life, language, energy and excitement, modernity, efficiency, rate of change, street life and colour, weather, beauty of the setting (harbour and peaks in a tropical forest), international character and 'sense' of the rest of the world. . . .

What do you like least about Hong Kong?
Bureaucracy, air pollution, crowding, uncertain commitment to democratic/freedom principles.

What advice would you have for anyone thinking of coming to live and work in Hong Kong?
Do it! Be patient. Everyone who comes from the West gets exhausted by HK after about 6 months then again at around 2 years. Then it grows on you and it's hard to leave – probably the next most common decision to depart comes after about seven years. Almost everyone who stays over two years is sorry to leave and dreams of schemes to return.

MICHIEL GEN – Exchange Student

How did you come to be living in Hong Kong?
Study, exchange programme at HKU

What was your first impression of Hong Kong?
Very impressive skyline, bustling cosmopolitan atmosphere, the most efficient and affordable public transport system I have ever seen. Very fast pace of living.

What was your visa status? Was it difficult to get such a visa?
Student visa. It wasn't difficult to obtain one, as HKU took care of the entire procedure

What sort of place did you live in? Was it easy to find accommodation?
Student hall. I can't remember the exact rent (HK$1,000-1,200/month) but it was quite cheap compared to private accommodation. I believe it was heavily subsidized by the university. The size of the accommodation left something to be desired according to European standards. Single room size was about two metres by four metres. It was easy to get this accommodation, the university arranged everything.

What was the social life like? Was it easy to make a new group of local friends?
My social life was very active. There was a sizable contingent of expats and other exchange students with whom it was easy to make contact. Making friends with Chinese students proved a little more difficult as they seemed rather shy and reluctant to speak English (with the exception of the authors of this book!). I decided to chose the more difficult (yet rewarding) path by focusing on meeting local people and spending less time with westerners. One of the reasons why I chose to go to HK was to learn about other cultures, after all. Anyway, I made a number of Chinese friends with whom I'm still in regular contact.

What do you like best about Hong Kong?
The food. Enormous variety of, naturally Cantonese cuisine but also other Chinese, Japanese, other Asian and Western styles. The local varieties being more affordable than others.

What do you like least about Hong Kong?
The climate in summer (too hot and humid). Dress accordingly!

What advice would you have for anyone thinking of coming to live and work in Hong Kong?
Make some local friends, learn some Cantonese, learn to eat with chopsticks, allow people a 'face-saving' way out of discussions and debates.

TONIO WANDMACHER – Exchange Student

How did you come to be living in Hong Kong?
I was studying at Hong Kong University (Cognitive Science).

What was your first impression of Hong Kong?
The immense population density; the unique fusion of Western and Chinese culture.

What was your visa status? Was it difficult to get such a visa?
Student visa. From abroad it was nearly impossible to get (via Chinese Embassy),
however, in Hong Kong it took just a day at the immigration office.

What sort of place did you live in? Was it easy to find accommodation?
Student hall, which costs about HK$1000/month. The student office helped me
very much; it would have been impossible to find anything else from abroad.

**What was the social life like? Was it easy to make a new group of local
friends?**
I spent most of the time with other foreigners (unfortunately!). My Chinese hall
mates were always kind and helpful, but it was difficult to make friends among
them. Still, I also made some Chinese friends (including the authors of this
book!).

What do you like best about Hong Kong?
The people, the breathtaking scenery, the public transport system, the fact that
you can find a small incense-fumed Buddhist temple right next to 40-storey
skyscrapers.

What do you like least about Hong Kong?
The obsession with economic wealth.

**What advice would you have for anyone thinking of coming to live and work
in Hong Kong?**

- Be open towards Chinese culture, try to understand the people!
- Get out of Lan Kwai Fong.
- Don't eat at Pizza Hut, go to a 'Chah Chaan Teng'.
- Go hiking, the nature reserves are wonderful.
- Learn at least some words of Cantonese.
- Use the Star Ferry instead of the MTR.

APPENDIX III

BIBLIOGRAPHY

Williamson, Andrew. *The Chinese Business Puzzle.* United Kingdom: howtobooks, 2003.

Harper, Damian et al. *Lonely Planet – China* (8th Edition). Australia: Lonely Planet Publications Pty Ltd, 2002.

Hunter & Sexton. *Contemporary China.* New York: St. Martin's Press, 1999.

Griffith, Susan. *Teaching English Abroad* (7th Edition). United Kingdom: Vacation Work Publications, 2004

China Benefits and Employment Terms. Hong Kong, Watson Wyatt Worldwide, 2001.

China Statistical Yearbook 2003: compiled by China National Bureau Statistics of China. Beijing: China Statistics Press, 2003.

China Watch 2004: Annual Country Forecast. Washington, D.C.: Orbis Publications, L.L.C, 2003.

Macau Statistical Yearbook 2002. Macau: Macau SAR, 2002.

Macau's Advantages. Macau: Macau Policy Research Institute, 2002.

Complete guides to life abroad from Vacation Work

Live & Work Abroad

Buying a House Abroad

Starting a Business Abroad

Available from good bookshops or direct from the publishers
Vacation Work, 9 Park End Street, Oxford OX1 1HJ
Tel 01865-241978 * Fax 01865-790885 * www.vacationwork.co.uk

In the US: available at bookstores everywhere
or from The Globe Pequot Press (www.GlobePequot.com)